THE DANGEROUS CASE OF DONALD TRUMP

THE DANGEROUS CASE OF DONALD TRUMP

37 PSYCHIATRISTS AND MENTAL HEALTH EXPERTS ASSESS A PRESIDENT

UPDATED AND EXPANDED WITH NEW ESSAYS

EDITED BY

BANDY X. LEE, M.D., M.DIV.,
ORGANIZER OF YALE'S "DUTY TO WARN" CONFERENCE

THOMAS
DUNNE
BOOKS

ST. MARTIN'S PRESS

NEW YORK

THOMAS DUNNE BOOKS.
An imprint of St. Martin's Press.

THE DANGEROUS CASE OF DONALD TRUMP: 37 PSYCHIATRISTS AND MENTAL HEALTH EXPERTS ASSESS A PRESIDENT. Copyright © 2017, 2019 by Bandy X. Lee. All rights reserved. Printed in the United States of America. For information, address St. Martin's Press, 175 Fifth Avenue, New York, N.Y. 10010.

www.thomasdunnebooks.com

www.stmartins.com

Designed by Omar Chapa

Library of Congress Cataloging-in-Publication Data is available upon request.

ISBN 978-1-250-21286-3 (hardcover)
ISBN 978-1-250-17946-3 (ebook)

Our books may be purchased in bulk for promotional, educational, or business use. Please contact your local bookseller or the Macmillan Corporate and Premium Sales Department at 1-800-221-7945, extension 5442, or by email at MacmillanSpecialMarkets@macmillan.com.

10   9   8   7   6   5   4   3

COPYRIGHT ACKNOWLEDGMENTS

*This work is dedicated to my grandfather, Dr. Geun-Young Lee,
who believed medical practice always involves social responsibility;
to my mother, Dr. Inmyung Lee, who continues the tradition;
and to Mirabelle and Blake, for their futures.*

CONTENTS

XIX   **FOREWORD TO THE SECOND EDITION**
       The Dire Warning of Mental Health Experts
       Jeffrey D. Sachs, Ph.D.

XXVII **PROLOGUE TO THE SECOND EDITION**
       Professions and Activism
       Stephen Soldz, Ph.D., and Bandy X. Lee, M.D., M.Div.

XLVII **FOREWORD TO THE FIRST EDITION**
       Our Witness to Malignant Normality
       Robert Jay Lifton, M.D.

LIII   **PROLOGUE TO THE FIRST EDITION**
       Professions and Politics
       Judith Lewis Herman, M.D., and Bandy X. Lee, M.D., M.Div.

1   **INTRODUCTION**
       Our Duty to Warn and to Protect
       Bandy X. Lee, M.D., M.Div.

19   **PART 1: The Trump Phenomenon**

21   Unbridled and Extreme Present Hedonism: How the
        Leader of the Free World Has Proven Time and Again
        He Is Unfit for Duty
        Philip Zimbardo, Ph.D., and Rosemary Sword

46   Pathological Narcissism and Politics: A Lethal Mix
        Craig Malkin, Ph.D.

64   I Wrote *The Art of the Deal* with Donald Trump: His
        Self-Sabotage Is Rooted in His Past
        Tony Schwartz

70   Trump's Trust Deficit Is the Core Problem
        Gail Sheehy, Ph.D.

78   Sociopathy
        Lance Dodes, M.D.

88   Donald Trump Is: (A) Bad, (B) Mad, (C) All of the Above
        John D. Gartner, Ph.D.

104   Why "Crazy Like a Fox" versus "Crazy Like a Crazy"
        Really Matters: Delusional Disorder, Admiration of Brutal
        Dictators, the Nuclear Codes, and Trump
        Michael J. Tansey, Ph.D.

120   Cognitive Impairment, Dementia, and POTUS
        David M. Reiss, M.D.

130   Donald J. Trump, Alleged Incapacitated Person: Mental
        Incapacity, the Electoral College, and the Twenty-Fifth
        Amendment
        James A. Herb, M.A., Esq.

143   **PART 2: The Trump Dilemma**

145   Should Psychiatrists Refrain from Commenting on
       Trump's Psychology?
       Leonard L. Glass, M.D., M.P.H.

154   On Seeing What You See and Saying What You Know: A
       Psychiatrist's Responsibility
       Henry J. Friedman, M.D.

163   The Issue Is Dangerousness, Not Mental Illness
       James Gilligan, M.D.

174   A Clinical Case for the Dangerousness of
       Donald J. Trump
       Diane Jhueck, L.M.H.C., D.M.H.P.

191   Health, Risk, and the Duty to Protect the Community
       Howard H. Covitz, Ph.D., A.B.P.P.

203   New Opportunities for Therapy in the Age of Trump
       William J. Doherty, Ph.D.

211   **PART 3: The Trump Effect**

213   Trauma, Time, Truth, and Trump: How a President
       Freezes Healing and Promotes Crisis
       Betty P. Teng, M.F.A., L.M.S.W.

228   Trump Anxiety Disorder: The Trump Effect on the
       Mental Health of Half the Nation and Special
       Populations
       Jennifer Contarino Panning, Psy.D.

237   In Relationship with an Abusive President
       Harper West, M.A., L.L.P.

254   Birtherism and the Deployment of the Trumpian
       Mind-Set
       Luba Kessler, M.D.

261   Trump's Daddy Issues: A Toxic Mix for America
       Steve Wruble, M.D.

273   Trump and the American Collective Psyche
       Thomas Singer, M.D.

289   Who Goes Trump? Tyranny as a Triumph of Narcissism
       Elizabeth Mika, M.A., L.C.P.C.

309   The Loneliness of Fateful Decisions: Social Contexts and
       Psychological Vulnerability
       Edwin B. Fisher, Ph.D.

332   He's Got the World in His Hands and His Finger on the
       Trigger: The Twenty-Fifth Amendment Solution
       Nanette Gartrell, M.D., and Dee Mosbacher, M.D., Ph.D.

345   **PART 4: Sociocultural Consequences**

347   Persistent Enslavement Systemic Trauma: The Deleterious
       Impact of Trump's Rhetoric on Black and Brown People
       Kevin Washington, Ph.D.

360   Traumatic Consequences for Immigrant Populations in the
       United States
       Rosa Maria Bramble, L.C.S.W.

373   To Trump, Some Lives Matter
       Ellyn Uram Kaschak, Ph.D.

385   The Charismatic Leader-Follower Relationship and
       Trump's Base
       Jerrold M. Post, M.D.

397   **PART 5. Humanity's Perpetuation and Survival**
399   The Myth of Nuclear War
       *James R. Merikangas, M.D., with Tarannum M.
       Lateef, M.D.*

412   The Age of Thanatos: Environmental Consequences of the
       Trump Presidency
       Lise Van Susteren, M.D., and H. Steven Moffic, M.D.

425   The Goldwater Rule and the Silence of American
       Psychiatry: A 2017 Symposium
       Nassir Ghaemi, M.D., M.P.H

437   Is the Commander in Chief Fit to Serve? A Nonpartisan
       Test that Marries U.S. Army Leadership Standards with
       Psychoanalytic Theory
       Prudence Gourguechon, M.D.

446   Disordered Minds: Democracy as a Defense Against
       Dangerous Personalities
       Ian Hughes, Ph.D.

458   Congress Should Establish an Alternative Body to Assess
       the President
       Norman Eisen, Esq., and Richard Painter, Esq.

471 **EPILOGUE**

Reaching Beyond the Professions

Noam Chomsky, Ph.D., and Bandy X. Lee, M.D., M.Div.

479 **APPENDIX**

Transcript of the Yale Conference (online)

FOREWORD TO THE SECOND EDITION

The Dire Warning of Mental Health Experts

JEFFREY D. SACHS, PH.D.

Donald Trump is a profound danger to Americans and to the rest of the world. He will remain a profound danger until he is no longer president, since the dangers clearly result from Trump's serious mental impairments that are untreated and are most likely impervious to treatment. The authors of this volume deserve our nation's gratitude and, most important, our deep attention and political response. Special thanks are due to the editor, Dr. Bandy X. Lee, who supplies (in economic jargon) the global public good of assembling this remarkable set of analyses while adding her own clear voice, leadership, and expertise.

The authors are all leading mental and public health professionals who are speaking out on behalf of public safety, against the misguided and misjudged "Goldwater rule" of the American Psychiatric Association (APA). As several authors make clear, the APA has a lot of soul-searching and self-correction to undertake. Its psychological counterpart has already been an institutional party to the government's regime of torture during the Bush administration and has generally refrained from educating the public regarding the imminent dangers caused by mentally impaired political leaders, perhaps out of fear of retribution from those leaders. A glimmer of hope for the APA is the association's recent attention to the mental health consequences of human-induced climate change despite the Trump administration's strident and hugely destructive efforts to block effective actions on climate change.

The new set of essays mostly highlights the profound public dangers of Trump's manifest psychological disorders. While the essays do not in general aim to settle on a single diagnosis (and many authors call urgently for an independent psychological examination), Ian Hughes's description of the "toxic triangle" of destructive leaders, susceptible followers, and conducive environments offers the reader a plausible starting point for assessing the dangers of Trump as president. As Hughes summarizes, the disorders common in these leaders "make it impossible for such persons to feel empathy for others, to view others as anything other than objects to be used or threats to be eliminated, and for whom the concept of equality is impossible to conceive."

The scintillating essay by Jerrold M. Post, expert in psychological profiling and author of the recent *Narcissism and Politics*, reminds us that Trump manifests a special relationship with his base. Trump is a "mirror-hungry" leader, that is, a narcissist whose private feelings of inadequacy must be quenched by the constant adulation of his followers, hence the nonstop rallies in front of Trump followers filled with chants of hatred, threats of violence, and constant references to Trump's serial lies and fantasy world. Yet the followers make the leader. In particular, Post describes the followers as "ideal-hungry" or "wounded" followers, who look to mirror-hungry leaders for salvation from some wounds or perceived injustices. Trump is not Adolf Hitler, but he shares many of Hitler's disorders, addiction to lies, and appeal to wounded followers through the dehumanization of target groups. In Trump's case, those include African Americans, Muslims, women, Hispanics, and migrants.

Dr. Lee and her colleagues have been in the forefront of warning society of the profound dangers of such an impaired individual in power. They have warned of the inevitable rise of violence, fear, and suffering that would follow. And Trump has proved them right. Trump has blood on his hands, and the threats continue to mount.

Like many past presidents, the blood starts with the reckless unleashing of U.S. military might through covert operations, drone attacks, and supplies of deadly munitions to killers. American bombs are taking the lives of children in Yemen, and America's overt and covert wars continue under Trump in Africa, the Middle East, and Asia. Trump aims to sell more than $100 billion of new advanced military hardware to Saudi Arabia despite the likelihood of escalating wars and deaths as a result. Trump's anti-Iran policies and rhetoric may foretell yet another major and catastrophic war in the Middle East. And on the economic side, his unilateral tariffs aimed at many countries, but most notably China, undermine global rules, global trust, and even perhaps global peace in the future.

Yet the toxicity goes far beyond conventional (if devastating) war and dangerously broken trade rules. Trump is also unleashing a new nuclear arms race that could end up in global nuclear annihilation. Any knowledgeable student of modern history knows of the numerous close calls, both deliberate and accidental, that have brought the world repeatedly to the brink of nuclear war. The *Bulletin of Atomic Scientists* has now advanced the Doomsday Clock to two minutes to midnight, the direst proximity to doomsday since 1953, when the thermonuclear arms race between the United States and the Soviet Union began.

Trump's recent call to withdraw from the Intermediate-Range Nuclear Force Treaty with Russia, against the counsel of foreign policy experts in the United States and Europe, not to mention Russia (including our age's preeminent peacemaker, Mikhail Gorbachev), is yet another marker of rising dangers. The essay by James R. Merikangas and Dr. Tarannum M. Lateef on the nuclear threat is powerful, poignant, and terrifying. As the authors put it: "Those who pretend that we are in the realm of politics when we are really in the realm of psychopathology make the situation even more dangerous, because they will not be prepared while the future of the planet and the human race are at stake."

The dangers stoked by Trump and his toxic triangle of conditions go beyond war. Trump is stoking mass violence in America. Hate crimes and deaths from mass shootings are soaring. And when they occur, as with the horrific attack on the synagogue in Pittsburgh, Trump's response is almost always more violence, calling for more guns, not fewer, and for the death penalty, while denying any role of his own toxic hate-filled speech. Herein is another sign of Trump's pathology, an utter inability to face the consequences of his own actions.

The authors powerfully document the enormous toll on society of this hate-filled political agenda. Rosa Maria Bramble describes the pain and suffering of migrants facing Trump's taunts and threats. Kevin Washington describes the pain felt by African Americans as "Persistent Enslavement Systemic Trauma" as opposed to posttraumatic stress disorder. Ellyn Uram Kaschak describes the suffering and anxiety of women in response to Trump's misogyny, once again under display by Trump during and after the Kavanaugh confirmation process. And several authors note the profound pain caused to children by the stresses of society and those faced by their own parents, not to mention the inhumane and blatantly illegal Trump administration policy of separating parents and children at the Mexican border.

Trump's responsibility for needless deaths and suffering extends to his reckless and corrupt repudiation of responsibility for human-induced climate change, as underscored by the important essay by Lise Van Susteren and H. Steven Moffic. Trump not only is endangering the world by repudiating the Paris Climate Agreement and putting oil industry lobbyists into positions of authority in the government; he is also failing to help the nation to prevent and respond effectively to the rising risks of extreme climate disasters, such as hurricanes, floods, and massive wildfires. The Trump administration's shockingly inadequate response to Hurricane Maria, which devastated Puerto Rico in September 2017, left thousands to die in the aftermath of the storm. Trump's characteristic response was to deny, flippantly and ignorantly, the deaths that had been meticulously assessed by two independent epidemiological studies. His palpable lack of empathy poisons not only his dealings with political adversaries but his substantive policies such as environmental policy.

The situation with Trump is so dangerous and unstable that an anonymous White House senior staffer wrote in the *New York Times* that a group embedded in the upper reaches of the administration was working day and night to stop the dangerous impulses of the president. Prudence Gourguechon notes that this might lead to the breakdown of the civilian chain of command over the military, if the military refuses to honor illegal commands by Trump. She quotes retired Lt. General Mark Hertling in noting that, "[T]he military is not palace guards. They take an oath to defend the Constitution of the United States against all enemies foreign and domestic."

We should appreciate that Trump poses a special threat not only because of his mental impairments but also because of the weakening of U.S. political institutions in recent decades. Public opinion is no check on Trump's reckless and illegal ways. He won the election with fewer votes than his opponent, and with only 27 percent of the vote of eligible voters and 19.5 percent of the U.S. population. His approval rating is persistently below his disapproval rating. His specific major policies, such as dismantling Obamacare, implementing tax cuts for the rich, withdrawing from the Paris Climate Agreement, withdrawing from the Iran nuclear agreement, opposition to gun control, separating children and parents at the border, and countless others, are policies a majority of Americans oppose. And yet the policies persist and many are enacted.

One reason is that American politics have become a game of big money, with Congress and the president catering to corporate interests rather than to the common good. As a result, Trump and the

Republican majority in Congress back the dictates of the oil and gas industry, Big Pharma, Wall Street, and the military-industrial complex (including the gun lobby). Campaign spending now exceeds $6 billion per cycle, with a disproportionate amount coming from wealthy donors and corporate interests. Combine Trump's personal mental disorders with the massive corruption of politics, and public opinion hardly stands a chance.

Many other contemporary trends multiply the risks. Russia has relentlessly meddled in U.S. politics (as, alas, the United States has meddled abroad), and perhaps helped Trump to eke out his narrow victory in the Electoral College. Time, and Special Prosecutor Robert Mueller, will no doubt add further insights. The two-party system also works less and less well to represent a population that both parties have increasingly alienated.

Consider this. Registered voters' party affiliations are divided roughly into thirds among Republicans, Democrats, and independents. The independents, in turn, divide their support roughly equally between the two parties, with modest shifts from election to election. Trump successfully captured the Republican Party's hard-right "base," representing roughly two-thirds of Republican voters and around one-quarter of the electorate. With independents leaning slightly toward the Republicans in 2016, but not specifically for Trump, the Republicans won a congressional majority while Trump won control of the Republican Party. In effect, Trump governs a majority party with core support from perhaps a quarter of the electorate. In a system of parliamentary proportional representation, Trump's power would be checked in a way that it is not in the U.S. two-party system.

Yet perhaps the most dangerous reason that Trump is not controlled is that the American president is now almost a despotic ruler when it comes to foreign policy. Congress has abdicated its responsibilities to declare war and oversee major foreign policy decisions. This is the tragedy of the U.S. pursuit of hegemonic global power after World War II. American wars, drone strikes, covert operations, and much else in foreign policy have essentially taken on the character of a one-man show, and, with Trump, a horrifyingly dangerous one at that.

It is in this context that Dr. Lee and her colleagues have taken the powerful, bold, and correct step of warning the public of Trump's severe mental impairments and the dire threat they pose to American and global safety. The American Psychiatric Association's position is simply wrong. Americans and their political representatives need to hear from learned psychiatrists and psychologists about the profound dangers of having a president whose widely documented behavior meets the many familiar pathological patterns to them, as detailed in the book. The mental health professionals who contributed to this volume are pointing out a clear and present danger that the general population would not otherwise understand. This is not politics as usual. Trump's vile behavior, as Dr. Robert J. Lifton has powerfully argued, must not become a "malignant normality."

The powerful message of this volume comes through loud and clear. Most importantly, Trump should submit to an independent psychological examination, not the sham that was conducted by his personal physician. But more than that, America and the world will be unsafe until Trump's power is dramatically curtailed. There are several avenues for accomplishing this, some discussed in the volume and others not. An independent body of experts could advise the cabinet and congressional leadership as to whether the president is fit to serve, and if not, to be removed by the Twenty-Fifth Amendment. Trump might face impeachment hearings relating to the Mueller investigation or for other possible high crimes and misdemeanors. And miracle of miracles, Congress might begin to act once again as a coequal branch of government, not a supine doormat of corporate lobbies and the Republican base.

We are on a dangerous course in stormy waters. This important volume will be vital in helping us to reach safe harbor.

Jeffrey D. Sachs, Ph.D., is University Professor and Director of the Center for Sustainable Development at Columbia University. A world-renowned intellectual, senior UN adviser, and best-selling author, his monthly newspaper columns appear in more than 100 countries. He is the co-recipient of the 2015 Blue Planet Prize. He has twice been named among Time *magazine's 100 most influential world leaders, called by* The New York Times, *"probably the most important economist in the world," and by* Time *magazine "the world's best known economist." A recent survey by* The Economist *ranked Prof. Sachs as among the world's three most influential living economists of the past decade. His most recent book is* A New Foreign Policy: Beyond American Exceptionalism *(2018).*

PROLOGUE TO THE SECOND EDITION

Professions and Activism

STEPHEN SOLDZ, PH.D., AND BANDY X. LEE, M.D., M.DIV.

The election of Donald Trump is a warning sign for American society. It signifies that decades-long trends toward economic inequality, environmental destruction, and the hollowing out of the content of U.S. democracy while maintaining some of its formal mechanisms are gaining steam. The election of Trump escalated many of the processes breaking down traditional institutions in the country.

Still, there is hope. The day after Trump's inauguration saw the largest collection of loosely coordinated demonstrations in human history, the Women's March. The president's Muslim ban saw thousands rush to airports to defend threatened immigrants. An unprecedented, at least in recent decades, number of new people have stepped up to run for political office. And the amazing ability of the Parkland, Florida, kids from the Marjory Stoneman Douglas High School to mobilize an unprecedented mass movement for gun control in a matter of weeks, a movement which has apparently shifted the political calculus in many parts of the country, shows how the combination of newly energized activists and social media can cause seismic shifts in record time. Just as the body's immune system kicks in at a time of descent into illness, these are the life-affirming impulses we spoke of in the first edition, and our hope for recovery toward health.

Professionals are an important component in this process, helping to provide checks on powerful institutions and alerting the public to wrongs. Professions operate with an implicit social contract with the broader society to contribute their special knowledge and training to the greater good. Professionals agree to follow a professional ethics code that binds them beyond the ordinary citizen. For example, lawyers are expected to act in the best interests of their clients and to adhere to attorney-client privilege. In exchange, these professionals are granted certain privileges not available to all in the wider society.

Professional ethical standards remain an ideal individual professionals can strive to fulfill, however imperfectly. For example, while horrific behavior by soldiers often accompanies war, for some, at least, the ideal of military honor can sometimes provide a counterweight to participation in those horrors. We saw this fifty years ago when Hugh Thompson intervened to stop the My Lai massacre (Wiener 2018) and, more recently, when military members and intelligence professionals refused considerable pressure to participate in the Bush-era torture program (Fallon 2017).

In considering professional ethics, it makes sense to distinguish between "risk management" and ethical reasoning. In our profession of mental health, most of what passes for ethics training consists primarily of risk management. Thus, we learn how to handle our professional records so that they will be a useful tool should we experience a malpractice complaint and to be consistent with the Health Insurance Portability and Accountability Act (HIPAA) of 1996. We avoid sleeping with our patients lest we find ourselves in serious trouble. What often is missing from this training is any deep engagement with fundamental ethical principles and ethical thinking. Thus, when professional psychology faced a fundamental crisis with the report that fellow professionals were participants in the Bush-era torture program, discussion among psychologists concerned with professional ethics centered largely on interpretations of the American Psychological Association's (APA) code of ethics rather than these psychologists' violation of fundamental ethical principles.

Health professionals pledge to use their knowledge and expertise to improve people's lives and "to do no harm." At times they must sacrifice their comfort and even family commitments to attend to their patients' needs. They also pledge to keep the confidences their patients communicate to them. In exchange, physicians and psychologists, among other professionals, are granted privileges such as an inviolable confidentiality of those communications, often even from law enforcement or the courts. In war, doctors are given such special status under the Geneva Conventions that the First Geneva Convention stipulates that:

> Medical personnel exclusively engaged in the search for, or the collection, transport or treatment of the wounded or sick, or in the prevention of disease, staff exclusively engaged in the administration of medical units and establishments . . . shall be respected and protected in all circumstances. (International Committee of the Red Cross n.d.)

These principles are incorporated into the World Medical Association's Physician's Pledge of the Declaration of Geneva developed in the wake of World War II, which some consider to be the modern-day Hippocratic Oath. The most relevant clauses from the Declaration are:

> AS A MEMBER OF THE MEDICAL PROFESSION:
> I SOLEMNLY PLEDGE to dedicate my life to the service of humanity;
> THE HEALTH AND WELL-BEING OF MY PATIENT will be my first consideration;
> I WILL RESPECT the autonomy and dignity of my patient;

I WILL MAINTAIN the utmost respect for human life;

I WILL NOT PERMIT considerations of age, disease or disability, creed, ethnic origin, gender, nationality, political affiliation, race, sexual orientation, social standing or any other factor to intervene between my duty and my patient;

. . .

I WILL PRACTISE my profession with conscience and dignity and in accordance with good medical practice;

. . .

I WILL SHARE my medical knowledge for the benefit of the patient and the advancement of healthcare;

. . .

I WILL NOT USE my medical knowledge to violate human rights and civil liberties, even under threat (World Medical Association 2017).

Despite minor differences, all medical professions share certain foundational ethical principles that are embodied in the Physician's Pledge. Among these are *beneficence, nonmaleficence, justice*, and respect for the *autonomy* of individuals. Beneficence refers to the obligation that health professionals are supposed to use their knowledge and expertise for the benefit of people, including both their patients and the wider public. Nonmaleficence refers to the famous "do no harm" clause and is often considered to be the first principle of health care, as in "first, do no harm." Thus, when consistent with beneficence, we health professionals should not apply ineffective or harmful treatments. This obligation also applies to the wider society, obligating us to take steps to prevent an infectious patient from infecting others, even if those others are not our patients.

Another important principle is respect for the autonomy of individuals. Thus, to the greatest degree possible, health professionals have a responsibility to educate their patients and the broader public in order to empower them to make informed judgments about what is in their best interests. Health professionals have more recently added justice as a basic value. Justice draws our attention to the importance of creating and ensuring more equal access, including for the poor and otherwise underserved, to decent high-quality health care and other important social goods such as healthy food and clean air and water, vital to maintaining health. It draws health professionals' attention to the broader social world and our obligations as professionals to work to make that world fairer.

Though not always identified as a separate principle, undergirding all these principles is that of *universality*, that all people regardless of nationality, ethnicity, race, or any other characteristic are equally entitled to the benefits and protections provided by the health professions. Thus, health professionals, at least insofar as they are practicing their professions, should not value Americans more highly than those from other countries or those from a dominant social group over others.

Both justice and universality direct health professionals to pay attention to the wider world beyond the clinic as they call upon us to serve the broader public, not just those who become our patients. And they direct attention toward the world of public policy and of "politics," broadly defined, as a way of collectively improving public health.

However, health professionals do not always live up to these aspirations. History, after all, is replete with examples of health professionals participating in human rights abuses. The horrors Nazi and Japanese doctors committed during World War II are extremes. But also to be remembered are abuses by U.S. health professionals, including the Tuskegee syphilis study in which physicians and public health workers deliberately allowed hundreds of poor African American patients and their families to go untreated for decades after effective treatments existed; the Guatemalan syphilis studies in which U.S. public health doctors deliberately introduced syphilis among prisoners and others in that country; and, in recent times, the involvement of psychologists, physicians, physician assistants, and other health professionals in the U.S. government's "enhanced interrogation" torture programs by the CIA and the Department of Defense. These horrors are especially disturbing, both because of the violation by the professionals of their ethical obligation to "do no harm," and because their expertise regarding people's physical and mental functioning gave them enhanced abilities to help generate immense suffering.

When inculcated into personal beliefs, professional ethics can provide an ideal to which health professionals aspire. They call us to exemplify the best human potentials, to help our patients, and to strive for a better world for them and us to live in. As part of this striving for a better world, it is incumbent upon health professionals to use our knowledge and expertise to call out injustices in the world that cause harm. Health professionals sometimes have privileged access to settings where abuses occur. They also have specialized knowledge that may allow them to identify or better explain the causes and effects of abuses.

For example, physicians in Turkey have played major roles, both participating in official torture of those in detention, and, at great personal risk, in reporting and publicizing this torture, as occurred after the 1980 coup (Cilasun 1991). Thus, it is particularly concerning that major attempts to deter physicians from reporting torture or, sometimes, even examining tortured prisoners (Human Rights Watch 2016; Stockholm Center for Freedom 2017) accompanied the turn in Turkey toward authoritarian strongman rule in the last few years. These efforts to suppress physicians in a perverse way testify to the power that health professionals have when calling attention to official abuses.

Similarly, in 2004 word spread that health professionals, especially psychologists and physicians, were helping to implement the Bush administration's torture program (Bloche and Marks 2005; Lewis 2005). This aroused many other health professionals to oppose this participation, and battles ensued in several professional associations. The American Medical Association and the American Psychiatric Association took the position that participation in interrogations of any kind—torturous or not, or whether national security or domestic law enforcement—was not appropriate, as such participation conflicts with their members' roles as healers (American Medical Association 2006). However, after issuing the statements, the two associations did little to follow up on them and thereafter largely ignored the government's torture program. The World Psychiatric Association recently adopted an analogous position banning psychiatrists worldwide from participating in any interrogations (Miles n.d.; Soldz 2017; World Psychiatric Association 2017).

In contrast, the main organization of psychologists in the United States, the American Psychological Association, took a different stand. While reiterating opposition to "torture" as defined by the Bush administration, it essentially ignored mounting evidence that psychologists were central players in designing and implementing torture and insisted rather that psychologists were essential participants in national security interrogations (American Psychological Association 2005; Coalition for an Ethical Psychology 2011a, 2011b; Soldz 2006). This move by the psychologists' organization aroused fierce opposition from many within and outside the Association (Coalition for an Ethical Psychology 2009; Pipher, Gonzalez, and Goodman 2017; Pope and Gutheil 2009; Soldz 2007, 2009, 2011). The struggle continued for over a decade, reaching a pinnacle in 2014–2015, after then *New York Times* Pulitzer Prize–winning reporter James Risen reported on emails he obtained documenting backchannel communication between CIA and White House officials and those of the association (Risen 2014, 2015; Soldz et al. 2015). The Association was compelled to initiate an outside investigation of Risen's claims by Chicago attorney David Hoffman. After a seven-month investigation, Hoffman documented a pattern of secret collaboration over several years between Association officials and those from the Department of Defense that resulted in the vetting of Association interrogation policies by the Department of Defense prior to their adoption by the Association (Hoffman et al. 2015). Thus, Hoffman argued that Association policies deliberately placed no restraints on military psychologists beyond those placed by the military themselves at a time when there was reason to believe that abusive interrogations might still be occurring. Not surprisingly, some are still contesting Hoffman's conclusions and the reforms that followed from them (Aldhous 2018a, 2018b).

Dr. Soldz spent a decade working to expose the roles of psychologists and other health professionals in the government's torture program and to change the Association's policies to be more consistent with those of the medical and psychiatric associations. On the one hand, as a citizen-professional concerned about the spread of brutality in our society, he acted on his outrage as a health professional that our government was resorting to officially authorized torture. While the United States has had a long and disturbing relationship with torture (Marks 1991; McCoy 2006, 2012; Otterman 2007), it seemed a major step toward the brutalization of society to adopt torture as official policy (Cole 2009). This official acceptance of torture could lead to acceptance of other forms of brutalization, both in other countries and against people in the United States. While acting as a citizen, he was simultaneously acting as a professional psychologist concerned that participation in torture was undermining the ethical basis of his profession. As a result of the actions of Dr. Soldz and other dozens of activists over many years, the Association changed its policies after Hoffman filed his report in 2015 (Aldhous 2015; Welch 2009).

This movement of psychologists against collusion in torture is one recent example of activism on the part of health professionals. It joins earlier examples of efforts by U.S. psychiatrists, including the American Psychiatric Association, to pressure the Soviet Union to stop using Soviet psychiatrists and mental hospitals as a way of punishing dissidents (Moran 2010); the organization of physicians and others against nuclear war in the 1980s; physicians joining other activists to push for a treaty banning land mines (Physicians for Human Rights 2018b); a decades-long fight by black physicians to integrate medical societies, to support civil rights efforts, and to push for equitable access to health care (Newkirk II 2017); and efforts by health professionals to push for universal health care that is not driven by profit, efforts that apparently are bearing fruit with the widespread endorsement of Medicare for all ("Physicians for a National Health Program" n.d.).

As these examples illustrate, activism by health providers is compatible with and even integral to professional responsibility toward society. Given all that we now know about prevention and population health, we would be dangerously neglectful to confine our professional responsibilities within the walls of private offices in order to maintain a fiction of professional neutrality. Medical neutrality means that we apply the same standards regardless of "age, disease or disability, creed, ethnic origin, gender, nationality, political affiliation, race, sexual orientation, social standing or any other factor" and speak out when necessary about potential harms, even harms caused and dangers powerful institutions pose, not that we mute our assessment for fear of appearances.

Dr. Lee, who has devoted her life to the study and prevention of violence, has argued forcefully that social, cultural, economic, and environmental factors are far more reliable predictors of violence than individual factors (Lee 2018). Based on this experience, after President Trump's election, she became concerned that the public health effects of having a psychologically unstable president would be highly consequential and widespread. Subsequent events unfortunately have shown only too clearly that her fears were well founded, as we have seen thousands of children separated from their migrant families in ways that may have permanently traumatized them; cruel hardships created for the 40 million Americans living in poverty in perhaps the greatest wealth transfer from the poor to the wealthy in U.S. history; white supremacist killings doubling while gun murder rates have escalated to levels not seen in twenty-five years; increased encouragement of violence against journalists in America and excusing of the murder of journalists abroad; reversal of the small steps that the United States has taken to reduce the threats from global warming; and a restructuring of the geopolitical order that has emboldened dictators, reignited a nuclear arms race, and generated a hostile political environment that does not bode well for future wars.

This is where the American Psychiatric Association's egregious use of ethical rules as a political tool under the Trump administration comes in. Preventing psychiatrists from adequately warning the public, or from drawing attention to a national mental health crisis as authoritative voices in the field before it became normalized and widespread, had enormous negative societal consequences—perhaps more widely consequential than torture. When the American Psychiatric Association might have taken a leadership role, since these harmful consequences were predictable, it did the opposite: it took the drastic step of expanding the so-called "Goldwater rule" into a gag rule. The original Goldwater rule had been part of a mandate to act—to "contribut[e] to the improvement of the community and the betterment of public health" by educating the public when asked about a public figure while refraining from making an explicit diagnosis. The new rule required psychiatrists to violate the first part of the same rule, the principle the rule fell under, as well as their professional responsibility to society as spelled out in the preamble of psychiatric ethics. All this happened within the first two months of the Trump presidency, but it did not stop there: on October 6, 2017, three days after the publication of the first edition of *The Dangerous Case of Donald Trump*, it issued a public statement that a "duty to warn" applies only to existing patients, even though we were invoking a societal duty to warn and not a patient-based duty. On January 9, 2018, six days after Dr. Lee revealed to the public that she had debriefed members of Congress, the American Psychiatric Association issued another statement prohibiting "armchair psychiatry" and "using psychiatry for political or self-aggrandizing purposes," even though Dr. Lee was speaking about public health consequences, not about personal mental health, and was specifically trying to prevent armchair psychiatry by calling for an evaluation. Furthermore, far from using psychiatry for political purposes, she was serving in a consultative role in strict accordance with its own guidelines, which encourage that psychiatrists "serve society by advising and consulting with the executive, legislative, and judiciary branches of the government" (American Psychiatric Association 2013). The Association's persistant sanctioning of Dr. Lee's speech, while stating that its rules applied also to nonmembers, even though she resigned over a decade ago because of the Association's excessive pharmaceutical industry ties, again perversely revealed the real and unique medical situation of this president and how important psychiatric input was.

Now that the dangers have vastly increased, in proportion to the time Mr. Trump has been in the presidency, the American Psychiatric Association, sadly, has become an epitome of institutional complicity and betrayal (Smith and Freyd 2014) and another example of how an organization charged with establishing ethical guidelines independent of political interests has rather become an agent of the state. Dr. Judith Herman points out with Dr. Lee in the Prologue to the First Edition how to avoid Soviet- or Chinese-style psychiatry. We must remember that the Declaration of Geneva Physician's Pledge was adopted in 1948 as a clarification of the health professional's humanitarian obligation, after the experience of Nazism, in recognition that *either* silence *or* active cooperation on the part of professionals with a dangerous regime could contribute to atrocities. Thus, it is imperative for principled mental health professionals to speak up, especially if they wish to help preserve the integrity and reputation of the field, even and especially if their own professional organization is involved.

Since the ethics conference Dr. Lee organized at Yale in 2017, thousands of mental health professionals have gathered to form the National Coalition of Concerned Mental Health Experts, to try to fill in gaps left by the leadership failure of the American Psychiatric Association. Some of its activities included partnering with mental health professionals working to alert the public to severe, psychologically harmful policies. Our colleagues' efforts exploded when word spread regarding the Trump administration's family-separation policies. Dr. Soldz's psychologist-psychoanalyst colleague Dr. Dana Sinopoli wrote a petition that obtained over eight thousand signatures from mental health professionals in a matter of days (Leher 2018). The National Coalition partnered with Dr. Sinopoli to deliver her letter to all members of Congress. Simultaneously, Physicians for Human Rights obtained more than twelve thousand signatures for a related health professional petition (Physicians for Human Rights 2018a). Subsequently, the American Psychological and Psychiatric Associations, along with other professional associations, such as that of pediatricians, alerted the press to the overwhelming psychological and medical research documenting the profound harms that can result from separating children from their parents. We believe the health professional community can feel proud of its role in joining with others to help reverse this profoundly immoral and harmful policy.

Similar activism occurred during the confirmation hearings for Brett Kavanaugh's appointment to the Supreme Court. When Dr. Christine Blasey Ford came forward with accusations that she had been sexually attacked by Kavanaugh while a teenager, much attention was focused upon gaps in her memory. It fell upon mental health professionals to explain the dynamics behind the long-term memory of traumatic events, how avoidance of those memories would have led to a delay in relating them, and why some details are heightened while others are blocked. These efforts helped many among the public to understand that these memory lapses were, in fact, consistent with her stated experiences and confirming rather than invalidating of her testimony. Rather, from Kavanaugh's behavior at the hearings, mental health professionals noted several psychological traits that pointed to his potential lack of fitness for office and possible active, problematic alcohol use and made a formal request to the FBI and the Senate Judiciary Committee that he undergo a fitness evaluation based upon the multiple allegations of assault (*Democracy Now!* 2018). The request gathered hundreds of signatures through the National Coalition and was buttressed by an unprecedented letter to the U.S. Senate signed by thousands of legal

professionals stating that Kavanaugh lacks the "judicial temperament" necessary for a seat on the Supreme Court. Of course, in this
instance as in so many others, the majority in Congress chose to ignore the evidence, and Kavanaugh was confirmed.

These varied experiences illustrate that there comes a point
where mental health and other health professionals' roles and their
roles as citizens begin to merge. There is also tension among professionals regarding how to act as purveyors of ideas and as doers. We
believe that our professional training teaches us to separate these
roles so that we can merge them thoughtfully: there comes a point
where ideas alone are insufficient for bringing the world to health
and safety, and action without careful thought becomes dangerous
for its potential to contribute to unintended results. These are healthy
tensions that will likely never receive a final resolution but will have
to be renegotiated generation by generation and struggle by struggle. It is our hope that the contributions to the present book will
help our generation explore the tensions we mental health professionals experience as we join with fellow citizens in efforts to do our
part in healing and coping with the dangerous territory facing our
country and the world.

*Stephen Soldz, Ph.D., is a clinical psychologist and psychoana-
lyst in Boston. He is Professor at the Boston Graduate School of
Psychoanalysis. Over the past decade he was a leader in efforts to
end U.S. torture and to remove psychologists from participation
in abusive interrogations and other problematic military and intelligence operations. Soldz is a past president of Psychologists for
Social Responsibility, a cofounder of the Coalition for an Ethical
Psychology, a member of the council of representatives of the
American Psychological Association, and an anti-torture adviser
for Physicians for Human Rights.*

*Bandy X. Lee, M.D., M.Div., is a forensic psychiatrist on the
faculty of Yale School of Medicine and a project group leader for*

the World Health Organization Violence Prevention Alliance. She teaches at Yale Law School, has spearheaded a number of prison reform projects, and has written more than one hundred peer-reviewed articles and chapters, edited thirteen academic books, and authored the textbook Violence.

References

Aldhous, Peter. 2015. "How Six Rebel Psychologists Fought a Decade-Long War on Torture—and Won." *Buzzfeed*, August 7. https://www.buzzfeednews .com/article/peteraldhous/the-dissidents?

———. 2018a. "Psychologists Are in a Nasty Fight About a Report on Torture." *Buzzfeed*, July 26. https://www.buzzfeednews.com/article/ peteraldhous/psychology-torture-guantanamo-interrogation.

———. 2018b. "In a Dramatic Vote, Psychologists Have Rejected a Plan to Allow Work with Terror Suspects." *Buzzfeed*, August 9. https://www .buzzfeednews.com/article/peteraldhous/apa-psychology-guanta namo-vote.

American Medical Association. 2006. *Report of the Council on Ethical and Judicial Affairs: Physician Participation in Interrogation (Res. 1, I-05).* Edited by Series American Medical Association. Vol. 2007. American Medical Association. https://web.archive.org/web/20111015024909/ http://www.ama-assn.org/ama1/pub/upload/mm/369/ceja_10a06 .pdf.

American Psychiatric Association. 2013. *Principles of Medical Ethics with Annotations Especially Applicable to Psychiatry.* Washington, DC: American Psychiatric Association. https://www.psychiatry.org/psychiatrists /practice/ethics.

American Psychological Association. 2005. *Report of the American Psychological Association Presidential Task Force on Psychological Ethics and National Security.* Washington, DC: American Psychological Association. http:// www.apa.org/pubs/info/reports/pens.pdf.

Bloche, M. G., and J. H. Marks. 2005. "Doctors and Interrogators at Guantanamo Bay." *New England Journal of Medicine* 353 (1): 6–8.

Cilasun, Ugur. 1991. "Torture and the Participation of Doctors." *Journal of Medical Ethics* 17 (Suppl): 21–22.

Coalition for an Ethical Psychology. 2009. "Coalition for an Ethical Psychology Calls for Independent Investigation of American Psychological Association." *ZNet*, May 5. http://www.zcommunications.org/znet/viewArticle/21384.

———. 2011a. "A Call for Annulment of the APA's PENS Report." Coalition for an Ethical Psychology. http://www.ethicalpsychology.org/materials/PENS_Annulment_Petition.pdf.

———. 2011b. "Background Statement on Annulment of the PENS Report." Coalition for an Ethical Psychology. http://www.ethicalpsychology.org/materials/PENS_Annulment_Background_Statement.pdf.

Cole, David. 2009. *The Torture Memos: Rationalizing the Unthinkable.* New York: The New Press.

Democracy Now! 2018. "Mental Health Experts Demand Psychological Assessment of Kavanaugh for Drinking, Instability." *Democracy Now!*, October 3. https://www.democracynow.org/2018/10/3/mental_health_experts_demand_psychological_assessment.

Fallon, Mark. 2017. *Unjustifiable Means: The Inside Story of How the CIA, Pentagon, and US Government Conspired to Torture.* New York: Regan Arts.

Hoffman, David H., Dannielle J. Carter, Cara R. Viglucci Lopez, Heather L. Benzmiller, S. Yasir Latifi, and Daniel C. Craig. 2015. "Report to the Special Committee of the Board of Directors of the American Psychological Association: Independent Review Relating to APA Ethics Guidelines, National Security Interrogations, and Torture." Chicago, IL: Sidley Austin, LLP. http://www.apa.org/independent-review/revised-report.pdf.

Human Rights Watch. 2016. "A Blank Check: Turkey's Post-Coup Suspension of Safeguards Against Torture." https://www.hrw.org/report/2016/10/25/blank-check/turkeys-post-coup-suspension-safeguards-against-torture.

International Committee of the Red Cross. n.d. "Treaties, States Parties, and Commentaries - Geneva Convention (I) on Wounded and Sick in Armed

Forces in the Field, 1949 - 24 - Article 24: Protection of Permanent Personnel - Commentary of 2016." Accessed October 9, 2018. https://ihl-data
-bases.icrc.org/applic/ihl/ihl.nsf/Comment.xsp?action=openDocument&
documentId=8BB42A7717B581D5C1257F15004A199F.

Lee, Bandy. 2018. "Violence Is a Societal Disorder." *US News & World Report*,
March 6. https://www.usnews.com/opinion/policy-dose/articles/2018
-03-06/prevent-violence-at-the-societal-level.

Leher, Brian. 2018. "The Separation Trauma of 'Zero Tolerance.'" *The Brian
Leher Show*, June 18. https://www.wnyc.org/story/separation-trauma
-zero-tolerance.

Lewis, Neil A. 2005. "Interrogators Cite Doctors' Aid at Guantánamo Prison
Camp." *New York Times*, June 24. http://www.nytimes.com/2005/06/24
/politics/24gitmo.html?ei=5094&en=0bb87618febc3438&hp=&
ex=1119585600&partner=homepage&pagewanted=print.

Marks, John D. 1991. *The Search for the "Manchurian Candidate."* New York:
Norton.

McCoy, Alfred W. 2006. *A Question of Torture: CIA Interrogation, from the Cold
War to the War on Terror*. The American Empire Project. New York:
Metropolitan Books/Henry Holt and Co. http://www.loc.gov/catdir
/enhancements/fy0625/2005051124-b.html http://www.loc.gov/catdir
/enhancements/fy0625/2005051124-d.html.

———. 2012. *Torture and Impunity: The US Doctrine of Coercive Interrogation*.
Madison: University of Wisconsin Press.

Miles, Steven H. n.d. "The WPA Declaration on Psychiatry and Interrogations: Why Now?" *Torture* 27 (3): 97–98.

Moran, Mark. 2010. "Former Soviet Dissidents Believed APA Pressure
Forced Change," November 19. https://psychnews.psychiatryonline
.org/doi/full/10.1176/pn.45.22.psychnews_45_22_023.

Newkirk II, Vann R. 2017. "The Fight for Health Care Has Always Been
About Civil Rights." *Atlantic*, June 27. https://www.theatlantic.com
/politics/archive/2017/06/the-fight-for-health-care-is-really-all-about
-civil-rights/531855/.

Otterman, Michael. 2007. *American Torture: From the Cold War to Abu Ghraib
and Beyond*. Ann Arbor, MI: Pluto Press.

"Physicians for a National Health Program." n.d. Accessed October 15, 2018. http://www.pnhp.org/.

Physicians for Human Rights. 2018a. "America's Health Professionals Appeal to Trump Administration: End Family Separation at Border Immediately." Physicians for Human Rights. June 14. http://physi ciansforhumanrights.org/press/press-releases/family-separation-letter .html.

———. 2018b. "Ridding the World of a Deadly Scourge—Physicians for Human Rights." Physicians for Human Rights. August 5. https://phr.org /impact/campaign-to-ban-landmines/.

Pipher, Mary, Juan Gonzalez, and Amy Goodman. 2017. "Psychologist, Author Mary Pipher Returns APA Award over Interrogation Policy." *Democracy Now!* (blog). August 29. https://web.archive.org/web /20071114072336/http://www.democracynow.org/article.pl?sid=07/08 /29/1514245.

Pope, Kenneth S., and Thomas G. Gutheil. 2009. "Psychologists Abandon the Nuremberg Ethic: Concerns for Detainee Interrogations." *International Journal of Law and Psychiatry* 32: 161–66.

Risen, James. 2014. *Pay Any Price: Greed, Power, and Endless War.* New York: Houghton Mifflin Harcourt.

———. 2015. "American Psychological Association Bolstered C.I.A. Torture Program, Report Says." *New York Times*, April 30. https://www .nytimes.com/2015/05/01/us/report-says-american-psychological -association-collaborated-on-torture-justification.html?referrer=&_r=1.

Smith, Carly Parnitzke, and Jennifer J. Freyd. 2014. "Institutional Betrayal." *American Psychologist* 69 (6): 575–87.

Soldz, Stephen. 2006. "Abusive Interrogations: A Defining Difference Between Psychiatrists and Psychologists." *CounterPunch*, December 12. http://www.counterpunch.org/soldz12122006.html.

———. 2007. "Letter to Committee on Intelligence." *Scoop*, November 5. http://www.scoop.co.nz/stories/HL0711/S00080/stephen-soldz-letter -to-committee-on-intelligence.htm.

———. 2009. "Closing Eyes to Atrocities: U.S. Psychologists, Detainee Interrogations, and Response of the American Psychological Association."

In *Interrogations, Forced Feedings, and the Role of Health Professionals: New Perspectives on International Human Rights, Humanitarian Law and Ethics*, edited by Ryan Goodman and Mindy Roseman, 103–42. Cambridge, MA: Harvard Human Rights Program at Harvard Law School.

———. 2011. "Psychologists, Torture, and Civil Society: Complicity, Institutional Failure, and the Struggle for Professional Transformation." In *United States and Torture: Interrogation, Incarceration, and Abuse*, ed. by Marjorie Cohn, 177–202. New York: New York University Press.

———. 2017. "Principles Determine Practice: Commentary on World Psychiatric Association Declaration on Participation of Psychiatrists in Interrogation of Detainees." *Torture* 27 (3): 96–97.

Soldz, Stephen, Nathaniel Raymond, Steven Reisner, Scott A. Allen, Isaac L. Baker, and Allen S. Keller. 2015. "All the President's Psychologists: The American Psychological Association's Secret Complicity with the White House and US Intelligence Community in Support of the CIA's 'Enhanced' Interrogation Program." https://assets.documentcloud.org /documents/2069718/report.pdf.

Stockholm Center for Freedom. 2017. "Doctors in Turkey Discouraged from Writing up Reports on Abuse, Torture." *Stockholm Center for Freedom* (blog). April 10. https://stockholmcf.org/doctors-in-turkey-discour aged-from-writing-up-reports-on-abuse-torture/.

Welch, Bryant. 2009. "The American Psychological Association and Torture: The Day the Tide Turned." *Huffington Post*. July 21. http://www .huffingtonpost.com/bryant-welch/the-american-psychologica_b _242020.html.

Wiener, Jon. 2018. "A Forgotten Hero Stopped the My Lai Massacre 50 Years Ago Today." *Los Angeles Times*, March 16. http://www.latimes.com /opinion/op-ed/la-oe-wiener-my-lai-hugh-thompson-20180316-story .html.

World Medical Association. 2017. "WMA—The World Medical Association-WMA Declaration of Geneva." https://www.wma.net /policies-post/wma-declaration-of-geneva/.

World Psychiatric Association. 2017. "World Psychiatric Association Declaration on Participation of Psychiatrists in Interrogation of Detainees: Statement Banning the Participation of Psychiatrists in Interrogation Procedures." *Torture* 27 (3): 94–95.

FOREWORD TO THE FIRST EDITION

Our Witness to Malignant Normality

ROBERT JAY LIFTON, M.D.

Our situation as American psychological professionals can be summed up in just two ideas—we can call them themes or even concepts: first, what I call *malignant normality*, which has to do with the social actuality with which we are presented as normal, all-encompassing, and unalterable; and second, our potential and crucial sense of ourselves as *witnessing professionals*.

Concerning malignant normality, we start with an assumption that all societies, at various levels of consciousness, put forward ways of viewing, thinking, and behaving that are considered desirable or "normal." Yet, these criteria for normality can be much affected by the political and military currents of a particular era. Such requirements may be fairly benign, but they can also be destructive to the point of evil.

I came to the idea of malignant normality in my study of Nazi doctors. Those assigned to Auschwitz, when taking charge of the selections and the overall killing process, were simply doing what was expected of them. True, some were upset, even horrified, at being given this task. Yet, with a certain amount of counseling—one can call it perverse psychotherapy—offered by more experienced hands, a process that included drinking heavily together and giving assurance of help and support, the great majority could overcome their anxiety sufficiently to carry through their murderous assignment. This was a process of *adaptation to evil* that is all too possible to initiate in such a situation. Above all, there was a *normalization of evil* that enhanced this adaptation and served to present participating doctors with the Auschwitz institution as the existing world to which one must make one's adjustments.

There is another form of malignant normality, closer to home and more recent. I have in mind the participation in torture by physicians (including psychiatrists), and by psychologists, and other medical and psychological personnel. This reached its most extreme manifestation when two psychologists were revealed to be among architects of the CIA's torture protocol. More than that, this malignant normality was essentially supported by the American Psychological Association in its defense of the participation of psychologists in the so-called "enhanced interrogation" techniques that spilled over into torture.

I am not equating this American behavior with the Nazi example but, rather, suggesting that malignant normality can take different forms. And nothing does more to sustain malignant normality than its support from a large organization of professionals.

There is still another kind of malignant normality, one brought about by President Trump and his administration. Judith Herman and I, in a letter to the *New York Times* in March 2017, stressed Trump's dangerous individual psychological patterns: his creation of his own reality and his inability to manage the inevitable crises that face an American president. He has also, in various ways, violated our American institutional requirements and threatened the viability of American democracy. Yet, because he is president and operates within the broad contours and interactions of the presidency, there is a tendency to view what he does as simply part of our democratic process—that is, as politically and even ethically normal. In this way, a dangerous president becomes normalized, and malignant normality comes to dominate our governing (or, one could say, our antigoverning) dynamic.

But that does not mean we are helpless. We remain a society with considerable openness, with institutions that can still be life-enhancing and serve truth. Unlike Nazi doctors, articulate psychological professionals could and did expose the behavior of corrupt colleagues and even a corrupt professional society. Investigative journalists and human rights groups also greatly contributed to that exposure.

As psychological professionals, we are capable of parallel action in confronting the malignant normality of Trump and his administration. To do so we need to combine our sense of outrage with a disciplined use of our professional knowledge and experience.

This brings me to my second theme: that of witnessing professionals, particularly activist witnessing professionals. Most professionals, most of the time, operate within the norms (that is, the criteria for normality) of their particular society. Indeed, professionals often go further, and in their practices may deepen the commitment of people they work with to that normality. This can give solace, but it has its perils.

It is not generally known that during the early Cold War period, a special governmental commission, chaired by a psychiatrist and containing physicians and social scientists, was set up to help the American people achieve the desired psychological capacity to support U.S. stockpiling of nuclear weapons, cope with an anticipated nuclear attack, and overcome the fear of nuclear annihilation. The commission had the task, in short, of helping Americans accept malignant nuclear normality. There have also been parallel examples in recent history of professionals who have promoted equally dangerous forms of normality in rejecting climate change.

But professionals don't have to serve these forms of malignant normality. We are capable of using our knowledge and technical skills to expose such normality, to bear witness to its malignance—to become witnessing professionals.

When I did my study of Hiroshima survivors back in 1962, I sought to uncover, in the most accurate and scientific way I could, the psychological and bodily experience of people exposed to the atomic bomb. Yet, I was not just a neutral observer. Over time, I came to understand myself as a witnessing professional, committed to making known what an atomic bomb could do to a city, to tell the world something of what had happened in Hiroshima and to its inhabitants. The Hiroshima story could be condensed to "one plane, one bomb, one city." I came to view this commitment to telling Hiroshima's story as a form of advocacy research. That meant combining a disciplined professional approach with the ethical requirements of committed witness, combining scholarship with activism.

I believe that some such approach is what we require now, in the Trump era. We need to avoid uncritical acceptance of this new version of malignant normality and, instead, bring our knowledge and experience to exposing it for what it is. This requires us to be disciplined about what we believe we know, while refraining from holding forth on what we do not know. It also requires us to recognize the urgency of the situation in which the most powerful man in the world is also the bearer of profound instability and untruth. As psychological professionals, we act with ethical passion in our efforts to reveal what is most dangerous and what, in contrast, might be life-affirming in the face of the malignant normality that surrounds us.

Finally, there is the issue of our ethical behavior. We talk a lot about our professional ethics having to do with our responsibility to patients and to the overall standards of our discipline. This concern with professional ethics matters a great deal.

But I am suggesting something more, a larger concept of professional ethics that we don't often discuss: including who we work for and with, and how our work either affirms or questions the directions of the larger society. And, in our present situation, how we deal with the malignant normality that faces us. This larger ethical model applies to members of other professions who may have their own "duty to warn."

I in no way minimize the significance of professional knowledge and technical skill. But our professions can become overly technicized, and we can be too much like hired guns bringing our firepower to any sponsor of the most egregious view of normality.

We can do better than that. We can take the larger ethical view of the activist witnessing professional. Bandy Lee took that perspective when organizing the Yale conference on professional responsibility,* and the participants affirmed it. This does not make us saviors of our threatened society, but it does help us bring our experience and knowledge to bear on what threatens us and what might renew us.

A line from the American poet Theodore Roethke brings eloquence to what I have been trying to say: "In a dark time, the eye begins to see."

Robert Jay Lifton, M.D., is Lecturer in Psychiatry at Columbia University and Distinguished Professor Emeritus of John Jay College and the Graduate Center of the City University of New York. A leading psychohistorian, he is renowned for his studies of the doctors who aided Nazi war crimes and from his work with survivors of the atomic bombing of Hiroshima. He was an outspoken critic of the American Psychological Association's aiding of government-sanctioned torture and is a vocal opponent of nuclear weapons. His research encompasses the psychological causes and effects of war and political violence and the theory of thought reform.

---

* Please see Appendix for the link to the Yale conference transcript.

PROLOGUE TO THE FIRST EDITION

Professions and Politics

JUDITH LEWIS HERMAN, M.D., AND BANDY X. LEE, M.D., M.DIV.

> Professions can create forms of ethical conversation that are impossible between a lonely individual and a distant government. If members of professions think of themselves as groups . . . with norms and rules that oblige them at all times, then they can gain . . . confidence, and indeed a certain kind of power.
>
> Timothy Snyder, *On Tyranny:*
> *Twenty Lessons from the Twentieth Century* (2017)

Soon after the presidential election of 2016, alarmed by the apparent mental instability of the president-elect, we both separately circulated letters among some of our professional colleagues, expressing our concern. Most of them declined to sign. A number of people admitted they were afraid of some undefined form of governmental retaliation, so quickly had a climate of fear taken hold. They asked us if we were not wary of being "targeted," and advised us to seek legal counsel. This was a lesson to us in how a climate of fear can induce people to censor themselves.

Others who declined to sign our letters of concern cited matters of principle. Psychiatry, we were warned, should stay out of politics;

otherwise, the profession could end up being ethically compromised. The example most frequently cited was that of psychiatrists in the Soviet Union who collaborated with the secret police to diagnose dissidents as mentally ill and confine them to prisons that fronted as hospitals (Medvedev and Medvedev 1971).

This was a serious consideration. Indeed, we need not look beyond our own borders for examples of ethics violations committed by professionals who became entangled in politics. We have recently witnessed the disgrace of an entire professional organization, the American Psychological Association, some of whose leadership, in cooperation with officials from the U.S. military, the CIA, and the Bush White House, rewrote its ethical guidelines to give legal cover to a secret government program of coercive interrogation and to excuse military psychologists who designed and implemented methods of torture (Hoffman et al. 2015; Risen 2014).*

Among the many lessons that might be learned from this notorious example, one in particular stayed with us. It seemed clear that the government officials responsible for abusive treatment of prisoners went to some lengths to find medical and mental health professionals who would publicly condone their practices. We reasoned that if professional endorsement serves as important cover for human rights abuses, then professional condemnation must also carry weight.

In 2005 the Pentagon organized a trip to the Guantánamo Bay detention camp for a group of prominent ethicists, psychiatrists, and psychologists. Participants toured the facility and met with high-ranking military officers, including the commanding general. They were not allowed to meet or speak with any of the detainees.

Dr. Steven Sharfstein, then the president of the American Psy-

---

* It should be noted that a majority of the American Psychological Association membership did not approve this revision of the Association's ethics code and tried to rescind it. They did not succeed, however, until the matter became a public scandal.

chiatric Association, was one of the invited guests on this trip. Apparently, what he saw and heard failed to convince him that the treatment of detainees fell within the bounds of ethical conduct. "Our position is very direct," he stated on return. "Psychiatrists should not participate on these [interrogation] teams because it is inappropriate" (Lewis 2005). Under Dr. Sharfstein's leadership, the American Psychiatric Association took a strong stand against any form of participation in torture and in the "interrogation of persons held in custody by military or civilian investigative or law enforcement authorities, whether in the United States or elsewhere" (American Psychiatric Association 2006).

Contrast this principled stand with the sorry tale of the American Psychological Association. Its involvement in the torture scandal illustrates how important it is for leaders in the professions to stand firm against ethical violations, and to resist succumbing to the argument that exceptional political circumstances, such as "the war on terror," demand exceptions to basic ethical codes. When there is pressure from power is exactly when one must abide by the norms and rules of our ethics.*

Norms and Rules in the Political Sphere

Norms and rules guide professional conduct, set standards, and point to the essential principles of practice. For these reasons, physicians have the *Declaration of Geneva* (World Medical Association 2006) and the American Medical Association *Principles of Medical Ethics* (2001), which guide the American Psychiatric Association's code for psychiatry (American Psychiatric Association 2013). The former confirms the physician's dedication to the humanitarian

---

* We hold no brief for the general moral superiority of the American Psychiatric Association, which has had its own ignominious history in the ways that its diagnostic code for many years reinforced institutional homophobia and misogyny. In the particular case that we are discussing, however, the APA was fortunate enough to have good leadership that resulted in a position of moral clarity.

goals of medicine, while the latter defines honorable behavior for the physician. Paramount in both is the health, safety, and survival of the patient.

Psychiatrists' codes of ethics derive directly from these principles. In ordinary practice, the patient's right to confidentiality is the bedrock of mental health care dating back to the ethical standards of the Hippocratic Oath. However, even this sacrosanct rule is not absolute. No doubt, the physician's responsibility is first and foremost to the patient, but it extends "as well as to society" (American Psychiatric Association 2013, p. 2). It is part of professional expectation that the psychiatrist assess the possibility that the patient may harm himself or others. When the patient poses a danger, psychiatrists are not merely allowed but mandated to report, to incapacitate, and to take steps to protect.

If we are mindful of the dangers of politicizing the professions, then certainly we must heed the so-called "Goldwater rule," or Section 7.3 of the APA code of ethics (American Psychiatric Association 2013, p. 6), which states: "it is unethical for a psychiatrist to offer a professional opinion [on a public figure] unless he or she has conducted an examination and has been granted proper authorization for such a statement." This is not divergent from ordinary norms of practice: the clinical approaches that we use to evaluate patients require a full examination. Formulating a credible diagnosis will always be limited when applied to public figures observed outside this intimate frame; in fact, we would go so far as to assert that it is impossible.

The Goldwater rule highlights the boundaries of practice, helps to preserve professional integrity, and protects public figures from defamation. It safeguards the public's perception of the field of psychiatry as credible and trustworthy. It is reasonable to follow it. But even this respectable rule must be balanced against the other rules and principles of professional practice. A careful ethical evaluation might ask: Do our ordinary norms of practice stop at the office of president? If so, why? If the ethics of our practice stipulate that the health of our patient and the safety of the public be paramount, then we should not leave our norms at the door when entering the political sphere. Otherwise, a rule originally conceived to protect our profession from scandal might itself become a source of scandal. For this very reason, the "reaffirmation" of the Goldwater rule in a separate statement by the American Psychiatric Association (2017) barely two months into the new administration seems questionable to us. The American Psychiatric Association is not immune to the kind of politically pressured acquiescence we have seen with its psychological counterpart.

A psychiatrist who disregards the basic procedures of diagnosis and treatment and acts without discretion deserves reprimand. However, the public trust is also violated if the profession fails in its duty to alert the public when a person who holds the power of life and death over us all shows signs of clear, dangerous mental impairment. We should pause if professionals are asked to remain silent when they have seen enough evidence to sound an alarm in every other situation. When it comes to dangerousness, should not the president of a democracy, as First Citizen, be subject to the same standards of practice as the rest of the citizenry?

Assessing dangerousness is different from making a diagnosis: it is dependent on the situation, not the person. Signs of likely dangerousness due to mental disorder can become apparent without a full diagnostic interview and can be detected from a distance, and one is expected to err, if at all, on the side of safety when the risk of inaction is too great. States vary in their instructions. New York, for example, requires that two qualifying professionals agree in order to detain a person who may be in danger of hurting himself or others. Florida and the District of Columbia require only one professional's opinion. Also, only one person need be in danger of harm by the individual, and the threshold is even lower if the individual has access to weapons (not to mention nuclear weapons).

The physician, to whom life-and-death situations are entrusted, is expected to know when it is appropriate to act, and to act responsibly when warranted. It is because of the weight of this responsibility that, rightfully, the physician should refrain from commenting on a public figure except in the rarest instance. Only in an emergency should a physician breach the trust of confidentiality and intervene without consent, and only in an emergency should a physician breach the Goldwater rule. We believe that such an emergency now exists.

Test for Proper Responsibility

When we circulated our letters of concern, we asked our fellow mental health professionals to get involved in politics not only as citizens (a right most of us still enjoy) but also, specifically, as professionals and as guardians of the special knowledge with which they have been entrusted. Why do we think this was permissible? It is all too easy to claim, as we did, that an emergency situation requires a departure from our usual practices in the private sphere. How can one judge whether political involvement is in fact justified?

We would argue that the key question is whether mental health professionals are engaging in political *collusion* with state abuses of power or acting in *resistance* to them. If we are asked to cooperate with state programs that violate human rights, then any involvement, regardless of the purported justification, can only corrupt, and the only appropriate ethical stance is to refuse participation of any sort. If, on the other hand, we perceive that state power is being abused by an executive who seems to be mentally unstable, then we may certainly speak out, not only as citizens but also, we would argue, as professionals who are privy to special information and have a responsibility to educate the public. For whatever our wisdom and expertise may be worth, surely we are obligated to share it.

It doesn't take a psychiatrist to notice that our president is mentally compromised. Members of the press have come up with their own diagnostic nomenclature, calling the president a "mad king" (Dowd 2017), a "nut job" (Collins 2017), and "emotionally unhinged"

(Rubin 2017). Conservative columnist George Will (2017) writes that the president has a "disorderly mind." By speaking out as mental health professionals, we lend support and dignity to our fellow citizens who are justifiably alarmed by the president's furious tirades, conspiracy fantasies, aversion to facts, and attraction to violence. We can offer a hand in helping the public understand behaviors that are unusual and alarming but that can all too easily be rationalized and normalized.

An important and relevant question that the public has been asking is this: Is the man simply crazy, or is he crazy like a fox? Is he mentally compromised or simply vile? When he lies, does he know he is lying, or does he believe his own lies? When he makes wild accusations, is he truly paranoid, or is he consciously and cunningly trying to deflect attention from his misdeeds?

We believe that we can help answer these questions by emphasizing that the two propositions are not mutually exclusive. A man can be both evil and mentally compromised—which is a more frightening proposition. Power not only corrupts but also magnifies existing psychopathologies, even as it creates new ones. Fostered by the flattery of underlings and the chants of crowds, a political leader's grandiosity may morph into grotesque delusions of grandeur. Sociopathic traits may be amplified as the leader discovers that he can violate the norms of civil society and even commit crimes with impunity. And the leader who rules through fear, lies, and betrayal may become increasingly isolated and paranoid, as the loyalty of even his closest confidants must forever be suspect.

Some would argue that by paying attention to the president's mental state, we are colluding with him in deflecting attention from that by which he should ultimately be judged: his actions (Frances 2017). Certainly, mental disturbance is not an excuse for tyrannical behavior; nevertheless, it cannot be ignored. In a court of law, even the strongest insanity defense case cannot show that a person is insane all the time. We submit that by paying attention to the president's mental state *as well as* his actions, we are better informed to assess his danger-ousness. Delusional levels of grandiosity, impulsivity, and the compul-sions of mental impairment, when combined with an authoritarian cult of personality and contempt for the rule of law, are a toxic mix.

There are those who still hold out hope that this president can be prevailed upon to listen to reason and curb his erratic behavior. Our professional experience would suggest otherwise; witness the numerous submissions we have received for this volume while orga-nizing a Yale conference in April 2017 entitled "Does Professional Responsibility Include a Duty to Warn?"* Collectively with our co-authors, we warn that anyone as mentally unstable as Mr. Trump simply should not be entrusted with the life-and-death powers of the presidency.

Judith Lewis Herman, M.D., is Professor of Psychiatry at Har-vard Medical School. She is a renowned expert in the traumas of interpersonal violence and author of the now-classic Trauma and Recovery. *She is a cofounder of the Victims of Violence Pro-gram in the Department of Psychiatry at Cambridge Health Alli-ance, a Distinguished Life Fellow of the American Psychiatric Association, and the recipient of numerous awards, including the Lifetime Achievement Award from the International Society for Traumatic Stress Studies.*

Bandy X. Lee, M.D., M.Div., is Assistant Clinical Professor in Law and Psychiatry at Yale School of Medicine. She teaches at Yale Law School, cofounded Yale's Violence and Health Study Group, and leads a Violence Prevention Alliance collaborators project for the World Health Organization. She is the author of more than one hundred peer-reviewed articles, editor of eleven academic books, and author of the textbook Violence.

---

* Please see Appendix for the link to the Yale conference transcript.

Acknowledgments

We thank Nanette Gartrell, Dee Mosbacher, Gloria Steinem, Robin Morgan, Jaine Darwin, Frank Putnam, and Grace Lee, for their helpful editorial comments and assistance in the preparation of this Prologue.

References

American Medical Association. 2001. *AMA Code of Medical Ethics: AMA Principles of Medical Ethics*. www.ama-assn.org/sites/default/files /media-browser/principles-of-medical-ethics.pdf.

American Psychiatric Association. 2006. *Position Statement on Psychiatric Participation in Interrogation of Detainees*. www.psychiatry.org/File %20Library/About-APA/Organization-Documents-Policies/Policies /Position-2014-Interrogation-Detainees-Psychiatric-Participation.pdf.

———. 2013. *Principles of Medical Ethics with Annotations Especially Applicable to Psychiatry*. www.psychiatry.org/psychiatrists/practice/ethics.

———. 2017. "APA Remains Committed to Supporting Goldwater Rule." www.psychiatry.org/news-room/apa-blogs/apa-blog/2017/03/apa -remains-committed-to-supporting-goldwater-rule.

Collins, Gail. 2017. "Trump Stays Buggy." *New York Times*, March 17. www .nytimes.com/2017/03/17/opinion/trump-stays-buggy.html.

Dowd, Maureen. 2017. "Mad Trump, Happy W." *New York Times*, March 4. www.nytimes.com/2017/03/04/opinion/sunday/mad-trump-happy-w .html?_r=0.

Frances, Allen. 2017. "An Eminent Psychiatrist Demurs on Trump's Mental State." *New York Times*, February 14. www.nytimes.com/2017/02/14 /opinion/an-eminent-psychiatrist-demurs-on-trumps-mental-state .html.

Hoffman, David H., Danielle J. Carter, Cara R. Viglucci Lopez, Heather L. Benzmiller, Ava X. Guo, S. Yasir Latifi, and Daniel C. Craig. 2015. *Report to the Special Committee of the Board of Directors of the American Psychological Association: Independent Review Relating to APA Ethics Guidelines, National Security Interrogations, and Torture* (revised). Chicago: Sidley Austin LLP.

Lewis, Neil A. 2005. "Guantánamo Tour Focuses on Medical Ethics." *New York Times*, Nov. 13. www.nytimes.com/2005/11/13/us/guantanamo -tour-focuses-on-medical-ethics.html.

Medvedev, Zhores, and Roy Medvedev. 1971. *A Question of Madness: Repression by Psychiatry in the Soviet Union.* New York: Vintage.

Risen, James. 2014. *Pay Any Price: Greed, Power, and Endless War.* New York: Houghton Mifflin.

Rubin, Jennifer. 2017. "Will Comey's Request Push Trump over the Edge?" *Washington Post*, March 6. www.washingtonpost.com/blogs/right-turn /wp/2017/03/06/will-comeys-request-push-trump-over-the-edge /?utm_term=.65aa62ca0657.

Snyder, Timothy. 2017. *On Tyranny: Twenty Lessons from the Twentieth Century.* New York: Crown/Archetype.

Will, George F. 2017. "Trump Has a Dangerous Disability." *Washington Post*, May 3. www.washingtonpost.com/opinions/trump-has-a-dangerous -disability/2017/05/03/56ca6118-2f6b-11e7-9534-00e4656c22aa_story .html?utm_term=.90f21a74dc93.

World Medical Association. 2006. *Declaration of Geneva.* www.wma.net /policies-post/wma-declaration-of-geneva/.

THE
DANGEROUS
CASE OF
DONALD
TRUMP

INTRODUCTION

Our Duty to Warn and to Protect

BANDY X. LEE, M.D., M.DIV.

Possibly the oddest experience in my career as a psychiatrist has been to find that the only people not allowed to speak about an issue are those who know the most about it. Hence, truth is suppressed. Yet, what if that truth, furthermore, harbored dangers of such magnitude that it could be the key to future human survival? How can I, as a medical and mental health professional, remain a bystander in the face of one of the greatest emergencies of our time, when I have been called to step in everywhere else? How can we, as trained professionals in this very area, be content to keep silent, against every other principle we practice by, because of a decree handed down from above?

I am not speaking of the long-standing "Goldwater rule," which is discussed in many places throughout this book and is a norm of ordinary practice I happen to agree with. I am rather speaking of its radical expansion, beyond the status we confer to any other rule, barely two months into the very presidency that has made it controversial. This occurred on March 16, 2017, when our professional organization essentially placed a gag order on all psychiatrists (American Psychiatric Association 2017), and by extension all mental health professionals. I am also speaking of its defect, whereby it does not have a countervailing rule, as does the rest of professional ethics, that directs what to do when the risk of harm from remaining silent outweighs the damage that could result from speaking about a public figure—which, in this case, could even be the greatest possible harm. Authors in this volume have been asked to respect the Goldwater rule and not to breach it unnecessarily, but I in turn respect their choices wherever their conscience has prompted them to take the professionally and socially radical step to help protect the public. Therefore, it would be accurate to state that, while we respect the rule, we deem it subordinate to the single most important principle that guides our professional conduct: that we hold our responsibility to the life and well-being of our patients and patient base as paramount.

My reasons for compiling this compendium are the same as my reasons for organizing the Yale conference by the title "Does Professional Responsibility Include a Duty to Warn?": the issue merits discussion, not silence, and the public deserves education, not further darkness. Over the course of preparing the conference, a number of prominent professionals in the field came forth to speak out. Soon after the 2016 presidential election, Dr. Herman (coauthor of the prologue to the first edition), an old colleague and friend, had written a letter urging President Obama to require that Mr. Trump undergo a neuropsychiatric evaluation before assuming the office of the presidency. Her cosignatories, Drs. Gartrell and Mosbacher (authors of the essay "He's Got the World in His Hands and His Finger on the Trigger") facilitated the letter's publication in the *Huffington Post* (Greene 2016). I also reached out to Dr. Lifton (author of the foreword to the first edition), whose "Mass Violence" meetings at Harvard first acquainted me with Dr. Herman years ago; together, they sent a letter to the *New York Times* (Herman and Lifton 2017). His ready agreement to speak at my conference sparked all that was to follow.

I encountered others along the way: Dr. Dodes (author of "Sociopathy"), who published a letter in the *New York Times* with thirty-five signatures (Dodes and Schachter 2017); Ms. Jhueck (author of "A

Clinical Case for the Dangerousness of Donald J. Trump"), who co-wrote and posted a letter to the head of New York City's Department of Health and Mental Hygiene with seventy signatures; Dr. Fisher (author of "The Loneliness of Fateful Decisions"), who expressed concerns at a key moment in a letter to the *New York Times* (Fisher 2017); and Dr. Gartner, author of "Donald Trump Is: (A) Bad, (B) Mad, (C) All of the Above," who initiated an online petition, which he delivered to the president's cabinet with seventy thousand signatures.

After the publication of the first edition, Prof. Sachs (author of the foreword to the second edition) got in touch, sharing concerns that mental health issues were imperiling the world; while former White House "Ethics Czars" Eisen and Painter (authors of "Congress Should Establish an Alternative Body to Assess the President") thought we should make mental "capacity" as important a national issue as "corruption" and "collusion." A number of Democratic Congress members also impressed me, including a former house majority and minority leader who reached out, and while I curtailed these meetings to be open also to consultations with Republicans, which never came, they revealed to me what truly concerned and capable leaders our country has (I was overwhelmed when one of them called me his "hero"). Communications such as these indicated to me the importance of dialogue among the different fields: while mental health professionals understand the phenomenon that is occurring, we do not have ways to intervene at the national level, and while politicians have the power to act nationally, they do not possess comprehensive understanding of mental health issues. My career in public health and prevention has regularly put me in contact with policymakers and specialists in other disciplines, but this instance particularly convinced me of this need.

It is difficult to conceive of professional activism under difficult conditions of governmental pressure without thinking of Dr. Soldz (coauthor of the prologue to the second edition), and it is for his ethical example that I invited him to contribute to this volume. Meanwhile, others had similar thoughts in mind: top CIA psychiatrist Dr. Post (author of "The Charismatic Leader-Follower Relationship and Trump's Base") contacted me, and I learned that he was on the original Carter Commission to establish a body for evaluating presidential fitness; Dr. Merikangas (author of "The Myth of Nuclear War") reached out with concerns about entrusting the nuclear launch codes in Mr. Trump's hands, while he as a naval officer handling them had to undergo rigorous mental health screening; and Dr. Gourguechon (author of "Is the Commander in Chief Fit to Serve?") established useful criteria for determining presidential capacity by consulting the *U.S. Army Field Manual*. At the same time, we tried to engage the American Psychiatric Association, as Dr. Ghaemi (author of "The Goldwater Rule and the Silence of American Psychiatry") had done, for a more responsible position than relegating psychiatry to a rarefied field that no one was to engage, which dealt with conditions that no one should speak about. At the time of this writing, the Association had not responded to the numerous protest letters, resignations of members including high-ranking officers, and requests for a vote, a commission to reexamine the Goldwater rule, even a discussion—or a response to a formal revision proposal Dr. Glass and twenty-one other authors submitted on June 28, 2018 (Begley 2018).

There are many more who influenced our course—too many to include in this volume and too many even to mention—but some names are: Dr. Eric Chivian, who cofounded the Nobel Prize–winning International Physicians for the Prevention of Nuclear War with Dr. Bernard Lown, who has been a personal inspiration through this endeavor; Dr. John Zinner, former surgeon of the U.S. Public Health Service and former director of family therapy studies for the National Institute of Mental Health, who has helped affirm the urgency of our cause; Drs. Brenda Burger, Susan Vaughan, Frank Yeomans, Otto Kernberg, and Justin Frank, who supported our efforts in professional ways; and Drs. Larry Sandberg, Richard C. Friedman, Kerry Sulkowicz, Stephanie Brandt, and Elaine Walker, who partnered with us against some of the harshest criticisms. Foremost in importance is Mr. Bill Moyers, who was the first to recognize the importance of our work and through this process became a good friend and an irreplaceable kindred spirit who cares about this world in much the same way.

The Yale Conference

- On April 20, 2017, Dr. Charles Dike of my division at Yale, as a member of the ethics committee of the American Psychiatric Association and distinguished fellow of the American Psychiatric Association, started the town hall–style meeting by reaffirming the relevance and reasons for the Goldwater rule. I also invited Drs. Lifton, Herman, and Gilligan (the last the author of "The Issue Is Dangerousness, Not Mental Illness"), with the purpose of bringing together the finest minds of psychiatry to address the quandary. They are all colleagues I have known for at least fifteen years and highly esteem not only for their eminence in the field but also for their ethics. They were beacons during other dark times. They abided by the Goldwater rule in that they kept the discussion at the level of dangerousness, without attempting to diagnose.

- The transcript of the meeting can be found in an online appendix, the link to which is at the end of this book. The conclusion from the conference was that we had a responsibility to society and not just to patients, as outlined in our own ethical guidelines, and that this entailed a duty to warn when the public's health and safety are at risk—and, we might now add, also a duty to protect.

- Assessing dangerousness requires a different standard from diagnosing so as to formulate a course of treatment. Dangerousness is about the situation, not the individual; it is more about the effects and the degree of impairment than the specific cause of illness; it does not require a full examination but takes into account whatever information is available. Also, it requires that the qualified professional err on the side of safety, and it may entail breaking other, ordinarily binding rules for urgent action.

Our nation is now living, in extremes, a paradigm that splits along partisan lines, and the quick conclusion will be that the speakers or contributors to this volume "must be Democrats" if they are casting a negative light on a Republican president. However, we are not all Democrats, and there are other paradigms. Mental health professionals practice within a paradigm of health versus disease. We apply science, research, observed phenomena, and clinical skill developed over years of practice in order to promote life and to prevent death. These goals cannot be contained within the purposes of a political party or the campaigns of a candidate. Rather, we are trained to maintain medical neutrality and to identify abnormalities in a standardized way while eliminating bias. In this sense, one might say that health professionals are pro-Trump, for we desire that he receive the same standard of care as anyone else, and not be short-changed because of political expediency. Just as we should not raise alarms for political reasons, we should not attenuate concerns for political acceptability or the mere appearance of professionalism. Minimizing a person's condition because of partisan benefits can be dangerous and immoral. It is a glimpse of this medical perspective that we hope to bring to the reader.

Our meeting gained national and international attention (Milligan 2017; Bulman 2017). While only two dozen physically attended the conference in an atmosphere of fear (mainly of the possibility that one might be gratuitously litigated against, or that they or their families might become the target of violent Trump supporters), hundreds, and later thousands, got in touch with me, and together we formed the National Coalition of Concerned Mental Health Experts (dangerouscase.org). We had tapped into a groundswell of a movement among mental health professionals (DeVega 2017). What was intended as a publication of the proceedings led to the first edition and then a second edition, with fifteen more authors! Many of the contributors here do not need an introduction, and I am humbled to have the opportunity to present such an assembly of brilliant and principled professionals.

A Compendium of Expertise

This volume consists of five parts, the first three being carried over from the original edition. The first part is devoted to answering the public's questions about Mr. Trump, with an understanding that no definitive diagnoses will be possible. In "Unbridled and Extreme Present Hedonism," Zimbardo and Sword discuss how the leader of the free world has proven himself unfit for duty as a result of his extreme ties to the present moment, without much thought for the consequences of his actions or for the future. In "Pathological Narcissism and Politics," Malkin explains that narcissism happens on a scale, and that pathological levels in a leader can spiral into psychosis and imperil the safety of his country through paranoia, impaired judgment, volatile decision making, and behavior called gaslighting. In "I Wrote *The Art of the Deal* with Donald Trump," Schwartz reveals how what he observed during the year he spent with Trump to write that book could have predicted a presidency marked by "black hole-level" low self-worth, fact-free self-justification, and a compulsion to go to war with the world.

In "Trump's Trust Deficit Is the Core Problem," Sheehy highlights the notion that beneath the grandiose behavior of every narcissist lies a pit of fragile self-esteem; more than anything, Trump lacks trust in himself, which may lead him to take drastic actions to prove himself to himself and to the world. In "Sociopathy," Dodes shows that someone who cons others, lies, cheats, and manipulates to get what he wants, and who doesn't care whom he hurts, may be not just repetitively immoral but also severely impaired, as sociopaths lack a central human characteristic, empathy. In "Donald Trump Is: (A) Bad, (B), Mad, (C) All of the Above," Gartner emphasizes the complexity of Trump's presentation, in that he shows signs of being "bad" as well as "mad," but also with a hypomanic temperament that generates whirlwinds of activity and a constant need for stimulation.

In "Why 'Crazy Like a Fox' versus 'Crazy Like a Crazy' *Really* Matters," Tansey shows that Trump's nearly outrageous lies may be explained by delusional disorder, about which Tansey invites the reader to make the call; even more frightening is Trump's attraction to brutal tyrants and also the prospect of nuclear war. In "Cognitive Impairment, Dementia, and POTUS," Reiss writes that a current vulnerability of our political system is that it sets no intellectual or cognitive standards for being president, despite the job's inherently requiring cognitive clarity; this lack of clarity can be even more serious if combined with other psychiatric disorders. In "Donald J. Trump, Alleged Incapacitated Person," Herb explains how, as a guardianship attorney (in contrast to a mental health professional), he is required to come to a preliminary conclusion about mental incapacity before filing a petition, which he does in his essay, while reflecting on the Electoral College and the Twenty-Fifth Amendment to the U.S. Constitution.

The second part of the book addresses the dilemmas that mental health professionals face in observing what they do and speaking out when they feel they must. In "Should Psychiatrists Refrain from Commenting on Trump's Psychology?" Glass argues against a technicality that would yield a simple yes-or-no answer to the Goldwater rule; instead, he advocates for a conscientious voicing of hazardous patterns, noting that the presence of mental illness is not as relevant as that of reliable functionality. In "On Seeing What You See and Saying What You Know," Friedman notes that technological advances that allow assessment and treatment from a distance, especially in underserved areas, have changed the clinician's comfort level with remote evaluations, even when detecting a totalitarian mind-set or a multidimensional threat to the world. In "The Issue Is Dangerousness, Not Mental Illness," Gilligan discusses the ethics of not diagnosing a public figure versus the duty to warn potential victims of danger; when invoking the latter, he emphasizes, what matters is not whether a person is mentally ill but whether he is dangerous, which is possible to assess from a distance.

In "A Clinical Case for the Dangerousness of Donald J. Trump," Jhueck notes that the United States legally confers mental health professionals and physicians considerable power to detain people against their will if they pose a danger due to likely mental illness—and Trump more than meets the requisite criteria. In "Health, Risk, and the Duty to Protect the Community," Covitz offers an ancient reference and two fables to illustrate just how unusual the mental health profession's response is to a dangerous president, as we do not to speak up in ways that would be unthinkable for our role with other members of society. In "New Opportunities for Therapy in the Age of Trump," Doherty claims that the Trump era has ruptured the boundary between the personal and the public, and while clients and therapists are equally distressed, integrating our roles as therapists and citizens might help us better help clients.

The book's third part speaks to the societal effects Mr. Trump has had, represents, and could cause in the future. In "Trauma, Time, Truth, and Trump," Teng points out the irony of seeing, as a trauma therapist, all the signs of traumatization and retraumatization from a peaceful election; she traces the sources of the president's sudden military actions, his generation of crises, his shaken notions of truth and facts, and his role in reminding patients of an aggressive abuser. In "Trump Anxiety Disorder," Panning describes a unique postelection anxiety syndrome that has emerged as a result of the Trump presidency and the task that many therapists face with helping clients manage the stress of trying to "normalize" behavior that they do not feel is normal for a president. In her essay "In Relationship with an Abusive President," West illustrates the dynamics of "other blaming" in individuals who have feelings of low self-worth and hence poor shame tolerance, which lead to vindictive anger, lack of accountability, dishonesty, lack of empathy, and attention-seeking, of which Trump is an extreme example.

In "Trump's Daddy Issues," Wruble draws on his own personal experiences, especially his relationship with his strong and successful father, to demonstrate what a therapist does routinely: uses self-knowledge as an instrument for evaluating and "knowing" the other, even in this case, where the other is the president and his followers. In "Birtherism and the Deployment of the Trumpian Mind-Set," Kessler portrays the broader background from which "birtherism" began and how, by entering into the political fray by championing this fringe sentiment, Trump amplifies and exacerbates a national "symptom" of bigotry and division in ways that are dangerous to the nation's core principles. In "Trump and the American Collective Psyche," Singer draws a connection between Trump's personal narcissism and the American group psyche, not through a political analysis but through group psychology—the joining of group self-identity with violent, hateful defenses is as much about us as about Trump.

In "Who Goes Trump?" Mika explains how tyrannies are "toxic triangles," as political scientists call them, necessitating that the tyrant, his supporters, and the society at large bind around narcissism; while the three factors animate for a while, the characteristic oppression, dehumanization, and violence inevitably bring on downfall. In "The Loneliness of Fateful Decisions," Fisher recounts the Cuban Missile Crisis and notes how, even though President Kennedy surrounded himself with the "best and the brightest," they disagreed greatly, leaving him alone to make the decisions—which illustrates how the future of our country and the world hang on a president's mental clarity. In "He's Got the World in His Hands and His Finger on the Trigger," Gartrell and Mosbacher note how, while military personnel must undergo rigorous evaluations to assess their mental and medical fitness for duty, there is no such requirement for their commander in chief; they propose a nonpartisan panel of neuropsychiatrists for annual screening.

The Second Edition

The original publication was an instant bestseller, depleting all major stocks across the country within two days of release, and remaining on the *New York Times* bestseller list for seven weeks. This is highly unusual for a multiauthored book by specialists, and this reception seemed an indication of the public's thirst for knowledge. Messages flooded into our website, marveling at how we predicted eighteen months ahead of time what would happen with this presidency—

that the dangers would continue to grow and eventually become uncontainable—when most believed that Mr. Trump would settle in and "pivot" toward greater normalcy. They gave us credit for decisively influencing public parlance toward "dangerousness" but did not know of the American Psychiatric Association's constant interventions to interfere with the public's and the media's ability to address it as a mental health issue. We came to witness a most extraordinary situation where the Association worked to sideline professionals who are most qualified to comment, ceding mental health debates to non-expert commentators: "I am not a mental health professional, but . . ." became a typical starting point of discussion by pundits in describing the puzzling behavior of the president. Nevertheless, demands for updates led to this second edition, and the general silencing of the profession made our mandate to educate all the more urgent.

Having largely achieved our aim of shifting public discourse from diagnosis to dangerousness in the first edition, we attempt to show how this psychological dangerousness in an individual could spread to sociocultural and geopolitical dangerousness through the office of the presidency. We are also pleased to include more diversity, which was initially difficult to achieve when people were fearful of speaking up. The fourth part thus addresses the sociocultural consequences of this presidency. In "Persistent Enslavement Systemic Trauma," Washington illustrates the harmful impact of Mr. Trump's rhetoric, given his propensity to use the dog-whistle language of white terrorism that perpetuates terror and trauma in African Americans and other marginalized groups; "posttraumatic stress disorder" is thus a misnomer for marginalized groups whose trauma is ongoing in the face of police brutality, environmental racism, and the pipeline-to-prison process. In "Traumatic Consequences for Immigrant Populations in the United States," Bramble documents the catastrophic consequences of the 2016 presidential election she witnesses as a bilingual practitioner and care provider for undocumented immigrants, "Dreamers," and refugees, who are now cast as criminals and rapists in the face of newly aggressive deportation policies.

In "To Trump, Some Lives Matter," Kaschak also objects to the phrase posttraumatic stress disorder, since "terror" better fits than "stress" what happens when black men are killed in their own apartments, when women are sexually assaulted with impunity, when indigenous people are murdered for defending their own land, and when innocent children are ripped from their families or kept in cages; under the Trump administration, some lives matter more than others. In "The Charismatic Leader-Follower Relationship and Trump's Base," Post gets to the bottom of Trump as a political phenomenon through the psychological defects of the president and his supporters: Trump's "mirror-hungry" personality and the "ideal-hungry" personality of his "base" fit together like a lock and key.

The final part is devoted to the perpetuation and survival of humanity and what is at stake if we do not heed the warning signs. In "The Myth of Nuclear War," Merikangas and Lateef, who have both experienced the horrific possibilities of nuclear war from different settings, outline how dangerously close to nuclear war the Trump administration is approaching, and the psychiatric and neurological signs that make the president too dangerously unstable to have the sole authority to launch nuclear and other weapons; they allege that there is no such thing as a "surgical strike" or a "punch in the nose," but only incineration or nuclear winter. In "The Age of Thanatos," Van Susteren and Moffic starkly state that the damage we are inflicting on the environment through the current leadership is akin to collective self-harm and suicidality, and that our current age is one of "death drive" or *Thanatos*—especially as we have only a few years left to act if we wish to avoid runaway climate change with disastrous consequences. In "The Goldwater Rule and the Silence of American Psychiatry," Ghaemi reminisces on a symposium he organized around the Goldwater rule a year earlier and, looking back, concludes that American psychiatry is following the lead of Soviet psychiatry by preserving false "neutrality" in a time of moral crisis; in a democracy, political leaders should release a full medical and psychiatric report to voters when they can order thousands to their deaths.

In "Is the Commander in Chief Fit to Serve?" Gourguechon notes that the unprecedented and shocking behavior of the president led to a great deal of attention being paid to the Twenty-Fifth Amendment to the Constitution but that little guidance existed on what the "ability to discharge the powers and duties of the office" means; marrying U.S. Army leadership standards with psychoanalytic theory, she devises a nonpartisan test of five points, which Trump fails on all counts. In "Disordered Minds," Hughes asserts that democracy can serve as a defense against the terrifying wastelands that result when a psychologically dangerous minority seizes power; since pathological leaders regularly go unrecognized, mental health professionals should work to increase public understanding.

Finally, in "Congress Should Establish an Alternative Body to Assess the President," Eisen and Painter discuss a limitation of the Twenty-Fifth Amendment, namely that, under the current design, it has not been invoked on a number of occasions when it perhaps should have been, which an alternative body to the Cabinet may help remedy.

A Follow-Up

I emphasized in the first edition that, in spite of its title, the main point of the book is not about Mr. Trump. That he is but a symptom of larger societal problems, and an accelerator and intensifier of those problems now that he is in a powerful office, became more pronounced with time. My concern has been the general state of health and the collective mental health of our nation, and my response was this book. While the conference I organized was deemed an "ice-breaker," and the book garnered high regard and endorsement from my most prominent colleagues, we also encountered obstacles: a handful of outspoken critics with heavy ties to the American Psychiatric Association (APA) and the pharmaceutical industry deliberately misrepresenting our work; the APA aggressively stifling an initial momentum so as to shape professional norms and to frame those who spoke out as unethical; and this perversion of ethical rules con-

tributing to a political culture ripe for tyrannical abuse. As a psychiatrist, I believe that there is no greater oppression than the hijacking of
the mind. While this has been occurring for at least a couple decades
through state-sanctioned propaganda masquerading as "news" (e.g.,
Fox News), the APA's control of the flow of information in the name of
"ethics," precisely at a time when professionals are most needed to
address a national mental health crisis, attests to the centrality of our
voice. Thought reform, in defiance of truth, works through the process of "milieu control," or the control of information and communication in the environment (Lifton 2012), and is the reason why the
mind is considered tyranny's battleground for power.

The hostile attacks and death threats I received also spoke to the
influence of our voice. In January 2018, after Mr. Trump tweeted that
his "Nuclear Button . . . is a much bigger & more powerful one" than
North Korean leader Kim Jong-Un's (BBC 2018), and I revealed to the
press my meeting with a dozen Congress members, under the invitation of former assistant U.S. attorney Sheila Nielsen, hostile messages via Twitter, email, and phone numbered up to one thousand
per day. Like Dr. Christine Blasey Ford, who went into hiding after
her testimony before the Senate Judiciary Committee against Brett
Kavanaugh's appointment to the U.S. Supreme Court, I, too, went into
hiding for a month, unable to get to my office or to step outside without a disguise. When the threats stopped, however, it was an even
greater letdown: it was a sign that our voices had become irrelevant
and the powers that be had won. I do not know what will happen
from here. At the time of this writing, dangers have increased expo-
nentially, and the nation has continued to grant malignant forces
even greater power, rather than contain them. Resistance movements
have fortified, but like any sickness, it has become a battle between
the force of the disease and the body's own immune response, where
the survival of the organism is still at stake.

Meanwhile, however, the camaraderie and mutual support
among many of the authors, the National Coalition, and the public
have been incredible. When I eventually returned to my office after

a month of hiding, having gained twenty pounds and lost half of my hair, waiting for me was a mountain of letters, thank-you cards, pictures of children, books, chocolate, poems, jokes, stories, and words of encouragement—all from the general public, who had heard of the threats I received. These were much more heartfelt, overwhelming the negative messages. For me, this is the true voice of the people, which I serve through my profession, not my profession's organization or any political figure. I still read every one of the hundreds of now highly positive emails that come in every day, and the messages of gratitude are the strongest persuasion that we did a public service. I also learn from the negative: there has been no better confirmation of our predictions of violence than the death threats and the very characteristic belligerence of Mr. Trump's followers. They know how they are supposed to respond, and do so as if on cue. Mr. Trump has also grown increasingly brazen in his endorsement and incitement of violence. But the quintessential lesson I have learned from studying violence for twenty years is that this arises from weakness, not strength, and we must carry on.

I am thankful to all the authors, for both the first and second editions, who have generously contributed their insights under the agreement that all book revenues would be donated to the public good, removing all financial conflicts of interest. I am especially grateful to Drs. Grace Lee, Nanette Gartrell, Dee Mosbacher, Edwin Fisher, and Leonard Glass for making this manuscript possible; Drs. Judith Herman and Robert Jay Lifton for their moral support; Dr. Thomas Singer and Ms. Betty Teng for their incomparable dedication and help with the authors' group; and Ms. Melissa Mendenhall for her passion and skillful co-leadership of the National Coalition of Concerned Mental Health Experts. And I thank the countless members of the Coalition who have devoted their time and effort to realizing many amazing projects, too numerous to enumerate here: Drs. Claire Silverman, Barbara Turk, Barbara Lavi, Susan Blank, Andrew Spitznas, David Schatz, Mary Intermaggio, Robin Freedman, Farrell Silverberg, Scott Banford, Robert MacDonald, Toni Aguilar, Susan Barth, Cherylynne Berger, Paula Bloom, Suzanne Burger, Frederick Burkle, Russell Cashin, Gabriele Chorney, Nancy Cohen, Howard Covitz, Barbara Gold, Mary Ann Hutchison, Françoise Jaffe, Diane Jhueck, Richard Kast, Gabriella King, Susan Lazar, Michael Leaver, James Lipot, Lynne Meyer, Debra Moore, Elyse Morgan, Jennifer Panning, Sara Pascoe, Stacy Pinkston, David Reiss, Neil Rubin, Nancy Schreiner, Maureen Schroeter, Lynn Shepler, Dana Sinopoli, Marcella Smithson, Lisa Stanton, Janet Sullivan, Rosemary Sword, Grant Syphers, Michael Tansey, Madeline Taylor, Nancy Thomas, Sarah Tuttle, Leslie Wagner, Bill Wedin, Harper West, and Jenifer Williams, among others; our legal consultants Attys. Sheila Nielsen, Craig Jenkins, Mark Bruzonsky, Connie Vasquez, and Debbie Matties; and our non–mental health professional contributors Mss. Phyllis Gould, Heather Hazelwood, Jen Senko, Messrs. David Dudine, and Jonathan Ambrose, among many others. I will forever cherish the support and solidarity that have happened in this space.

I would like to express my appreciation for Dr. Robert Rohrbaugh, who as deputy chair for education made the initial conference at Yale possible; Dr. Howard Zonana, who as director of the Law and Psychiatry Division has been a role model along with Dr. Madelon Baranoski, ethicist; and Dr. John Krystal, who, as department chair, demonstrated true leadership when he treaded the careful lines to do what he must to protect the department but at the same time allowed me to speak my principles (in spite of my causing him "A Heck of a Year"—as he entitled his state of the department address!). I thank Mr. Scott Mendel, the most intellectually astute literary agent one could ask for; Mr. Stephen Power, the most brilliantly insightful editor one could have; Ms. Gabrielle Gantz, who deftly handled the numerous publicity requests; and Ms. Janine Barlow, who took care of everything behind the scenes. I am grateful to Atty. Glen Feinberg, specialist of psychiatric law; Atty. Max Stern, civil rights counsel; Atty. Ronald London, First Amendment lawyer; and Atty. Henry Kaufman, the publisher's counsel. I thank Drs. Bernard Lown, Regis DeSilva, Anne Davenport, Leon Golub, and Harold Bursztajn for their friendship and sustained support through my personal journey, as well as my family, Drs. Soon-Hyung Lee, Sun-Hyung Lee, Yoo Sung Lee, Patricia Lee, and Alan Chan. Finally, I would like to share my gratitude for the inspiration of my grandfather, Dr. Geun-Young Lee, who was the Dr. Rudolf Virchow of his time and place, and my mother, Dr. Inmyung Lee, whose constant concern for humanity and whose passing in 2016 are the direct reasons for my embarking on this cause.

Bandy X. Lee, M.D., M.Div., is a forensic psychiatrist at Yale School of Medicine and a project group leader for the World Health Organization Violence Prevention Alliance. She earned her degrees at Yale, interned at Bellevue, was chief resident at Mass. General, and was a research fellow at Harvard Medical School. She was also a fellow of the National Institute of Mental Health. She has taught at Yale Law School, College, and Schools of Medicine and Public Health. She has spearheaded several prison reform projects, including of New York City's Rikers Island jail complex, and consults globally with governments on violence prevention. She has written more than one hundred peer-reviewed articles and chapters, edited thirteen academic books, and authored the textbook Violence.

References

American Psychiatric Association. 2017. "APA Remains Committed to Supporting Goldwater Rule." www.psychiatry.org/news-room/apa-blogs/apa-blog/2017/03/apa-remains-committed-to-supporting-goldwater-rule.

BBC, 2018. "Trump to Kim: My nuclear button is 'bigger and more powerful.'" *BBC*, January 3. www.bbc.com/news/world-asia-42549687.

Begley, Sharon. 2018. "Psychiatrists Call for Rollback of Policy Banning Discussion of Public Figures' Mental Health." *STAT News*, June 28. www.statnews.com/2018/06/28/psychiatrists-goldwater-rule-rollback/

Bulman, May. 2017. "Donald Trump Has 'Dangerous Mental Illness,' Say Psychiatry Experts at Yale Conference." *Independent*, April 21. www

.independent.co.uk/news/world/americas/donald-trump-dangerous
-mental-illness-yale-psychiatrist-conference-us-president-unfit-james
-gartner-a7694316.html.

DeVega, Chauncey. 2017. "Psychiatrist Bandy Lee: 'We Have an Obligation
to Speak About Donald Trump's Mental Health Issues . . . Our Survival as a Species May Be at Stake.'" *Salon*, May 25. www.salon.com
/2017/05/25/psychiatrist-bandy-lee-we-have-an-obligation-to-speak
-about-donald-trumps-mental-health-issues-our-survival-as-a-species
-may-be-at-stake/.

Dodes, Lance, and Joseph Schachter. 2017. "Mental Health Professionals
Warn About Trump." *New York Times*, February 13. www.nytimes.com
/2017/02/13/opinion/mental-health-professionals-warn-about-trump
.html?mcubz=1.

Fisher, Edwin B. 2017. "Trump's Tweets Attacking Obama." *New York Times*,
March 6. www.nytimes.com/2017/03/06/opinion/trumps-tweets
-attacking-obama.html?mcubz=1.

Greene, Richard. 2016. "Is Donald Trump Mentally Ill? 3 Professors of
Psychiatry Ask President Obama to Conduct 'A Full Medical and
Neuropsychiatric Evaluation.'" *Huffington Post*, December 17. www
.huffingtonpost.com/richard-greene/is-donald-trump-mentally_b
_13693174.html.

Herman, Judith L., and Robert Jay Lifton. 2017. "'Protect Us from This
Dangerous President,' 2 Psychiatrists Say." *New York Times*, March 8.
www.nytimes.com/2017/03/08/opinion/protect-us-from-this-danger
ous-president-2-psychiatrists-say.html?mcubz=1&_r=0.

Lifton, Robert Jay. 2012. *Thought Reform and the Psychology of Totalism: A
Study of 'Brainwashing' in China*. Chapel Hill: University of North
Carolina Press.

Milligan, Susan. 2017. "An Ethical Dilemma: Donald Trump's Presidency
Has Some in the Mental Health Community Re-evaluating Their
Role." *U.S. News & World Report*, April 21. www.usnews.com/news/the
-report/articles/2017-04-21/mental-health-professionals-debate-ethics
-in-the-age-of-trump.

PART 1

THE TRUMP PHENOMENON

UNBRIDLED AND EXTREME PRESENT HEDONISM

How the Leader of the Free World Has Proven Time
and Again He Is Unfit for Duty

PHILIP ZIMBARDO AND ROSEMARY SWORD

In the summer of 2015, we commenced what would become an ongoing discussion about Donald Trump. He had just thrown his hat in the ring as a Republican presidential candidate, and our initial conversation was brief: he was in it for the publicity. For us, as for many Americans, Donald Trump had been in the periphery of our consciousness for years, first as a well-publicized New York City businessman and later as a mediocre television personality. And like most, we didn't take him seriously. Why would we have? He had no political experience, and he failed to show any real interest in philanthropy, much less in helping the American people or non-Trump businesses. His products were made outside the United States, and multiple lawsuits indicated he didn't pay those small businesses that supplied him with goods and services. He had also created Trump University, for people who wanted to get certified in business administration, at a fee of $43,000 for one year. It was a scam—the same lessons were available online for free for anyone, and the mentors who were supposed to give students personal guidance were rarely available. Students who took Trump University to court won their lawsuits, and Trump U got dumped. Simply put, Donald Trump was a businessman interested primarily in personal gain, sometimes using unscrupulous methods.

We also knew that, for decades, Trump had flip-flopped, switching political parties—first a Democrat, then a member of the Reform Party, then a Republican, then a Democrat, and finally a Republican again. Surely, it seemed, "The Donald" was in the running merely to gain media coverage, to place himself in a better position to make even more big deals and to up-level his product line: Donald J. Trump.

Then, as the months progressed, we became increasingly concerned that, given his "straightforward" or "outsider" presentation and his charisma, he would appeal to people who were unaware of the dangers of narcissism in extremis, or of the offensive behaviors that can accompany it. While we are not trying to diagnose here (which would be close to impossible in any case), we would like to call the reader's attention to associated behaviors that include but are not limited to condescension, gross exaggeration (lying), bullying, jealousy, fragile self-esteem, lack of compassion, and viewing the world through an "us-vs.-them" lens. Having observed the schoolyard bully tactics Trump employed during the Republican debates, and his absurdly boastful presentation during interviews, we felt it was important to raise awareness about this set of behaviors. So, in January 2016, we published an online *Psychology Today* column about bullies and the hostile social environments they create in schools and businesses (Sword and Zimbardo 2016a).

As Trump's campaign, and his narcissism, gained momentum, so did our efforts to make people aware of the potential dangers he posed for our democracy. In March 2016 we published a column about the narcissistic personality (Sword and Zimbardo 2016b). In it, we shared clinically documented narcissistic behaviors, hoping it would be easy for readers to come to their own conclusions that Trump fit every example. We did not mention his numerous romantic dalliances, or the growing number of sexual harassment lawsuits he faced, or his three marriages, in which he traded up for younger, more beautiful women. Each of these, on its own, is not exceptional, but it doesn't take a mental health professional to determine that these behaviors, coupled with his ever-shifting political party affiliations (changes that could be viewed as having been made to bolster his image and ego), indicated that this person's main focus was self-interest, and were incongruent with one important character trait the American people have come to appreciate in their president—at least up until November 2016: stability.

Furthermore, through our observations, it was glaringly apparent, based on Zimbardo's time perspective theory (Zimbardo and Boyd 2009), later developed into time perspective therapy by Sword and Sword (Zimbardo, Sword, and Sword 2012), that Trump embodied a specific personality type: an *unbridled, or extreme, present hedonist*. As the words suggest, present hedonists live in the present moment, without much thought of any consequences of their actions or of the future. An extreme present hedonist will say whatever it takes to pump up his ego and to assuage his inherent low self-esteem, without any thought for past reality or for the potentially devastating future outcomes from off-the-cuff remarks or even major decisions. Trump's behavior indicates that his time perspectives are totally *unbalanced*. It's not necessary for him to take the Zimbardo Time Perspective Inventory (either the long or short forms) in order for us to come to this conclusion. Our assertion that Trump qualifies as among the most extreme present hedonists we have ever witnessed comes from the plethora of written and recorded material on him, including all his interviews, hundreds of hours of video, and his own tweets on his every personal feeling.

What follows is meant to help readers understand how we've come to the conclusion that Donald Trump displays the most threatening time perspective profile, that of an extreme present hedonist, and is therefore "unfit for duty."

Time Perspective Theory and Time Perspective Therapy (TPT)

We are all familiar with the three main time zones: the past, the present, and the future. In TPT, these time zones are divided into subsets: *past positive* and *past negative*, *present hedonism* and *present fatalism*, and *future positive* and *future negative*. When one of these time perspectives is weighed too heavily, we can lose out on what's really happening now and/or lose sight of what could happen in our future. This can cause us to be unsteady, unbalanced, or temporally biased.

Being out of balance in this way also shades the way we think, and negatively impacts our daily decision making. For instance, if you are stuck in a past negative experience, you might think that from now on everything that happens to you will be negative. Why even bother planning for your future? you might think. It's just going to continue to be same old bad stuff. Or, if you are an extreme present hedonist adrenaline junky intent on spiking your adrenal glands, then you might engage in risky behaviors that unintentionally endanger you or others because you are living in the moment and not thinking about the future consequences of today's actions. If you are out of balance in your future time perspective, constantly thinking and worrying about all the things you have on your endless to-do list, you might forget about or miss out on the everyday, wonderful things happening in your life and the lives of your loved ones in the here and now.

SIX MAIN TIME PERSPECTIVES IN TPT

1. **Past positive people** focus on the good things that have happened.
2. **Past negative people** focus on all the things that went wrong in the past.
3. **Present hedonistic people** live in the moment, seeking pleasure, novelty, and sensation, and avoiding pain.
4. **Present fatalistic people** feel that planning for future decisions is not necessary because predetermined fate plays the guiding role in one's life.

5. **Future positive people** plan for the future and trust that things will work out.
6. **Future negative people** feel the future is predetermined and apocalyptic, or they have no future orientation.

THREE MAIN TP BIASES

1. **Past bias:** Good and bad things happen to everyone. Some of us view the world through rose-colored glasses (past positive), whereas others see the world through a darker lens (past negative). We have found that people who focus primarily on the past value the old more than the new; the familiar over the novel; and the cautious, conservative approach over the daring, more liberal or riskier one.

2. **Present bias:** People who live in the present are far less, or not at all, influenced by either past experiences or future considerations. They focus only on the immediate present—what's happening *now* (present hedonism). Decisions are based on immediate stimulus: internal hormonal signals, feelings, smells, sounds, the attractive qualities of the object of desire, and what others are urging them to do. Present-biased people who are influenced by past negative experiences are likely to feel stuck in the mire of the *past now* (present fatalism).

3. **Future bias:** No one is born thinking about how to plan for the future. A number of conditions, including living in a temperate zone (where it's necessary to anticipate seasonal change), living in a stable family or stable economic/political society (where a person learns to trust promises made to him), and becoming educated, can create future-positive-oriented people. In general, future-oriented people do very well in life. They are less aggressive, are less depressed, have more energy, take care of their health, have good impulse control, and have more self-esteem. Those stuck in the past, and locked into negative memories, feel fatalistic about the present and may have lost the ability even to conceive of a hopeful future (future negative).

Healthy Versus Unhealthy Time Perspectives

Through years of research, we have discovered that people who live healthy, productive, optimistic lives share the following traits—what we call an "ideal time perspective":

- High past positive/low past negative;
- Low present fatalism/moderate selected present hedonism; and
- Moderately high future-positive orientation.

Conversely, we have found that people with pessimistic time perspectives, usually due to trauma, depression, anxiety, stress, or posttraumatic stress, share the following time perspective profile:

- High past negative/low past positive;
- High present fatalism and/or high present hedonism; and
- Low future/no future orientation.

Having a dose of selected present hedonism in one's overall time perspective profile is important because enjoying oneself and having fun is a healthy part of life. Yet, too much of a good thing can cause numerous problems.

Present Hedonism and Arrested Emotional Development

As just mentioned, present hedonists live and act in the moment, frequently with little to no thought of the future, or the consequences of their actions. Most children and teenagers are present hedonists. Each day, they build on past experiences, but their concept of the future is still under development. People suffering from arrested emotional development, usually caused by a childhood trauma, are also present hedonists. Without therapy, the ability to mature emotionally beyond the age of trauma is difficult to impossible. When they reach adulthood, they may be able to hide their lack of emotional maturity for periods, but then, when in a stressful situation, they revert to behaving the emotional age they were when they were first traumatized. Depending on the degree to which the childhood trauma affected the person suffering from arrested emotional development, they may find that, over time, their present-hedonistic time perspective has morphed into extreme present hedonism.

Without proper individual assessment, we can only make a best guess as to whether Donald Trump suffers from arrested emotional development, which may or may not be a factor in his extreme present hedonism. Yet, with access to the extensive amount of print and video media exposing his bullying behavior, his immature remarks about sex, and his childlike need for constant attention, we can speculate that the traumatizing event was when he was sent away to military school at the age of thirteen. According to one of his biographers, Michael D'Antonio, Trump "was essentially banished from the family home. He hadn't known anything but living with his family in a luxurious setting, and all of a sudden he's sent away" (Schwartzman and Miller 2016). This would help explain his pubescent default setting when confronted by others.

Extreme Present Hedonism

An extreme present hedonist will say or do anything at any time for purposes of self-aggrandizement and to shield himself from previous (usually negatively perceived) activities, with *no* thought of the future or the effect of his actions. Coupled with a measure of paranoia, which is the norm, extreme present hedonism is the most unpredictable and perilous time perspective due to its "action" component. Here's how it works:

The extreme present hedonist's impulsive thought leads to an impulsive action that can cause him to dig in his heels when confronted with the consequences of that action. If the person is in a position of power, then others scramble either to deny or to find ways to back up the original impulsive action. In normal, day-to-day life, this impulsiveness leads to misunderstandings, lying, and toxic relationships. In the case of Donald Trump, an impulsive thought may unleash a stream of tweets or verbal remarks (the action), which then spur others to try to fulfill, or deny, his thoughtless action.

Case in point: Trump's impulsive tweet "How low has President Obama gone to tapp [*sic*] my phones during the very sacred election process. This is Nixon/Watergate. Bad (or sick) guy!" (Associated Press 2017) caused members of his staff to scramble to find evidence to make the false and slanderous claim "real." That one extreme present hedonistic tweet has led, ironically, to multiple investigations into the Trump campaign's possible Russian connections at the expense of taxpayers' hard-earned dollars.

Another concerning characteristic of extreme present hedonists is the often unwitting—we like to give some extreme present hedonists the benefit of the doubt—propensity to dehumanize others in order to feel superior. This lack of foresight and compassion is also a trait of narcissism and bullying, which we address later in this chapter.

Donald Trump's Extreme Present Hedonistic Quotes

It could be argued that almost anyone can be presented in a negative light when scrutinized or quoted out of context. However, when one runs for the highest office in the land, and then wins that prize, such scrutiny is expected. In the case of Donald Trump, a rich trove of recorded examples gives us a strong picture of the inner workings of his unbalanced psyche. The following well-known quotes, which we've organized into categories—some of them overlap multiple categories—compiled by Michael Kruse and Noah Weiland for *Politico Magazine* ("Donald Trump's Greatest Self Contradictions," May 5, 2016) illustrate his extreme present hedonistic penchant for offroading from his script and/or saying or tweeting whatever pops into his mind, making things up, repeating fake news, or simply lying:

DEHUMANIZATION
- "Sometimes, part of making a deal is denigrating your competition" (*The Art of the Deal*, 1987).

- "When Mexico sends its people, they're not sending their best . . . They're sending people that have a lot of problems, and they're bringing those problems with us. They're bringing drugs. They're bringing crime. They're rapists. And some, I assume, are good people" (Republican rally speech, June 16, 2015).

- "Written by a nice reporter. Now the poor guy. You ought to see this guy" (remark made while contorting his face and moving his arms and hands around awkwardly, at a campaign rally in South Carolina, November 24, 2015, about journalist Serge Kovaleski, who has arthrogryposis, a congenital condition that can limit joint movement or lock limbs in place).

LYING

- "Made in America? @BarackObama called his 'birthplace' Hawaii 'here in Asia'" (Twitter, November 18, 2011).

- "I watched when the World Trade Center came tumbling down . . . And I watched in Jersey City, New Jersey, where thousands and thousands of people were cheering as that building was coming down. Thousands of people were cheering" (at a rally in Birmingham, Alabama, November 21, 2015). The next day, *This Week* host, George Stephanopoulos, pointed out that "the police say that didn't happen." Trump insisted otherwise: "It was on television. I saw it happen."

- "In addition to winning the Electoral College in a landslide, I won the popular vote if you deduct the millions of people who voted illegally" (Twitter, November 27, 2016).

MISOGYNY

- "You could see there was blood coming out of her eyes. Blood coming out of her—wherever" (remarks during CNN interview with regard to Megyn Kelly, following the previous night's Fox News debate co-moderated by Kelly in which Kelly asked Trump about his misogynistic treatment of women, August 7, 2015).

- "Look at that face! Would anybody vote for that? Can you imagine that, the face of our next president? . . . I mean, she's a woman, and I'm not supposed to say bad things, but really, folks, come on. Are we serious?" (remarks in *Rolling Stone* interview with regard to Republican presidential candidate Carly Fiorina, September 9, 2015).

- "When you're a star, they let you do it. You can do anything . . . Grab 'em by the pussy . . . You can do anything" (off-camera boast recorded over a hot mic by *Access Hollywood* in 2005 and published by the *Washington Post* in October 2016).

PARANOIA

- "The world is a vicious and brutal place. We think we're civilized. In truth, it's a cruel world and people are ruthless. They act nice to your face, but underneath they're out to kill you . . . Even your friends are out to get you: they want your job, they want your house, they want your money, they want your wife, and they even want your dog. Those are your friends; your enemies are even worse!" (*Think Big: Make It Happen in Business and Life*, 2007).

- "My motto is 'Hire the best people, and don't trust them'" (*Think Big: Make It Happen in Business and Life*, 2007).

- "If you have smart people working for you, they'll try to screw you if they think they can do better without you" (*Daily Mail*, October 30, 2010).

RACISM

- "You haven't been called, go back to Univision" (when dismissing Latino reporter Jorge Ramos at an Iowa rally, August 2015).

- "Donald J. Trump is calling for a total and complete shutdown of Muslims entering the United States" (at a rally in Charleston, South Carolina, December 2015).

- "Look at my African American over here. Look at him" (at a campaign appearance in California, June 2016).

SELF-AGGRANDIZEMENT
- "I'm, like, a really smart person" (during an interview in Phoenix, Arizona, July 11, 2015).

- "It's very hard for them to attack me on my looks, because I'm so good looking" (in an interview on NBC's *Meet the Press*, August 7, 2015).

- "I'm speaking with myself, number one, because I have a very good brain and I've said a lot of things. . . . My primary consultant is myself" (from MSNBC interview, March 16, 2016).

Trump also exhibits two generally known personality traits that, when combined with extreme present hedonism, amplify our concern: *narcissism* and *bullying behavior*. In order to help readers understand the complexities of narcissists and bullies, how these two characteristics dovetail with extreme present hedonism, and demonstrate how the president displays these predispositions, we've condensed years of study on these two subjects.

The Narcissistic Personality

I alone can fix it.

Donald Trump, Republican National Convention, July 2016

In the early 1900s, Sigmund Freud introduced narcissism as part of his psychoanalytic theory. Throughout the ensuing decades, it was refined and sometimes referred to as megalomania or severe egocentrism. By 1968, the condition had evolved into the diagnosable *narcissistic personality disorder*. Narcissistic people are out of balance in that they think very highly of themselves while simultaneously thinking very lowly of all those whom they consider their inferiors, which is mostly everybody. Narcissists are emotional, dramatic, and can lack compassion and empathy, as those traits are about feeling for others.

What follows are some of the symptoms of narcissistic personality disorder. (Note that because this is about narcissists, we use the term *you*.)

- **Believing that you're better than others:** This is across the board in your world; you look down your nose at other people.

- **Fantasizing about power, success, and attractiveness:** You are a superhero, among the most successful in your field; you could grace the cover of *GQ* or *Glamour* magazine, and you don't realize this is all in your mind.

- **Exaggerating your achievements or talents:** Your ninth-place showing in the golf tournament becomes first place to those who weren't there and, if you're brazen enough, even to those who were. Although you plunked poorly on a guitar in high school before you lost interest in the instrument, you tell others you took lessons from Carlos Santana.

- **Expecting constant praise and admiration:** You want others to acknowledge when you do anything and everything, even if it's taking out the garbage.

- **Believing that you're special and acting accordingly:** You believe you are God's gift to women/men/your field/the world, and that you deserve to be treated as such by everyone. They just don't know this.

- **Failing to recognize other people's emotions and feelings:** You don't understand why people get upset with you for telling it the way you think it is or what you think they did wrong.

- **Expecting others to go along with your ideas and plans:** There is only one way and that's your way, so you get upset when others share their thoughts or plans because surely theirs aren't as good as yours.

- **Taking advantage of others:** You take your parent's/friend's car/tools/credit card/clothing without asking, or cut in line in front of an elderly person, or expect something much more significant in return for doing a small favor. "What's the big deal?"

- **Expressing disdain for those whom you feel to be inferior:** "That homeless person isn't even wearing a coat or shoes in freezing weather. What an idiot!"

- **Being jealous of others:** You, and not so-and-so, deserved the award/trophy/praise and recognition. Also, if you think someone is more attractive/intelligent/clever or has a more prestigious car/significant other/house, you hate and curse him.

- **Believing that others are jealous of you:** You believe everybody wants to be you.

- **Having trouble keeping healthy relationships:** Your family and friends don't understand you, so you don't stay in touch with them anymore. You lose interest in your romantic relationships each time someone better comes along; you have recurring unsatisfying affairs.

- **Setting unrealistic goals:** You believe that one day you will be a CEO/president/great musician/artist/best-selling author, marry a movie star, or have Bill Gates's billions.

- **Being easily hurt and rejected:** You don't understand why people purposefully hurt your feelings, and either it takes a long time for you to get over it or you don't ever get over it.

- **Having a fragile self-esteem:** Underneath it all, you are just a delicate person, which makes you special, and you don't understand why people don't see this about you.

- **Appearing tough-minded or unemotional:** Read: You act like Mr. Spock.

While some of these symptoms may come across as simply elevated personal confidence or high self-esteem, they're different in people who have a healthy dose of confidence and self-esteem because whereas these people don't value themselves more than they value others, the narcissist looks down on others from his lofty pedestal. The narcissistic personality frequently appears to be a conceited, pompous braggart who dominates conversations and has a sense of entitlement. He wants the best of whatever is available, and when he doesn't get his way, he may become annoyed or angry. He becomes Mr. or Ms. Petulant in action.

Interestingly, what lies underneath this personality type is often very low self-esteem. Narcissists can't handle criticism of any kind, and will belittle others or become enraged or condescending to make themselves feel better when they perceive they are being criticized. It's not unusual for a narcissistic personality to be blind to his own behavior because it doesn't fit his view of his perfect and dominant self. But a narcissistic personality can spot one of his kind a mile away, and will either put down or generally avoid that other mindless competing narcissist.

Unfortunately, narcissistic people may find their relationships falling apart. After a while, folks don't want to be around them; all their relationships (personal, work, or school) become problems.

Sometimes their finances are troublesome, too, because it's hard to keep up their image without expensive accoutrements.

The Bully Personality

> *I hope Corrupt Hillary Clinton chooses Goofy Elizabeth Warren*
> *as her running mate. I will defeat them both*
>
> Donald Trump, Twitter, May 6, 2016

Bullying is defined as systematically and chronically inflicting physical hurt and/or psychological distress on one or more people, whether they are students at school, peers in the workplace, or family members. Research indicates that some bullies may suffer from narcissistic personality disorder, while others may have difficulty interpreting or judging social situations and other people's actions—they interpret hostility from others when none was meant. For example, a person unintentionally bumps into a bully, who views this accident as an act of aggression; he therefore overreacts, which triggers the bully response of seeking revenge.

Bullying behavior is often learned at home from family members, such as parents or older siblings who display this form of aggression. Generally, bullying behavior is caused by stress in the bully's life. Bullies have often been abused or are driven by their insecurities. They typically want to control and manipulate others to feel superior. The anger they feel as a result of their hurt is directed toward others. Their targets are those whom they consider weaker than they and/or different.

A bully's actions are intentional: to cause emotional or physical injury to one or more people, usually on a repeated basis. Many readers might recall basic types of bully as portrayed in film or on television, such as Biff in *Back to the Future* or Eddie Haskell on the television show *Leave It to Beaver*. As the decades have unfolded and our technology has evolved, so have the numbers and types of bullies.

- **Physical bullying** occurs when people use physical actions to gain power and control over their targets. It's easiest to identify and most likely what people think of when they think of bullying.

- **Verbal bullying** involves using words, statements, and name-calling to gain power and control over a target. Typically, verbal bullies use relentless insults to belittle, demean, and hurt others.

- **Prejudicial bullying** is based on prejudices people have toward people of different races, religions, or sexual orientations. This type of bullying can encompass all the other types of bullying. When prejudicial bullying occurs, those who are somehow considered "different" are targeted and the door is opened to hate crimes.

- **Relational aggression**, frequently referred to as **emotional bullying**, is a sneaky, insidious type of bullying that manifests as social manipulation. The goal of the relational bully is to ostracize others to gain social standing and to control others.

- **Cyberbullying** refers to using the Internet, cell phones, or other technology to harass, threaten, embarrass, or target another person; cyberbullying usually involves a teen or tween. If an adult is involved in this harassment, it is called **cyber-harassment** or **cyberstalking**. This form of bullying has gained momentum, as there is much less risk of being caught.

- **Sexual bullying** consists of repeated, harmful, and humiliating actions (sexual name-calling, crude comments, vulgar gestures, uninvited touching or sexual propositioning) that target a person sexually. It can occur in a group and can be considered a show of bravado among the perpetrators; when done one on one, it can lead to sexual assault.

If you take into account the sexual harassment/assault lawsuits that have targeted Trump over the years, you will find that he has displayed every one of these bullying types. Bullying is not "normal" and is therefore unacceptable behavior—or, at least, it was unacceptable up until the 2016 presidential election. Culturally in the past, bullying was considered a normal rite of passage (while this line of thinking may never have been realistic); it is certainly not so today. With extreme bullying becoming increasingly pervasive, often with tragic results, we can no longer view it as simply a part of growing up, much less a part of being a grown-up.

The Trump Effect

I'm gonna bomb the shit out of them!

Donald Trump during campaign rally in Fort Dodge,
Iowa, November 13, 2015

One person *can* affect an entire nation, and nowhere do we see this more clearly than with "the Trump Effect," which was originally defined as an increase in bullying in schools caused by the rhetoric used by Donald Trump during his campaign. This particular definition of the Trump Effect—not to be confused with definitions that refer, for example, to the stock market, to Trump's publicly skirting the truth, or to the uptick in populism in Europe—gained traction in the media as campaign season deepened and Donald Trump won the election.

In short order, the bullying crept beyond schools to include religious and racial bullying by adults. At least four mosques were burned to the ground. Jewish cemeteries across our nation have been desecrated. Two innocent Indian engineers were shot while having dinner, as was a white American who tried to intervene. One of the engineers died, but not before his killer yelled racial slurs at him that culminated in "Get out of my country!" More recently, articles about the Trump Effect have largely been replaced by continuing coverage of Trump's tweets, his odd behavior, and his campaign team's possibly illegal ties to Russia. However bizarre it may seem, the Trump Effect exists, and is a growing phenomenon.

A report from Maureen Costello of the Southern Poverty Law Center's (SPLC) Teaching Tolerance project, "The Trump Effect: The Impact of the 2016 Presidential Campaign on Our Nation's Schools," lays out in no uncertain terms the dire consequences of Donald Trump's behavior. It indicates that immigrant students, children of immigrants—close to one-third of pupils in American classrooms are the children of foreign-born parents—African Americans, and other students of color were fearful, while their friends worried for them and wanted to protect them.

Yet, many children were not afraid at all. Rather, some used the name "Trump" as a taunt or chant as they ganged up on others. Muslim children were called terrorists; those of Mexican descent were told that they or their parents would be deported; children of color were afraid they would be rounded up and put into camps. The bullying caused some of these children to have panic attacks and suicidal thoughts.

One consistent theme across grade levels emerged: the students understood that the behavior on display was not okay. Also, our research revealed that the great many people who witness such bullying do nothing, and many of these passive bystanders feel prolonged shame for their inaction against this injustice experienced by friends and classmates—another negative fallout of bullying, beyond its targeted victims.

While the long-term impact of these noxious experiences on children's well-being may be impossible to measure, the students were stressed and anxious in a way that threatened their health, their emotional state, and their schoolwork. It is common knowledge that stressed students have a more difficult time learning, and in fact, the report indicated that there were many instances in which anxiety was having an impact on grades and was affecting students' ability to concentrate. All students, though, regardless of whether they are members of a targeted group, are vulnerable to the stresses of the Trump Effect.

If we dive a little deeper, we realize that children are a reflection of their upbringing. More than likely, the angry acting-out of some students toward others in our schools is a reflection of what they observe in their homes. So, how has a small but active segment of our population been reacting to Donald Trump's presidency? Statistics show that they have become even more emboldened and, in recent months, have taken to engaging in hate crimes against Jews as well as Muslims and Mexicans; speculation about Trump's approval of white supremacist/anti-Semitic groups has emboldened them.

According to the SPLC, in the two-week period between Election Day and February 9, 2017, there were seventy anti-Jewish incidents and thirty-one anti-Muslim incidents, the majority being bomb threats. These figures are proportional to the respective populations of Jews and Muslims in the United States, which means Jews and Muslims have a roughly equal chance of being victimized.

The recent rash of desecrations of Jewish graveyards and places of worship, and the burning of mosques, should be extremely concerning to all of us as Americans, as we are a nation composed largely of immigrants. These insults against the identity of Jews and Muslims promote the dehumanization of our fellow human beings. Although the president was eventually forced to condemn the acts of anti-Semitism, in our research for this chapter, we could find little evidence of his condemnation of the attacks against American Muslims. This reluctance to serve and protect segments of his population is yet another sign for bullies that their behavior is acceptable to the man in charge.

A Scary Venn Diagram

In Donald Trump, we have a frightening Venn diagram consisting of three circles: the first is extreme present hedonism; the second, narcissism; and the third, bullying behavior. These three circles overlap in the middle to create an impulsive, immature, incompetent person who, when in the position of ultimate power, easily slides into the role of tyrant, complete with family members sitting at his proverbial "ruling table." Like a fledgling dictator, he plants psychological seeds of treachery in sections of our population that reinforce already negative attitudes. To drive home our point, here are what we consider to be two of Trump's most dangerous quotes:

- "If she gets to pick her judges, nothing you can do, folks. Although the Second Amendment people—maybe there is, I don't know" (remark made during a campaign rally in Wilmington, North Carolina, August 9, 2016); and

- "I could stand in the middle of Fifth Avenue, shoot somebody, and I wouldn't lose any voters" (remark made during a campaign appearance in Sioux City, Iowa, January 23, 2016).

Before Donald Trump, it was unfathomable for American citizens to consciously consider voting for, and then inaugurating, a person as unbalanced as this president. Admittedly, it's possible, as Guy Winch points out in his February 2, 2016, *Psychology Today* article, "Study: Half of All Presidents Suffered from Mental Illness." According to Winch, many of our previous presidents may have suffered from mental health issues, including depression (Abraham Lincoln), bipolar disorder (Lyndon Johnson), alcoholism (Ulysses S. Grant), Alzheimer's disease (Ronald Reagan), and transient bouts of extreme present hedonism (John F. Kennedy and Bill Clinton). We have also survived a president who blatantly lied to cover his criminal tracks before he was caught in those lies (Richard Nixon). In the past, Americans have pulled together and worked to overcome our differences. We moved forward collectively as one great country. Unfortunately, in more recent times, it appears we have become a bipolar nation, with Donald Trump at the helm as his followers cheer him on and others try to resist him.

The Results

In presenting our case that Donald Trump is mentally unfit to be president of the United States, we would be remiss if we did not consider one more factor: the possibility of a neurological disorder such as dementia or Alzheimer's disease, which the president's father, Fred Trump, suffered from. Again, we are not trying to speculate diagnoses from afar, but comparing video interviews of Trump from the 1980s, 1990s, and early 2000s to current video, we find that the differences (significant reduction in the use of essential words; an increase in the use of adjectives such as *very*, *huge*, and *tremendous*; and incomplete, run-on sentences that don't make sense and that could indicate a loss of train of thought or memory) are conspicuously apparent. Perhaps this is why Trump insists on being surrounded by family members who love and understand him rather than seasoned political advisers, who may note, and then leak, his alarming behavior.

Whether or not Donald Trump suffers from a neurological disorder—or narcissistic personality disorder, or any other mental health issue, for that matter—will, undeniably, remain conjecture unless he submits to tests, which is highly unlikely given his personality. However, the lack of such tests cannot erase the well-documented behaviors he has displayed for decades and the dangers they pose when embodied in the president of the United States.

In line with the principles of *Tarasoff v. Regents of the University of California* 17 Cal. 3d 425 (1976), known as the "Tarasoff doctrine," it is the responsibility of mental health professionals to warn the citizens of the United States and the people of the world of the potentially devastating effects of such an extreme present-hedonistic world leader, one with enormous power at his disposal. On the whole, mental health professionals have failed in their duty to warn, in a timely manner, not only the public but also government officials about the dangers of President Donald Trump. Articles and interviews intent on cautioning the masses prior to the election fell on deaf ears, perhaps in part because the media did not afford the concerned mental health professionals appropriate coverage, perhaps because some citizens discount the value of mental health and have thrown a thick blanket of stigma over the profession, or perhaps because we as mental health professionals did not stand united. Whatever the reason, it's not too late to follow through.

When an individual is psychologically unbalanced, *everything* can teeter and fall apart if change does not occur. We wonder how far-reaching, in our society over time, the effects of our unbalanced president's actions will be and how they will continue to affect us as individuals, communities, a nation, and a planet. We believe that Donald Trump is the most dangerous man in the world, a powerful leader of a powerful nation who can order missiles fired at another nation because of his (or a family member's) personal distress at seeing sad scenes of people having been gassed to death. We shudder to imagine what actions might be taken in broader lethal confrontations with his personal and political enemies.

We are gravely concerned about Trump's abrupt, capricious 180-degree shifts and how these displays of instability have the potential to be unconscionably dangerous to the point of causing catastrophe, and not only for the citizens of the United States. There are two particularly troubling examples: (1) his repeatedly lavishing praise on FBI director James Comey's handling of an investigation into Hillary Clinton's emails and then, in early May 2017, abruptly and abusively firing Comey for the very investigation that garnered such praise, but in this case actually because of Comey's investigation into the Trump campaign's ties to Russia; and (2) his stating during the campaign that NATO was obsolete and then, later, unexpectedly stating that NATO was necessary and acceptable. As is the case with extreme present hedonists, Trump is "chumming" for war, possibly for the most selfish of reasons: to deflect attention away from the Russia investigation. If another unbalanced world leader takes the bait, Trump will need the formerly "obsolete" and now-essential NATO to back him up.

We as individuals don't have to follow our nation's leader down a path headed in the wrong direction—off a cliff and into a pit of past mistakes. We can stand where we are at this moment in history and face forward, into a brighter future that *we* create. We can start by looking for the good in one another and for the common ground we share.

In the midst of the terrorist attacks on places of worship and cemeteries mentioned earlier, something wonderful emerged from the ashes: a spirit of overwhelming goodness in humanity. In the wake of the attacks, Jews and Muslims united: they held fund-raisers to help each other repair and rebuild; they shared their places of worship so that those burned out of theirs could hold gatherings and services; and they offered loving support to those who'd faced hatred. By observing ordinary people engaging in acts of everyday heroism and compassion, we have been able to witness the best aspects of humanity. *That's* us! *That's* the United States of America!

A final suggestion for our governmental leaders: corporations and companies vet their prospective employees. This vetting process frequently includes psychological testing in the form of exams or quizzes to help the employer make more informed hiring decisions and determine if the prospective employee is honest and/or would be a good fit for the company. These tests are used for positions ranging from department store sales clerk to high-level executive. Isn't it time that the same be required for candidates for the most important job in the world?

Philip Zimbardo, Ph.D., Professor Emeritus at Stanford University, is a scholar, educator, and researcher. Zimbardo is perhaps best known for his landmark Stanford prison study. Among his more than five hundred publications are the best seller The Lucifer Effect *and such notable psychology textbooks as* Psychology: Core Concepts, *8th edition, and* Psychology and Life, *now in its 20th edition. He is founder and president of the Heroic Imagination Project (heroicimagination.org), a worldwide nonprofit teaching people of all ages how to take wise and effective action in challenging situations. He continues to research the effects of time perspectives and time perspective therapy.*

Rosemary Sword is codeveloper of Time Perspective Therapy and coauthor of The Time Cure: Overcoming PTSD with the New Psychology of Time Perspective Therapy *(in English, German, Polish, Chinese, and Russian);* The Time Cure Therapist Guidebook *(Wiley, 2013);* Time Perspective Therapy: Transforming Zimbardo's Temporal Theory into Clinical Practice *(Springer, 2015);* Time Perspective Theory *(Springer, 2015);* Living and Loving Better with Time Perspective Therapy *(McFarland, 2017); and* Time Perspective Therapy: An Evolutionary Therapy for PTSD *(McFarland, forthcoming). Sword and Zimbardo write a popular column for* PsychologyToday.com *and contribute both to* AppealPower, *a European Union online journal, and to* Psychology in Practice, *a new Polish psychological journal. Sword is also developer of Aetas: Mind Balancing Apps (www. discoveraetas.com).*

References

Associated Press. 2017. "President Trump's Claim That Obama Wiretapped Him Basically Died This Week." *Time,* March 24. http://amp.timeinc .net/time/4713187/donald-trump-obama-wiretap-fact-check/ ?source=dam.

Kruse, Michael, and Noah Weiland. 2016. "Donald Trump's Greatest Self Contradictions." *Politico Magazine,* May 5. www.politico.com/magazine /story/2016/05/donald-trump-2016-contradictions-213869.

"Mental Health Experts Say Donald Trump Is Unfit to Serve." 2017. *The Last Word with Lawrence O'Donnell.* MSNBC, February 21. www.msnbc.com /the-last-word/watch/mental-health-experts-say-trump-is-unfit-to -serve-882688067737.

Psychology Today Editorial Staff. 2017. "Shrinks Battle Over Diagnosing Donald Trump," January 31. www.psychologytoday.com/blog /brainstorm/201701/shrinks-battle-over-diagnosing-donald-trump.

Schwartzman, Paul, and Michael E. Miller. 2016. "Confident. Incorrigible. Bully: Little Donny Was a Lot Like Candidate Donald Trump." *Washington Post,* June 22. www.washingtonpost.com/lifestyle/style

/young-donald-trump-military-school/2016/06/22/f0b3b164-317c-11e6
-8758-d58e76e11b12_story.html?utm_term=.961fefcee834.

Stetka, Bret. 2017. "As Presidents Live Longer, Doctors Debate Whether to
Test for Dementia." NPR, February 17. www.npr.org/sections/health
-shots/2017/02/17/514583390/as-our-leaders-live-longer-calls-for
-presidential-dementia-testing-grow-louder.

Sword, Rosemary, and Philip Zimbardo. 2016a. "Bullies." *PsychologyToday
.com*, January 24. www.psychologytoday.com/blog/the-time-cure
/201601/bullies.

———. 2016b. "The Narcissistic Personality: A Guide to Spotting Narcissists." *PsychologyToday.com*, March 29. www.psychologytoday.com/blog
/the-time-cure/201603/the-narcissistic-personality.

Winch, Guy. 2016. "Study: Half of All Presidents Suffered from Mental
Illness." *PsychologyToday.com*, February 2. www.psychologytoday.com
/blog/the-squeaky-wheel/201602/study-half-all-presidents-suffered
-mental-illness.

Zimbardo, Philip, and John Boyd. 2009. *The Time Paradox*. New York: Atria.

Zimbardo, Philip, Richard Sword, and Rosemary Sword. 2012. *The Time
Cure*. San Francisco, CA: Wiley.

PATHOLOGICAL NARCISSISM AND POLITICS

A Lethal Mix

CRAIG MALKIN, PH.D.

> My twitter has become so powerful that I can actually make my enemies tell the truth.
>
> Donald J. Trump, tweet from October 17, 2012

In 1952, a young Richard Nixon, rising star in the Republican Party, had been handpicked as Eisenhower's running mate, and by all accounts, the Republicans made a sound choice. Nixon's great strength was the message he'd pounded like a drumbeat into voters' ears: Washington needed a major cleanup, a White House full of good moral upstanding people. The elites, like the previous administration under Harry Truman and Eisenhower's opponent, Adlai Stevenson—a brilliant orator and skilled lawyer—had ruined it for everyone with their corruption, communism, and cronyism ("pay for play," as we've come to call it).

America embraced the message for a time—the Ike-Nixon team held a substantial lead in the polls—but just as he and Eisenhower were gearing up to stump for votes on their "whistle stop" tours of the country—Nixon on his train, the Nixon Express, Eisenhower on his, the Look Ahead, Neighbor—Nixon became embroiled in a potentially career-ending controversy. Stories erupted of a secret slush fund of money from his supporters that he used to live the high life: a mink coat for his wife, Pat; lavish dinners for himself and his friends; and—worst of all—special favors for those who'd subsidized him. The story, courtesy of the *New York Post*'s Leo Katcher, spread like wildfire, fueled by an especially incendiary headline: *Secret Rich Men's Trust Fund Keeps Nixon in Style Far Beyond His Salary.*

Public outcry was loud and clear: Nixon should resign as Eisenhower's running mate. As late election season disasters go, this one was a juggernaut; behind the scenes, the entire team scrambled to rescue a troubled campaign. With no solution in sight, Nixon made a bold decision: he'd appeal directly to the American people by laying bare every financial detail of his life. His wife, Pat, was reportedly mortified at the thought of his sharing their economic history with the entire country, but Nixon remained undeterred.

On the evening of September 23, 1952, Nixon sat before a TV audience of 60 million, his alarmed wife beside him, mostly off screen, and went through each and every one of his accounts: what he owned and what he owed, line by line. Nixon reassured viewers that an independent audit had found no wrongdoing and that he hadn't used a penny of the money he'd been given for personal gain. But, he confessed, there was one gift that had brought personal benefit that he couldn't bear to return:

> It was a little cocker spaniel dog in a crate . . . sent all the way from Texas. Black and white spotted. And our little girl—Tricia, the six-year-old—named it Checkers. And you know, the kids, like all kids, love the dog and I just want to say this right now, that regardless of what they say about it, we're gonna keep it.

Though Nixon was unsure how successful he'd been, and political opinion was divided along party lines, the speech worked with the American public, earning him a place in people's hearts and securing his position on the Republican ticket. Eisenhower and Nixon trounced their opponents, and President Eisenhower assumed office as the thirty-four[th] commander in chief.

To some, Nixon's comeback wasn't surprising. Despite his unassuming hangdog look, Nixon brought a blend of brutal ambition and relentless determination to politics that few had seen before. And he used that same drive to survive one defeat after another, including, later, his losses to John F. Kennedy in 1960 as president of the United States and Pat Davis, in 1962, as governor of California. The last defeat was supposed to be his curtain call in politics; famously, in his "final" press conference, he dourly announced, "Just think what you're going to be missing. You won't have Nixon to kick around anymore." But if Nixon worried about being kicked, he certainly didn't show it. He remained in politics, and continued to thrive, ultimately becoming president of the United States in 1968.

Everything finally seemed to be going Nixon's way, despite his trouble leaving behind his nickname from the 1950s, "Tricky Dick." He even enjoyed accolades for bringing U.S. troops back from Vietnam, opening diplomatic relations with Communist China, and kibitzing with Neil Armstrong and Buzz Aldrin after they walked on the moon. Even with the carnage of Vietnam looming in the background, he appeared to have a largely successful first term, and sailed to victory again in 1972, to serve his second term.

If the fund scandal ambushed Nixon, the next threat crept up on him like a thief in the night. After months of rumblings about Tricky Dick's dirty dealings, he finally came face-to-face with the scandal that brought him down once and for all: Watergate. As details of illegal wiretappings, blackmail, and burglaries trickled out, Nixon's dark side came fully into the light. Here, the public learned, was a self-serving suspicious man who secretly taped every Oval Office conversation, arranged the break-in at the Democratic National Committee (DNC) headquarters, and—when distressed—paced the White House halls, holding court with portraits. Here was a man who swore lividly about the Jews taking over, employed unsavory characters like former FBI agent-cum-mercenary, G. Gordon Liddy, and spent much of his time becoming belligerently drunk while Cambodia was carpet-bombed.

Strangely, this profanity-prone, paranoid tyrant both was—and wasn't—the man people thought they knew: a comeback king, resilient in defeat, humble in victory, but always, behind the scenes it seems, on the precipice of some self-made disaster. This was the paradox of Nixon.

Nixon's story, as fascinating as it is terrifying, tells us a great deal about the relationship between personality and politics. What's most surprising about Nixon is the fact that his apparently contradictory character appears to be rather *un*remarkable among presidents and politicians. That is, Nixon displayed a combination of intense ambition, authority, grandiosity, arrogance, entitlement, subterfuge, and self-importance that appears to have been common in the Oval Office throughout history. Nixon was a narcissist.

Narcissism: The Good, the Bad, and the Ugly

Despite what you may have read, *narcissist* isn't a diagnosis and it never has been. *Narcissism* isn't a diagnosis either. Narcissism, in fact, is best understood as a trait that occurs, to varying degrees, in all of us: *the drive to feel special, to stand out from the other 7 billion people on the planet, to feel exceptional or unique.*

Instead of thinking of narcissism as all or none, think of it along a spectrum, stretching from zero on the low end, signifying no drive to feel special, to moderate at 5, and finally, spiking to 10 at the extreme:

0	5	10

Moderate narcissism (around 4 to 6) is where we have the healthiest amount of the trait. Lower and higher on the scale present problems. If you imagine feeling special like a drug, moderate ("healthy") narcissism gives us a little boost when we need it, a way to press on when the world and sometimes common sense tell us our reach might exceed our grasp. According to 30 years of research, the vast majority of happy healthy people around the world feel a little special, even if privately. Healthy narcissism isn't simply self-confidence, self-care, or self-esteem. It's a *slightly* unrealistically positive self-image. Think of it as rose-colored glasses for the self—the glasses are strong enough to tint the world, but not so opaque they blind us to reality.

Healthy narcissism comes with a host of benefits. Moderately narcissistic teens are less anxious and depressed and have far better relationships than their low and high narcissism peers. Likewise, corporate leaders with moderate narcissism are rated by their employees as far more effective than those with too little or too much. And in our team's research, we're finding that people with healthy narcissism are happier, more optimistic, and more consistently self-confident than those at the low or high end of the spectrum.

When someone scores well above average in narcissistic traits (picture above 6 on the spectrum), they earn the label *narcissist*. There are many types of narcissists, though we're most familiar with the *extroverted* kind (a.k.a obvious, overt, or grandiose, in the research): ambitious, outgoing charismatic individuals, often drawn to the spotlight. Most politicians, actors, and celebrities exhibit this louder, chest-thumping brand of narcissism. Presidents seem to be especially likely to rank high in extroverted narcissism.

In fact, psychologist Ronald J. Deluga, of Bryant College, used biographical information to calculate a Narcissistic Personality Inventory score (a tool for measuring extroverted narcissism) for every commander in chief, from George Washington through Ronald Reagan. He found that high-ego presidents like Richard Nixon and Ronald Reagan ranked higher than more soft-spoken leaders like Jimmy Carter and Gerald Ford, but almost all presidents scored high enough to be considered "narcissists."

A more recent study led by psychologists Ashley L. Watts and Scott O. Lilienfeld of Emory University yielded similar results, but also revealed something that helps explain Nixon's dual nature: as the presidents' narcissism scores increased, so did their likelihood of facing impeachment proceedings, "abusing positions of power, tolerating unethical behavior in subordinates, stealing, bending or breaking rules, cheating on taxes, and having extramarital affairs." The authors' conclusion: narcissism is a double-edged sword, much as we've seen in Nixon's and Bill Clinton's case—and as we may be seeing in Donald Trump's case.

Donald Trump's brand of narcissism is clearly the obvious, loud kind, and it certainly comes with a downside. While he's extremely extroverted—he was, after all, the star of his own reality TV show—he also demonstrates many of the worst qualities we see in a narcissist. He brags: "I'll be the best jobs president God ever created." He boasts: "It's in my blood. I'm smart," he assured a crowd at a South Carolina rally. "Really smart." And he freely insults people, mocking their looks ("Rosie O'Donnell is a fat Pig"), their talent (Meryl Streep is "one of the most overrated actresses in Hollywood"), and—perhaps because they mattered most to him as a TV star—their ratings. He sparked a Twitter feud with Arnold Schwarzenegger, accusing him of killing Trump's beloved show, *The Celebrity Apprentice*.

> *Wow, the ratings are in and Arnold Schwarzenegger got "swamped" (or destroyed) by comparison to the ratings machine, DJT. So much for being a movie star—and that was season 1 compared to season 14. Now compare him to my season 1.*
>
> Donald J. Trump, Tweet from January 6, 2017

But perhaps the most startling display of Trump's numbers obsession took place when he had his press secretary, Sean Spicer, hold a briefing, the principal subject of which was the *size* of his inauguration crowd. Many watched and listened in disbelief while reporters pressed the question: why is this topic the central point of the administration's first press briefing?

A preoccupation with size is certainly laughably Freudian, but is it reason enough to question Trump's leadership capacity? When does the double-edged sword of narcissism—Trump's or any other president's—turn dangerous? That answer is more complicated than it seems, but it turns, in part, on whether or not their narcissism is high enough to count as an illness.

Pathological narcissism begins when people become so addicted to feeling special that, just like with any drug, they'll do anything to get their "high," including lie, steal, cheat, betray, and even *hurt* those closest to them. Imagine this starting around 9 on the spectrum and getting worse as we approach 10. At these points, you're in the realm of narcissistic personality disorder (NPD).

For a detailed description of NPD, see the latest edition of the *Diagnostic and Statistical Manual* (DSM-V), but for now, here's a simple explanation. People with NPD have a strong need, in every area of their life, to be treated as if they're special. To those with NPD, other people are simply mirrors, useful only insofar as they reflect back the special view of themselves they so desperately long to see. If that means making others look bad by comparison—say, by ruining their reputation at work—so be it. Because life is a constant competition, they're also usually riddled with envy over what other people seem to have. And they'll let you know it. At the heart of pathological narcissism, or NPD, is what I call *Triple E*:

- *Entitlement*, acting as if the world and other people owe them and should bend to their will
- *Exploitation*, using the people around them to make themselves feel special, no matter what the emotional or even physical cost to others (battering away at their self-esteem or running them into the ground with late-night work projects)
- *Empathy-impairment*, neglecting and ignoring the needs and feelings of others, even of those closest to them, because their own need to feel special is all that matters

Exploitation and entitlement (or EE, in the research) are linked to just about every troubling behavior pathological narcissists demonstrate: aggression when their ego is threatened, infidelity, vindictiveness, extreme envy, boasting, name-dropping, denial of any problems or wrongdoing—even workplace sabotage.

As people become more addicted to feeling special, they grow ever more dangerous. Here's where pathological narcissism often blends with *psychopathy*, a pattern of remorseless lies and manipulation. Psychopaths may carry on affairs, embezzle funds, ruin your reputation, and still greet you with a smile, without feeling any guilt, shame, or sadness.

Unlike NPD, psychopathy is marked not by impaired or blocked empathy but a complete *absence* of it (apart from being able to parrot words that *sound* like empathy, known as "cognitive empathy"). In fact, some neuroimaging evidence suggests that psychopaths don't experience emotions the same way non-psychopaths do. The emotion centers of their brains simply fail to light up when they confess shameful events, say, cheating on a spouse or punching a friend, or when they see pictures of people in pain or suffering or anguish.

When NPD and psychopathy combine, they form a pattern of behavior called *malignant narcissism*. This isn't a diagnosis, but a term coined by psychoanalyst Erich Fromm and elaborated on by personality disorder expert, Otto Kernberg, to describe people so driven by feeling special that they essentially see other people as pawns in their game of kill or be killed, whether metaphorically or literally. Hitler, who murdered millions, Kim Jong-un, who's suspected of ordering his uncle's and brother-in-law's deaths, and Vladimir Putin, who jokes about "liquidating journalists"—no doubt all fall in the category of malignant narcissist (among possessing other pernicious traits, like sadism, or delight in hurting others).

The problem is not all malignant narcissists are as overtly dangerous as people like Hitler, Putin, or Kim Jong-un, especially in democracies like the U.S., where it's still presumably illegal to kill people who disagree with you—even if they do write articles you don't like. That means if we're trying to determine whether or not a pathologically narcissistic president poses a threat to our country or the world, we'll also have to look to subtler indicators than a penchant for murder. We need to examine whether or not they can perform their jobs, one of the most important of which is to preserve the safety of our country—and the world.

Mentally Ill Leaders: Are They Functional or Impaired?

The diagnosis of a mental illness—NPD or any other—is not by itself a judgment about whether a person is a capable leader. Steve Jobs, by all accounts, had NPD—yelling at staff, questioning their competence, calling them "shit"—but he also galvanized Apple's engineers into developing the iMac, the iPod, and the iPhone. No doubt more than a few shareholders would have objected to Job's re-removal (he'd already been ousted for his nasty attitude once) from the company. He may have had what mental health clinicians call "high functioning" NPD—he was narcissistic enough to show Triple E, but still able to be incredibly productive, maintain decent (enough) family relationships and friendships, and mostly keep his angry explosions from completely blowing up the workplace.

What mental health experts concern themselves with most when it comes to assessing the *dangers* of mental illness are "functional impairments." That is, how much do the symptoms of a person's mental illness interfere with their ability to hold down a job, maintain meaningful relationships, and—most importantly—manage their intense feelings, such as anger or sadness or fear, without becoming a danger to themselves or others? This is particularly important when it comes to positions as powerful as president of the United States. Steve Jobs calling another CEO "a piece of shit" has far less troubling implications than the leader of the free world telling a volatile dictator he's "very dumb."

In other words, in tackling the question of whether or not a leader's narcissism is dangerous, it's not enough to say they're mentally

ill; I've helped many clients over the years with active psychotic illness, who have wonderful loving relationships and maintain steady
jobs, even while anxiously worrying, for example, about devices
being implanted in their teeth. Equating mental illness with incapacity merely stigmatizes the mentally ill.

When it comes to the question of whether or not someone who's
mentally ill can function, *danger is the key—to self or others*. This is
where pathological narcissism and politics can indeed become a toxic,
even lethal, mix. When peace at home and abroad are at stake—not
just the feelings of coworkers, friends, or partners—pathological narcissism unchecked could lead to World War III.

The greatest danger, as we saw with Nixon, is that pathological
narcissists can lose touch with reality in subtle ways that become extremely dangerous over time. When they can't let go of their need to
be admired or recognized, they have to *bend* or *invent* a reality in
which they remain special despite all messages to the contrary. In
point of fact, they become *dangerously* psychotic. It's just not always
obvious until it's too late.

Just like narcissism and most traits or conditions, psychosis lies
on a spectrum. On the low end, people become "thought-disordered,"
that is, use tortured logic, deny embarrassing facts, and show horrendous judgment. On the upper end, they may have auditory and
visual hallucinations and paranoid delusions. As their special status
becomes threatened, people with NPD bend the truth to fit their story
of who they are. If reality suggests they're not special, but flawed,
fragile, and—even worse—mediocre, then they simply ignore or
distort reality.

Did Nixon's psychotic deterioration, for example, lead to more
carnage in Vietnam? One biographer claims he bombed the country,
at least once, to impress his friends, and that Henry Kissinger, the
secretary of state, kept Nixon's rashest decisions in check, making
sure any escalation of conflict cleared a committee of military experts.

Did Nixon foment more unrest internally than the U.S. would
have seen otherwise? Certainly, his "the press is the enemy" mantra,

which dated back to his anger over the slush fund scandal, pitted the administration against the people. Paranoia is easy to catch when the POTUS suffers from it; everyone starts looking over their shoulders for danger when the free world's leader says it surrounds us. Turmoil, rage, and distrust swirled through the 1970s. Are we living through that again?

Did Nixon make decisions of state while drunk, drowning the pain of his persecution, imagined or real? Given the widespread reports of how much he drank, it's hard to imagine he didn't. Multiple biographers report his staff scrambling to contain his threatened actions, including IRS audits, against the people on his burgeoning "Enemies List."

Did Nixon ever draw counsel from the paintings he spoke to? Did he follow it?

These all constitute dangerous functional impairments for a leader. They're the foreign and domestic policy equivalent of leaping from a building, believing you can fly. And they're all part of the *psychotic spiral* that afflicts pathological narcissists confronted with the troubling truth that they're not as special as they think they are.

The Psychotic Spiral
If we wish to preserve the safety of our country and the world, we have to remain vigilant to the signs of the psychotic spiral in pathologically narcissistic leaders:

Increasing Paranoia
Increasing Paranoia: Pathological narcissists abhor admitting to vulnerability—feeling scared, insecure, unsure of themselves— because they don't trust people to support them when they're upset, a problem called *insecure attachment* in the research. They don't even like people knowing they're upset (except over feeling attacked). So they divide the world into good and bad, friend and enemy, in simple black-and-white terms, the advantage being that if they want to

feel safe again, if they want to feel assured of their special status, all they need do is flee (or eliminate) their enemies and cozy up to their friends.

In other words, pathological narcissists in a psychotic spiral *project*, imagining the danger they feel inside themselves (anxiety, panic, confusion, doubts) is coming from *outside*, so that they can escape or destroy it. Unfortunately, because the sense of danger is internal (their insecurity), they have to step up their efforts to attack their enemies in order to feel safe.

Imagine this on a global scale, where enemies are Communists or Muslims or immigrants or any kind. Nixon was far happier complaining about Communist threats than recognizing his errors and correcting them. How often did that lead to additional violence in Vietnam? Could such "splitting" as it's called lead to unnecessary violence again?

Impaired Judgment

As pathological narcissists become increasingly thought-disordered, their vision becomes clouded. That's because if you see the world not as it is, but as you *wish* or *need* it to be in order to preserve the belief you're special, you lose touch with crucial information, brute facts, and harsh realities. On a global scale that means, as it did with Nixon, that if it feeds your ego, step up military action. The precariousness of the world or careful assessments of the dangers of a military assault don't matter at this point; displays of power and superiority are soothing when pathological narcissists feel like they're falling apart inside.

The resulting chaos can be hard to keep up with (and fruitless in the end) as we saw with Nixon's staff chasing after his drunken calls and egregious rants about the Jews working against him. In a startlingly parallel lapse of judgment, Trump reportedly boasted to the Russian ambassador about the impressiveness of his intelligence assessment, spilling secrets Israel shared (without their permission).

Volatile Decision Making

This sign of a psychotic spiral is particularly troubling. Impaired judgment naturally leads to reactivity and ill-conceived plans. If all that matters to a pathologically narcissistic leader is any action that preserves their special status (at least in their mind), then reality, circumstance, and facts cease to matter. Which means that what a leader says from day to day or even hour to hour may shift based on what feels best, not what's best for the country.

Right after his staff and appointees spread the message that Trump fired FBI director James Comey, who was investigating his campaign's and administration's ties to Russia, for incompetence and on the recommendation of the deputy attorney general, Rod Rosenstein, the president blithely contradicted the statement.

"I'd already decided to fire him," Trump proudly proclaimed, as though what mattered most was proving he could make his own decisions, not the appearance, at least, of neutrality or a separation of powers. Trump went on to call Comey "crazy, a nut job" and said that firing him relieved the "pressure" of the Russia investigation.

Whether or not this is a sign of thought disorder, at the very least, it shows a remarkable lack of self-preservation. Trump totally ignored that Nixon, too, fired those investigating him—and with fatal consequence.

Gaslighting

Often, people with NPD resort to an insidious strategy called *gaslighting*—a term drawn from the 1938 play about a man who persuaded his wife she was crazy by, among other means, dimming the gaslights and claiming he'd never touched them. As people with NPD become increasingly psychotic, they're determined to convince others that they're the "crazy" ones who can't see reality for what it is. Gaslighting reassures pathological narcissists that their own grip on reality remains firm because they can't bear to acknowledge their sanity is slipping away. We might ask if we're seeing this now, as Trump and his closest advisers appear on TV claiming he didn't make statements that journalists often simply play back—or if it's a tweet, flash an image—to prove that he did indeed say what he said.

Lately, these incidents have become commonplace. Many in the press and public at large now refer to them as *alternative facts*, alluding to Trump spokesperson Kellyanne Conway's now infamous "explanation" for why Sean Spicer had berated the press for misreporting Trump's inauguration size: "this was the largest audience to ever witness an inauguration, period, both in person and around the globe," Spicer peevishly told a stunned press corps. This turned out to be patently false, though Conway defended the statement, saying Spicer had simply been providing "alternative facts."

Those who embrace Trump's reality, where the mainstream media lies and remains "the enemy," signify their support with red hats bearing the inscription MAGA (Make America Great Again). Those who *believe* what the news reports about Trump have donned the symbol of resistance—pink pussy hats, a reference to his now infamous hot mic comments about women, "I just grab 'em by the pussy . . ."

That the country is currently split—and our shared reality with it—seems without question at this point.

Spotting Lethal Leaders: How to Save the World

Currently, it's up to you to decide if the evidence cited points to functional impairments in Trump or any other politician. That's not something mental health professionals in the United States are allowed to do—not yet.

Nevertheless, we have in our midst people already trained to provide functional and risk assessments based *entirely* on observation—forensic psychiatrists and psychologists as well as "profilers" groomed by the CIA, the FBI, and various law enforcement agencies. They spend their whole lives learning to predict how people behave.

We could, if we wish, assemble a panel of politically independent specialists within government to provide these assessments.

That means suspending the Goldwater rule—or at least allowing risk assessment (to the country, to the world) to take precedence over the sanctity of current ethics.

If pathological narcissists, in their reality-warping efforts to feed their addiction, bring themselves to the precipice of disaster, why should we, as nations, allow them to pull us into the abyss with them?

It's *this* urgent existential question that faces democracies throughout the world today.

Craig Malkin, Ph.D., is author of the internationally acclaimed Rethinking Narcissism, *a clinical psychologist, and Lecturer for Harvard Medical School with twenty-five years of experience helping individuals, couples, and families. His insights on relationships and narcissism have appeared in newspapers and magazines such as* Time, *the* New York Times, *the* Sunday Times, *Psychology Today, Women's Health, the* Huffington Post, *and* Happen Magazine. *He has also been featured multiple times on NPR, CBS Radio, and the Oprah Winfrey Network channel, among other stations and shows internationally. Dr. Malkin is president and director of the Cambridge, Massachusetts–based YM Psychotherapy and Consultation Inc., which provides psychotherapy and couples workshops.*

References

Ackerman, R. A., E. A. Witt, M. B. Donnellan, K. H. Trzesniewski, R. W. Robins, and D. A. Kashy. 2011. "What Does the Narcissistic Personality Inventory Really Measure?" *Assessment* 18 (1): 67–87.

Alicke, Mark D., and Constantine Sedikides. 2011. *Handbook of Self-Enhancement and Self-Protection.* New York: Guilford Press.

Baumeister, Roy F., and Kathleen D. Vohs. 2001. "Narcissism as Addiction to Esteem." *Psychological Inquiry* 12 (4): 206–10.

Brown, Jonathon D. 2010. "Across the (Not So) Great Divide: Cultural Similarities in Self-Evaluative Processes." *Social and Personality Psychology Compass* 4 (5): 318–30.

———. 2012. "Understanding the Better Than Average Effect: Motives (Still) Matter." *Personality and Social Psychology Bulletin* 38 (2): 209–19.

Deluga, Ronald J. 1997. "Relationship Among American Presidential Charismatic Leadership, Narcissism, and Rated Performance." *The Leadership Quarterly* 8 (1): 49–65.

Drew, Elizabeth. 2007. *Richard M. Nixon: The American Presidents Series: The 37th President, 1969–1974.* New York: Macmillan.

Farrell, John A. 2017. *Richard Nixon: The Life.* New York: Doubleday.

Grijalva, E., D. A. Newman, L. Tay, M. B. Donnellan, P. D. Harms, R. W. Robins, and T. Yan. 2014. "Gender Differences in Narcissism: A Meta-Analytic Review." *Psychological Bulletin* 141 (2): 261–310.

Grijalva, Emily, and Daniel A. Newman. 2014. "Narcissism and Counter-productive Work Behavior (CWB): Meta-Analysis and Consideration of Collectivist Culture, Big Five Personality, and Narcissism's Facet Structure." *Applied Psychology* 64 (1): 93–126.

Grijalva, Emily, Peter D. Harms, Daniel A. Newman, Blaine H. Gaddis, and R. Chris Fraley. 2014. "Narcissism and Leadership: A Meta-Analytic Review of Linear and Nonlinear Relationships." *Personnel Psychology* 68 (1): 1–47.

Hill, Patrick L., and Daniel K. Lapsley. 2011. "Adaptive and Maladaptive Narcissism in Adolescent Development." (2011): 89–105.

Hill, Robert W., and Gregory P. Yousey. 1998. "Adaptive and Maladaptive Narcissism Among University Faculty, Clergy, Politicians, and Librarians." *Current Psychology* 17 (2–3): 163–69.

Isaacson, Walter. 2011. *Steve Jobs.* New York: Simon and Schuster.

Jakobwitz, Sharon, and Vincent Egan. 2006. "The Dark Triad and Normal Personality Traits." *Personality and Individual Differences* 40 (2): 331–39.

Lapsley, D. K., and M. C. Aalsma. 2006. "An Empirical Typology of Narcissism and Mental Health in Late Adolescence." *Journal of Adolescence* 29 (1): 53–71.

Malkin, Craig. 2015. *Rethinking Narcissism: The Bad—and Surprising Good—About Feeling Special.* New York: HarperCollins.

Malkin, Craig, and Stuart Quirk. 2016. "Evidence for the Reliablity and

Construct Validity of the Narcissism Spectrum Scale." *Research in progress.*

Pailing, Andrea, Julian Boon, and Vincent Egan. 2014. "Personality, the Dark Triad and Violence." *Personality and Individual Differences* 67: 81–86.

Penney, Lisa M., and Paul E. Spector. 2002. "Narcissism and Counterproductive Work Behavior: Do Bigger Egos Mean Bigger Problems?" *International Journal of Selection and Assessment* 10 (1–2): 126–34.

Raskin, Robert N., and Calvin S. Hall. 1979. "A Narcissistic Personality Inventory." *Psychological Reports* 45 (2): 590.

Reidy, Dennis E., Amos Zeichner, Joshua D. Foster, and Marc A. Martinez. 2008. "Effects of Narcissistic Entitlement and Exploitativeness on Human Physical Aggression." *Personality and Individual Differences* 44 (4): 865–75.

Ronningstam, Elsa. 1998. *Disorders of Narcissism: Diagnostic, Clinical, and Empirical Implications.* 1st ed., Washington, DC: American Psychiatric Press.

Sosik, John J., Jae Uk Chun, and Weichun Zhu. 2014. "Hang On to Your Ego: The Moderating Role of Leader Narcissism on Relationships Between Leader Charisma and Follower Psychological Empowerment and Moral Identity." *Journal of Business Ethics* 120 (1): 65–80.

Spain, Seth M., Peter Harms, and James M. LeBreton. 2014. "The Dark Side of Personality at Work." *Journal of Organizational Behavior* 35 (S1): S41–S60.

Summers, Anthony, and Robbyn Swan. 2000. *The Arrogance of Power: The Secret World of Richard Nixon.* New York: Viking.

Taylor, Shelley E., Jennifer S. Lerner, David K. Sherman, Rebecca M. Sage, and Nina K. McDowell. 2003. "Portrait of the Self-Enhancer: Well Adjusted and Well Liked or Maladjusted and Friendless?" *Journal of Personality and Social Psychology* 84 (1): 165.

Watts, Ashley L., Scott O. Lilienfeld, Sarah Francis Smith, Joshua D. Miller, W. Keith Campbell, Irwin D. Waldman, Steven J. Rubenzer, and Thomas J. Faschingbauer. 2013. "The Double-Edged Sword of Grandiose Narcissism." *Psychological Science* 24 (12): 2379–89. doi: 10.1177/09567976 13491970.

Wink, Paul. 1992. "Three Types of Narcissism in Women from College to Mid-Life." *Journal of Personality* 60 (1): 7–30.

Woodworth, Michael, and Stephen Porter. 2002. "In Cold Blood: Characteristics of Criminal Homicides as a Function of Psychopathy." *Journal of Abnormal Psychology* 111 (3): 436.

Young Mark S., and Drew Pinsky. 2006. "Narcissism and Celebrity." *Journal of Research in Personality* 40 (5): 463–71.

I WROTE *THE ART OF THE DEAL* WITH DONALD TRUMP

His Self-Sabotage Is Rooted in His Past

TONY SCHWARTZ

Why does President Trump behave in the dangerous and seemingly self-destructive ways he does?

Three decades ago, I spent nearly a year hanging around Trump to write his first book, *The Art of the Deal*, and got to know him very well. I spent hundreds of hours listening to him, watching him in action, and interviewing him about his life. To me, none of what he has said or done over the past four months as president comes as a surprise. The way he has behaved over the past two weeks—firing FBI director James B. Comey, undercutting his own aides as they tried to explain the decision, disclosing sensitive information to Russian officials, and railing about it all on Twitter—is also entirely predictable.

Early on, I recognized that Trump's sense of self-worth is forever at risk. When he feels aggrieved, he reacts impulsively and defensively, constructing a self-justifying story that doesn't depend on facts and always directs the blame to others.

The Trump I first met in 1985 had lived nearly all his life in survival mode. By his own description, his father, Fred, was relentlessly demanding, difficult, and driven. Here's how I phrased it in *The Art of the Deal*: "My father is a wonderful man, but he is also very much a business guy and strong and tough as hell." As Trump saw it, his older brother, Fred Jr., who became an alcoholic and died at age 42, was overwhelmed by his father. Or as I euphemized it in the book: "There were inevitably confrontations between the two of them. In most cases, Freddy came out on the short end."

Trump's worldview was profoundly and self-protectively shaped by his father. "I was drawn to business very early, and I was never intimidated by my father, the way most people were," is the way I wrote it in the book. "I stood up to him, and he respected that. We had a relationship that was almost businesslike."

To survive, I concluded from our conversations, Trump felt compelled to go to war with the world. It was a binary, zero-sum choice for him: You either dominated or you submitted. You either created and exploited fear, or you succumbed to it—as he thought his older brother had. This narrow, defensive outlook took hold at a very early age, and it never evolved. "When I look at myself in the first grade and I look at myself now," he told a recent biographer, "I'm basically the same." His development essentially ended in early childhood.

Instead, Trump grew up fighting for his life and taking no prisoners. In countless conversations, he made clear to me that he treated every encounter as a contest he had to win, because the only other option from his perspective was to lose, and that was the equivalent of obliteration. Many of the deals in *The Art of the Deal* were massive failures—among them the casinos he owned and the launch of a league to rival the National Football League—but Trump had me describe each of them as a huge success.

With evident pride, Trump explained to me that he was "an assertive, aggressive" kid from an early age, and that he had once punched a music teacher in the eye and was nearly expelled from elementary school for his behavior.

Like so much about Trump, who knows whether that story is true? What's clear is that he has spent his life seeking to dominate others, whatever that requires and whatever collateral damage it creates along the way. In *The Art of the Deal*, he speaks with street-fighting relish about competing in the world of New York real estate: They are "some of the sharpest, toughest, and most vicious people in the world. I happen to love to go up against these guys, and I love to beat them." I never sensed from Trump any guilt or contrition about anything he'd done, and he certainly never shared any misgivings publicly. From his perspective, he operated in a jungle full of predators who were forever out to get him, and he did what he must to survive.

Trump was equally clear with me that he didn't value—nor even necessarily recognize—the qualities that tend to emerge as people grow more secure, such as empathy, generosity, reflectiveness, the capacity to delay gratification, or, above all, a conscience, an inner sense of right and wrong. Trump simply didn't traffic in emotions or interest in others. The life he lived was all transactional, all the time. Having never expanded his emotional, intellectual, or moral universe, he has his story down, and he's sticking to it.

A key part of that story is that facts are whatever Trump deems them to be on any given day. When he is challenged, he instinctively doubles down—even when what he has just said is demonstrably false. I saw that countless times, whether it was as trivial as exaggerating the number of floors at Trump Tower or as consequential as telling me that his casinos were performing well when they were actually going bankrupt. In the same way, Trump would see no contradiction at all in changing his story about why he fired Comey and thereby undermining the statements of his aides, or in any other lie he tells. His aim is never accuracy; it's domination.

The Trump I got to know had no deep ideological beliefs, nor any passionate feeling about anything but his immediate self-interest. He derives his sense of significance from conquests and accomplishments. "Can you believe it, Tony?" he would often say at the start of late-night conversations with me, going on to describe some new example of his brilliance. But the reassurance he got from even his biggest achievements was always ephemeral and unreliable—and that appears to include being elected president. Any addiction has a predictable pattern: the addict keeps chasing the high by upping the ante in an increasingly futile attempt to re-create the desired state. On the face of it, Trump has more opportunities now to feel significant and accomplished than almost any other human being on the planet. But that's like saying a heroin addict has his problem licked once he has free and continuous access to the drug. Trump also now has a far bigger and more public stage on which to fail and to feel unworthy.

From the very first time I interviewed him in his office in Trump Tower in 1985, the image I had of Trump was that of a black hole. Whatever goes in quickly disappears without a trace. Nothing sustains. It's forever uncertain when someone or something will throw Trump off his precarious perch—when his sense of equilibrium will be threatened and he'll feel an overwhelming compulsion to restore it. Beneath his bluff exterior, I always sensed a hurt, incredibly vulnerable little boy who just wanted to be loved.

What Trump craves most deeply is the adulation he has found so fleeting. This goes a long way toward explaining his need for control and why he simply couldn't abide Comey, who reportedly refused to accede to Trump's demand for loyalty and whose continuing investigation into Russian interference in the election campaign last year threatens to bring down his presidency. Trump's need for unquestioning praise and flattery also helps to explain his hostility to democracy and to a free press—both of which thrive on open dissent.

As we have seen countless times during the campaign and since the election, Trump can devolve into survival mode on a moment's notice. Look no further than the thousands of tweets he has written attacking his perceived enemies over the past year. In neurochemical terms, when he feels threatened or thwarted, Trump moves into a fight-or-flight state. His amygdala is triggered, his hypothalamic-pituitary-adrenal axis activates, and his prefrontal cortex—the part of the brain that makes us capable of rationality and reflection—shuts down. He reacts rather than reflects, and damn the consequences. This is what makes his access to the nuclear codes so dangerous and frightening.

Over the past week, in the face of criticism from nearly every quarter, Trump's distrust has almost palpably mushroomed. No importuning by his advisers stands a chance of constraining him when he is this deeply triggered. The more he feels at the mercy of forces he cannot control—and he is surely feeling that now—the more resentful, desperate, and impulsive he becomes.

Even 30 years later, I vividly remember the ominous feeling when Trump got angry about some perceived slight. Everyone around him knew that you were best off keeping your distance at those times, or, if that wasn't possible, that you should resist disagreeing with him in any way.

In the hundreds of Trump's phone calls I listened in on with his consent, and the dozens of meetings I attended with him, I can never remember anyone disagreeing with him about anything. The same climate of fear and paranoia appears to have taken root in his White House.

The most recent time I spoke to Trump—and the first such occasion in nearly three decades—was July 14, 2016, shortly before *The New Yorker* published an article by Jane Mayer about my experience writing *The Art of the Deal*. Trump was just about to win the Republican nomination for president. I was driving in my car when my cell phone rang. It was Trump. He had just gotten off a call with a fact-checker for *The New Yorker*, and he didn't mince words.

"I just want to tell you that I think you're very disloyal," he started in. Then he berated and threatened me for a few minutes. I pushed back, gently but firmly. And then, suddenly, as abruptly as he began the call, he ended it. "Have a nice life," he said, and hung up.

Tony Schwartz is the author of several books, including The Art of the Deal, *which he coauthored with Mr. Trump. He also wrote* The Power of Full Engagement: Managing Energy, Not

Time *(with Jim Loehr) and* The Way We're Working Isn't Working, *a* New York Times *and* Wall Street Journal *bestseller. He is also CEO and founder of The Energy Project, a consulting firm that helps individuals and organizations solve intractable problems and add more value in the world by widening their worldview.*

TRUMP'S TRUST DEFICIT IS THE CORE PROBLEM

GAIL SHEEHY, PH.D.

The narcissism and paranoia are issues, but the biggest concern is that Donald Trump trusts no one. This will be his downfall—or maybe ours.

In a world spinning radically out of control, can we trust President Trump to rely on his famous "instincts" as he alienates U.S. allies and plays brinksmanship with our enemies? Writing from the perspective of his first one hundred days, and from a year and a half of reporting on the president-elect, I can't help worrying how much closer the day of reckoning has to come on charges of collusion with Russia before he needs a war to provide the ultimate distraction?

The fundamental bedrock of human development is the formation of a capacity to trust, absorbed by children between birth and eighteen months. Donald Trump has boasted of his total lack of trust: "People are too trusting. I'm a very untrusting guy" (1990). "Hire the best people, and don't trust them" (2007). "The world is a vicious and brutal place. Even your friends are out to get you: they want your job, your money, your wife" (2007).

His biographers have recorded his worldview as saturated with a sense of danger and his need to project total toughness. As we know, his father trained him to be a "killer," the only alternative to being a "loser." Trump has never forgotten the primary lesson he learned from his father and at the military school to which he was sent to be toughened up still further. In Trump's own words, "Man is the most vicious of all animals, and life is a series of battles ending in victory or defeat."

In the biography *Never Enough*, Trump describes to Michael D'Antonio his father's "dragging him" around tough neighborhoods in Brooklyn when he collected the rents for the apartments he owned. Fred Trump always told the boy to stand to one side of the door. Donald asked why. "Because sometimes they shoot right through the door," his father told him.

Today, this man lives mostly alone in the White House, without a wife or any friends in whom to confide, which he would never do anyway, because that would require admitting vulnerability.

Leon Panetta, former CIA director and defense chief under Clinton, stated on Fox Business channel in February 2017, "The coin of the realm for any president is trust—trust of the American people in the credibility of that president." In the nearly two years that Donald Trump has been in our face almost daily, he has sown mistrust in all his Republican rivals, alienated much of the conservative Republican bloc he needs in the House for legislative success, ignored congressional Democrats, and viciously insulted Democratic leaders, calling them liars, clowns, stupid, and incompetent, and condemning Barack Obama as "sick" and Hillary Clinton as "the devil." When he represents the American people abroad, his belligerent behavior and disrespect for leaders of our closest allies rips apart the comity and peace-keeping pledges built over decades. Yet, he never hesitates to congratulate despots, such as Turkey's Erdogan, Egypt's General Sisi, and, most lavishly of all, Russia's Putin.

As president, Trump is systematically shredding trust in the institutions he now commands. Having discredited the entire seventeen-agency intelligence community as acting like Nazis, he also dismissed the judiciary because of one judge's Hispanic background and another's opposition to his travel [née Muslim] ban. Even his Supreme Court justice, Neil Gorsuch, said it was "disheartening" and "demoralizing" to hear Trump disparage the judiciary. Not content to smear the media on a daily basis, Trump borrowed a phrase used by Lenin and Stalin to brand the American media as an "enemy of the people."

By his own words, Trump operates on the assumption that everyone is out to get him. The nonmedical definition of paranoia is the tendency toward excessive or irrational suspiciousness and distrustfulness of others. For a man who proclaims his distrust of everyone, it is not surprising that Trump drew closest to him two legendary conspiracy theorists: Stephen Bannon and Gen. Michael Flynn.

And even after he was forced to fire his choice for top national security adviser after Flynn blatantly lied, Trump's White House desperately stonewalled congressional investigators to keep them from getting their hands on documents that could prove Flynn's paid collusion with Russia on Trump's behalf. The closer that case comes to a criminal referral to the Justice Department, the closer Trump's survival instincts will propel him to a wag-the-dog war.

A leader who does not trust his subordinates cannot inspire trust. Though Trump boasts of fierce personal loyalty, he himself is loyal only until he isn't. Among his anxious aides, only Jared Kushner, it seems, may be safe, deputized as Trump's de facto secretary of state. Where Trump succeeds in inspiring trust is by giving his subordinates the license to lie. In fact, this virus of licentiousness has spread from the White House to congressional Republicans, to wit the stunt that exposed Rep. Devin Nunes as unfit to lead the House Intelligence Committee probe into Trump operatives' possible collusion with Russia. As the chaos of the White House rolled with a crisis-a-day fever into the month of May, a hide-and-seek commander in chief began sending out his most trusted national security advisers to defend him (Gen. James "Mad Dog" Mattis, Gen. H. R. McMaster, and the muted secretary of state, Rex Tillerson) and then cut the legs out from under them with his own blurted half-truths.

We hear repeatedly that Trump as a manager likes chaos. I asked a deputy White House counsel under Obama, a decorated former officer in Iraq and former White House counsel to President Obama, how such a management style impacts trust. "Trump explicitly or implicitly manages the situation so it's never possible for his advisers to know where they stand," he said. "It's the opposite of what you want in a high-functioning organization." Trump's anxious aides must know just how easy it is to fail his loyalty test, or to be the fall guy if a scapegoat is needed. While publicly they may defend him, it is clear to reporters that White House staffers are leaking information constantly. The leaks can only exacerbate Trump's mistrust, perpetuating a vicious circle.

His failure to trust or to inspire trust is even more dangerous on a global scale. He sees alliances such as NATO as suspect (until he changes his mind); he sees trade agreements such as NAFTA as ripping off America (until he changes his mind three or four times in the same week). "This is because Trump's worldview is that we live in a snake pit where everybody is out for themselves," observes the former White House counsel. He and his co-conspiracy theorist adviser Bannon take everything that the left-behind white working class hates about globalization and they turn it into personalized enemies: Muslims, Mexicans, and refugees whom they believe are taking away their jobs. "Those people aren't like us," is the alt-right message; "they're polluting our culture."

In the course of his first one hundred days, Trump appeared to be increasingly out of touch with the reality in which the majority of us live. His pathological propensity to lie is not the worst of it—his monomaniacal attachment to his lies is, such as the transparent one in his March 4 twitterstorm accusing President Obama of putting a tap on his phone. It raises the question: Is this president floating in his own alternate reality?

When I attended Dr. Bandy Lee's Yale town hall meeting to write about it for *The Daily Beast*, I cited insights delivered there by two of the authors in this book. Dr. Robert Jay Lifton, the eminent former professor of psychiatry at Yale University and today at Columbia University, elaborated in a follow-up interview, "Trump creates his own extreme manipulation of reality. He insists that his spokesmen defend his false reality as normal. He then expects the rest of society to accept it—despite the lack of any evidence." This leads to what Lifton calls "malignant normality"—in other words, the gradual acceptance by a public inundated with toxic untruths of those untruths until they pass for normal.

Dr. James F. Gilligan is a psychiatrist and author who has studied the motivations behind violent behavior over his twenty-five years of work in the American prison systems. "If we psychiatrists who have experience in assessing dangerousness, if we give passive permission to our president to proceed in his delusions, we are shirking our responsibility," Gilligan said. Today a senior clinical professor of psychiatry at NYU School of Medicine, Gilligan told Dr. Lee's town hall attendees, "I don't say Trump is Hitler or Mussolini, but he's no more normal than Hitler."

We don't have to rely on psychiatrists to see that this president is not consistent in his thinking or reliably attached to reality. We have had vastly more exposure to Donald Trump's observable behavior, his writing and speaking, than any psychiatrist would have after listening to him for years. It is therefore up to us, the American public, to call him on it. And some of the most experienced hands in and around the White House are doing so.

Presidential historian Douglas Brinkley believes that Donald Trump represents a very different subculture from any commander in chief. "He represents the New York building business—where you don't let your right hand know what your left hand is doing," says Brinkley. "In Trump's world, he must win at all costs. It's not about character or public service or looking out for your band of brothers."

The president to whom Trump is most often compared is Richard Nixon. John Dean, the famous White House counsel who testified against his fellow conservative Republican, compared Trump to that notably paranoid president. "Nixon was two personae—in public and with his top aides, he was trusted. But in private, his deeply paranoid and vengeful dark side came out."

Asked for the best example, Dean snapped, "He had zero empathy!" Just like Trump. "Nixon let twenty-two thousand more Americans die in Vietnam [after he sabotaged the 1968 Paris peace talks], plus who knows how many Cambodians and Laotians and Vietnamese, all to ensure his election." It took forty years before Nixon's worst crime was revealed: treason. That was when then-presidential candidate Nixon was heard on tape (from recordings ordered by President Johnson) scuttling the Vietnam peace talks to derail the reelection campaign of the Democratic candidate. Nixon sent a message to the South Vietnamese negotiators that they should withdraw from the peace talks and wait for him to be elected, at which point he would give them a much better deal.

Sound familiar? Fifty years later, Donald Trump's go-between with Russian officials, General Flynn, hinted to Putin's ambassador that Russia could get a much better deal if it didn't retaliate against Obama's sanctions and instead sat tight until Trump was elected. Also, Trump frequently tweeted about his eagerness to lift those sanctions—that is, until his fantasy bromance with Putin looked like it could arouse a federal investigation. Trump's appetite for vengeance is also matched by Nixon's with his long "Enemies List." No two modern presidents have had a more serious case of "political hemophilia," in the phrase of the latest Nixon biographer, John Farrell, by which he means: "Once wounded, these men never stop bleeding."

To the dismay of even conservative observers, Trump appears totally indifferent to the truth. *Time* magazine gave Trump an opportunity to clarify his refusal to correct his long string of falsehoods. What the March 23 interview produced instead was an astonishing revelation of his thinking: He states what he wants to be true. If his statement is proven false, he is unfazed, and confidently predicts that the facts will catch up with his belief: "I'm a very instinctual person, but my instinct turns out to be right." Even when the top sleuth in the country, FBI director James Comey, condemned Trump as a fabulist, Trump ignored the public rebuke and bragged about his ability to persuade millions of his paranoid version of Obama as "sick" and surreptitiously spying on him.

"Narcissistic people like Trump want more than anything to love themselves, but desperately want others to love them, too," wrote professor and chair of the Psychology Department at Northwestern University, Dan P. McAdams, in *The Atlantic*. "The fundamental goal in life for a narcissist is to promote the greatness of the self, for all to see."

Yet, what is an extreme narcissistic personality such as Trump to do when he fails to win glorification? "Trump, from his own writings, has shown massive hypersensitivity to shame or humiliation," says Dr. Gilligan. Yet, how does he dodge the humiliation when he is exposed as sacrificing the nation's security on the altar of his infantile need to impress Russian officials by giving away sensitive foreign intelligence?

Beneath the grandiose behavior of every narcissist lies the pit of fragile self-esteem. What if, deep down, the person whom Trump trusts least is himself? The humiliation of being widely exposed as a "loser," unable to bully through the actions he promised during the campaign, could drive him to prove he is, after all, a "killer." In only the first four months of his presidency, he teed up for starting a war in three places, Syria, Afghanistan, and North Korea. It is up to Congress, backed up by the public, to restrain him.

Gail Sheehy, Ph.D., as author, journalist, and popular lecturer, has changed the way millions of women and men around the world look at their life stages. In her fifty-year career, she has written seventeen books, including her revolutionary Passages, *named one of the ten most influential books of our times. As a literary journalist, she was one of the original contributors to* New York *magazine and, since 1984, has written for* Vanity Fair. *A winner of many awards, three honorary doctorates, a Lifetime Achievement Award in 2012 by Books for a Better Life, she has regularly commented on political figures, including in her acclaimed biography of Hillary Clinton,* Hillary's Choice.

SOCIOPATHY

LANCE DODES, M.D.

"Crazy like a fox or just crazy?" This question has surrounded Donald Trump since his campaign for president. The question is whether a person who is repetitively immoral—who cons others, lies, cheats, and manipulates to get what he wants, doesn't care whom he hurts just as long as he is gratifying himself—whether such a person's indifference to the feelings of others for personal gain is just being clever: crazy like a fox. Or are these actions a sign of something much more serious? Could they be expressions of significant mental derangement?

The answer to that question is emphatically, "Yes." To understand why, it's necessary to understand the psychological condition called "sociopathy," and why sociopathy is such a severe disturbance.

Caring for others and trying not to harm them is a fundamental quality of not just humans, but many mammals. Normal people, as well as normal wolves, dolphins, and elephants, appreciate when another of their species is in pain or danger and, unless fighting over territory or sexual partners, react to protect one another. Such caring and cooperation has major survival value for any species, and its clear evolutionary advantages have made these qualities basic across much of the animal kingdom. In humans, the ability to sense the feelings of one another, care about one another, and try to avoid harming one another even to the extent of placing ourselves at a disadvantage (think of animals that will stand all together to protect against a threat) is called empathy. It is a characteristic of all people no matter what individual emotional conflicts and issues they have. Unless they are sociopaths.

The failure of normal empathy is central to sociopathy, which is marked by an absence of guilt, intentional manipulation, and controlling or even sadistically harming others for personal power or gratification. People with sociopathic traits have a flaw in the basic nature of human beings. Far from being clever like a fox, they are lacking an essential part of being human. This is why sociopathy is among the most severe mental disturbances.

Yet, we are a culture that admires external success in wealth and power, regardless of how it is achieved. People with sociopathic qualities who are able to achieve high status and power precisely because of their manipulations and cheating are, therefore, sometimes seen as not only psychologically healthy, but superior. This contributes to the confusion: "How crazy can someone be who is so successful?" It has even been said that Mr. Trump couldn't possibly have serious mental problems because he got to be president.

Indeed, there are generally two life paths for people with severe sociopathy. Those who are unskilled at manipulating and hurting others, who are not careful in choosing their victims, who are unable to act charming well enough to fool people, have lives that often end in failure. They are identified as criminals or lose civil court battles to those they've cheated, or are unable to threaten their way back to positions of power. But those who are good at manipulation, at appearing charming and caring, at concealing their immoral or illegal behavior, and can bully their way to the top, do not end up as outcasts or in prison. There is a term for these people: "successful sociopaths." They are the ones who most fool others into thinking they are "crazy like a fox." Even their characteristic rages may appear almost normal. Instead of having a visible tantrum, they may simply fire people, or sue them. As their power increases, their ability to disguise their mental disturbance may also increase, concealed behind a wall of underlings who do the dirty work, or armies of lawyers who threaten those who are currently seen as the enemy. What is important to understand is that their success is on the outside. They are no different from those who are less skilled at concealing their lack of empathy, even if they require an expert to recognize them. They are still severely emotionally ill.

Diagnostic Labels

The word "sociopathy" is sometimes used interchangeably with "psychopathy," though some have defined the words a bit differently. Sociopathy is also a major aspect of the term, "malignant narcissism," and is roughly synonymous with the official (Diagnostic and Statistical Manual, or DSM) psychiatric diagnostic term, "antisocial personality disorder." All refer to a disturbance in an individual's entire emotional makeup (hence the term "personality" disorder in the DSM).

A label can never capture everything about a person, though. This may create diagnostic confusion if laypersons expect any individual to fit exactly into their conception of the problem. Cold-blooded murderers and cruel, sadistic rulers may treat their pets kindly, for instance. Consequently, it is the *traits* of sociopathy that are important to recognize in order to evaluate anyone or assess his fitness to hold a position of power. This is, in fact, the way the DSM does it. Each label has a set of observable behaviors that define it, and these groupings change often. We are now on the fifth version of the DSM, and there will be many more to come as knowledge, understanding, and even diagnostic fads change. Traits, however, are fixed. Therefore, in assessing whether a person is "sociopathic," what we really need to know is whether he has the observable, definitive traits that indicate the condition.

Without being concerned about a formal diagnostic label, it's useful to consider the traits of antisocial personality disorder as defined in the current DSM:

> A pervasive pattern of disregard for and violation of the rights of others, occurring since age 15 years, as indicated by three (or more) of the following:
>
> 1. Failure to conform to social norms with respect to lawful behaviors;
> 2. Deceitfulness, as indicated by repeated lying . . . or conning others for personal profit or pleasure;
> 3. Impulsivity or failure to plan ahead;
> 4. Irritability and aggressiveness, as indicated by repeated physical fights or assaults;
> 5. Reckless disregard for safety of self or others;
> 6. Consistent irresponsibility, as indicated by repeated failure to sustain consistent work behavior or honor financial obligations;
> 7. Lack of remorse, as indicated by being indifferent to or rationalizing having hurt, mistreated, or stolen from another; and
> 8. Evidence of conduct disorder [impulsive, aggressive, callous, or deceitful behavior that is persistent and difficult to deter with threats or punishment] with onset before age 15 years.

Other systems of diagnosis use different words for the essential sociopathic traits: *sadistic*, unempathic, cruel, devaluing, immoral, primitive, callous, predatory, bullying, dehumanizing.

The term "primitive" as a descriptor of sociopathic traits deserves special attention. The word derives not from ancient historical times, but from ancient personal times: the early years of life. It helps to explain why there is a multiplicity of defects in these people.

In early development, everything is happening at once. Major emotional capacities are developing alongside major cognitive capacities. Children must develop ways to manage emotional distress: anxiety, confusion, disappointment, loss, fear, all while they are growing in their capacity to think, and sorting out what is real and what is their imagination. We all develop systems to do this, to tolerate and control our emotions, understand and empathize with the people around us, and tell the difference between reality and wishes or fears.

But not people with the early, primitive emotional problems seen in sociopathy. They do not tolerate disappointments; instead, they fly into rages and claim that the upsetting reality isn't real. They make up an alternative reality and insist that it is true. This is the definition of a delusion. When it is told to others, it is basically a lie. As described earlier, successful sociopaths may not look very "crazy," but this capacity to lose touch with reality shows up when they are stressed by criticism or disappointment. Later, when they are less stressed, they explain their loss of reality with rationalizations or simply more lies.

The primitive nature of people with sociopathic traits can also be seen through the findings of brain research. In early life, along with its psychological developments, the brain is developing physically. It is notable that people with sociopathic traits have been found to have abnormalities in the prefrontal cortex and the amygdala regions of their brains, areas closely associated with essential cognitive and emotional functions.

Psychological Mechanisms in Sociopathy

People with sociopathic traits employ specific abnormal emotional mechanisms. Primary among these is "projective identification." "Projection" by itself refers to a belief that others have feelings or thoughts which are actually in the mind of the individual doing the projecting. Commonly, these are aggressive and dangerous feelings, which are managed by being projected to others, who are then seen as aggressive and dangerous. When this process occurs regularly, it is simply called paranoia. "Projective identification" is the most serious version of paranoia. The "identification" part of the term refers to seeing others not just as having threatening characteristics, but as entirely dangerous people—people who have to be attacked or destroyed.

This psychological mechanism contributes to loss of reality, rage outbursts, and attacks on others. When it is combined with a lack of empathy and its corresponding lack of guilt for harming others, the danger from such people is enormous.

Projective identification is not the only defective psychological mechanism in sociopaths. Because of the incapacity to realistically appraise (or care for) people, others are alternately seen as evil or good, according to the projection in use at the moment. The sociopath may treat people as though they are great friends, charmingly complimenting them on how wonderful they are, then abruptly turn on them as the enemy. Loyalty is highly prized by sociopaths because it serves their personal ends, but there is no real relationship. Dividing the world into good and bad in an unstable, fluctuating way is called "splitting."

Although sociopathy always means a lack of empathy, there is one way in which severe sociopaths do have a certain, frightening type of empathy. It is the empathy of the predator. A tiger stalking his prey must have an ability to sense the prey's fear, or at least to be aware of the small signs of that fear (Malancharuvil 2012). The tiger is "empathic" with its prey, but not sympathetic or caring. Successful sociopaths are like that. They are closely attuned to their victim's emotional state. Does the victim buy what the sociopath is selling? Does he need false reassurance, a compliment on his intelligence or appearance, a lying promise, or a friendly gesture to keep him thinking the sociopath is honorable? The successful sociopath's predatory "empathy" reflects a definite perceptive acumen, making him a genius at manipulation. When this works, it produces a disastrous trust in him. Yet, like the tiger, he is unconcerned about the welfare of his target.

The pathological emotional problems in sociopathy make one another worse. An inability to have a consistent realistic view of the world, or to maintain emotionally genuine relationships, leads to more paranoia. The weakness in impulse control which arises from enraged reactions to imagined slights and produces reckless, destructive behavior, leads to a greater need to deny criticism with more lies to tell oneself and everyone else, and an increasing distance from reality. The more a sociopath needs to scapegoat others the more he genuinely hates them, making him even more aggressive and sadistic. Life is devoted to endless destruction in the service of an endless quest for power and admiration, unmitigated by basic empathy or guilt.

Donald Trump

Because Mr. Trump has been a very public figure for many years, and because we have been able to hear from many who have known him for a long time, we are in an excellent position to know his behaviors—his speech and actions—which are precisely the basis for making an assessment of his dangerousness, whether we assess him using the official DSM criteria for antisocial personality disorder (APD), as below, or whether we apply our knowledge of malignant narcissism, both of which include the signs and symptoms of sociopathy. Let us consider these in turn.

Lack of Empathy for Others; Lack of Remorse; Lying and Cheating

Mr. Trump's mocking the disability of a handicapped reporter, unconcern for the safety of protesters at a rally ("Get rid of them!"), sexually assaulting women, threatening physical harm to his opponent in the election (alluding to gun owners eliminating her), repeatedly verbally attacking a family who lost their son fighting for the country, personally degrading people who criticize him (calling them insulting names, as he did in both the Republican primaries and the general election), a history of cheating people he's hired by not paying them what he owes, creating the now forced-to-disband Trump University, targeting and terrifying minority groups, all provide overwhelming evidence of profound sociopathic traits, which are far more important than trying to assign any specific diagnostic label.

Loss of Reality

Mr. Trump's insistence on the truth of matters proven to be untrue ("alternative facts") is well-known. His insistence has occurred both repeatedly and over a long time, even when such denial is not in his interest and it would be better for him to acknowledge that he spoke in error. He has falsely claimed that President Obama is not an American and that he wiretapped Mr. Trump's building, that his own loss in the vote total of the general election was caused by illegal aliens, that he had the largest inauguration crowd in history, etc. Together, these show a persistent loss of reality.

Rage Reactions and Impulsivity

Mr. Trump's rages have been reported on multiple occasions in the press, leading to sudden decisions and actions. He fired and subsequently threatened the director of the FBI after hearing him testify in unwanted ways before Congress, launched more than 50 missiles within 72 hours of seeing a disturbing image on the news—reversing his stated Middle East policy, precipitously violated diplomatic norms, creating international tensions (as with reports of threatening to invade Mexico, hanging up on the prime minister of Australia, antagonizing Germany, France, Greece, and others), issued illegal executive orders, apparently without vetting them with knowledgeable attorneys, and so on.

Conclusion

Donald Trump's speech and behavior show that he has severe sociopathic traits. The significance of this cannot be overstated. While there have surely been American presidents who could be said to be narcissistic, none have shown sociopathic qualities to the degree seen in Mr. Trump. Correspondingly, none have been so definitively and so obviously dangerous.

Democracy requires respect and protection for multiple points of view, concepts that are incompatible with sociopathy. The need to be seen as superior, when coupled with lack of empathy or remorse for harming other people, are in fact the signature characteristics of tyrants, who seek the control and destruction of all who oppose them, as well as loyalty to themselves instead of to the country they lead.

The paranoia of severe sociopathy creates a profound risk of war, since heads of other nations will inevitably disagree with or challenge the sociopathic leader, who will experience the disagreement as a personal attack, leading to rage reactions and impulsive action to destroy this "enemy." A common historical example is the creation, by sociopathic leaders, of an international incident to have an excuse to seize more power (suspend constitutional rights, impose martial law, and discriminate against minority groups). Because such leaders will lie to others in government and to their citizens, those who would check the sociopath's power find it difficult to contradict his claims and actions with facts. Would-be tyrants also typically devalue a free press, undermining journalists' ability to inform and resist the move toward war and away from democracy.

Mr. Trump's sociopathic characteristics are undeniable. They create a profound danger for America's democracy and safety. Over time these characteristics will only become worse, either because Mr. Trump will succeed in gaining more power and more grandiosity with less grasp on reality, or because he will engender more criticism producing more paranoia, more lies, and more enraged destruction.

Lance Dodes, M.D., is a Training and Supervising Analyst Emeritus at the Boston Psychoanalytic Society and Institute and retired Assistant Clinical Professor of Psychiatry at Harvard Medical School. He is the author of many academic articles and book chapters describing a new understanding of the nature and treatment of addiction, and three books: The Heart of Addiction; Breaking Addiction; *and* The Sober Truth. *He has been honored by the Division on Addictions at Harvard Medical School for "Distinguished Contribution" to the study and treatment of addictive behavior, and been elected a Distinguished Fellow of the American Academy of Addiction Psychiatry.*

References

Aragno, Anna. 2014. "The Roots of Evil: A Psychoanalytic Inquiry." *Psychoanalytic Review* 101 (2): 249–88.

Malancharuvil, Joseph M. 2012. "Empathy Deficit in Antisocial Personality Disorder: A Psychodynamic Formulation." *American Journal of Psychoanalysis* 72 (3): 242–50.

Watt, Douglas. 2007. "Toward a Neuroscience of Empathy: Integrating Affective and Cognitive Perspectives." *Neuropsychoanalysis* 9 (2): 119–40.

DONALD TRUMP IS:
A) BAD
B) MAD
C) ALL OF THE ABOVE

JOHN D. GARTNER, PH.D.

Donald Trump is so visibly psychologically impaired that it is obvious even to a layman that "something is wrong with him." Still, putting a name to that disturbance has been a challenge for two reasons. First, because of the Goldwater gag order, discussed extensively in Part 2 of this book, which has forced mental health professionals to censor themselves, despite how alarmed they might be; and second, Trump's is a genuinely complex case. Like the story of the blind men and the elephant, many writers have tried to analyze and diagnose Trump, and have gotten pieces of the elephant right. What is missing is the whole elephant. There are *a lot* of things wrong with him— and together, they are a scary witch's brew.

One of the most recurrent debates, and a genuine mystery, is to what extent is Trump just a really bad person and to what extent is he really crazy? Psychoanalyst Steven Reisner has written in *Slate*, "This is not madness. Impulsivity, threats, aggression, ridicule, denial of reality, and the mobilization of the mob that he used to get there [to the presidency] are not symptoms. It is time to call it out for what it is: evil" (Reisner 2017). According to this view, Donald Trump is "crazy like a fox." That is, his abnormal persona is an act, a diabolical plan to manipulate the public's worst instincts for fun, power, and profit.

When Trump tweeted about his imaginary inauguration crowd size and about Obama having tapped his phones, was there any part of him that believed this "denial of reality"? If so, then Michael Tansey ("Why 'Crazy Like a Fox' versus 'Crazy Like a Crazy' *Really* Matters"), who writes here about Trump having delusional disorder, may be right that Trump is not crazy like a fox but "crazy like a crazy."

My old boss Paul McHugh, longtime chairman of psychiatry at Johns Hopkins University School of Medicine, used to say that "a dog can have both ticks and fleas." I will argue that Trump can be both evil *and* crazy, and that unless we see how these two components work together, we will never truly understand him. Nor will we recognize how much danger we are in.

Bad: Malignant Narcissism

"The quintessence of evil" was how Erich Fromm (1964) described *malignant narcissism*, a term he introduced in the 1960s. Fromm, a refugee from Nazi Germany, developed the diagnosis to explain Hitler. While Fromm is most well known as one of the founders of humanistic psychology (whose basic premise, ironically, is that man's basic nature is good), the Holocaust survivor had a lifelong obsession with the psychology of evil. Malignant narcissism was, according to Fromm, "the most severe pathology. The root of the most vicious destructiveness and inhumanity."

The modern figure most associated with the study of malignant narcissism is my former teacher Otto Kernberg (1970), who defined the syndrome as having four components: (1) narcissistic personality disorder, (2) antisocial behavior, (3) paranoid traits, and (4) sadism. Kernberg told the *New York Times* that malignantly narcissistic leaders such as Hitler and Stalin are "able to take control because their inordinate narcissism is expressed in grandiosity, a confidence in themselves, and the assurance that they know what the world needs" (Goode 2003). At the same time, "they express their aggression in cruel and sadistic behavior against their enemies: whoever does not submit to them or love them." As Pollock (1978) wrote, "the malignant narcissist is pathologically grandiose, lacking in conscience and behavioral regulation[,] with characteristic demonstrations of joyful cruelty and sadism."

Much has been written in the press about Trump having narcissistic personality disorder. Yet, as critics have pointed out, merely being narcissistic is hardly disqualifying. However, normal narcissism and malignant narcissism have about as much in common as a benign and malignant tumor. The latter is far rarer, more pathological and dangerous, and, more often than not, terminal. It's the difference between life and death.

Narcissism

Narcissistic personality disorder is described in this book by Craig Malkin ("Pathological Narcissism and Politics: A Lethal Mix"). Trump finds himself to be uniquely superior ("Only I can fix it"), and appears to believe that he knows more than everyone about everything, despite his lack of experience, study, intellectual curiosity, or normal attention span. Since he took office, an amusing video montage has made its way through social media in which, in the course of three minutes, Trump brags about being the world's greatest expert in twenty different subject areas. "No one knows more about [fill in the blank] than me," he repeats over and over.

Antisocial Personality Disorder

In his piece in this book, Lance Dodes describes antisocial personality disorder, or "Sociopathy." Antisocials lie, exploit, and violate the rights of others, and they have neither remorse nor empathy for those they harm.

While we will not give a final diagnosis here, the fact-checking website PolitiFact estimated that 76 percent of Trump's statements were false or mostly false (Holan and Qui 2015), and *Politico* estimated that Trump told a lie every three minutes and fifteen seconds (Cheney et al. 2016).

We have ample evidence of Trump's pervasive pattern of exploiting and violating the rights of others. According to New York State attorney general Eric Schneiderman, Trump University was a "straight up fraud . . . a fraud from beginning to end" (Gass 2016). Also, dozens of lawsuits attest to Trump's pattern and practice of not paying his contractors. Finally, there is Trump's pattern of serial sexual assault, which he bragged about on tape even before a dozen women came forward, whom he then called liars.

Trump is allergic to apology and appears to feel no remorse of any kind. It is as if being Trump means never having to say you're sorry. When political consultant Frank Luntz asked Trump if he had ever asked God for forgiveness, Trump said, "I'm not sure I have . . . I don't think so" (Scott 2015). His unrepentance notwithstanding, he also boasted that he had "a great relationship with God."

And empathy? Even Trump's former mentor, the notorious Roy Cohn, lawyer for gangsters and Joseph McCarthy, said that when it came to his feelings for his fellow human beings, Trump "pisses ice water" (Lange 2016).

Paranoia

Paranoia is not a diagnosis but, rather, a trait that we see in some conditions. When Donald Trump was asked to document his false claim that "thousands and thousands" of New Jersey Muslims openly celebrated the attacks of 9/11, he cited a link to Infowars, the website of radio talk show host Alex Jones. Jones, nicknamed "the king of conspiracies," believes that the American government was behind the September 11 attacks, that FEMA is setting up concentration camps, and that the Sandy Hook school shooting was a hoax. Yet, according to Trump, Jones is one of the few media personalities he trusts. "Your reputation is amazing," Trump told Jones when he appeared as a guest on Jones's show on December 2, 2015. Trump vowed that if he were elected president, "you will find out who really knocked down the World Trade Center."

In the same week, both the *New York Times* (Haberman 2016) and the *Washington Post* (*Washington Post* Editorial Board 2016) ran front-page stories on Trump as a conspiracy theorist. Before the election, Right Wing Watch (Tashman 2016) accumulated a list of fifty-eight conspiracies that Trump had proclaimed or implied were true. Of course, that list has grown since then. Many are truly bizarre. For example, not only is Obama a Muslim born in Kenya but, according to Trump, he had a Hawaiian government bureaucrat murdered to cover up the truth about his birth certificate ("How amazing, the state health director who verified copies of Obama's birth certificate died in a plane crash today. All others lived," Trump said); Antonin Scalia was murdered ("[T]hey say they found a pillow on his face, which is a pretty unusual place to find a pillow"); later, fake news websites sponsored by the Russians laid this "murder" at Hillary's feet; and Ted Cruz's father aided the Kennedy assassination, the mother of all conspiracy theories ("What was he doing with Lee Harvey Oswald shortly before the death? Before the shooting? It's horrible").

And still the world was shocked when Trump accused Barack Obama of illegally wiretapping Trump Tower. Why were we surprised?

When you combine these three ingredients, narcissism, antisocial traits, and paranoia, you get a leader who feels omnipotent, omniscient, and entitled to total power; and who rages at being persecuted by imaginary enemies, including vulnerable minority groups who actually represent no threat whatsoever. With such a leader, all who are not part of the in-group or who fail to kiss the leader's ring are enemies who must be destroyed.

Sadism

Because he is a sadist, the malignant narcissist will take a bully's glee in persecuting, terrorizing, and even exterminating his "enemies" and scapegoats. When a protester was escorted out of a Trump rally, Trump famously said, "I'd like to punch him in the face," in a tone that suggested it would genuinely bring him great pleasure. Narcissists often hurt others in the pursuit of their selfish interests:

> A notable difference between normal narcissistic personality disorder and malignant narcissism is the feature of sadism, or the gratuitous enjoyment of the pain of others. A narcissist will deliberately damage other people in pursuit of their own selfish desires, but may regret and will in some circumstances show remorse for doing so, while a malignant narcissist will harm others and enjoy doing so, showing little empathy or regret for the damage they have caused.

We often see Trump "punch down," demeaning and humiliating people weaker than he. In fact, a substantial portion of the thirty-four thousand tweets he has sent since he joined Twitter can be described as cyberbullying. Sometimes he will send the same nasty tweet six times across a day's news cycle in order to maximally humiliate his victim.

Erich Fromm saw evil up close, thought about it throughout his life, and applied his genius to boil it down to its psychological essence. A malignant narcissist is a human monster. He may not be as bad as Hitler, but according to Fromm, he is cut from the same cloth. "The Egyptian Pharaohs, the Roman Caesars, the Borgias, Hitler, Stalin, Trujillo—they all show certain similar features," Fromm writes. Malignant narcissism is a psychiatric disorder that makes you evil. What's scary is that's not even the worst of it.

Mad

Before the 2016 election, I wrote an article for the *Huffington Post* (Gartner 2016) warning about Trump. At that point, in June 2016, there was still a strong hope that Trump would "pivot" and become more presidential—a hope based on the assumption that while he might be a wicked opportunist and a con man, he was still a rational actor, and thus would change tack when it was in his own best interest. I wrote, "[T]he idea that Trump is going to settle down and become presidential when he achieves power is wishful thinking. Success emboldens malignant narcissists to become even more grandiose, reckless and aggressive. Sure enough, after winning the nomination, there has been no 'pivot' towards more reasonable behavior and ideas, just the opposite. He has become more shrill, combative, and openly racist." After riding his angry base to the White House, to alter his behavior to a saner presentation after the election would have been in Trump's best interest. As Rob Reiner put it on *Real Time with Bill Maher*, "People don't understand why Trump doesn't just stop acting mentally ill? Why can't he just stop being mentally ill?" Why? Because his illness is not a ruse. It can't just be turned off when it's convenient.

According to Fromm, "malignant narcissism is a madness that tends to grow in the life of the afflicted person." In *The Heart of Man*, Fromm argues that malignant narcissism "lies on the borderline between sanity and insanity." In more benign forms of narcissism, "being related to reality curbs the narcissism and keeps it within bounds," but the malignant narcissist recognizes no such boundaries. His grandiose fantasy trumps reality.

The thing that distinguishes the malignant narcissistic leader from a run-of-the-mill psychotic patient is his power to coerce and seduce others to share his grandiose and persecutory delusions. "This Caesarian madness would be nothing but plain insanity," Fromm writes, "were it not for one factor: by his power Caesar has bent reality to his narcissistic fantasies. He has forced everyone to agree he is god, the most powerful and wisest of men—hence his megalomania seems to be a reasonable feeling."

According to Fromm's description of the disorder, Trump lives on the border of psychosis. Does he ever go over the border? Is it all for effect, to rile up his base, deflect blame, and distract from his shortcomings, or does Trump actually believe the crazy things he says? If you take Donald Trump's words literally, you would have to conclude that he is psychotic.

A delusion is technically defined as a "rigidly held, demonstrably false belief, which is impervious to any contradictory facts." Is he "crazy like a fox," asks Michael Tansey (2017b), or simply "crazy like a crazy?" With Trump, it's often genuinely difficult to know, but as Tansey makes frighteningly clear, this is not a trivial academic distinction. Literally, the fate of the entire world may depend on the answer:

> Surpassing the devastation of climate, health care, education, diplomacy, social services, freedom of speech, liberty, and justice for all, nothing is more incomprehensible than the now-plausible prospect of all-out nuclear war . . . Because of this existential threat, it is absolutely urgent that we understand the differences between a president who is merely "crazy like a fox" (shrewd, calculating, the truth is only spoken when it happens to coincide with one's purposes) versus what I have termed "crazy like a crazy" (well-hidden-core grandiose and paranoid delusions that are disconnected from reality). (Tansey 2017b)

Insight into this question comes from, of all sources, Joe Scarborough, host of the popular MSNBC show *Morning Joe*. After Trump claimed that Trump Tower had been bugged by Barack Obama, Scarborough tweeted, "His tweets this weekend suggest the president is not crazy like a fox. Just crazy."

Some of Trump's false claims can be seen as giving him a perverse strategic advantage. For example, his claim that Obama was not born in the United States appealed to the racist portion of the electorate who were already inclined to see a black president as foreign and illegitimate. Other false statements of his seem more blatantly crazy, precisely because they offer him no discernible strategic advantage. Take his false claim that he had the biggest inaugural crowd in history. On the first day of his presidency, he lost credibility with the entire world with that demonstrably false claim—as Groucho Marx said, "Who are you going to believe, me or your lying eyes?"—when there was no longer any need to motivate his base, which was already ecstatically celebrating his inauguration. He needed to broaden his base and shore up his authority as president, but did the opposite.

On *Morning Joe* on April 3, Joe Scarborough and Donny Deutsch, both of whom had known Trump personally for over a decade, came to two conclusions: first, that Trump must suffer from a mental illness, because his behavior since ascending to the presidency had been so irrationally self-destructive; and second, that Trump had gotten dramatically worse since he was inaugurated.

Scarborough: People, stop tweeting at me "How could you not have known?" We've known this guy for ten, eleven, twelve years. We had misgivings, but it's safe to say neither you [Donny Deutsch] nor I thought it would be this bad. We were concerned. Really, really concerned, but never thought this guy would be this much of a petulant brat. We didn't think he would wake up every day and hit his hand with a hammer.

Deutsch: I also think it's time. I know the psychiatric community has the Goldwater rule about not diagnosing from a distance. I just think he's not a well guy. Period.

Scarborough: During the campaign, he would do things that were offensive to us [that energized his base], but that's not like hitting your hand with a hammer. What he's doing now is *not* in his self-interest. Then you start saying how well is he [pointing to his own head] when he's doing things that any sane rational person would know would hurt him politically?

For these same reasons, Michael Tansey suggests that Trump may meet DSM-V criteria for delusional disorder, which require evidence of a delusion lasting longer than a month in the absence of a more serious psychotic disorder such as schizophrenia or bipolar disorder type 1, which would in themselves explain the presence of delusional thinking.

Trump doesn't show signs of being schizophrenic, but we should explore where he fits on the bipolar spectrum. He definitely has the hypomanic temperament I wrote about in my two books, *The Hypomanic Edge: The Link Between (a Little) Craziness and (a Lot) of Success in America* (2005) and *In Search of Bill Clinton: A Psychological Biography* (2008). Hypomanic temperament is genetically based, running in the families of people with bipolar relatives, but it represents a milder and more functional expression of the same traits as mania. Historically, hypomanic temperament has received little attention compared to bipolar disorder, but the founders of modern psychiatry, Eugen Bleuler, Emil Kraepelin, and Ernst Kretschmer, first described these personalities early in the twentieth century (Bleuler 1924; Kraepelin 1908, 1921; Kretschmer 1925). In an article in *The New Republic* (Gartner 2005), I summarized the traits of hypomanic temperament as follows:

> Hypomanics are whirlwinds of activity who are filled with energy and need little sleep, less than 6 hours. They are restless, impatient and easily bored, needing constant stimulation and tend to dominate conversations. They are driven, ambitious and veritable forces of nature in pursuit of their goals. While these goals may appear grandiose to others, they are supremely confident of success—and no one can tell them otherwise. They can be exuberant, charming, witty, gregarious but also arrogant. They are impulsive in ways that show poor judgment, saying things off the top of their head, and acting on ideas and desires quickly, seemingly oblivious to potentially damaging consequences. They are

risk takers who seem oblivious to how risky their behavior truly is. They have large libidos and often act out sexually. Indeed all of their appetites are heightened.

This description sounds an awful lot like Trump who reports, "I usually sleep only four hours a night" (1987), which by itself is usually a pretty reliable indicator of hypomania Indeed, he boasts about it: "How can you compete against people like me if I sleep only four hours?" He claims to work seven days a week and, in a typical eighteen-hour day, to make "over a hundred phone calls" and have "at least a dozen meetings." He also tweeted, "Without energy you have nothing!"—hence his taunt of Jeb Bush as "a low energy person ," by contrast, a charge that proved quite effective. Like most hypomanics, Trump is easily distracted. We could add attention deficit disorder to the Trump differential, except attention deficit disorder almost always goes with the territory for hypomanics. "Most successful people have very short attention spans. It has a lot to do with imagination," Trump wrote with Meredith McIver in *Think Like a Billionaire* in 2004. He is correct. The same rapidity of thought that helps engender creativity makes it difficult for one to stay on one linear track of ideas without skipping to the next. Like most hypomanics, Trump trusts his own ideas and judgment over those of anyone and everyone else, and follows his "vision, no matter how crazy or idiotic other people think it is."

One of my dictums when working with hypomanic patients is that "nothing fails like success." If they succeed in achieving one of their wildly ambitious goals, there is often a noticeable uptick in their hypomania, sometimes even precipitating a full-blown hypomanic episode, which, unlike hypomanic temperament, is a diagnosable disorder. They become more aggressive, irritable, reckless, and impulsive. Now seemingly confirmed in their grandiosity, they drink their own Kool-Aid and feel even more invincible and brilliant. They pursue even bolder, riskier, and more ambitious goals, without listening to dissent, doing their due diligence, or considering contradictory facts. Their gut is always right. Once, Trump was asked whom he went to for advice. With a straight face, he said, "Myself." Trump is Trump's most trusted adviser. In the same vein, with the increase in grandiosity comes a corresponding increase in paranoia over the fools and rivals who might nay-say the hypomanic's insights, impede his progress, or destroy him out of jealousy or ignorance.

In fact, this is a pattern for Trump. In 1988, after the publication of his best-selling book *The Art of the Deal*, Trump's celebrity really took off. His response was an increase in his hypomania, according to *Politico* writer Michael Kruse (2016) in his article "1988: The Year Trump Lost His Mind":

> [H]is response to his surging celebrity was a series of manic, ill-advised ventures. He cheated on his wife, the mother of his first three children. In business, he was acquisitive to the point of recklessness. He bought and sold chunks of stocks of companies he talked about taking over. He glitzed up his gaudy yacht, the yacht the banks would seize less than three years later. He used hundreds of millions of dollars of borrowed money to pay high prices for a hotel and an airline—and his lenders would take them, too. And he tussled for months with game-show magnate Merv Griffin for ownership of his third casino in Atlantic City, the most expensive, gargantuan one yet, the Trump Taj Mahal, which led quickly to the first of his four corporate bankruptcy filings.

During that period, Trump the storied dealmaker went on a buying binge, and made impulsive, ill-advised investments, often paying the asking price without negotiating at all. As Kruse wrote in his *Politico* piece:

> That spring, though, he purchased the Plaza Hotel because he openly coveted the Manhattan landmark, so much so that he paid more for it than anybody anywhere ever had

spent on a hotel—$407.5 million—[for] a hotel that wasn't turning enough profit to service the debt to which Trump [was] committed.

And in the fall, he agreed to buy the Eastern Airlines [*sic*] Shuttle, which he wanted to rename the Trump Shuttle, for a sum that analysts and even his own partners considered excessive—more than the airline itself thought the shuttle was worth. . . .

"It was not a lengthy financial analysis," [said] Nobles [president of Trump Shuttle], describing it as "back-of-the-envelope" and "very quick. . . . Donald said, 'I really want to buy it.'"

Trump could be the poster child for the dictum that when it comes to hypomanics, nothing fails like success. Kruse continued:

If Trump's current campaign is the culmination of a lifelong effort to turn his name into a brand, his brand into money and all of it into power, 1988 was the first sustained look at what the man who is the shocking favorite to be the Republican Party's nominee does when he gets ahold of it. It was the year when Trump's insatiable appetites and boundless ego—this early, spectacular show of success—nearly did him in.

Fast-forward twenty-eight years, to 2016, when Trump once again achieved success beyond anyone's wildest imaginings. He became addicted to rallies, where he excited crowds with his hypomanic charisma, and where they in turn threw gasoline on the fire of his hypomanic grandiosity. This culminated in the Republican National Convention, at which Trump made a grandiose statement that encapsulates it all: "Only I can fix it."

David Brooks (2016) is not a mental health professional, but he astutely commented on what appeared to him to be Trump's increasing hypomania:

He cannot be contained because he is psychologically off the chain. With each passing week, he displays the classic symptoms of medium-grade mania in more disturbing forms: inflated self-esteem, sleeplessness, impulsivity, aggression and a compulsion to offer advice on subjects he knows nothing about.

His speech patterns are like something straight out of a psychiatric textbook. Manics display something called "flight of ideas." It's a formal thought disorder in which ideas tumble forth through a disordered chain of associations. One word sparks another, which sparks another, and they're off to the races. As one trained psychiatrist said to me, compare Donald Trump's speaking patterns to a Robin Williams monologue, but with insults instead of jokes.

Trump's first hypomanic crash resulted only in a few bankruptcies, but while he is president, the consequences could be on a scale so vast it's difficult even to contemplate.

Let's put these two moving parts together, bad and mad. Trump is a profoundly evil man exhibiting malignant narcissism. His worsening hypomania is making him increasingly more irrational, grandiose, paranoid, aggressive, irritable, and impulsive. Trump is bad, mad, and getting worse. He evinces the most destructive and dangerous collection of psychiatric symptoms possible for a leader. The worst-case scenario is now our reality.

Often as therapists we are called on to help our patients see that their life circumstances are not as catastrophic as they might feel. In the case of Trump, however, our job is the opposite: to warn the public that the election of Donald Trump is a true emergency, and that the consequences most likely will be catastrophic.

It's a catastrophe that might have been avoided if we in the mental health community had told the public the truth, instead of allowing ourselves to be gagged by the Goldwater rule. "See something, say nothing" appears to be the APA's motto when it comes to national security. History will not be kind to a profession that aided the rise of an American Hitler through its silence.

John D. Gartner, Ph.D., is a clinical psychologist. He taught in the Department of Psychiatry at Johns Hopkins University Medical School for twenty-eight years. He is the author of In Search of Bill Clinton: A Psychological Biography *and* The Hypomanic Edge: The Link Between (a Little) Craziness and (a Lot of) Success in America. *He practices in Baltimore and New York.*

References

Bleuler, Eugen. 1924. *Textbook of Psychiatry*. New York: Macmillan, p. 485.

Brooks, David. 2016. "Trump's Enablers Will Finally Have to Take a Stand." *New York Times*, August 5.

Cheney, Kyle, et al. 2016. "Donald Trump's Week of Misrepresentations, Exaggerations, and Half-Truths." *Politico*, September 25.

Fromm, Erich. 1964. *The Heart of Man*. New York: American Mental Health Foundation, p. 63.

Gartner, John. 2005. *The Hypomanic Edge: The Link Between (a Little) Craziness and (a Lot of) Success in America*. New York: Simon and Schuster.

———. 2008. *In Search of Bill Clinton: A Psychological Biography*. New York: St. Martin's Press.

———. 2015. "Donald Trump and Bill Clinton Have the Same Secret Weapon." *The New Republic*, August 25.

———. 2016. "What Is Trump's Psychological Problem?" *Huffington Post*, June 9.

Gass, Nick. 2016. "New York AG: Trump U 'Really a Fraud from Beginning to End.'" *Politico*, September 25.

Goode, Erica. 2003. "The World; Stalin to Saddam: So Much for the Madman Theory." *New York Times*, May 4.

Haberman, Maggie. 2016. "Even as He Rises, Donald Trump Entertains Conspiracy Theories." *New York Times*, February 29.

Holan, Angie, and Linda Qui. 2015. "2015 Lie of the Year: The Campaign Misstatements of Donald Trump." PolitiFact, December 21.

Kernberg, O. 1970. "Factors in the Psychoanalytic Treatment of Narcissistic Personalities." *Journal of the American Psychoanalytic Association* 18: 51–85.

Kraepelin, Emil. 1908. *Lectures on Clinical Psychiatry*. Bristol, UK: Thoemmes, pp. 129–30.

———. 1921. *Manic Depressive Insanity and Paranoia*. Edinburgh: Livingstone, pp. 125–31.

Kretschmer, Ernst. 1925. *Physique and Character*. New York: Harcourt and Brace, pp. 127–32.

Kruse, Michael. 2016. "1988: The Year Donald Lost His Mind." *Politico*, March 11.

Lange, Jeva. 2016. "Donald Trump Turned His Back on His Closest Friend When He Heard He Had AIDS." *The Week*, April 8.

Pollock, G. H. 1978. "Process and Affect." *International Journal of Psychoanalysis* 59: 255–76.

Reisner, Steven. 2017. "Stop Saying Donald Trump Is Mentally Ill." *Slate*, March 15.

Scott, Eugene. 2015. "Trump Believes in God, but Hasn't Sought Forgiveness." CNN.com, July 8.

Tansey, Michael. 2017a. "Part VIII. Delusional Disorder." *Huffington Post*, February 24.

———. 2017b. "Part X. Trump and the Codes: Why 'Crazy Like a Fox' vs. 'Crazy Like a Crazy' *Really* Matters." *Huffington Post*, March 19.

Tashman, Brian. 2016. "58 Conspiracy Theories (and Counting): The Definitive Trump Conspiracy Guide." *Right Wing Watch*, May 27.

Trump, Donald. 1987. *The Art of the Deal*. New York: Random House.

Washington Post Editorial Board. 2016. "Donald Trump's Campaign of Conspiracy Theories." *Washington Post*, February 19.

WHY "CRAZY LIKE A FOX" VERSUS "CRAZY LIKE A CRAZY" *REALLY* MATTERS

Delusional Disorder, Admiration of Brutal Dictators, the Nuclear Codes, and Trump

MICHAEL J. TANSEY, PH.D.

Since becoming president, Donald Trump has made increasingly staggering statements contradicted by irrefutable evidence to the contrary (videos, photos, tweets), such that we have no choice but to consider whether his psychological disturbance is far more severe than what has widely been proposed as *merely* narcissistic personality disorder, *merely* antisocial personality disorder, or *merely* pathological lying.

Delusional Disorder

I begin with a presentation of the exceedingly rare diagnosis of delusional disorder, which may help us understand why DT makes such jaw-dropping statements. I am intending not to diagnose but to educate the general public so that each person can make his or her own informed assessment. (The criteria from the *Diagnostic and Statistical Manual*, 5th ed., are easily observable, simple behavioral characteristics that even a fifth-grader could understand.) I will then examine the final five minutes of a meandering, free-flowing, fifteen-minute videotaped speech DT delivered to the CIA the morning after Trump's inauguration, to see if the diagnosis can provide a lens through which to make sense of three egregious, separate, and startling statements contained in a mere five minutes.

Delusional disorder is coded as 297.1 (F22) for the purpose of insurance coverage for treatment. Those with delusional disorder scoff at the notion that there is a problem in the first place, such that insurance coverage for treatment is irrelevant. This "stealth" disorder is exceptionally beguiling because such individuals can seem perfectly normal, logical, high functioning, and even charming so long as the delusion itself is not challenged. Delusional disorder is described as "one of the less common *psychotic* disorders in which patients have delusions that differ from classical symptoms of schizophrenia." Psychosis is defined as "a condition in which there is profound loss of contact with external reality." The schizophrenic person tends to display bizarre behavior, hallucinations, and overtly disordered thinking. Whereas in schizophrenia the disconnection tends to be highly visible and all-encompassing, the less serious delusional disorder is neither bizarre nor readily apparent to the outside observer:

- Delusions are beliefs that exist despite indisputable, factual evidence to the contrary.

- Delusions are held with absolute certainty, despite their falsity and impossibility.

- Delusions can have a variety of themes, including grandeur and persecution.

- Delusions are not of the bizarre variety ("I am being poisoned by the CIA") but, rather, seem like ordinary figures of speech except that *each word is meant literally*: e.g., "I alone am the chosen one, invincible, extraordinary beyond words, the very best of the best in every way."

- Delusional people tend to be extremely thin-skinned and humorless, especially regarding their delusions.

- Delusions are central to the person's existence, and questioning them elicits a jolting and visceral reaction.

- Delusional disorder is chronic, even lifelong, and tends to worsen in adulthood, middle age, and beyond.

- Words and actions are consistent and logical if the basic premise of the delusion is accepted as reality: "Because I am superior to all, it follows that I would never apologize because I am never wrong."

- General logical reasoning and behavior are unaffected unless they are very specifically related to the delusion.

- The person has a heightened sense of self-reference ("It's always all about me"), and trivial events assume outsize importance when they contradict ("You are a con man, not a great businessman") or, conversely, support the delusional belief ("These adoring crowds recognize that I am extraordinary beyond measure"), making trivial events, whether positive or negative, hard to let go of and move past ("Have I mentioned my greatest ever electoral landslide?").

Delusional disorder may help us make sense of the last five minutes of DT's CIA address (CNN videos 2017), which contain three staggering statements that lead us to think, "He can't possibly mean that." In the tenth minute, DT declared he was "a thousand percent behind" the CIA, and accused the Fake Media, "some of the most dishonest people on the planet . . . of making it sound like I had a feud" with the intelligence community, when the truth is the "exact opposite." Anyone in the audience with a cell phone who doubted his own memory could instantly have googled DT's innumerable tweets about the incompetence and dishonesty of the "so-called intelligence community," a position he has since reverted to. Did DT actually believe that the truth was defined by his words and not hard facts to the contrary? Why would he merely lie despite knowing that each and every person in attendance knew there was not an iota of truth to the claim? His stunning falsehood lacks the shrewdness of the typical pathological liar. If he had been hooked up to a reliable lie detector test and were in fact delusional, he would have passed with flying colors because he literally believes every word he says, despite irrefutable facts to the contrary. He takes it as a given that the world around him will conform to his own warped view of events, and that those who do not believe so are irrational enemies backed by the Fake Media.

A minute later in the speech, he described his disappointment that, as he began his inaugural address, it was raining, but then he claimed, with a finger to the sky, "God looked down and said, 'We're not going to let it rain on your speech.'" He then insisted that the rain stopped immediately and it became "really sunny" before it "poured right after I left." Again, anyone at the CIA that day with a cell phone could immediately have watched the video demonstrating clearly that the drizzle on Inauguration Day *started* as DT began to speak, and that it never got sunny. It never subsequently poured. Again, did he believe every word he was saying? If the answer is yes, this would be compelling evidence of underlying delusional disorder leaking through the veneer of normality.

The third statement, of course, was his insistence that the inaugural grounds were packed "all the way to Washington Monument." Despite his badgering the National Park Service to come up with photo angles that might suggest a larger crowd, the aerial shots clearly showed that DT's audience was many hundreds of thousands fewer than Obama's in 2009. Again, DT claimed this was another example of Fake News, because the photos did not accord with his certainty of his personal reality. Again, his otherwise inexplicable insistence can be explained only by an understanding of grandiose, delusional detachment from reality.

These three incidents of demonstrably factually false statements made in the space of five minutes exemplify scores of other completely false claims: He has claimed to know more than all the generals. He has said he has the best temperament of anyone ever to be president. He still bellows (Sarlin 2016) that the black and brown teenagers wrongly convicted of raping and brutally beating a woman jogger in the 1989 "Central Park Five" case are guilty, this despite the fact that the actual rapist confessed nine years after the crime and knew intimate details of the scene, and despite the rapist's DNA matching a sample from the crime scene. DT insists he saw on TV thousands of Muslims in New Jersey celebrating the collapse of the World Trade Center towers on September 11, 2001. He insists that he was the very best high school baseball pro prospect in New York City (Maddow 2016). He has bragged that, "in a movement like the world has never seen," he won the presidency by the greatest electoral landslide since Reagan when, in fact, he trailed five of the previous seven electoral totals. And so on, and so on. The fact that he lost the popular vote by three million, because it does not comport with his grandiose delusions, he explains away by declaring that these votes were made by were fraudulent voters, despite study after bipartisan study demonstrating at most a few thousand illegal votes nationwide.

Though the term *solipsism* comes from philosophy, not psychology, it appears relevant to this discussion: "Solipsism is the belief that the person holding the belief is the only real thing in the universe. All other persons and things are merely ornaments or impediments to his happiness."

DT lies regularly and reflexively, telling the truth only when it randomly suits his purposes. Yet, pathological lying does not nearly seem to account for the staggering, self-aggrandizing statements I have referred to. Does he actually believe what he is saying based upon underlying delusions of grandeur? Had he been hooked up to a lie detector test during his CIA speech, would he have passed without so much as a blip, as I believe?

You now have the simple diagnostic criteria. You make the call.

Why Does Trump Admire Brutal Dictators?

Thomas Jefferson insisted that an "informed citizenry" is the best protection for democracy. It is therefore extremely disconcerting that a staggering percentage of Americans cannot name our president during the Civil War or the country from whom we won our independence. Even more worrisome is that DT himself did not understand that there are three branches of the federal government and that judges cannot simply "sign bills into law." During a late campaign interview (Stephanopoulos 2016), he was unaware that Russia had not only invaded but had been occupying Crimea for two years. In his first global tour, he commented that he was happy to be in Israel after coming from the Middle East.

In keeping with Jefferson's warning, if in fact DT harbors an underlying delusional disorder, from a clinical perspective, his delusions would likely be grandiose and paranoid in nature. This would help us to answer once and for all the question of why, during the 2016 presidential campaign and beyond, DT has repeatedly and openly expressed admiration for Kim Jong-un of North Korea, Bashar al-Assad of Syria, Iraq's Saddam Hussein, and especially Vladimir Putin. *There is considerable evidence to suggest that absolute tyranny is DT's wet dream.* The unopposed dictator is the embodiment of the ability to demand adulation on the one hand and to eradicate all perceived enemies with the simple nod of the head on the other. With statues and thirty-foot portraits everywhere attesting to his godlike status, there would be no problem whatsoever with critical Fake Media, marching protesters, pesky appellate courts, or the slightest political opposition. Such is the awesome power of the despots whom DT so inexplicably reveres.

Here are statements (Keneally 2016) DT made about each during his campaign, followed by brief illustrations that barely scratch the surface of their hideous brutality:

- **Kim Jong-un:** "You gotta give him credit . . . when his father died, he goes in, he takes over these tough generals and he's the boss. It's incredible. He wiped out the uncle, wipes out this one, that one. It's incredible." Kim's uncle was ripped out of a large government meeting as an example and summarily executed by a machine-gun-toting firing squad, along with seven of his aides. Kim's aunt, his father's sister, was poisoned. All their remaining children and grandchildren were killed. He executed one general with a *firing squad of antiaircraft missiles at close range* and another, bound to a post, with a mortar round, while requiring multitudes to watch, including their families. His entire country is quite literally starving to death while he finances his nuclear ambitions.

- **Bashar al-Assad:** "I think in terms of leadership, he's getting an A and our president is not doing so well." In his struggle to stay in power, Assad has ruthlessly suppressed his countrymen, resulting in hundreds of thousands of deaths of civilian men, women, and children, many by gassing. If deposed, he will be charged with crimes against humanity.

- **Saddam Hussein:** "Okay, so he was a very bad guy. But you know what he did so well? He killed terrorists. He did that so good! He didn't read them their rights. They didn't talk. You were a terrorist, it's over!" Hussein is universally regarded as perhaps the most monstrous tyrant of the last several decades. Among his countless atrocities, in what has been described as "the worst chemical-weapons attack in human history," he gassed more than 100,000 of his Kurdish citizens, then hunted down tens of thousands of survivors, whom he buried alive, for a total of 180,000 murdered in this slaughter alone.

- **Vladimir Putin:** "If he says great things about me, I'm going to say great things about him. He's really very much of a leader . . . very strong control over his country . . . and look, he has an eighty-two-percent approval rating!" Stunning comments. DT states clearly that his radiant view of Putin required *only* that he be flattered by him. In fifteen years of Putin's tyranny, journalists who dissent are shot in the back of the head. Dissidents who flee the country are regularly stalked and murdered, with poison the favored method, KGB style. Others in asylum are in constant fear for their lives, including the former world chess champion and current chairman of the Human Rights Foundation, Garry Kasparov, and the Russian Olympic runner who blew the whistle on Russia's pervasive doping program, Yuliya Stepanova. Either DT is incomprehensibly naïve regarding Putin's popularity at home—the 82 percent rating was fabricated—or he was swooning from the compliment when Putin called him "bright" (*not* a "genius," as DT has bragged ever since).

In addition, during the campaign, DT spoke of "fighting for peaceful regime-change" if elected. (America is not ruled by a regime.) He bloviated that he would "blow out of the water" the seven small Iranian boats whose sailors had harrassed and given the finger to our "beautiful destroyers." He bragged that "Russia and I would get along really well." He suggested that maybe "the Second Amendment people" might be able to stop Hillary; that his supporters should patrol voting sites to ensure he was being treated fairly, and that he would love to "hit and hit and hit [his critics from the DNC] until their heads spin and they'll never recover."

He insisted that he will "bomb the shit out of ISIS" and order our soldiers to kill their presumed families. He repeatedly goaded supporters to rough up hecklers at his speeches and pontificated that NFL players who refuse to stand for the national anthem should find another country. He quoted Mussolini's "Better to live one day as a lion than a hundred years as a sheep," and he expressed genuine bewilderment about why we build nuclear weapons if we don't use them.

In the clinical assessment of such frightening characteristics, why would DT admire grotesque tyrants while never praising our own past presidents but boasting that he himself could be the greatest in history, "except maybe Abe Lincoln"? From childhood throughout life, we all look for role models to emulate, especially when trying to navigate new and unfamiliar life challenges and transitions. We select inspirational people, often from a different time or place, who guide us by their example of how to get it right. We search for what has been called an "ego ideal" who best personifies our own highest intentions.

Whether or not his admiration for despots derives from an underlying delusional disorder, grandiose and paranoid in nature, DT is drawn to leaders who already fit his fundamental personality makeup. While anticipating the presidency, he looked for role models for how to preside, what that would look like, which leaders performed in ways that were inspiring. For Obama, it was Kennedy, Reagan, Dr. King, and Mandela. Bill Clinton turned to JFK; and Hillary to Eleanor Roosevelt. George W. Bush modeled his leadership after Jesus and Winston Churchill. For DT, it was Hussein, Jong-un, Assad, and Putin. Those guys know how to run a tight ship!

Once elected, certainly DT, many argued, would moderate his words and actions in a so-called "soft pivot." When a person is character-disordered or worse—especially one who always blames others, never apologizes or displays accountability, and who never for an instant believes there is anything wrong with himself—the only possibility for change is for him to become worse, not better. In fact, all DT's despicable traits have been frighteningly exacerbated by his ascension to the presidency. *He has tried to become more of the tyrant he wants to be, not less.*

And since becoming president, what has DT's attitude been toward brutal dictators? He has congratulated President Rodrigo Duterte of the Philippines for dealing with his country's drug problems in the "right way," with the vigilante slaughter of nearly ten thousand people merely *suspected* of using or dealing drugs. In April, DT invited him to the White House, though Duterte has not yet come.

He has expressed support and approval to President Recep Erdogan of Turkey, another invitee to the White House, who has engaged in a harsh, systematic purge of all opposition over the past year while arrogating dictatorial powers to himself alone over what had previously been a democratically elected government. During his Washington visit, Erdogan unleashed his bodyguard thugs to savagely repel peaceful protesters in front of the Turkish embassy.

Despite their clashes and nuclear saber rattling, DT has referred to Kim Jong-un as a "smart cookie," one whom he continues to admire for the insanely harsh methods Kim has used to maintain control over North Korea since his father's death. Bizarrely, Kim, too, has been invited to the White House. Ditto President Abdel-Fattah al-Sissi, who has viciously ruled Egypt with an iron fist since taking office in 2013.

By contrast, shortly after his inauguration DT insulted Prime Minister Malcolm Turnbull of Australia in a phone call, reportedly slamming the phone down, and he childishly refused to shake the hand of German chancellor Angela Merkel, with live television cameras broadcasting the world over, during her April visit to the White House. Australia and Germany have long been among our closest allies. DT also stunningly shoved aside, while all the world watched, the prime minister of Montenegro, Dusko Marcovic, in his haste to get to the front row for a group photo op during a G20 conference.

Far beyond his staggering affinity for monstrous tyrants, Trump, since coming to office, has railed against a critical free press; vilified millions of marching protesters as paid professionals; denigrated our federal appeals courts for thwarting his Muslim travel ban as unconstitutional; abruptly fired forty-six United States Attorneys; and, shockingly, fired FBI director James Comey for what DT brazenly admitted was Comey's ongoing investigation of potential collusion between Russia and the 2016 Trump campaign.

The day following Comey's abrupt departure, despite the mind-boggling optics, DT welcomed Russian ambassador Sergey Kislyak and Russian foreign minister Sergey Lavrov to the White House, and allowed Russian film crews into the meeting, while blocking American press and photographers.

Days later, reports circulated that DT had shared, without permission, highly classified information given to the United States by Israel, possibly leading to the deaths of embedded Israeli spies. DT reportedly did so in an impulsive and boastful way, seeming to try to impress the Russians. The event has rattled our allies, who now feel they cannot trust the United States with intelligence, and thus exposed and endangered the intelligence sources who provided the information. In addition, he reportedly bragged to the Russians about firing FBI director Comey, whom he called a "nut job," and expressed relief that the Russia-Trump campaign collusion investigation was over. (It is not.)

His honeymoon with Putin has already cooled, but what is DT capable of when the bromance ends? Given his mental instability, his thirst for adulation is rivaled only by his obsession for vengeance, even for the tiniest of slights. What happens when he discovers that Putin has been playing him like a fiddle or when Putin potentially humiliates him on the world stage? As Trump stated dozens of times during the primary, "As long as they're nice to me, I'll be nice to them. But if they get nasty and hit me, I'll hit back much, much harder."

Checks and balances? Hey, nobody writes checks anymore. And you can't see his balances until his IRS audit is completed!

The Constitution? Believe me, those are rules, and rules are meant to be broken. Besides, rules are for losers, and DT's a winner. He's a winner!

Like the despots he idolizes, DT intends to rule, not lead; to control, not compromise. The 2016 presidential election was not about traditional Republican-versus-Democratic views. Quite literally, it was about apocalypse, not politics.

This can't be happening? It can and it is. Jefferson's warning has never been more relevant.

Why "Crazy Like a Fox" versus "Crazy Like a Crazy" Really Matters

DT's penchant for brutality alone would be disconcerting. Yet, given the evidence of delusional disorder, we must ask why the distinction of "crazy like a fox" versus "crazy like a crazy" even matters. Although there are several areas in which DT's particular version of personality disorder is vital to understand, none is more compelling or terrifying than his control of the nuclear codes. Surpassing the devastation of climate, health care, education, diplomacy, social services, freedom of speech, and liberty and justice for all, nothing is more incomprehensible than the now-plausible prospect of all-out nuclear war. For all but the few remaining survivors who witnessed the atomic bombing of Japan and its aftermath, we simply have nothing in our own experiences to imagine instantaneous annihilation. Quite literally, we are here one second and vaporized the next, along with everyone and everything.

Because of this very real existential threat, it is absolutely urgent that we comprehend the titanic differences between a president who is merely "crazy like a fox" (shrewd, calculating, and convinced that the truth is spoken only when it happens to coincide with his purposes) versus what I have termed "crazy like a crazy" (possessing well-hidden, core grandiose and paranoid delusions that are disconnected from factual reality). To illustrate the differences, let's look at two actual episodes from recent American history and consider how DT might act faced with similar circumstances.

The 3:00 a.m. Call: President Carter

In 1979, near the end of Jimmy Carter's presidency, the nightmare phone call (Sagan 2012) came at 3:00 a.m., awakening Carter's national security adviser, Zbigniew Brzezinski, with the news that 250 Soviet nuclear missiles were bearing down on America. Knowing that he still had five or six minutes to act and that mistakes could cause false alarms, Brzezinski directed an aide to find further verification. The aide immediately called back, this time to report that *2,500* missiles were incoming. As Brzezinski prepared to call President Carter to advise a full-fledged counterattack, he elected not to wake his sleeping wife, reasoning that she would be dead in a matter of minutes. As he was reaching to phone the president, a third call came in announcing that the report of the incoming missiles was a false alarm caused by a computer glitch.

It is extremely disconcerting to note that false alarms and accidents are by no means a rare occurrence.

The Cuban Missile Crisis: President Kennedy

Unlike the nightmarish false alarm of 1979, lasting five minutes, which few were aware of, the Cuban Missile Crisis of October 1962 lasted thirteen white-knuckle days, played out before the entire world in a series of very real, terrifying actions and reactions between America and the USSR. At several junctures, the world was within an eyelash of all-out nuclear holocaust. The gist of the crisis entailed Russia's intention to place nuclear missiles in Cuba in response to the United States' having deployed nuclear sites close to Russia's borders in Turkey and Italy. The Joint Chiefs of Staff unanimously pressured President John F. Kennedy to preemptively attack Cuban missile sites already in place, with the rationale that Russia would back down and not counterattack, especially given its much smaller nuclear capability. Fortunately, JFK had the equanimity to hold off and follow the advice of his civilian advisers, notably RFK and Secretary of Defense Robert McNamara.

Interviewed many years later, McNamara described leaving the White House late in the crisis. Marveling at a beautiful sunset, he thought that it might well be the last any of us would ever see. Government families in DC, as well as those from cities and towns everywhere, were fleeing to remote regions in the hope of surviving a nuclear attack.

The standoff climaxed when Russia agreed to remove the existing missile sites from Cuba and to build no new ones in exchange for the United States' public commitment never to invade Cuba. Saving face, JFK also secretly agreed to remove the missiles from Turkey and Italy. The world exhaled.

The "crazy like a fox" characterization of DT needs little explanation. The phrase describes someone who may appear "crazy" (e.g., erratic, irrational, impulsive) on the surface, but whose seemingly crazy external behavior is a cleverly designed strategy to mislead, distract, and deceive others into responding in precisely the manner that is secretly desired. This is indeed one aspect of DT's behavior. Someone who is "crazy like a fox," during that given moment, is actually the exact opposite of crazy.

When insisting that the Fake Media created the feud between him and the intelligence community, such a person would fail a reliable lie detector test because he would know he was lying.

The most jarring evidence yet of DT's "crazy like a crazy" delusional disorder came with his early morning tweets (subsequently deleted) in March that his Trump Tower phones had been wiretapped by a "bad (or sick!) Obama"; the tweets included insane comparisons to Watergate and McCarthyism. DT's actions immediately generated bipartisan criticism, and there was a complete lack of evidence from anyone, anywhere, that he had been targeted for surveillance. The suspicion that one is being wiretapped is an absolutely classic expression of paranoid delusions.

When insisting that the Fake Media created the feud between him and the intelligence community, DT would unequivocally have passed a lie detector test because he believed the delusion was actually true. "Crazy like a fox" defines a person whose apparent external irrationality masks underlying rational thinking. "Crazy like a crazy" characterizes a person whose apparent external rationality masks underlying irrational thinking.

Returning to our historical examples of nuclear emergencies, is there anyone who could possibly believe DT would have shown Brzezinski's grace under pressure had he himself received that 3:00 a.m. call? If, indeed, Trump harbors grandiose and paranoid delusions (for which there is mounting evidence), he would have launched missiles faster than he fires off paranoid tweets on a Saturday morning.

Given the thirteen days of excruciating tension during the very real nuclear threat of the Cuban Missile Crisis, is there anyone who possibly believes that DT could have demonstrated JFK's composure, wisdom, and judgment, especially in the face of unanimous pressure from his military advisers? If DT were indeed merely "crazy like a fox," it would still be a huge stretch—but, increasingly, that appears not to be the case.

Michael J. Tansey, Ph.D. (www.drmjtansey.com), is a Chicago-based clinical psychologist, author, and teacher. He is a graduate of Harvard University (A.B., 1972, in personality theory) and Northwestern University Feinberg School of Medicine (Ph.D., 1978, in clinical psychology). In addition to his full-time practice, he was an assistant professor teaching and supervising students, interns, residents, and postdoctoral fellows. He has been in private practice for more than thirty-five years, working with adults, adolescents, and couples. Along with a coauthored book on empathy and the therapeutic process, he has written numerous professional journal articles as well as twenty-five blogs for the Huffington Post.

References

Chang, Laurence; Kornbluh, Peter, eds. (1998). "Introduction." The Cuban Missile Crisis, 1962: A National Security Archive. http://nsarchive .gwu.edu/nsa/cuba_mis_cri/declass.htm.

CNN.com video. 2017. January 21. www.youtube.com/watch?v=4v -Ot25u7Hc.

Keneally, Meghan. 2016. "5 Controversial Dictators and Leaders Donald Trump Has Praised." ABC News.com, July 6.

Maddow, Rachel. 2016. *The Rachel Maddow Show.* MSNBC, October 27.

Sagan, Scott. 2012. The National Security Archive, George Washington University, Washington, DC, March 1.

Sarlin, Benjy. 2016. NBC News, October 7.

Stephanopoulos, George. 2016. *This Week with George Stephanopoulos*. ABC News, July 31.

Wright, David. 2015. TK. Union of Concerned Scientists. November 9, http://blog.vcsusa.org/david-wright/nuclear-false-alarm-950.

COGNITIVE IMPAIRMENT, DEMENTIA, AND POTUS

DAVID M. REISS, M.D.

Obviously, it is difficult to conceive of a more stressful, demanding job than being POTUS. Leaving aside all the serious, critical, and snarky questions we hear regarding presidential "vacations," golf outings, and so on, the office demands the ability to be emotionally and cognitively alert and intact, and fully "on duty" at a moment's notice, 24/7. Potentially, the lives and well-being of millions of people are at stake in any number of the presidential decisions required to be developed over time, with appropriate advice and counseling, or within minutes, without any prior notice regarding the specific details or options.

It goes without saying that the position of POTUS inherently requires an almost inhuman degree of cognitive clarity at all times, regardless of the personal situation or circumstances of the man or woman holding the office. It is not surprising that the idea of a "dual presidency," at least some division of tasks, has been considered at different times (Rediff.com n.d., Smith 2015) (including, briefly, during the last election cycle) (Lerer 2016), although implementation of the idea has never seemed practically or politically possible.

In general, the populace values exuberance, energy, and experience as essential qualities in a POTUS, some would say with each cycle which traits are considered of primary importance at different times. Historically, longings for an experienced leader and the seeking of a "paternal," even "grandfatherly," presidential persona and political presence have often yielded male candidates who are in their senior years, with Donald Trump being the oldest person to be sworn in as POTUS.

With age comes experience and, it is hoped, wisdom—but also, medically, concerns regarding cognitive decline. It is now recognized that while some neurological functioning has peak efficiency during earlier adult years (e.g., physical reaction time), in general, cognitive functioning remains remarkably intact until quite late in the life cycle (with minor deterioration during the seventies and a more measurable decline after age eighty, but such decline certainly is not universal) of the *healthy* older adult (Levin 2016, Ramer 2013). Thus, the key issue to be addressed is not age-related cognitive decline but *illness-related* cognitive decline and decline related to other non-age-dependent physiological factors (the use of prescribed medications, a history of past or present substance abuse, a history of injury to the head, etc.). In general, older persons are more likely to be using multiple prescribed medications than younger persons, and many medications may have a subtle negative impact upon cognition, but that is not an age-related issue in and of itself.

Therefore, concerns regarding the cognitive abilities of a POTUS can be divided into five general areas: (1) innate, baseline, intellectual/cognitive skills and ability; (2) impairment due to an ongoing neurological deterioration (Alzheimer's disease or other types of dementia); (3) impairment caused by acute illness (especially in older individuals; even a urinary tract infection can negatively impact cognition); (4) toxic effects of prescribed medications or use of illicit substances; and (5) cumulative effects of head trauma and/or use of licit or illicit toxic agents (an issue that has received much more attention, clinically and publicly, vis-à-vis sports-related concussion injury).

Baseline Intellectual and Cognitive Skills

The current political system sets no intellectual or cognitive standards (or physical/medical well-being standards) for someone to become POTUS. Clearly, this is a vulnerability. Equally as clearly, the question of where any "line should be drawn" regarding health or, in particular, intellectual and cognitive prowess, as well as how and by whom those parameters would be measured, in my opinion, make it practically unlikely that any such standards will ever be implemented. In essence, we rely upon the candidates to voluntarily divulge their medical history (which Trump did not do with any indication of clinical validity), and we rely upon the voting populace to determine if a candidate's intellectual abilities "measure up," an inherently flawed system, as the populace has access only to prepackaged presentations and observations of a candidate in debates and while he or she is giving speeches—hardly an adequate database for accurately gauging intellectual ability.

Based upon the limited information available, persons with professional training could provide public opinions regarding a candidate's intellect, but the database that even professionals can use remains inadequate and incomplete, and differentiation between objective and clinically "solid" opinions versus politically based propaganda is an insurmountable problem.

At the current time, I view this as a problem without any solution in the near future.

Impairment Due to an Ongoing Neurological Deterioration

In the vernacular, the term *Alzheimer's* is often used nonspecifically to refer to dementing illness, which is not clinically accurate, as deterioration of cognitive functioning can occur due to multiple different degenerative neurological disease processes. However, with regard to the issue at hand, the important question is whether a degenerative process is present, not necessarily a specific diagnosis. Other than in certain relatively uncommon acute illnesses, cognitive decline due to degenerative neurological disorders is a relatively slow process that can begin insidiously. As just noted, but not commonly appreciated, absent other factors, "normal aging" is a very infrequent cause of significant cognitive impairment prior to true "old age" (i.e., above eighty years). It is not unusual for early indications of a degenerative process to be "excused" or minimized as age-related and not seen as particularly significant acutely (which they may not be) or recognized as implying a problematic prognosis.

This is an area in which sophisticated clinicians may notice, *even from public appearances and interactions*, that a person is exhibiting indications suggestive of an early stage of a dementing process. Without a full medical history and without formal testing, no diagnosis can be provided based upon such observation, but certainly a trained observer can identify cause for concern and *suggest the prudence of obtaining a formal evaluation*.

However, it is obviously problematic for many reasons to rely upon unsolicited opinions from practitioners whose level of expertise, objectivity, and ulterior motivations may be suspect (legitimately or defensively/manipulatively). This is, in fact, what has occurred regarding the candidacy and election of Donald Trump. Multiple experts have voiced concern, some referring to an inherent "duty to warn." Multiple differing opinions have been expressed, ranging from denial of any evidence necessitating concern; to suggestions of the need for a formal evaluation; to speculation about, provision of, and even rumor of specific diagnoses.

Objectively, I personally do not see how any informed clinician would not notice a significant difference between the cognitive performance of Trump in videos from fifteen years ago to his current presentation. Objectively, I personally do not see how any informed clinician cannot conclude that there is reason for concern and/or a formal evaluation.

Yet, at the same time, the videos from the past were produced under very different situations (vis-à-vis planning, scripting, stress, and in some cases, editing), and it has been my stance that the promulgation of anything beyond a general warning, along with education regarding the "differential diagnoses" (i.e., *possible* causes for the apparent change), is not clinically supported without additional data, as well as being ethically questionable.

Thus, in my opinion, it has been appropriate and, in fact, prudent for clinicians to speak out regarding their concerns of possible neurological deterioration, but the public discussion has been so muddied that serious and legitimate concerns voiced have had no practical impact.

Although the presidency of Donald Trump is still young and, in the view of many, including me, quite problematic, with very high and dangerous risks present, in essence we have probably already "dodged a bullet" at least once. During the first 1984 debate between Ronald Reagan and Walter Mondale, Reagan obviously experienced a moment of disorganization. A brief lapse can happen to anyone under stress and need not be assumed to indicate the presence of pathology (e.g., Rick Perry's forgetting "the third department" he wished to disband during the 2012 primary debate). In retrospect, Reagan's "becoming lost" appeared more significant. There were already public concerns regarding his medical status, and it was later reported that friends and family were well aware that a degenerative disease was progressing (Corn 2011). Yet, there was no significant expression of public concern by clinicians, and the issue was, out of (in my opinion, misplaced) "politeness," not seriously raised within the political discourse. Perhaps if clinicians had spoken up, there could have been a reasonable call for appropriate medical records or evaluation. It might have backfired, and the election could have been determined on the spot, but personally, I always wonder what might have happened if, in the second debate, in a sincere and diplomatic manner, Mondale had directly raised the question to Reagan: "Sir. The last time we met, you appeared to have a moment of significant confusion. What would the consequences be if that occurred during a national emergency?" It is conceivable that Reagan could have deftly deflected the question, and Mondale would have been pilloried, his campaign essentially ended. Yet, it is also conceivable that if Reagan had some awareness of his difficulties, the question could have led to his becoming acutely disturbed and discombobulated—perhaps revealing his vulnerability and swinging the election in the other direction. We will never know, and thankfully whatever neurological impairment Reagan suffered while in office did not (to anyone's knowledge) ever lead to any inappropriate action, behavior, or decision. Nonetheless, that is not a risk the country should look forward to taking again.

While neurological degenerative disease can occur even at relatively young ages, this is quite uncommon, and perhaps the wisest course would be for there to be a legal imperative for candidates above a certain age to undergo neuropsychological testing to rule out the process of a progressive illness. It would still be problematic to determine exactly what tests should be administered, who should administer them, and where a "cut-off" for eligibility/determination of "fitness to serve" should be set. It is conceivable that a bipartisan effort based upon clinical knowledge could at least set standards for disqualifying a candidate for whom there is objective medical evidence of a progressive disorder.

Short of such a procedure, in my opinion, qualified professionals should not hesitate to carefully, judiciously express any concerns they may have, providing as much educative information as possible—while appreciating that, practically, the situation will remain confusing and controversial to a large segment of the population and that pernicious manipulation by unscrupulous clinicians cannot be avoided.

Impairment Caused by Acute Illness and Toxic Effects of Prescribed Medications or Illicit Substances

Any number of medical conditions can negatively impact cognition in any person, regardless of age—although, in general, as age progresses, vulnerability to cognitive impairment increases. Similarly, many medications very legitimately and appropriately prescribed for medical purposes can result in side effects ranging from mild word-finding difficulties (not uncommon with anticholinergic agents) to more significant cognitive slippage or confusion and even overt delirium. It goes without saying that those risks are higher with use of specific psychotropic medications and, of course, illicit drugs or alcohol. Acute side effects are very often reversible, while some agents (definitely alcohol; other illicit drugs; controversially, some rather common medications generally considered benign) may result in irreversible cognitive problems.

However, practically, identifying these issues in a candidate does not appear to be nearly as problematic as addressing the question of a degenerative process. Simply by the release of objective and clinically sound medical records, including a toxicological screen and consideration of potential medication side effects (with formal neuropsychological testing performed if indicated by the clinical history and findings), issues of acutely impaired cognitive functioning can be identified and often remedied. Or, at least such as in the possibility of illicit drug use, or mild, insignificant side effects (e.g., some simple word-finding difficulties due to use of anti-hypertensives) be made public. If any such findings cannot be remedied, then the situation would essentially fall into section (2) as described above.

Cumulative Effects of Head Trauma and/or Use of Licit or Illicit Toxic Agents

It is now recognized and generally accepted that a history of even "mild" head trauma, especially if there have been multiple events, as well as past use of licit or illicit psychoactive agents, can produce acute cognitive impairment that lasts longer than was previously thought and can trigger an ongoing cognitive deterioration (the specific mechanism of which is not yet well understood). Increasing evidence is being obtained from those who participated in contact sports (and even relatively non-contact sports that involve use of the head, e.g., soccer; as well as victims of domestic violence or abuse that involved blows to the head), can suffer from increasing cognitive difficulties as they age, even years after the injuries/exposure occurred and even if acute symptomatology did not seem particularly severe. While the medical details regarding CTE (Chronic Traumatic Encephalopathy) (Boston University CTE Center 2017) remain controversial and under investigation, it cannot be denied that many persons with a history of head trauma or substance abuse suffer from cognitive decline that is not related to Alzheimer's Syndrome or other "typical" degenerative neurological disorders. However, determining the presence and severity of any such decline (and establishing a prognosis) is somewhat more complicated than determining the presence or absence of a well-established disease process.

Thus, this is not an issue that is practically different than described in (2) above, but it is an area of a person's medical history that (to this day) often remains overlooked and deserves appropriate consideration and evaluation within any review of a candidate's medical history.

Summary

No reasonable person would want someone with compromised cognitive/intellectual functioning to serve as POTUS. However, to date, there is no process or procedure (beyond voluntary release of medical records) that provides the public with any reliable knowledge regarding whether a candidate for the office of POTUS suffers from cognitive impairment or is at high risk for cognitive degeneration.

Others have discussed the very problematic aspects of the candidacy of Donald Trump with regard to acute psychiatric illness and chronic characterological dysfunction/pathology. Especially in a person for whom questions of acute or chronic psychiatric issues come into play (issues that inherently impact cognition, judgment, decision making, etc.), additional or superimposed neurologically based cognitive impairment becomes even more critical. Yet, absent the specific circumstances of the Trump candidacy/election, the candidate selection and electoral processes do not in any manner take into account the medical and neurological knowledge gained since the time of the Founding Fathers—knowledge that continues to expand, and will continue to expand, with ever-increasing sophistication and understanding.

Nevertheless, applying clinical/medical knowledge to a political process is practically complex and daunting with regard to issues of objectivity, the setting of parameters (e.g., for qualification/disqualification), and the avoidance of ill-informed and/or malicious manipulation. The process of taking into account a candidate's cognitive abilities and status is fraught with danger. Those who speak out must do so carefully, not without risk, and to a populace that *should* be reasonably skeptical.

This is, indeed, a very "slippery slope." However, it is far wiser to attempt to maintain an appropriate balance upon that slope than to totally ignore its presence and remain in total denial regarding the potential risks to the country and the world.

David M. Reiss, M.D., attended Northwestern University (chemical/biomedical engineering; medical school) and has maintained a private psychiatric practice in California since 1982. Dr. Reiss has evaluated/treated more than twelve thousand people; has served as interim medical director of Providence Hospital (Massachusetts), and has recently been associated with the Brattleboro Retreat (Vermont). He is a California-qualified medical examiner and a member of professional organizations, including the Society for the Exploration of Psychotherapeutic Integration, the Sports Lawyers Association, and the International Psychohistory Association. Dr. Reiss has appeared in all media formats addressing clinical issues and psychological aspects of social and political phenomena.

References

Corn, David. 2011. "How Close Did Lesley Stahl Come to Reporting Reagan Had Alzheimer's While in Office? Very Close." *Mother Jones*, January 20. www.motherjones.com/politics/2011/01/reagan -alzheimers-family-feud-lesley-stahl.

Rediff.com. n.d. "Dual Presidency Theory." Rediff.com. http://pages.rediff
.com/dual-presidency-theory/731558.

Lerer, Lisa. 2016. "Hillary Clinton Brings Back Talk of Dual Presidency."
Boston Globe, May 17. www.bostonglobe.com/news/nation/2016/05/16
/hillary-clinton-brings-back-talk-dual-presidency/PHde6zkoaUOnD
3bFWV7PgM/story.html.

Levin, Michael C. 2016. "Memory Loss." *Merck Manual Professional Version*
(online). www.merckmanuals.com/professional/neurologic-disorders
/symptoms-of-neurologic-disorders/memory-loss.

Ramer, Jessica. 2013. "How Does Aging Affect Reaction Time?" LiveStrong
.com. www.livestrong.com/article/442800-how-does-aging-affect
-reaction-time/.

Smith, Jeff. 2017. "David Orentlicher, Two Presidents Are Better Than One:
The Case for a Bipartisan Executive Branch." *European Journal of
American Studies* [online], Reviews 2015-4, document 10. http://ejas
.revues.org/11162.

Boston University CTE Center. 2017. "What Is CTE?" Boston University CTE
Center. www.bu.edu/cte/about/what-is-cte/.

DONALD J. TRUMP, ALLEGED INCAPACITATED PERSON

Mental Incapacity, the Electoral College, and the Twenty-Fifth Amendment

JAMES A. HERB, ESQ.

Donald J. Trump became an "alleged incapacitated person" on October 4, 2016, when I filed a petition to determine his mental incapacity in the Palm Beach County Circuit Court. I claim legal standing to commence such a proceeding as an adult and a resident of Florida, and based on the fact that Trump's apparent lack of mental capacity to function could impact me and possibly the whole world, in addition to him.

Before the Election

I have a B.A. and M.A. in political science, and have always been a political junkie of sorts. I followed the televised Watergate hearings leading up to President Nixon's resignation in 1974. I taught a course on the Constitution and politics after I received my law degree. I followed the impeachment proceedings of President Clinton. I lived through each day of *Bush v. Gore*, but nothing prepared me for Trump's presidential campaign, which started with a ride down an escalator. Perhaps the symbolism was prophetic: instead of ascending to the heights, he was descending to the depths, and taking us all with him. How low could an escalator go? I never imagined that Trump's style of campaigning could thrive in our society.

Like many, I assumed that Trump would not get the Republican nomination for president. Then, in July 2016, he did. I started to agonize over the possibility of a Trump presidency. It was true, of course, that two hurdles still stood between Trump's nomination and what I believed might be the Apocalypse. One was the general election, to take place on November 8, 2016. The second (should Trump win) was the voting of the Electoral College, to take place on December 19, 2016. Was there anything that I, a simple probate attorney, an ordinary citizen, could do?

I started to review the public record regarding things Trump had said and done. I compiled a list of two hundred items that I believed reflected his mental disability to discharge the duties of a president. The list could have been substantially larger, but I stopped at two hundred.

There was a lot of commentary on the Internet about Trump's mental state. There were also Internet petitions seeking a determination (by someone) that Trump lacked the mental capacity to be president. No one suggested a court proceeding. I reviewed the Goldwater rule (discussed in more detail in part 2 of this book) and its apparent prohibition of certain mental health professionals from diagnosing the mental health of a public official from afar. The irony of this is that I, not a mental health professional and perhaps less formally trained to make such a diagnosis, in no way come under the Goldwater rule prohibition. To the contrary, part of my job as a guardianship attorney is to come to a preliminary conclusion about the mental incapacity of a person *before* I file a petition to determine incapacity.

Once, when I tuned in to watch a Trump rally on TV, he was reciting lyrics from a song titled, "The Snake," about a tenderhearted woman who rescues a half-frozen snake, only to be fatally bitten by it once it has revived. The snake says, "You knew damn well I was a snake before you took me in." I thought Trump was speaking about himself, and the American people were the tenderhearted woman.

It turned out he was speaking about immigrants as being vicious snakes.

This story is similar to other animal fables, perhaps best illustrated by the story of the scorpion and the frog, which is told in various forms. In one telling, a scorpion asks a frog to carry him on his back in a swim across a pond. The frog is reluctant, fearful of the scorpion's sting. The scorpion argues that he obviously won't sting the frog, because if he does, they will both drown. So, they start crossing the pond, and midway across, the scorpion stings the frog. Just before they sink below the surface of the water, the frog asks the scorpion why he has stung him. The scorpion replies, "I can't control my nature."

I was concerned that we might end up with a scorpion king in the White House, someone who was unable to control a dangerous part of his nature.

Having practiced guardianship law for almost forty years, I believed that it might be appropriate to start an "incapacity" proceeding in Palm Beach County (where Trump maintains a residence at Mar-a-Lago), and, ultimately, to have a three-person examining committee appointed to interview Trump and file reports as to whether he lacked the mental capacity to be president. While I have handled many incapacity proceedings, I would be dealing with someone who was clearly not a *normal* abnormal person.

If the court had proceeded and ultimately determined that Trump was incapacitated, it could not have prevented him from running—Trump met the age and other eligibility requirements to be president as set forth in the Constitution—but such a determination would have been an appropriate consideration for the electorate in going to the polls and deciding for whom to vote.

My petition was ready to go in mid-August 2016, but instead of filing it, I decided to speak to various people about it. These people were not part of any presidential campaign and were not political party officials. I spoke to lawyers, nonlawyers, and retired judges. I spoke to Republicans, Democrats, and Independents. To me, it wasn't an issue of partisan politics; it was an issue of the survival of our democracy. I also thought long and hard about proceeding. Did I wish to antagonize someone who might become president? Did I want to antagonize someone so vindictive, so litigious? Might I be sued for defamation? Might my life, as I knew it, end?

I decided that the issue was so extremely important to everyone in our country, and possibly to everyone in the world, that I felt compelled to file the petition to determine incapacity, as a patriotic duty.

I filed the petition a little more than a month before the November 8, 2016, election. It alleged that Trump was or might be incapacitated to seek or retain employment, based on the following factual information: (1) that his actions/statements appeared to support a diagnosis of histrionic personality disorder, DSM-V 301.50, meeting diagnostic criteria 1 through 8; and (2) that his actions/statements appeared to support a diagnosis of narcissistic personality disorder, DSM-V 301.81, meeting diagnostic criteria 1 through 9. I attached my list of two hundred supporting statements made by Trump during the course of his campaign.

The first judge assigned to the case recused herself. The second assigned judge ordered that I explain why my petition ought not be dismissed, and to address whether a state court could restrict Trump from seeking the presidency, given that Trump met the sole eligibility requirements to be president as set forth in Article II, Section 1, Clause 5 (at least thirty-five years old, a U.S. resident for fourteen years, and a natural born citizen), of the Constitution.

The day before the election, the court dismissed my incapacity proceeding.

After Election Day: The Electoral College

After Election Day (and before the date for the Electoral College to meet and vote), I asked that the court reconsider its decision, arguing that the issue of whether Trump was mentally incapacitated was not moot, given that the president is selected by members of the Electoral College, and not by a direct vote of the electorate. Perhaps the Electoral College could save us.

I argued that it was the *original intent* of the Framers of the Constitution, as explained in Alexander Hamilton's Federalist No. 68, March 12, 1788, that the electors were to provide wisdom and judgment (beyond that held by the general public) in making the selection of the president. The president is to be selected by the "sense of the people" operating through electors selected by the people for that particular purpose. The election of the president "should be made by men most capable of analyzing the qualities adapted to the station, and acting under circumstances favorable to deliberation and to a judicious combination of all the reasons and inducements, which were proper to govern their choice." Hamilton also wrote, "A small number of persons, selected by their fellow citizens from the general mass, will be most likely to possess the information and discernment requisite to so complicated an investigation." The process of election through electors "affords a moral certainty, that the office of president, will seldom fall to the lot of any man, who is not in an eminent degree endowed with the requisite qualifications."

I pointed out that Supreme Court Justice Robert H. Jackson (who was also the architect of the international war crimes trials of Nazi leaders as well as the lead American prosecutor at Nuremberg) said that the plan originally contemplated was "that electors would be free agents, to exercise an independent and nonpartisan judgment as to the men best qualified for the Nation's highest office." Justice Jackson went on: "This arrangement miscarried. Electors, although often personally eminent, independent, and respectable, officially became voluntary party lackeys and intellectual nonentities to whose memory we might justly paraphrase a tuneful satire:

> They always voted at their Party's call
> And never thought of thinking for themselves at all.

"As an institution, the Electoral College suffered atrophy almost indistinguishable from *rigor mortis*" (*Ray v. Blair*, 343 U.S. 214, 232 [1952], Justice Robert H. Jackson dissenting).

I added that the Framers intended electors to be persons of "superior discernment, virtue, and information," who would select the president "according to their own will" and without reference to the immediate wishes of the people (*Ray v. Blair*, 343 U.S. 214, 232 [1952], Justice Robert H. Jackson dissenting). That "Electors constitutionally remain free to cast their ballots for any person they wish and occasionally they have done so" (U.S. Senate 2013).

While a state court determination that Trump lacked "mental capacity" to be president would *not* automatically have disqualified him from serving, such a determination would have been vital information for members of the Electoral College to have. Having as much relevant information as possible is a prescription from the Founders to the members of the Electoral College, necessary for members to perform their function properly.

The court did not change its holding. Trump was selected by the Electoral College on December 19, 2016, and was inaugurated on January 20, 2017.

After Inauguration: The Twenty-Fifth Amendment

I saw no "presidential pivot" by Trump in his first ten days in office, so, on January 30, 2017, I filed a second petition to determine incapacity.

In those first ten days, Trump espoused at least two delusional beliefs. One was as to the size of the crowd at his inauguration; a second was that Secretary Clinton had won the popular vote in the presidential election only because between three million and five million illegal votes had been cast.

Also in those first ten days, Trump issued various executive orders that demonstrated his mental inability to comprehend the following: what is and is not legal (the immigration ban); what he can and cannot do without getting funding approval from Congress (building a border wall with Mexico); and what is and is not in the best interest of our country's security (Steve Bannon is in, and certain Cabinet-level officers are out). Trump alienated Mexico; alienated nations across the world with his immigration ban; displayed an inability to vet issues and actions with appropriate parts of the U.S. government before taking action; and displayed a total inability to anticipate (or even consider) the impact of his statements and actions.

My petition asserted that in order for him to continue as president, he needed to have the mental capacity to:

- separate fact from fiction;
- think through an issue or matter before speaking or taking action;
- be able and willing to learn about issues;
- apply coherent decision making to fact;
- communicate coherently;
- be consistent (without vacillating or "flip-flopping") with statements he makes;
- comprehend likely results from saying certain things or taking certain actions;
- differentiate between acceptable decisions and horrendous decisions;
- be willing to understand, protect, and defend the U.S. Constitution, including its provisions that relate to the functioning of the executive branch and the rights of citizens under the Bill of Rights;
- keep himself from committing high crimes and misdemeanors as that term appears in the U.S. Constitution, Art. II, Sec. 4, regarding impeachment;
- make agreements and keep those agreements;
- learn about and conduct foreign policy on behalf of the United States;
- deal reasonably and effectively with other people;
- not be delusional;
- understand basic democratic principles, including: the importance of a free and fair election (and the importance of not claiming it is

"rigged" before it has occurred); the undemocratic nature of intending to jail his election rival; and the danger of propounding multiple conspiracy theories against him; and

- be stable (i.e., not having mental instability) in his thoughts and speech.

I asserted that the statements of Trump support a determination that he suffers from *narcissistic personality disorder*, which would make him mentally incapable of continuing as president, and that he:

- has a grandiose sense of self-importance;
- is preoccupied with fantasies of unlimited success, power, or brilliance;
- believes that he is special and unique;
- requires excessive admiration;
- has a sense of entitlement (i.e., has unreasonable expectations of especially favorable treatment or automatic compliance with his expectations);
- is interpersonally exploitive (i.e., takes advantage of others to achieve his own ends);
- lacks empathy, being unwilling or unable to recognize or identify with the feelings and needs of others; and
- shows arrogant, haughty behaviors or attitudes.

I asserted that the statements of Trump support a determination that he suffers from *histrionic personality disorder*, which would make him mentally incapable of continuing as president, and that he:

- has had interactions with others that are often characterized by inappropriate sexually seductive or provocative behavior;
- displays rapidly shifting and shallow expressions of emotions;
- has a style of speech that is excessively impressionistic and lacking in detail;

- shows self-dramatization, theatricality, and exaggerated expression of emotion; and
- is suggestible (i.e., easily influenced by others or circumstances).

I asserted that Trump appears to suffer from delusional beliefs, which would make him incapable of continuing as president, citing various of the more than two hundred troubling statements made by him during the election campaign.

I asserted that the U.S. Constitution does have provisions that deal with the inability of a president (once in office) to discharge the powers and duties of that office, being Sections 3 and 4 of the Twenty-Fifth Amendment.*

---

* Sections 3 and 4 of the Twenty-Fifth Amendment state:

Section 3. Whenever the President transmits to the President pro tempore of the Senate and the Speaker of the House of Representatives his written declaration that he is *unable* to discharge the powers and duties of his office, and until he transmits to them a written declaration to the contrary, such powers and duties shall be discharged by the Vice President as Acting President.

Section 4. Whenever the Vice President and a majority of either the principal officers of the executive departments or of such other body as Congress may by law provide, transmit to the President pro tempore of the Senate and the Speaker of the House of Representatives their written declaration that the President is *unable* to discharge the powers and duties of his office, the Vice President shall immediately assume the powers and duties of the office as Acting President.

Thereafter, when the President transmits to the President pro tempore of the Senate and the Speaker of the House of Representatives his written declaration that no *inability* exists, he shall resume the powers and duties of his office unless Vice President and a majority of either the principal officers of the executive department or of such other body as Congress may by law provide, transmit within four days to the President pro tempore of the Senate and the Speaker of the House of Representatives their written declaration that the President is *unable* to discharge the powers and duties of his office. Thereupon Congress shall decide the issue, assembling within forty-eight hours for that purpose if not in session. If the Congress, within twenty-one days after receipt of the latter written declaration, or, if Con-

Section 3 provides for a voluntary (and possibly temporary) relinquishment of the powers and duties of the president to the vice president, who becomes acting president. The president transmits a written declaration to the president *pro tempore* of the Senate and the Speaker of the House that he is unable to discharge the powers and duties of his office. This relinquishment continues until the president transmits to them a written declaration to the contrary.

Section 3 has been invoked three times in our history—once in 1985, by Ronald Reagan (colon cancer surgery), for about eight hours; once in 2002, by George W. Bush (colonoscopy), for less than two hours; and once in 2007, by George W. Bush (colonoscopy), for less than two hours. We have accordingly had two acting presidents: George H. W. Bush and Richard B. Cheney. These relinquishments were (and were intended to be) temporary.

Section 4 provides for an involuntary relinquishment of the office. If the vice president and a majority of the Cabinet officers transmit to the president *pro tempore* of the Senate and the Speaker of the House their written declaration that the president is unable to discharge the powers and duties of his office, the vice president immediately becomes acting president.

However, it doesn't end there. If the president transmits to the president *pro tempore* of the Senate and the Speaker of the House his written declaration that no inability exists, he resumes his office—unless the vice president and a majority of the Cabinet officers transmit to the president *pro tempore* of the Senate and the Speaker of the House their written declaration that the president is unable to discharge his office. Congress then decides the issue. If Congress determines by a two-thirds' vote of both houses that the president is unable

---

gress is not in session, within twenty-one days after Congress is required to assemble, determines by two-thirds vote of both Houses that the President is unable to discharge the powers and duties of his office, the Vice President shall continue to discharge the same as Acting President; otherwise, the President shall resume the powers and duties of his office [emphasis added].

to serve, the vice president continues to serve as acting president; otherwise, the president resumes the powers and duties of his office.

I asserted that the Florida state court had the power to determine that Trump was mentally incapacitated to serve as president. While such a determination is not self-executing—that is, it does not automatically remove him from office—it could provide the basis on which a removal relinquishment could go forward under the Twenty-Fifth Amendment.

On February 21, 2017, the court dismissed my second petition, and I filed a notice of appeal of that decision to the Florida Fourth District Court of Appeal. The appeal is pending.

I filed my appellate brief on May 1, 2017. My "May Day/Mayday" brief asks the appellate court to order the trial court to proceed with the incapacity proceeding against Trump, to the ultimate determination of whether he is mentally incapacitated to serve as president. If the appellate court agrees with me and grants my requested relief, this procedure will go forward.

Quo Vadis

Perhaps given a holding that he lacks mental capacity to be president, Trump will follow the voluntary proceeding set forth in Section 3 of the Twenty-Fifth Amendment, and declare himself to be unable to discharge the powers and duties of his office. Given the somewhat bizarre nature of our current *Alice in Wonderland* world, though, this may not be out of the question. If he does not choose a voluntary relinquishment under Section 3, then Section 4 of the Twenty-Fifth Amendment sets forth an involuntary procedure involving the vice president, the Cabinet, and the Congress. This section has never been invoked. Perhaps now is the time.

All are equal before the law. As far as Florida guardianship law is concerned, Trump has the right to be protected from himself—just like anyone else. But, for now, Trump is an alleged incapacitated person, and will remain so until there is a determination otherwise.

To be continued . . .

James A. Herb, M.A., Esq., has practiced law in Florida for forty years. He is a Florida Supreme Court–certified circuit court mediator, a certificated arbitrator, and a professional member of the National College of Probate Judges. He is author of four chapters in Florida law practice books and has chaired or spoken at more than fifty legal seminars.

Reference

U.S. Senate. 2013. *The Constitution of the United States of America, Analysis and Interpretation.* 112th Congress, 2nd Session, Senate Document No. 112-9.

PART 2

THE TRUMP DILEMMA

SHOULD PSYCHIATRISTS REFRAIN FROM COMMENTING ON TRUMP'S PSYCHOLOGY?

LEONARD L. GLASS, M.D., M.P.H.

You might think the answer is obvious, but it isn't.

Obviously "No"

There's a historical basis for objecting to mental health professionals injecting their opinions into political debate: the Goldwater rule (Friedman 2017). Psychiatrists' painful experience of suffering legal humiliation for offering their armchair diagnoses of Barry Goldwater in 1964 chastened the leaders of mental health organizations, who then acted to protect their professions' reputation by including in their code of ethics a prohibition against the diagnosis of public figures.

The central argument is that one can claim professional authority to comment on an individual's mental functioning only if one has followed the precepts of the profession for a bona fide evaluation: that is, a thorough vis-à-vis interview buttressed by a personal history derived from the patient and reliable family sources, a complete mental status examination, a physical exam, relevant lab studies, and so on. Otherwise, any opinion offered by a mental health professional, though it would be seen as valid by the public, would, some hold, lack the accepted foundation to be appropriately taken as such.

Recently, the American Psychiatric Association's Ethics Committee expanded its interpretation of the Goldwater rule to prohibit *any* comment by psychiatrists on a public figure that included reference to their professional status (American Psychiatric Association 2017).

Other "no" arguments opposed to such diagnoses are essentially variations on the theme of protecting the guild from disgrace: mental health professionals might speak in biased, uninformed, or merely disparate ways, and this could discredit the psychological professions, which are always vulnerable to critique and often not taken seriously, as seen in cartoons in *The New Yorker* and in other, less affectionate forms of ridicule.

But, Less Obviously, "Yes"

The Goldwater rule, especially in its expanded interpretation, makes an error in categorizing: it conflates a "professional opinion" (i.e., a clinical assessment that is the basis for the care of a patient) with "the opinion of a professional" commenting in a *nonclinical* role (i.e., as a mental health expert offering his perspective in the public square). There is *no patient* in the latter instance, and hence the standards for providing only a clinically derived assessment with the patient's authorization and with due regard for the patient's confidentiality are not applicable: again, here there *is no patient*. For example, you might be interested in "the opinion of a professional" when deciding on an investment or a catering menu, or when reading an op-ed in the *New York Times*.

By the same token, I question the literal application of the so-called Tarasoff duty to warn, so named after the landmark legal case from which it arose. The Tarasoff duty is relevant when, in a doctor-patient relationship, the professional becomes aware of a concrete threat to a third party. In those circumstances, the duty to warn overrides the patient's right to confidentiality. But where there is no doctor-patient relationship, the duty to warn is more metaphoric— that is, we professionals can "connect the dots" and alert the public to what appears to us to be a pattern of irrationality, impulsivity, and intolerance of divergent views that suggests a dangerous vulnerability in a man occupying the most powerful of positions. Our duty to warn is an expression of our concerns as *citizens* possessed of a particular expertise; not as *clinicians* who are responsible for preventing predictable violence from someone under our care.

The public could benefit from psychologically expert commentary on phenomena that are, on the face of it, confusing. Indeed, one of the explicit ethical principles guiding physicians is to make "relevant information available to . . . the general public" (American Psychiatric Association 2013). For instance, what to make of a person who characteristically proclaims his successes and never acknowledges his mistakes, who instead blames and vilifies others (e.g., the generals who planned the mission, the Fox News analyst whose opinion Trump proclaimed as fact, the press who exposed the problem, the leakers/whistleblowers who alerted the press). While it may seem obvious to some that such a person is driven to inflate himself out of insecurity, some not very psychologically sophisticated segments of the public may well take his boasts at face value. Thus, it is precisely the role of trained professionals to offer expert perspectives to the public at large.

While it's true that, in the case of Donald Trump, we professionals don't have the data we traditionally rely on in a clinical setting, it's also true that, thanks to Trump's facility in garnering public attention, the many years he has been in the news, and most especially the abundance of videotaped evidence of his behavioral reactions, there is an impressive quantity of Donald Trump's emotional responses and spoken ideation for us to draw on. While the prior understanding of the Goldwater rule sought to prevent speculation about the inner, unobservable workings of a public figure's mind, the newly propounded interpretation blocks psychiatrists from helping to explain widely available and readily observed behaviors.

As for the prohibition against identifying oneself as a psychiatrist when commenting on a public figure, consider the orthopedist interviewed on local television who is asked to assess the implications of the injury sustained by the local team's quarterback in today's game played on the opposite coast. Is she prohibited from offering her professional opinion because she hasn't examined the football star? Of course, her opinion is conditioned by her not having examined him or seen the X-rays, but this is so obvious and implicit that it often isn't stated. (It would be prudent to do so, lest there be any doubt about the certainty of her opinion.) Psychiatrists' being gagged by their professional association bespeaks that association's profound lack of respect for and confidence in the maturity and judgment of its members.

By attempting to preclude psychiatry as a profession from the public discussion, the American Psychiatric Association is, inescapably, devaluing the relevance and importance of the very profession it imagines it is protecting.

Now, it is undoubtedly true that mental health professionals are not exempt from bias and that some would speak without due reflection and circumspection. Though professionals are trained to bear in mind the potential confounding influence of their own attitudes and feelings, they're human and fallible. I think a more appropriate action by the American Psychiatric Association would be to urge members to recognize the need for discretion when speaking out, rather than compelling them to choose between submitting to a gag rule or risk being found in violation of its ethical code. Such a policy would recognize the dictates of the individual psychiatrist's conscience to engage with the public and not require that his or her moral prompting be subordinated to protect the psychiatric profession from appearing less than scientifically respectable because some members might speak out in an insufficiently considered way.

I do respect the difference between, on the one hand, making a diagnosis of a public person one hasn't examined and, on the other, offering a professionally informed perspective. Diagnosing is intrinsically more specific and requires a more substantial level of confidence rooted in the professional procedures and discipline in which a more definitive conclusion is grounded. Offering a definitive medical diagnosis without a thorough personal evaluation and the consent of the person being assessed can easily degenerate into speculation and name-calling, which discredits the clinician making the less than optimally founded diagnosis. Nonetheless, one can acknowledge the limitations of relying on publicly available evidence and the lack of certainty inherent in that foundation and still offer valuable professional perspectives on the apparent psychological impediments of a public figure.

In the End, It's a Matter of Opinion

I believe that either a "yes" or a "no" answer to the question of the legitimacy of a professional making a statement about a public figure's mental fitness without a personal examination can be made on firm moral ground. In withholding comment, one places a premium on the traditional methodology and restraint of the profession, but also privileges the public image of the profession over a psychiatrist's right to abide by the dictates of individual conscience. By offering an opinion conditioned on the publicly available data (but lacking the sources one relies on in clinical practice), one prioritizes the professional duty to engage with and educate the public and to identify hazards that are most starkly evident and comprehensible to the clinician's eye.

To demonize those conscientiously holding either view is, I feel, the only indefensible position.

Why I Choose to Speak Out

These are frightening times. The current occupant of the White House is widely perceived as erratic and vindictive (Chollet, Kahl, and Smith

2017; Remnick 2017; Shelbourne 2017; Tumulty 2017).* Yet, those very elements of his character may well have endeared him to his base. He speaks without hesitation or reflection, and repudiates "political correctness." That convinces some that he is authentic, saying things that they've felt but have feared to say out loud. He appears to be easily moved to anger and heedless retaliation. That, too, could be appealing to people who feel powerless and oppressed by an economic system and the societal changes that haven't preserved their status or allowed them to fulfill their dreams and potential. I can identify with those feelings—ironically, even better now, because I am experiencing a variation on the powerlessness I've just described. It would be comforting to believe I had a forceful advocate who possessed the authority and motivation to fix what worries me. Alas, the shoe is on the other foot. (Although, I have profound doubts about how sincerely motivated Mr. Trump is to pursue the interests of the truly powerless.)

Yet, I can feel a sense of community with those who share my apprehension by raising an alarm in the hope that others will be comforted by seeing that their concerns are shared. Still others may feel empowered with a heightened, psychiatrically informed understanding of the nature of the danger, and may be better equipped to respond effectively by virtue of what I and others write.

The Essentially Dangerous Nature of Donald Trump as Commander in Chief

What I and many others discern in Mr. Trump's behavior and speech is a pattern of *impulsivity* that leads to vengeful attacks on those who challenge him. He doesn't seem to pause to consider the validity of facts and perspectives that are unfamiliar or displeasing to him. He presents himself as "knowing more than the generals" and having

---

* As discerned by videotaped exchanges and acknowledging the limitations of relying on such material as opposed to a traditional and in-person psychiatric evaluation.

"great" plans that are sure to succeed: "You will be sick of winning," he has said. This combination of *overconfidence* and rash reactions may have been an asset in the world of real estate deals, where the stakes are financial, personal, and presumably recoverable. But "shooting from the hip" without feeling the need to obtain a genuine understanding of complex matters has much graver consequences when the safety of the nation and the global environment are on the line.

Viewed from a mental health perspective, a person who constantly extols his abilities and feels driven to diminish and ridicule others (and here I am not speaking of political campaigning, where promoting oneself vis-à-vis one's opponents is part of the game) often arises from *profound insecurity*, the very opposite of the supreme confidence that is being projected.

This may seem contradictory, that someone who has succeeded in one realm of life will keep insisting that he is masterful in unrelated areas, areas where he has, in fact, no demonstrated competence, but it soothes such a person's inner doubts and, simultaneously, may appeal mightily to those who crave an all-powerful ally.

This impulsivity, the need to support an insupportably inflated image of oneself, added to a profound inability to acknowledge what one doesn't know, all augur profound psychological interference with the rational and considered exercise of power. *We* need to understand this, all the more so because it is the very awareness that Mr. Trump himself and his acolytes feel they mustn't acknowledge to themselves and us, the people whose safety he is entrusted to protect. Our understanding that this is a recognizable personality style that predictably impedes reliable judgment and a sound, considered response to crises allows us to take appropriate action within the law to contain and limit the damage that we can clearly envision and, collectively, must try to prevent.

Is Donald Trump Mentally Ill?

In my opinion, this is decidedly *not* the question to be addressed, for two reasons: First, mental illness per se is not incompatible with reliably functioning at a high level, e.g., Abraham Lincoln (depression), Winston Churchill (bipolar disorder). Second, without a bona fide psychiatric examination, any speculation about a definitive diagnosis can be seen (and sometimes be) just that, speculation. To compound matters, it's counterproductive because of its irrelevance (see my first point) and because the uncertain conclusions facilitate the easy dismissal of genuine, observable, and profound impediments in Mr. Trump's capacity to deal thoughtfully and reliably with the complex and grave responsibilities of being a reliable president and commander in chief.

To put it another way, operationally and day to day, we don't know and can't tell if Mr. Trump knows that what he is saying is demonstrably not true. What we *do* know is that he can't be relied upon to recognize having been wrong; nor does he seem to able to learn from experience such that he could avoid repeating the same untruth or another the next day, possessed as he appears to be of the same absolute conviction that characterized his previous error.

Conclusion

Donald Trump's presidency confronts the psychiatric profession and, much more important, our country with the challenge of dealing with an elected leader whose psychological style (marked by impulsivity, insistence on his own infallibility, vengeful retaliation, and unwarranted certainty in uncertain circumstances) is a profound impediment to sound decision making and presages the erratic and ill-considered exercise of enormous power.

Leonard L. Glass, M.D., M.P.H., is an associate professor of psychiatry (part time) at Harvard Medical School and a senior attending psychiatrist at McLean Hospital. Dr. Glass was president of the Boston Psychoanalytic Society and Institute, chair of its Ethics Committee, and a distinguished life fellow of the American Psychiatric Association until he resigned in protest of the Goldwater rule in April 2017. Dr. Glass pressed the need for reform of the Goldwater rule directly with the APA, in a peer-reviewed journal article, and, after the first edition of this book, in interviews on PBS, CNN, NPR, op-eds in the Boston Globe, *and in other national and international media.*

ON SEEING WHAT YOU SEE AND SAYING WHAT YOU KNOW

A Psychiatrist's Responsibility

HENRY J. FRIEDMAN, M.D.

Can experienced psychiatrists well trained in both psychiatry and psychoanalysis and seasoned by decades of clinical work actually turn off their powers of observation? And if they could, why would they choose to do so? As important, why should the public be deprived of our expertise? These are relevant and necessary questions to ask before exploring the question of how to process the experience of being exposed to President Donald Trump in the media. Such a series of questions and concerns would be entirely unnecessary were it not for the position taken by the American Psychiatric Association that insists it is unethical for psychiatrists to comment on or diagnose a public figure such as President Trump unless you have seen him in your office. There is a certain irony in this position because if, as a psychiatrist, you examined him in person, you would be prohibited, by ethical standards of confidentiality, from revealing anything about his diagnosis without his permission to do so, even if you had concluded that he was in some way unfit for office.

The American Psychiatric Association came to the Goldwater rule after *Fact Magazine* had surveyed psychiatrists, asking them to diagnose Barry Goldwater, who was running for the presidency against Lyndon Johnson in 1964. A majority of those responding felt that Goldwater's endorsement of the use of nuclear weapons in the Cold War with the Soviet Union justified giving him a diagnosis of paranoia (even paranoid schizophrenia) in some form or another. This fact alone was felt to be sufficient for many to use this diagnosis in responding to the question asked by the magazine. Goldwater successfully sued the magazine for libel; the resulting panic and concern expressed in the APA's adoption of the Goldwater rule was understandable at the time but would certainly have been expected to be modified in response to the very different world that has evolved since the early 1970s. Changes in the world of media, such as the presence of cable news with its 24/7 cycle of reporting and broadcasting visual images of events and leaders, should have led, in my opinion, to the abandonment of the Goldwater rule. Instead, the Ethics Committee of the APA decided, without polling the members, to double down on the Goldwater rule by extending it beyond the realm of diagnosis to include any and all comments on the mental functioning of this or any president or prominent public figure.

In addition to changes in the availability of coverage on TV, there has been an evolving use of phone and Skype in the distant treatment of patients in both psychotherapy and psychoanalysis. Many contemporary psychiatrists no longer feel that their patient must be present in the consulting room with them. While clinicians vary in their comfort and experience with phone and Skype therapies, there is a definite trend toward these modalities as essential if one is to conduct a full-time practice and extend treatment into underserved areas. This shift in attitude toward "remote" treatment conducted through previously untried communication methods is relevant to why commenting on President Trump's mental function feels not only comfortable but necessary.

Because of the constant exposure to Donald Trump on TV news and his open expression of his thinking in rapidly expressed tweets and a multitude of other extemporaneous, unscripted remarks, a trained observer cannot avoid noting the style of his thinking and his reaction to the existence of frustrating realities that challenge his version of events. In this regard, observations about President Trump require some professional clarification concerning the concepts of paranoid thinking and character. The applicability of these concepts to the president can be considered by the nonclinical observer, thus facilitating a more enlightened, critical-thinking public better capable of acting in its interest.

Paranoid thinking, when persistent, is indicative of a paranoid character structure. This means that an individual with such a basic character will consistently produce ideas and responses that find exaggerated danger and malevolent intent in others and in the situations he encounters. The major totalitarian leaders of the twentieth century have all manifested paranoid thinking. Their destructive behavior has been an enactment of their disturbed ideation. Inevitably we have watched as such individuals have taken over entire countries, always acting to increase their power by suppressing freedom of the press and media, jailing or killing the political opposition, and militarizing their political power. Hence, the resemblance between Hitler and Stalin with regard to the senseless murder of millions of people for reasons of pure paranoid-based ruthlessness once they had entered the leader's mind as "enemies of the people."

When attention is called to the resemblance between Hitler and Trump, it tends to elicit a veritable storm of objection. Those who object so strongly are, in effect, calling attention to Hitler's actions in immediately taking over the press and arresting or killing his opposition. While it is true that the restraints operating in our country have prevented Trump from moving as swiftly as Hitler did, this can be attributed to the balance of powers and the greater strength of our democratic traditions rather than to any sense that Trump's patterns of emotional thinking are greatly different from those that motivated Hitler.

The totalitarian mind is remarkably reproducible because it depends upon paranoid ideation presented in a dramatic fashion designed to mobilize both fear and hate, particularly in the less well-educated citizens. Trump, like Hitler, began with his insistence on identifying the United States as in decline, a decline, in Trump's case, caused by our first African American president, who, according to Trump, had left our country in a mess, an "American carnage." This, despite the actual spectacular record of President Obama in saving the economy after the crash of 2008, preventing the worst recession from becoming another Great Depression, the extension of health care to the poor and middle class, and the general spreading of enlightened attitudes toward minorities and women.

The insistence that grave danger exists in reality because it exists in one's mind is the hallmark of the dictator. For Hitler, the Jews represented an existential threat; for Trump, it is illegal immigrants and Mexicans in particular. Also, the disregard for facts, the denial that "factualization" is a necessity before making an assertion of danger or insisting on the nefarious intent of a large group (i.e., the Jews for Hitler, the Muslims for Trump) is typical of paranoid characters who need an enemy against whom to focus group hate.

Many critics of Trump, particularly journalists but also those in the mental health field, have focused on his so-called narcissism, his need to be constantly approved of, the childlike nature of his character. In this they are minimizing the significance of his paranoid beliefs and, in so doing, are relegating his psychological dysfunction to a much higher level than is actually the case. This is also true of those who believe he is simply using his attack on illegal immigrants and Muslims to feed his base. In doing so, they are suggesting that he himself knows better, that he knows that he is merely using these ideas because they will appeal to the white working-class men who make up the bulk of his voters. Yet, this overlooks and minimizes the more ominous probability: that he actually is paranoid and that there is an overlap of his personal hatreds and those of his followers. Together, they represent a desire to undo the impact of all that has changed since Franklin Delano Roosevelt, the New Deal, and the general liberalization of society and life in the United States.

Progress within our liberal democracy can hardly be said to have been rapid. Rather, it has been slow, coming in bursts of activity followed by the integration of the change, but that integration has always been opposed by those who found the particular change unacceptable. The civil rights movement established a new identity for African Americans, one in which they refused to accept a designation as inferior individuals expected to be treated as second-class or lesser citizens. Their ability to use passive resistance and marching to achieve recognition of their right to equal status was furthered by the registration of black voters against local resistance and the establishment of their votes as a powerful determinant in both state and national elections. The combined power of African American, women, and liberal voters resulted in the election of the first African American president, a result that led many liberals, including President Obama, to believe that the United States had at last arrived at a postracial position as a society. Unfortunately, this proved to be anything but the case. Instead of proving to be the sign of decreased racism, the very fact of a black man in the White House appeared to generate a degree of hatred and resistance to President Obama that was, if anything, a grim reminder of the legacy of slavery and the split in the United States between the North and the South that has never come close to actually healing or even scarring over.

In his successful campaign to capture the Republican Party nomination, candidate Trump used the racism of the white working class to engage their enthusiastic support by attacking each of the other Republican candidates in terms never seen before in such a competition. Mostly, however, he depended upon his populist appeal to his followers' discontent and disdain for the establishment. What tended to get lost even in the process of securing the nomination was his ability to make things up and, at the same time, to believe them himself. Trump managed a variation on Descartes's "I think, therefore I am": "I think it, therefore it is." This reckless relationship to reality on Trump's part has continued to represent a reliably occurring part of his character; no fact that he believes to be true, often after reading it on some alt-right website, is fact-checked or questioned.

This form of grandiosity is part of the paranoia that clearly dominates Trump's thinking.

Am I making a diagnosis of President Trump? Well, yes and no—and even maybe—but whatever it is I am doing, there is one thing that I am refusing to do: to deny what I am hearing and seeing coming from Trump himself on the TV news and in the printed reliable press. The effort on the part of CNN, MSNBC, the *New York Times*, and the *Washington Post* to keep the public informed about Trump and his administration has undoubtedly been a crucial element in preventing him from doing more harm, from going the really radical route of Hitler. Hence, his attack on the press, accusing real reporting of facts as being "fake news," is an attenuated version of the more extreme takeover of the media that is usual in totalitarian governments. Trump hasn't been able or willing to seize the news media and close them down, but he has tried by insisting that those who question his campaign's involvement with the Russian interference with our election are refusing to accept that there is no basis for investigating this possibility. Some reporters, such as Thomas Friedman, Rachel Maddow, and Lawrence O'Donnell, have suggested that Trump is "crazy." Recently, in relationship to his firing of FBI director James Comey, many have made the observation that President Trump is "unhinged." These descriptions are made by intelligent nonpsychiatrists who are limited in using such terms to describe their impression of the man and his thinking. Donny Deutsch on *Morning Joe* actually spoke out against the Goldwater rule and asked when the psychiatrists were going to comment on what they see in watching President Trump. Deutsch emphasized the need to ignore the Goldwater rule in favor of supporting those who correctly doubt that Trump's mental state is compatible with the office he currently inhabits.

A paranoid, hypersensitive, grandiose, ill-informed leader such as Donald Trump, who has surrounded himself with a Cabinet and a set of advisers who either are unable to bring him out of his paranoid suspicions and insistences or, worse, identify with his positions, represents a multidimensional threat to our country and the world. The most common concern I hear from my patients is that Trump's impulsivity will result in a nuclear war with North Korea. The intensity of this concern tends to mask an awareness of what has already begun in the United States, namely, an erosion of the just and decent society that has been evolving since FDR's New Deal. That society reached the pinnacle of decency under the presidency of Barack Obama, a leader who personified what it means to be a stable leader of a great and powerful nation. Trump's need to destroy everything that Obama achieved derives from the paranoid character's hatred of goodness in others whose achievements he cannot attain, understand, or tolerate. This degree of destructiveness in any individual makes him a poor candidate for therapy of any sort. The goodness of any therapist, his or her competence, and his or her ability to provide needed responsiveness can and will be targeted for destruction. Treating such individuals is always arduous and rarely effective, and yet they often present when in trouble as motivated to receive help. Once they have managed to solve the problem that has brought them to therapy, they quickly reveal a lack of investment in the therapy or the therapist.

This brings us to the question of analyzing President Trump from a distance; is it possible, is it ethical, and who is to decide this issue? In particular, does the stance of the APA, with its newly minted version of the Goldwater rule, prevent a psychiatrist-psychoanalyst from attempting such an analysis? A classical psychoanalyst would scoff at the idea that any psychoanalysis could be done from a distance, whether by telephone or by Skype. For such an analyst, both analyst and analysand must be present in the consulting room, so that observations of the patient who is practicing free association can be made continuously. The unconscious is to be found and interpreted to the patient at the moment of interaction. Judged by the criteria of classical psychoanalysis, no analysis of candidate or President Trump is possible. But taken from the perspective of an interpersonal or relational psychoanalyst, it is possible to think psychoanalytically about him only from a distance. Because of the unlikely possibility that Trump could form a significant attachment to a therapist, we need to see him as a fit subject for descriptive reflection rather than treatment of any kind; we need to believe what we see in all that he reveals to us without hesitation or inhibition. As important, we need to emphasize that these revelations cannot be normalized; nor will they change. Trump challenges us with the question "Are you going to believe me, or are you going to believe your lying eyes?"

Whatever Trump thinks at the moment is translated into tweets or speech with no regard for linking his idea with any previously stated idea or with any context that should be obviously relevant to what he is now asserting. He may be beyond the scope of even the most broadly defined idea of applied psychoanalysis, but what he does gives us ample access to is his characteristic style of responding to others who oppose him. His critics often treat him as if he were childish—that is, were merely acting like a child rather than a mature adult—suggesting that, as a child, he can still "grow up." The problem with such an approach is that it is a manifestation of wishful thinking, and it is incorrect in that it grossly underestimates the importance of Trump's adult paranoid character with its belief in an apocalyptic vision of a weak, diminished United States that only he can save from the liberal Democrats who oppose his authority. Any attempt to "understand" Trump from the perspective of his childhood or of what he is reenacting from the past is, in all probability, a hopeless and unnecessary task. Character formation of the paranoid typology becomes so autonomous that, once it has solidified, it is practically meaningless to try to find an explanation for its existence in a particular individual.

Ultimately, the response to the Trump administration will have to come from the electorate. All the policies that he wants to promote may not in themselves be absolutely ruinous to our country. The poor and disenfranchised will undoubtedly suffer, but the real danger will be from the president's paranoid character, which will continue to be present and active for as long as he is in office. Perhaps the observations of this psychiatrist-psychoanalyst, and of others in the mental health field, will help clarify why the threat of President Trump exceeds the issue of his policies, and resides instead in his core paranoid personality. When, as a psychiatrist, I watch commentators and reporters struggling to understand or explain President Trump's latest irrational position—as when he lies about when and why he decided to fire James Comey or the claimed details of his exchanges with Comey before the firing occurred—I wish that I could help them understand his paranoid character and why there should be no surprise that Trump has behaved in this way. They should be prepared to witness many more situations in which Trump feels betrayed and turns on those who have previously served him. Paranoids are always finding betrayal in those surrounding them, and react with retaliatory anger—Hitler and Stalin, by murdering their newly minted enemies; and Trump, by firing them. Psychiatric knowledge and terminology will save reporters and the public from remaining confused and attempting to find explanations of behavior that could easily be understood if Trump's paranoid character were always kept in mind. This is the only way to ensure the preservation and viability of our democracy and our national security.

Henry J. Friedman, M.D., is an associate professor of psychiatry, Harvard Medical School (part time), on the editorial boards of Psychoanalytic Quarterly, the American Journal of Psychoanalysis, *and the* Journal of the American Psychoanalytic Association, *with main interests in the therapeutic action of psychoanalysis and analytic psychotherapy. Friedman is also chair of the "Meet the Author" at the biannual meetings of the American Psychoanalytic Association.*

THE ISSUE IS DANGEROUSNESS, NOT MENTAL ILLNESS

JAMES GILLIGAN, M.D.

Psychiatrists in America today have been told by two different official organizations that they have two diametrically opposite professional obligations, and that if they violate either one, they are behaving unethically. The first says they have an obligation to remain silent about their evaluation of anyone if that person has not given them permission to speak about it publicly. The second says they have an obligation to speak out and inform others if they believe that person may be dangerous to them, even if he has not given them permission to do so. The first standard is the Goldwater rule of 1973, which prohibits psychiatrists from offering a professional opinion in public about the mental health of anyone whom they have not personally examined. The second is the Tarasoff decision, which in 1976 ruled that psychiatrists have a positive obligation to speak out publicly when they have determined, or should have determined, that an individual is dangerous to another person or persons, in order both to warn the potential victim(s) of the danger they are in and to set in motion a set of procedures that will help protect the potential victim(s).

From both an ethical and a legal standpoint, the second of those two rulings trumps the first.

Insofar as psychiatrists function as clinicians, their primary duty is to their individual patients. Yet, psychiatry, like every other medical specialty, involves more than just clinical practice (that is, diagnosing and treating one patient at a time after those patients have already become ill). It is also a branch of public health and preventive medicine, and in that aspect of its functioning, we owe society a primary duty, for that is the level at which primary and secondary prevention can prevent individuals from becoming ill or violent in the first place, and injuring or killing others if either their illness or their behavior is contagious. In fact, this level of intervention can even prevent the whole society from becoming vulnerable to epidemics of illness, injury, and death. Clinical psychiatry, from a public health standpoint, is merely tertiary prevention, and it represents the least useful contribution we can make to the public health, compared to primary and secondary prevention (Gilligan 2001). From that standpoint, we have a positive obligation to warn the public when we have reason to believe, based on our research with the most dangerous people our society produces, that a public figure, by virtue of the actions he takes, represents a danger to the public health—whether or not he is mentally ill.

An intellectual precursor to the Goldwater rule was a comment that one of the most influential and brilliant German intellectuals made not long before the rise of Hitler. In his essay on "Science as a Vocation," Max Weber (1917) argued that intellectuals and scholars should not utter political opinions or say anything that could be regarded as "partisan." They could talk about politics in general, but they should not say anything that could be taken as support for or opposition to any particular party or politician.

I have always been troubled by that opinion, because it appears to me to have encouraged the intellectual and professional leaders of Germany to remain silent, even in the face of enormous and unprecedented danger. It does not seem to me that the German Psychiatric Association of the 1930s deserves any honor or credit for remaining silent during Hitler's rise to power. On the contrary, it appears from our perspective today to have been a passive enabler of the worst atrocities he committed—as were most German clergymen, professors, lawyers, judges, physicians, journalists, and other professionals and intellectuals who could have, but did not, speak out when they saw a blatantly obvious psychopath gaining the power to lead their country into the worst disaster in its history. Our current president does not have to be a literal reincarnation of Hitler—and I am not suggesting that he is—in order for the same principles to apply to us today.

The issue that we are raising is not whether Trump is mentally ill. It is whether he is dangerous. Dangerousness is not a psychiatric diagnosis. One does not have to be "mentally ill," as both law and psychiatry define it, in order to be dangerous. In fact, most mentally ill people do not commit serious violence, and most violence is committed by people who are not mentally ill. The association between violence and mental illness is very tenuous at best. Only about 1 percent of the perpetrators of homicide in this country are found to be "not guilty by reason of insanity." The rest are declared by our courts to be mentally healthy but evil, as those concepts are used in relevance to people's "criminal responsibility" for whatever violence they have committed.

President Trump may or may not meet the criteria for any of the diagnoses of mental disorders defined in the *Diagnostic and Statistical Manual* of the American Psychiatric Association, or for many of them, but that is not relevant to the issue we are raising here.

Also, the most reliable data for assessing dangerousness often do not require, and are often not attainable from, interviewing the individuals about whom we are forming an opinion. Such individuals often (though not always) deny, minimize, or attempt to conceal the very facts that identify them as being dangerous. The most reliable data may come from the person's family and friends and, just as important, from police reports; criminal histories; medical, prison, and judicial records; and other publicly available information from third parties. However, in Trump's case, we also have many public records, tape recordings, videotapes, and his own public speeches, interviews, and "tweets" of his numerous threats of violence, incitements to violence, and boasts of violence that he himself acknowledges having committed repeatedly and habitually.

Sometimes a person's dangerousness is so obvious that one does not need professional training in either psychiatry or criminology to recognize it. One does not need to have had fifty years of professional experience in assessing the dangerousness of violent criminals to recognize the dangerousness of a president who:

- **Asks what the point of having thermonuclear weapons is if we cannot use them.** For example, in an interview with Chris Matthews on an MSNBC town hall meeting, he said, "Somebody hits us within ISIS, you wouldn't fight back with a nuke?" When Matthews remarked that "the whole world [is] hearing a guy running for president of the United States talking of maybe using nuclear weapons. No one wants to hear that about an American president," Trump replied, "Then why are we making them?" Another MSNBC host, Joe Scarborough, reported that Trump had asked a foreign policy adviser three times, "If we have them, why can't we use them?" (Fisher 2016).

- **Urges our government to use torture or worse against our prisoners of war.** Throughout his presidential campaign, Trump repeatedly said that "torture works," and promised to bring back "waterboarding" and to introduce new methods "that go a lot further." After being reminded that there were by then laws prohibiting these practices, he responded by insisting that he would broaden the laws so that the United States would not have to play "by the rules," as ISIS did not do so (Haberman 2016).

- **Urged that five innocent African American youths be given the death penalty for a sexual assault even years after it had been proven beyond a reasonable doubt to have been committed by someone else.** In 1989, Trump spent $85,000 placing ads in New

York City's four daily papers calling for the return of the death penalty to New York State so that five African American youths who had been wrongfully convicted of raping a woman in Central Park could be executed, and he was still advocating the same penalty in 2016, fourteen years after DNA evidence and a detailed confession had proved that a serial rapist had actually committed the crime (Burns 2016).

- **Boasts about his ability to get away with sexually assaulting women because of his celebrity and power.** Trump was recorded saying, of his way of relating to women, that "I just start kissing them. It's like a magnet. . . . I don't even wait. And when you're a star they let you do it. You can do anything. Grab 'em by the pussy. You can do anything" ("Donald Trump's Lewd Comments About Women" 2016).

- **Urges his followers at political rallies to punch protesters in the face and beat them up so badly that they have to be taken out on stretchers.** In an editorial, the *New York Times* has quoted the following remarks by Trump at his rallies: "I'd like to punch him in the face, I'll tell you"; "In the good old days this doesn't happen, because they used to treat them very, very rough"; "I love the old days. You know what they used to do to guys like that when they were in a place like this? They'd be carried out on a stretcher, folks"; "If you see somebody getting ready to throw a tomato, knock the crap out of them, would ya? Seriously. Just knock the hell out of them. I will pay for the legal fees, I promise you." He even complained that his supporters were not being violent enough (even though many had assaulted protesters severely enough to be arrested and tried for assault and battery): "Part of the problem, and part of the reason it takes so long [to remove protesters], is because nobody wants to hurt each other anymore, right?" (*New York Times* Editorial Board 2016).

- **Suggests that his followers could always assassinate his political rival, Hillary Clinton, if she were elected president or, at the very least, throw her in prison.** He has led crowds in chants of "Lock her up! Lock her up!" In his words, "If she gets to pick her judges, nothing you can do, folks. Although the Second Amendment people—maybe there is, I don't know" (remark made during rally on August 9, 2016).

- **Believes he can always get away with whatever violence he does commit.** He said, "I could stand in the middle of Fifth Avenue and shoot somebody, and I wouldn't lose voters" (remark made at rally on January 23, 2016).

And so on and on and on—in an endless stream of threats of violence, boasts of violence, and incitements to violence.

While Trump has not yet succeeded in undoing the rule of law to such a degree as to become a dictator, it is clear that he speaks the language of dictatorship. Only dictators assassinate or imprison their personal political rivals and opponents.

Trump did not confess that he personally assaulted women himself; he boasted that he had. That is, he acknowledged having done so repeatedly, and gotten away with it, not as an expression of personal feelings of guilt and remorse for having violated women in this way but, rather, as a boast about the power his celebrity had given him to force women to submit to his violations of their dignity and autonomy.

As for inciting violence by his followers against his enemies, he sometimes used the same tactic that Henry II used to incite his followers to assassinate Thomas Becket, by implication rather than by an explicit order: "What miserable . . . traitors have I nourished and promoted in my household, who let their lord be treated with such shameful contempt by a low-born clerk!" Of course, his vassals got the point, and did what Henry had made clear he wanted done.

In this regard, however, Trump sometimes went further than his historical predecessors and explicitly, rather than implicitly, encouraged his followers to "punch protestors in the face," and "beat them up so badly that they'll have to be taken out on stretchers." Indeed, a number of his supporters did assault anti-Trump dissenters, and are now being tried for assault and battery. The defense of some has been that they were merely doing what Trump had asked them to do, though the courts may reject that defense on the grounds that Trump was indeed as indirect (notwithstanding that he was just as clear) as Henry II.

If psychiatrists with decades of experience doing research on violent offenders do not confirm the validity of the conclusion that many nonpsychiatrists have reached, that Trump is extremely dangerous—indeed, by far the most dangerous of any president in our lifetimes—then we are not behaving with appropriate professional restraint and discipline. Rather, we are being either incompetent or irresponsible, or both.

However, while all psychiatrists, by definition, have studied mental illness, most have not specialized in studying the causes, consequences, prediction, and prevention of violence, which is considered a problem in public health and preventive medicine. Nor have most studied the principles on which the assessment of current and future dangerousness is based, regardless of whether any particular individual is mentally ill, and regardless of what diagnosis or diagnoses, if any, he may merit according to the criteria outlined in DSM-V.

That is why it is so important and so appropriate for those few of us who have done so—whether by investigating the psychology of Nazi doctors and Japanese terrorists, as Robert Lifton has done; or by studying sexual violence (rape, incest, etc.), as Judith Herman has done; or by examining murderers and rapists (including those who have committed "war crimes") in prisons and jails throughout the world, as I did while working with the World Health Organization's Department of Violence and Injury Prevention on the epidemiology and prevention of violence—to warn the potential victims, in the interests of public health, when we recognize and identify signs and symptoms that indicate that someone is dangerous to the public health.

One implication of this is that we need to identify the potential causes of injury and illness before they have harmed any given population of potential victims as severely or extensively as they would if allowed to go unchecked. In other words, we need to recognize the earliest signs of danger before they have expanded into a full-scale epidemic of lethal or life-threatening injury. The analogy here is to the proverb about how to get a frog to become unaware that it is being boiled to death: place it in a pot of cold water and then heat the water up bit by bit. Something analogous to that is the danger with the Trump presidency.

The United States has been blessed with a little over two centuries of democracy. That is actually a rather short period in comparison with the millennia of monarchy. However, it is long enough to have made most of us complacent, and perhaps overconfident, with respect to the stability of our democracy. In fact, if we are prone to making a mistake in this regard, we are far more likely to underestimate the fragility of democracy than we are to become unnecessarily alarmist about it.

Here again, it is the behavioral scientists who have studied violence (including but not limited to psychiatrists) who owe it to the public to share what we have learned before we experience the epidemic of violence that would be unleashed by the collapse or undermining of the rule of law, the system of checks and balances, the freedom of the press, the independence and authority of the judiciary, the respect for facts, the unacceptability of deliberate lying, the prohibition on conflicts between a political leader's private interests and the public interest, and the even stronger prohibition on physically assaulting one's political rivals or opponents and threatening to imprison or even assassinate them—in other words, dictatorship—all of which have been characteristic of Donald Trump's public statements throughout his electoral campaign and presidency.

To wait until the water reaches boiling temperature, or our democracy collapses, before we begin saying anything about the fact that the water is warming already would mean that anything we said or did in the future would come too late to be of any help. Let us not make the same mistake that the German Psychiatric Association did in the 1930s.

There is an unfortunate and unnecessary taboo in the social and behavioral sciences generally against regarding politics and politicians as appropriate and legitimate subjects for discussion, inquiry, and conclusions. On the contrary, if a psychiatrist or psychologist, or any other behavioral scientist, expresses an opinion that is relevant to the political debates that occur in our country, he is likely to be accused of being "partisan" rather than "professional," or engaging in a discussion that is "just political" rather than "scientific."

I would argue that the opposite is true. At a time when more and more medical scientists are urging us to practice "evidence-based medicine," isn't it even more important that we learn to practice "evidence-based politics"? But of course we cannot do that unless we are willing to apply the methods and accumulated knowledge of all the social and behavioral sciences to this subject, and to publicize the conclusions we reach so that all our fellow citizens, which means all our fellow voters, can benefit from the knowledge we have gained through our clinical, experimental, and epidemiological research into the causes and prevention of violence—concerning which data from politics and economics certainly figure prominently (Gilligan 2011; Lee, Wexler, and Gilligan 2014).

If we are silent about the numerous ways in which Donald Trump has repeatedly threatened violence, incited violence, or boasted about his own violence, we are passively supporting and enabling the dangerous and naïve mistake of treating him as if he were a "normal" president or a "normal" political leader. He is not, and it is our duty to say so, and to say it publicly. He is unprecedentedly and abnormally dangerous.

This is not to inform the public of something it does not already know, for most people in the lay public already appear to know it. Most voters voted against Trump. As our most recent Nobel Prize winner in Literature, Bob Dylan, has put it, "You don't need a weatherman to know which way the wind blows!"

In fact, Trump's dangerousness is so obvious that he might be said to have preempted the role other people might otherwise have to play in warning the public as to how dangerous he is. For, in his many public statements on that subject, he himself has warned us about how dangerous he is far more clearly and eloquently than we have been able to do, or need to do. Our role here is not so much to warn the public ourselves, but merely to heed the warnings Trump himself has already given us, and to remind the public about them.

In that regard, one final clarification is in order. Trump is now the most powerful head of state in the world, and one of the most impulsive, arrogant, ignorant, disorganized, chaotic, nihilistic, self-contradictory, self-important, and self-serving. He has his finger on the triggers of a thousand or more of the most powerful thermonuclear weapons in the world. That means he could kill more people in a few seconds than any dictator in past history has been able to kill during his entire years in power. Indeed, by virtue of his office, Trump has the power to reduce the unprecedentedly destructive world wars and genocides of the twentieth century to minor footnotes in the history of human violence. To say merely that he is "dangerous" is debatable only in the sense that it may be too much of an understatement. If he even took a step in this direction, we will not be able to say that he did not warn us—loudly, clearly, and repeatedly. In that case, the fault will not be his alone. It will also be ours.

James Gilligan, M.D., is Clinical Professor of Psychiatry and Adjunct Professor of Law at New York University. He is a renowned violence studies expert and author of the influential Violence: Our Deadly Epidemic and Its Causes, *as well as* Preventing Violence *and* Why Some Politicians Are More Dangerous

Than Others. *He has served as director of mental health services for the Massachusetts prisons and prison mental hospital, president of the International Association for Forensic Psychotherapy, and as a consultant to President Clinton, Tony Blair, Kofi Annan, the World Court, the World Health Organization, and the World Economic Forum.*

References

Burns, Sarah. 2016. "Why Trump Doubled Down on the Central Park Five." *New York Times*, October 17.

"Donald Trump's Lewd Comments About Women." 2016. Transcript and video. *New York Times*, October. 8.

Fisher, Max. 2016. "Donald Trump, Perhaps Unwittingly, Exposes Paradox of Nuclear Arms." *New York Times*, August 3.

Gilligan, James. 2001. *Preventing Violence: An Agenda for the Coming Century.* London and New York: Thames and Hudson.

———. 2011. *Why Some Politicians Are More Dangerous Than Others.* Cambridge, UK: Polity Press.

Haberman, Maggie. 2016. "Donald Trump Again Alters Course on Torture." *New York Times*, March 15.

Heilpern, Will. 2017. "Trump Campaign: 11 Outrageous Quotes." CNN.com, January 19. cnn.com/2015/12/31/politics/gallery/donald-trump-campaign-quotes/index.html.

Lee, Bandy X., Bruce E. Wexler, and James Gilligan. 2014. "Political Correlates of Violent Death Rates in the U.S., 1900–2010: Longitudinal and Cross-Sectional Analyses." *Aggression and Violent Behavior* 19: 721–28.

New York Times Editorial Board. 2016. "The Trump Campaign Gives License to Violence." *New York Times*, March 15. www.nytimes.com/2016/03/15/opinion/the-trump-campaign-gives-license-to-violence.html.

Weber, Max. 1917. "Science as a Vocation." In *From Max Weber,* tr. and ed. by H. H. Gerth and C. Wright Mills. Repr. New York: Free Press, 1946.

A CLINICAL CASE FOR THE DANGEROUSNESS OF DONALD J. TRUMP

DIANE JHUECK, L.M.H.C., D.M.H.P.

Mental illness in a U.S. president is not necessarily something that is dangerous for the citizenry he or she governs. A comprehensive study of all thirty-seven U.S. presidents up to 1974 determined that nearly half of them had a diagnosable mental illness, including depression, anxiety, and bipolar disorder (Davidson, Connor, and Swartz 2006). Notably, however, personality disorders were not included in this study, even though they can be just as debilitating. This addition would most certainly have increased the number of presidents with mental illness to something well past 50 percent. Yet, psychiatric illness alone in a president is not what causes grave concern. A second and crucial part of the equation is: Is the president dangerous by reason of mental illness?

Favoring civil liberties, U.S. law gives a lot of latitude for behavioral variation. When the law allows, even requires, that mental health professionals and physicians detain people against their will for psychiatric reasons, they must demonstrate that those people are a danger to themselves or others, or are gravely disabled. Initially, we need to look at what it means to be a danger to others due to mental illness. It is important to separate mental symptoms from things such as poor judgment or opinions and points of view that differ from one's own, which the law clearly permits. In the United States, it must be a disturbance of cognition, emotion regulation, or behavior, as described in the fifth edition of the *Diagnostic and Statistical Manual of Mental Disorder* (DSM-V), that is driving the patterns of dangerous behavior. Additionally, the magnitude of the perceived harm must be considered. Is it that feelings are being hurt? Or is there actual damage being perpetrated? Are there patterns of behavior and statements of intent that reasonably indicate that harm is imminent? Does the person carry weapons or any other instruments of harm?

People holding high political office inevitably cause some form of harm, whether they intend to or not. Leaders must often select what they think are the best options from a list of bad ones in areas as complex as military policy, the allocation of limited resources, or the line between safety nets and deregulation. When an individual in high office makes decisions, some people may be hurt in some way because of the sheer magnitude of that individual's power. A good leader will attempt, to the extent he or she can, to minimize that harm and to comfort those impacted, but damage is still unavoidable. This remains an unfortunate effect of governing large groups of people. This is also the very reason it is more, not less, important that the leader of the United States be mentally and emotionally stable. As president, Donald J. Trump has control over our executive branch and its agencies; is commander in chief of our military; has unilateral authority to fire nuclear weapons (which the secretary of defense authenticates but cannot veto). For the leader of the free world, inappropriate words alone may create a snowball effect that ultimately results in devastating harm to others.

The MacArthur Violence Risk Assessment Study has a number of indicators for whether an individual will commit future violence. Some examples include: a past history of violence, a criminal or substance-abusing father, personal chemical abuse, having a generally suspicious nature, and a high score on the Novaco Anger Scale.

In regard to categories of mental health disorder, and perhaps counterintuitively, major illnesses (such as schizophrenia) have a lower rate of harm to others than personality disorders. "Psychopathy, [antisocial personality disorder] as measured by a screening version of the Hare Psychopathy Checklist, was more strongly associated with violence than any other risk factor we studied" (Monahan 2001). The twenty-item Hare checklist measures interpersonal and affective presentation, social deviance, impulsive lifestyle, and antisocial behavior (Hart, Cox, and Hare 1995).

The president, in a position of great power and making critical decisions, should theoretically meet higher standards of mental stability. Also, having access to a nuclear arsenal capable of destroying the world many times over, he should be of lower risk of violence than the average citizen. Despite these higher standards, our response is the opposite, for there is protection of public perception to consider: the president is supposed to be our protector, and he is unwell and harmful. The more unwell and unwilling to admit of any disturbance (in an extreme-case scenario), the more a mental health detention may need to be considered—and how would that appear to the public? Or, if we did not act, would we continue to deny until we were at a point of no return? Additionally, those who dare apply these mental health principles, such as those who dare apply justice to our First Citizen, may find themselves at risk of their jobs, their security, or even their personal safety—by the president or that segment of our society currently feeling empowered by the rise of the present regime, who would be driven around the emotional bend if these actions were successful. A complex web of factors requires consideration, which is why public education and collaboration with other professionals (e.g., politicians, lawyers, social psychologists) is highly important.

There is a preponderance of information in the public record regarding Donald J. Trump's aberrant behavior. The following list of incidents is neither all-inclusive nor deeply analytical. Each topic is a potential theme for an entire book in its own right. The intent here is to isolate enough indicators of record to reach a reasoned conclusion about whether President Trump's patterns of behavior indicates a clinically relevant "danger to others."

During a rally in Wilmington, North Carolina, Trump stated, "Hillary wants to abolish, essentially abolish the Second Amendment. . . . And by the way, if she gets to pick her judges, nothing you can do, folks. Although [for] the Second Amendment people, maybe there is, I don't know." A reporter covering this incident was moved to say, "While the remark was characteristically glib, it finds Trump again encouraging violence at his rallies. Worse, it marks a harrowing jump from threatening protestors to suggesting either an armed revolt or the assassination of a president" (Blistein 2016). It was not just journalists who heard Trump's statement in these terms: "The former head of the CIA, retired Gen. Michael Hayden, told CNN's Jake Tapper, 'If someone else had said that outside the hall, he'd be in the back of a police wagon now with the Secret Service questioning him'" (Diamond and Collinson 2016). It is true also for medical and mental health professionals: if a patient had said that, an emergency certificate would have been signed, and the person taken to the nearest emergency room for further questioning and evaluation.

Trump has said that he did not mean the statement the way it sounded. A common explanation by his defenders of aggressive and untoward remarks made by him in public settings is that what he said was a joke. This in no way discounts the dangerousness of his remark. In fact, his deeming the remark so lightly as to consider that it could be a joke would in itself be concerning. Moreover, his holding life-and-death matters themselves to be inconsequential may indicate serious pathology and risk—which cannot fully be ruled out without a detailed examination. This statement, in this context, exemplifies the "willingness to violate others" and the lack of empathy that characterize antisocial personality disorder (American Psychiatric Association 2016, pp. 659–60). In modern history, no other candidate for president of the United States has joked about his followers murdering his opponent.

In his response to the release by the *Washington Post* of the now-infamous "Grab 'em by the pussy" video, Trump the candidate stated that the audio was recorded more than ten years ago and did not represent who he is. The recording was made by *Access Hollywood*'s Billy Bush on September 16, 2005. It includes the following comments from the newly married Trump when he sees actress Arianne Zucker outside the bus where he is being recorded: "I better use some Tic Tacs, just in case I start kissing her." (Sound of Tic Tacs being dispensed.) "You know I'm automatically attracted to beautiful—I just start kissing them. It's like a magnet. Just kiss. I don't even wait" (Fahrenthold 2016). During the course of the video, he is on record as saying even more disturbing and assaultive things regarding women.

After this video was aired, a significant number of Republican senators, representatives, governors, political appointees, and others stated publicly that they would not endorse Trump for office. Lisa Murkowski, Republican senator from Alaska, stated, "The video that surfaced yesterday further revealed his true character," she said. "He not only objectified women, he bragged about preying upon them. I cannot and will not support Donald Trump for President—he has forfeited the right to be our party's nominee. He must step aside" (2016). Brian Sandoval, Republican governor from Nevada, declared, "This video exposed not just words, but now an established pattern, which I find to be repulsive and unacceptable for a candidate for President of the United States" (Graham 2016). While senators and representatives have a more complicated relationship to Trump as president, governors and political appointees are more removed from him politically and warrant closer inspection. Of note, with less to lose politically, both these groups had a higher percentage of members state that they would not endorse Trump. Of the fifteen Republican governors who went on record, 53 percent stated that they would not endorse the nominee for president. Two of the seven who said they would endorse him now have jobs in his administration, as vice president and United Nations ambassador. Of the twenty-three Republican political appointees who made statements on record, an astounding 87 percent of them said they would not endorse or vote for Trump. Only three said they would (Graham 2016). Therapists of mental health across the country report having to expand their practices to include what is being called "election trauma." "What I'm seeing with my clients, particularly with women who experienced sexual abuse when younger, is that they are being re-wounded, re-traumatized," said Atlanta licensed professional counselor Susan Blank. "They can't escape it. It's all around them, written large on the national stage" (LaMotte 2016).

Among the many truly disturbing behaviors of this man now serving as the leader of the free world is his relationship to his daughter Ivanka. What follows are some of the more unsettling things Trump has said about her while knowingly being recorded:

- "You know who's one of the great beauties of the world, according to everybody? And I helped create her. Ivanka. My daughter Ivanka. She's 6 feet tall, she's got the best body" (King 2016).

- During an interview with Howard Stern when Ivanka was twenty-two years old (Cohen 2016): "I've said that, if Ivanka weren't my daughter, perhaps I'd be dating her" ("Donald Trump Nearly Casually Remarks . . ." 2006).

- And in another appearance on the Howard Stern radio show, in response to Stern's saying, "By the way, your daughter . . ." Trump responded, "She's beautiful." Stern added, "Can I say this? A piece of ass," to which Trump replied, "Yeah" (Kaczynski 2016).

- To a reporter about Ivanka: "Yeah, she's really something, and what a beauty, that one. If I weren't happily married and, ya know, her father . . ." (Solotaroff 2015).

- On Fox's *Wendy Williams Show*, in 2013: "Ivanka, what's the favorite thing you have in common with your father?" Williams asked.

"Either real estate or golf," Ivanka replied. "Donald?" Williams asked Trump. "Well, I was going to say sex, but I can't relate that to . . ." Trump answers, gesturing to Ivanka (Feyerick 2016).

One of the first acts of mass citizen resistance against Trump's presidency occurred the day after his inauguration, when much of the country went to the streets in protest. The 2017 Women's March was the largest protest gathering in the history of the United States. Researchers Jeremy Pressman and Erica Chenowith (2017) estimate that more than four million people participated nationwide. They calculate that approximately three hundred thousand people marched in other countries, partly in response to an assaultive attitude and behavior against women unprecedented in a U.S. president.

A great danger to vulnerable groups and the potential for human rights abuses arise from the type of individuals Trump's psychopathy leads him to look to for affirmation and support. Unable to tolerate criticism and perceived threats to his ego, and with a documented obsessive need to be admired, he has notably selected as his advisers either family members or people who, in clinical jargon, "enable" his illness. This is one of the more significant ways in which he has become a danger to others as president. Members of vulnerable communities often write and speak about grave concerns regarding those whom he is choosing to guide him. Using his proposed federal budget as a lens, Jessica González-Rojas writes, "It outlines President Trump's spending priorities and program cuts that make clear his utter contempt for communities of color, and it edges this country and its moral compass closer to the nativist vision espoused by the likes of White House advisers Steve Bannon and Stephen Miller, and Attorney General Jeff Sessions" (González-Rojas 2017).

His mental health symptoms, including impulsive blame-shifting, claims of unearned superiority, and delusional levels of grandiosity, have been present in his words from his very first campaign speech: "They're bringing drugs. They're bringing crime. They're rapists, and some, I assume, are good people" (Elledge 2017).

"I would build a Great Wall, and nobody builds walls better than me, believe me, and I'll build them very inexpensively. I will build a great, great wall on our southern border and I will have Mexico pay for that wall, mark my words" (Gamboa 2015). Regarding U.S. district judge Gonzalo Curiel, who was born in Indiana, Trump claimed it was a conflict of interest for the judge to hear a fraud case against Trump University, telling CNN, "He's a Mexican. We're building a wall between here and Mexico" (Finnegan 2016).

Trump's unhinged response to court decisions, driven as they appear to be by paranoia, delusion, and a sense of entitlement, are of grave concern. While president of the United States, he has on more than one occasion questioned the legitimacy of the court, as in this example: "We had a very smooth roll-out," he insisted, claiming that "the only problem with the [Muslim] ban was the 'bad court' that halted it" (Friedman, Sebastian, and Dibdin 2017). In February 2017, he tweeted, "The opinion of this so-called judge, which essentially takes law-enforcement away from our country, is ridiculous and will be overturned!" To which Representative Jerry Nadler responded, on February 8, 2017: "@realDonaldTrump's conduct—attacking judges + undermining independent judiciary—is inappropriate and dangerous." According to the Department of Homeland Security, at least 721 individuals and their families were denied the entry they had expected at U.S. borders under a ban soon deemed illegal by more than one court. At least 100,000 visas were revoked, according to a Justice Department lawyer (Brinlee 2017).

"We're hearing from really, really scared people," said Rachel Tiven, CEO of Lambda Legal, a nonprofit legal advocacy organization for LGBTQ rights. She adds, "We're seeing a fear of an atmosphere of intolerance that began with Trump's campaign." In the same article, Kris Hayashi, executive director of the Transgender Law Center, states, "It was clear in 2016 that we saw an upswing in anti-trans legislation, more than we'd ever seen before . . . We anticipated that was not going to lessen but increase in 2017" (Grinberg 2016). "These are situations that put fear, not just into the individual who is targeted, but the entire community," said Heidi Beirich, director of the Southern Poverty Law Center's (SPLC) Intelligence Project, in a *Boston Globe* article about increased hate-based crimes at schools in Massachusetts. The SPLC reports that a record 16,720 complaints were filed nationwide with the Office for Civil Rights of the U.S. Department of Education in 2016, which they state is a 61 percent increase over the previous year (Guha 2017).

The American Association of University Professors' national council has approved the following resolution (2016): "Since the election of Donald J. Trump almost two weeks ago, the US has experienced an unprecedented spike in hate crimes, both physical and verbal, many of them on college and university campuses. . . . These have been directed against African Americans, immigrants, members of the LGBTQ community, religious minorities, women, and people with disabilities. In some instances, the perpetrators have invoked the president-elect in support of their heinous actions." Within the resolution, the council affirms the concept of free speech, stating, "No viewpoint or message may be deemed so hateful or disturbing that it may not be expressed. But threats and harassment differ from expressions of ideas that some or even most may find repulsive. They intimidate and silence."

Two social psychologists at the University of Kansas conducted a study on prejudice that involved surveying an even split of four hundred Trump and Clinton supporters. The scientists noted that "Trump's campaign over the preceding 18 months featured a procession of racist and ethnocentric rhetoric, with repeated insults, gross generalizations, and other derogatory speech hurled at Mexicans, Muslims, and women." So they asked one hundred of the Trump and one hundred of the Clinton supporters to rate their personal feelings toward a variety of social groups that the Trump campaign had disparaged at one time or another over the course of the race: Muslims, immigrants, Mexicans, fat people, and people with disabilities. All study participants were also polled on groups that Trump had not publicly maligned: alcoholics, adult film stars, rich people, members of the National Rifle Association, and Canadians. When the participants were surveyed again after the election, Crandall and White found that "Both personal and general prejudices remained unchanged for both sets of supporters with regard to the groups that Trump had not publicly targeted. But for the groups that Trump *had* disparaged, both Trump and Clinton supporters reported slightly lower levels of personal animus, and significantly higher levels of perceived acceptance for discriminatory speech. . . . In short: The perceived norm had shifted." Research suggests that individual expressions of prejudice and potential violence depend highly on perceived social norms; Trump surely had the effect of changing those norms (Crandall and White 2016).

Sometimes overlooked is the extent to which this president's mental health issues are harming our children. His impact is pervasive enough to have earned a label: "the Trump Effect." It has been used specifically to describe the trauma American children are experiencing because of Trump's candidacy and now presidency. "We have a bully in our midst, some therapists and school counselors say, traumatizing the most vulnerable of us. That bully is the 2016 presidential campaign, including the so-called 'Trump Effect.'" SPLC Teaching Tolerance director Maureen Costello has said, "I'm concerned children are coming to school every day terrified, anxious, disappointed, fearful. Feeling unwanted" (LaMotte 2016).

As the issue of Trump's mental illness was not of intense national concern until he ran for office and assumed the presidency, assessment by individuals with intimate understanding of what that job entails are useful for analyzing his dangerousness. It is instructive to remove the variable of political ideology from our determination and narrow our review to the perspective of Republicans only. In August 2016, a letter signed by fifty such individuals was published in the *New York Times*. While some of their concern centers on lack of experience, a portion of the letter made more direct reference to Trump's mental and emotional stability: "The undersigned individuals have all served in senior national security and/or foreign policy positions in Republican Administrations, from Richard Nixon to George W. Bush. We have worked directly on national security issues with these Republican Presidents and/or their principal advisers during wartime and other periods of crisis, through successes and failures. We know the personal qualities required of a President of the United States. None of us will vote for Donald Trump. From a foreign policy perspective, Donald Trump is not qualified to be President and Commander-in-Chief. Indeed, we are convinced that he would be a dangerous President and would put at risk our country's national security and well-being." A president, they continue, ". . . must be willing to listen to his advisers and department heads; must encourage consideration of conflicting views; and must acknowledge errors and learn from them . . . must be disciplined, control emotions, and act only after reflection and careful deliberation . . . must maintain cordial relationships with leaders of countries of different backgrounds and must have their respect and trust," and must be able and willing "to separate truth from falsehood" in order to aspire to be president and commander in chief, with command of the U.S. nuclear arsenal. They conclude: "We are convinced that in the Oval Office, he would be the most reckless President in American history."

Hillary Clinton's remark "A man you can bait with a tweet is not a man we can trust with nuclear weapons" was not just campaign hyperbole (Broad and Sanger 2016). The president of the United States has approximately 2,000 deployed nuclear warheads at his or her disposal and has the authority to order these weapons to be launched even if our country has not yet been attacked. Weapons fired against the United States from a submarine would take about twelve minutes to hit Washington, D.C. Missiles fired from most continents would reach this country in around thirty minutes. The nightmare scenario of this unstable, impulsive, blame-shifting, and revenge-obsessed individual having mere minutes to make the kind of decision required in such a scenario is of the gravest concern possible in our era.

In an interview on Fox News, then–Vice President Dick Cheney stated, "He [the president] could launch a kind of devastating attack the world's never seen. He doesn't have to check with anybody. He doesn't have to call the Congress. He doesn't have to check with the courts. He has that authority because of the nature of the world we live in" (Rosenbaum 2011). The entire focus in the missile launch decision process is on whether the launch command is authentic, not whether it is reasonable. Ron Rosenbaum describes the case of Maj. Harold Hering, who, during the period when Nixon was displaying erratic behavior, was troubled by a question he was not allowed to ask. "Maj. Hering decided to ask his question anyway, regardless of consequences: How could he know that an order to launch his missiles was 'lawful'? That it came from a sane president, one who wasn't 'imbalance[d]' or 'berserk?' as Maj. Hering's lawyer eventually, colorfully put it." Hering was a career military officer and asked the question while attending a missile training class. He was discharged from the air force for asking it. To this day, Harold Hering's question remains unanswered.

If we who have come together to write this book are accurate in our assessments, one must ask why Donald J. Trump's dangerousness was not addressed earlier in his life? The extensive public record on him shows that he has been insulated by inherited wealth and that his father had similar mental health disturbances. As we are all witnessing now, with his politically inexperienced daughter and son-in-law taking key advisory positions at the White House, Trump has distanced himself from possible checks and balances while enabling his own disorder: a lack of insight and confirmation-seeking that make certain mental disorders particularly dangerous in a position of power.

A substantive change in the level of his dangerousness came with his assumption of the role of leader of the free world. Although an argument can be made that, by taking this office, he has shaken the global political structure to the extent that the U.S. presidency is rapidly losing that standing. His narcissistic traits (manifesting in blatant lying, impulsive and compulsive decision making against rational interests, and immature relational abilities) are creating a leadership gap that other political actors may well seek to fill. Yet, it is impossible for him, through the lens of his mental dysfunction, to evaluate his actual presentation and impact.

As the ultimate representative of our nation, Donald J. Trump is normalizing previously outrageous behaviors, negatively impacting everyone from leaders of other nations to our own children. From the outset of his presidency, although clearly absent a mandate from the population he now governs, he has repeatedly declared himself "the greatest," or "tremendous," or "knowing more than anyone," and other statements consistent with narcissistic personality disorder, with regard to an "expectation of being viewed as superior without commensurate achievements" (American Psychiatric Association 2013, p. 669). He exhibits extreme denial of any feedback that does not affirm his self-image and psychopathic tendencies, which affords him very limited ability to learn and effectively adjust to the requirements of the office of president. Rather, he consistently displays a revenge-oriented response to any such feedback. Holding this office at once feeds his grandiosity and claws at the fragile sense of self underneath it. His patterns of behavior while in the role of president of the United States have potentially dire impact on every individual living not only in this nation but across the entire globe. The earth itself is in peril, both from the urgent issues that are not being addressed while an unstable man sits in the Oval Office and by the new urgencies he creates. Mr. Trump is and has demonstrated himself to be a danger to others—not just one person or a few, but possibly to *all* others.

Diane Jhueck, L.M.H.C., D.M.H.P., has operated a private therapy practice for several decades. In addition, she performs mental health evaluations and detentions on individuals presenting as a danger to self or others. In a previous social justice career, she was a women's specialist at the United Nations, in New York City. She founded the Women's and Children's Free Restaurant, an empowerment project that has been in operation for thirty years. She also founded the People's AIDS Project and was an assistant regional manager for Feeding America. She has directed agencies addressing food aid, domestic violence, apartheid, low-income housing, and LGBTQ rights.

Acknowledgments

I thank Bandy Lee, M.D., for her exceptional assistance in the preparation of this chapter.

References

American Association of University Professors (AAUP). 2016. "The Atmosphere on Campus in the Wake of the Elections." AAUP.org, November 22. www.aaup.org/news/atmosphere-campus-wake-elections#.WP-oOMa1tPb.

American Psychiatric Association. 2013. *Diagnostic and Statistical Manual of Mental Disorders*. 5th ed. Arlington, VA: American Psychiatric Association, pp. 659–60, 669.

Blistein, Jon. 2016. "Donald Trump Hints at Hillary Clinton Assassination." *Rolling Stone*, August 9. www.rollingstone.com/politics/news/donald-trump-hints-at-hillary-clinton-assassination-w433591.

Brinlee, Morgan. 2017. "27 Real Things Trump Has Actually Said Since Becoming President." Bustle, February 13. www.bustle.com/p/27-real-things-trump-has-actually-said-since-becoming-president-37189/amp.

Broad, William J., and David E. Sanger. 2016. "Debate Over Trump's Fitness Raises Issue of Checks on Nuclear Power." *New York Times*, August 4. www.nytimes.com/2016/08/05/science/donald-trump-nuclear-codes.html.

Cohen, Claire. 2016. "Donald Trump Sexism Tracker: Every Offensive Comment in One Place." *The Telegraph*, June 4. www.telegraph.co.uk/women/politics/donald-trump-sexism-tracker-every-offensive-comment-in-one-place/.

Crandall, Chris S., and Mark H. White II. 2016. "Donald Trump and the

Social Psychology of Prejudice." *Undark,* November 17. https://undark
.org/article/trump-social-psychology-prejudice-unleashed/.

Davidson, J. R., K. M. Connor, and M. Swartz. 2006. "Mental Illness in U.S.
Presidents Between 1776 and 1974: A Review of Biographical Sources."
The Journal of Nervous and Mental Disease, January 194 (1): 47–51. http://
journals.lww.com/jonmd/Abstract/2006/01000/Mental_Illness_In_U
_S__Presidents_Between_1776_and.9.aspx.

Diamond, Jeremy, and Stephen Collinson. 2016. "Trump: Gun Advocates
Could Deal with Clinton." CNN, August 10. www.cnn.com/2016/08/09
/politics/donald-trump-hillary-clinton-second-amendment/.

"Donald Trump Nearly Casually Remarks About Incest with Daughter
Ivanka." 2006. *The View.* Season 9. Episode 119. March 6. www.youtube
.com/watch?v=DP7yf8-Lk80.

Elledge, John. 2017. "Here Are 23 Terrifying Things That President Trump
Has Done in the Last Seven Days." January 26. www.newstatesman
.com/world/2017/01/here-are-23-terrifying-things-president-trump
-has-done-last-seven-days?amp.

Fahrenthold, David A. 2016. "Trump Recorded Having Extremely Lewd
Conversation About Women in 2005." *Washington Post,* October 8.
www.washingtonpost.com/politics/trump-recorded-having-extremely
-lewd-conversation-about-women-in-2005/2016/10/07/3b9ce776-8cb4
-11e6-bf8a-3d26847eeed4_story.html?utm_term=.8e1252766ffe.

Feyerick, Diane. 2016. "Donald Trump's Uncomfortable Comments About
His Daughter Ivanka." CNNuTube, October 12. Accessed April 9, 2017.
https://youtu.be/GcnBuE3ExWo.

Finnegan, Michael. "'It's Going to Be a Big, Fat, Beautiful Wall!': Trump's
Words Make His California Climb an Even Steeper Trek." *Los Angeles
Times,* June 3, 2016. Accessed April 11, 2017. www.latimes.com/politics
/la-na-pol-trump-california-campaign-20160602-snap-story.html.

Friedman, Megan, Michael Sebastian, and Emma Dibdin. "11 of the
Craziest Things President Trump Said at His Latest Rollercoaster of a
Press Conference." *Cosmopolitan,* February 16, 2017. www.cosmopolitan
.com/politics/amp8943522/trump-press-conference-crazy-moments/.

Gamboa, Suzanne. "Donald Trump Announces Presidential Bid by Trashing Mexico, Mexicans." NBCNews.com. NBCUniversal News Group, June 16, 2015. Accessed April 11, 2017. www.nbcnews.com/news/latino /donald-trump-announces-presidential-bid-trashing-mexico-mexicans -n376521.

González-Rojas, Jessica. "Trump's First 100 Days: A Blueprint to Hurt People of Color." *Rewire*, April 24, 2017. Accessed April 27, 2017. https:// rewire.news/article/2017/04/24/trumps-first-100-days-blueprint-hurt -people-color/.

Graham, David A. "Which Republicans Oppose Donald Trump? A Cheat Sheet." *The Atlantic*, November 06, 2016. Accessed April 7, 2017. www .theatlantic.com/politics/archive/2016/11/where-republicans-stand-on -donald-trump-a-cheat-sheet/481449/.

Grinberg, Emanuella. "What a Trump Presidency Could Mean for LGBT Americans." CNN, November 11, 2016. Accessed April 11, 2017. https:// amp.cnn.com/cnn/2016/11/11/politics/trump-victory-lgbt-concerns /index.html.

Guha, Auditi. "Campuses Wrestle with Wave of Hate-Based Incidents Since Election." *Rewire*, April 24, 2017. Accessed April 27, 2017. https://rewire .news/article/2017/04/24/campuses-wrestle-wave-hate-based -incidents-since-election/.

Hart, S.D., D. N. Cox, and R. D. Hare. *Manual for the Psychopathy Checklist: Screening Version* (PCL:SV). 1995. Toronto, ON: Multi-Health Systems.

Kaczynski, Andrew. "Donald Trump to Howard Stern: It's Okay to Call My Daughter a 'Piece of Ass.'" CNN, October 9, 2016. Accessed April 9, 2017. www.cnn.com/2016/10/08/politics/trump-on-howard-stern/.

King, Shaun. " Donald Trump Is a Pervert." New York *Daily News*, June 22, 2016. www.nydailynews.com/news/politics/king-donald-trump -pervert-article-1.2683705.

LaMotte, Sandee. "Is the 'Trump Effect' Damaging Our Psyches?" CNN, October 14, 2016. Accessed April 7, 2017. www.cnn.com/2016/10/14 /health/trump-effect-damaging-american-psyche/.

"A Letter from G.O.P. National Security Officials Opposing Donald Trump." 2006. *New York Times*, August 8. www.nytimes.com/interactive/2016/08 /08/us/politics/national-security-letter-trump.html.

Monahan, J. The MacArthur Violence Risk Assessment: Executive Summary. 2001. Accessed April 6, 2017. www.macarthur.virginia.edu/risk.html.

Murkowski, Lisa. "Full Statements on Donald Trump from Alaska Sens. Lisa Murkowski and Dan Sullivan." *Alaska Dispatch News*, December 12, 2016. Accessed April 7, 2017. www.adn.com/politics/2016/10/08/full-statements-from-sens-lisa-murkowski-and-dan-sullivan-on-donald-trump/.

Pressman, Jeremy, and Erica Chenowith. "Crowd Estimates, 1.21.2017." Google, January 26, 2017. Accessed April 11, 2017. University of Connecticut and University of Denver. https://docs.google.com/spreadsheets/d/1xa0iLqYKz8x9Yc_rfhtmSOJQ2EGgeUVjvV4A8LsIaxY/htmlview?sle=true.

Rosenbaum, Ron. "How Cold War Maj. Harold Hering Asked a Forbidden Question That Cost Him His Career." *Slate Magazine,* February 28, 2011. Accessed April 11, 2017. www.slate.com/articles/life/the_spectator/2011/02/an_unsung_hero_of_the_nuclear_age.html.

Solotaroff, Paul. "Trump Seriously: On the Trail with the GOP's Tough Guy." *Rolling Stone*, September 9, 2015. Accessed April 9, 2017. www.rollingstone.com/politics/news/trump-seriously-20150909.

HEALTH, RISK, AND THE DUTY TO PROTECT THE COMMUNITY

HOWARD H. COVITZ, PH.D., A.B.P.P.

Don't go loose-lipped among your people (but)
Don't stand idly by either as your neighbor bleeds;
I am God.

Leviticus 19:16*

This collected volume of essays is about the investigation of a tension between two goods, a balancing act that is at least as old as the Bible. Leviticus (see epigraph) argues for a version of confidentiality that is almost unlimited: "Don't go loose-lipped among your people." Indeed, the psalmist would specify further:

Who is the man who desires life. . . .
Guard your tongue against speaking ill and
your lips against uttering gossip. (Psalms 34:12)

---

* My own translation from the Hebrew. A literal take on this passage might be "Go not rumoring among your people; Stand not on the blood of your neighbor: I am God."

Looking back to the Leviticus text, we see that an exception is immediately rendered, as there would be times when speaking up was necessary to protect another from harm. In traditional cantillation, the halfway melody mark of the sentence (*esnachtah*) is immediately before "I am God." The intent of the ancient writer seems to be: Oh, yes, there is a tension between Confidentiality and the Duty to Warn and recognizing this tension holds the essence of Godliness . . . or Goodness, as we might say today. And after two to three millennia, the mental health community is just beginning to recognize this dialectic. This, indeed, is *the* dialogue that developed within the community of practitioners during and after the 2016 U.S. presidential election. This tension is known as the one between the Goldwater rule, which protects a limited privacy for public figures, and the duty to warn those who may be at risk of serious harm from the very same public figures.

At least three complexities stand in the way of offering up a simple solution: Are mental health professionals duty-bound to speak their truth about a presidential candidate's fitness for duty, or should they, rather, be constrained by professional ethics from doing so? What are the measurements by which we evaluate the first? What are the injuries of its absence? Is it a matter of a personal decision, or a decision by the community in which one lives?

The second difficulty has to do with the following: When we investigate the wellness of an individual, are we focused on his freedom from disabling characteristics that compromise his own life or, rather, do we concern ourselves with whether he is a danger to himself or others? Finally, we will briefly turn to how we evaluate risk, whether publicly shared or not.

Two Types of Mental Illness

More than eighty years ago, in a polemic against religion and politically based theories, Freud asked, "Does psychoanalysis lead toward a particular *Weltanschauung*?" (Freud, Sprott, and Strachey, 1933,

p. 158). Answering this question in the negative, Freud chose empirical science over what he considered to be illusion and emotion. His new psychotherapies would, if Freud had his way, rely on no assumptions whatever about the good life, but solely on scientific methodology and clear-minded examination of the observable. While this may seem perfectly reasonable, let me point out that the sciences—as is the case with the purest of them all, mathematics—depend not only on the correctness of the investigators' logical moves but also on the postulates or axioms we begin with.

Let me, then, state my own position: While in the natural sciences, it is assumed that researches and classification systems are generally independent of values, in the psychological and social sciences, such theoretical neatness is a luxury. Psychological theories of health are inextricably intertwined with the views of a healthy polity, with the need to protect the community, and with a vision of the good life. When we apply knowledge from one group to another, we speak of an error of *cultural bias*. Even science cannot be thoroughly free of assumptions and values.

Whatever paradigms one selects for describing mental health and mental illness, there will be questions of how the individual processes feelings, thoughts, and actions. Consider, for instance, anxiety. Humankind has developed anxiety as an adaptive signal to the body to prepare for danger—danger from another person or from a feral predator. However, if the anxiety expresses itself in eating disorders or digestive failure or in facial tics, we see it as maladaptive. Similar constructions can be offered for other responses, such as depression, anger, guilt, and shame.

On the other side is the arguable value in examining mental structures that foster civilized behavior and a capacity for nondestructive membership in *polities of mutual concern*. These, too, are adaptive and promote wellness both in the individual and in groups. These two perspectives are joined in a three-part definition of emotional health. The healthy person has:

- the capacity to recognize his own wishes and impulses and those of others with clarity;
- the ability to determine whether the actions that express these impulses are likely to cause avoidable damage to himself or others, and when such actions or speech are deemed safe; and
- the agency necessary to act upon those impulses without intrusive anger, anxiety, depression, guilt, prohibition, or shame.

Those who either are incapable of or disinterested in measuring the impact they may have on another or on others may well appear symptom-free, functional, and at times even quite successful in their work lives, but they are typically not so in their relationships. In very general terms, those who suffered internally were thought to be living with *symptomatic disturbances*, while the latter group was described as having character pathology, or *personality disorders*.

Here, too, our discussion gets more than a little messy. As noted earlier, what constitutes healthy interpersonal relationships varies from culture to culture; perhaps a recognition of this messiness contributed to the unwillingness of some mental health professionals to define what is meant by a healthy individual or a well community. And here, too, we cannot escape making certain postulates about the good life.

Freud focused on the puzzling development of conscience. He reasoned that the child begins life with a sense that all are present to serve him. A youngster eventually recognizes that others exist but not initially that they are complex beings with their own thoughts and relationships. Freud discovered that the child's life changes dramatically when he realizes that others are *subjects*, just as he is: *subjects in their own right* (Covitz 2016). Until that time, the child understands others more or less only in their capacities to satisfy his needs: as either good or bad, as satisfying his demands or not. When the child accepts the complexity of family relationships and is able to understand that Mom and Dad have an independent relationship, he has begun to embrace them as subjects (i.e., as doers) with their own thoughts, feelings, and relationships. He has, Freud would say, developed a conscience (an *uber-Ich*, or a "Guiding I"). Those who fail to accept others as *subjects in their own right* comprise the personality-disordered subgroup of humanity.

Let me be a little more specific as to the typical characteristics seen in personality-disordered individuals.

1. Such people are generally incapable of understanding and responding in an emotionally empathic way to how another feels. They may well, in an intellectual way, be able to know how others react or even what they might be thinking, but this has little bearing on how they treat others, who remain objects to them, like pieces on a chessboard to be moved about in order to win the game.

2. This black-and-white thinking effectively splits the world into friend or foe, into those who support him and all those others who are against him. Such a person may, indeed, grow to be incapable of bigotry—for, to be bigoted or racist or sexist, one must feel allegiance to a group. Still and all, they may have no qualms about using bigotries for their own purposes.

3. Lacking the need to evaluate how their actions may impact others, these people react more quickly, and with less skepticism about the correctness of their actions.

4. Such individuals have not yet developed respect for others' thinking, relationships, or efforts, which leads them to put little value in the accomplishments of others. As such, they tend not to recognize the necessity for maintaining extant organizations, government

structures, conventional practices, and laws. They may appear civilized but are not safely socialized.

5. Due to the aforementioned (points 1–4), their thinking is focused but lacks nuance. They demonstrate no apparent ability to see more than one not-unreasonable view: a monomania of sorts. These views, additionally, can flip to their opposite, since what makes any new attitude acceptable to them is under the control of a "my will be done" syndrome, no matter what that will is.

6. Finally (following on 1–5), they display a limited capacity to distinguish the real from the wished for or imagined, and demonstrate a ready willingness to distort the truth.

Two Fables

There are two distinct general types of emotional illness: those that precipitate symptoms in the individual and those that represent a risk to relationships and the communities in which the person lives. This leads directly into our second concern: Is the mental health of a powerful leader to be measured by the person's relationship to oneself or by one's ability to be safe and constructive in a *polity of mutual concern*?

I'll ask the reader to imagine two fables and some thought experiments.

Fable 1. The Policeman

I was driving down Old York Road in my police cruiser when I saw this driver, a funny-looking kind of old guy. He was driving his brand-new Bentley, so I assumed he was pretty safe, even though he was weaving just a little haphazardly. Y'know, a little erratic. He had his window open and was calling some immigrant-looking pedestrians pretty angry names. I pulled him over. He had a small arsenal of automatic weapons up front and what looked like an RPG launcher on the backseat. I asked him: "What's with all the weapons, sir?"

He says, "Officer, I've got a license and Montgomery County is Open Carry. I have every right to go where I want. Anyhow, it's a pretty dangerous world out there. You know, there are a lot of immigrants, and I think I saw Muslims dancing in Wall Park."

I go back to my cruiser and call the station house. "Sarge. Any report of dancing foreigners in the park?" Sarge asks me what I've been smoking; I understand his intent. So, I go back to the guy's car. "Sir, I cannot confirm any disturbance going on in Wall Park." "Officer, I saw it myself, and I should know because I have a lot of money." The man then goes on and on talking trash about people who are different, saying that everybody who disagrees with him is a liar and one of them might have killed a Kennedy and another one should be sent to the Women's Detention Center because she's the world's biggest crook. Then he tells me it's not raining and that it never rains when he's riding in his Bentley. Meanwhile, the water's pouring off my Stetson. He starts swearing about the township commissioners and accusing them of being stupid. In any case, I have choices, don't I? I think to myself, I could say any of the following:

1. "Sir. You be careful now, and have a blessed day."
2. "Sir. I just wanna say that your car is the tiger's roar. Be careful, now!"
3. "Sir. I think you might be batshit crazy, but I can't be sure, so, have a good day."
4. "Sir. Take me for a ride in your car, please, and gimme a good job, and we'll forget about all this silliness."

or

5. "Sir, would you step out of the car and we'll take a ride and see if we can't settle down those images in your head of Muslims dancing in the park? By the way: Were they barefoot?"

Fable 2. The Casual Customer and the Man in the Psychotherapist's Office

A person comes into my psychoanalytic office or, for that matter, sits down next to me at Starbucks carrying a small-caliber handgun. I ask the reader to imagine that, in listening to him, I recognize the six characteristics I've just described. In any case, imagine further that time is up on our meeting or that our coffee is finished. I've not administered any objective tests. The man shows no signs of anxiety; he has only expressed disdain for others, and assuredly no shame or guilt. He seems to be oriented in time and space. Still, I have a strong if tentative diagnostic impression that this man suffers from serious character disorders. What shall I do, and what is my ethical duty to do as a citizen, and/or as a citizen possessing special training?

But back to President Trump. I've gone back, in my mind, to Leviticus time after time since the election. It occurred to me more than once that the behaviors of candidate, President-elect, and now President Trump may have been—as is the case with the television persona Stephen Colbert presented for many years—an act.

As a psychologist and psychoanalyst with more than forty years of experience, I cannot say with certainty, for instance, whether Trump's sexist comments and claims of sexual acting out, his unempathic responses to the Khans (who'd lost their soldier son overseas) or to a handicapped man at his rally, or his calls for violence at those rallies were no more than performance art. Perhaps, in his heart of hearts, I thought, Mr. Trump has an empathic soul, does not split the world into with-him and against-him groups, and is a careful and nuanced thinker. Perhaps, even, Mr. Trump knows the difference between alternate reality and reality, and perhaps he simply uses alternate reality as a strategic ploy. I did consider this and concluded, nonetheless, that his actions still showed severe gaps. After all, and briefly, the damage to the Khans was done, the lies were believed by tens of millions of Trump's followers, violent rhetoric at his meetings produced real harm, and Mr. Trump has irresponsibly alienated (so far) five of our closest trading partners.

The Simple Arithmetic of Risk Management

Since the attack on the Twin Towers and the Pentagon of September 11, 2001, the leaders in the United States and other nation states have communicated to their citizens the need to be vigilant. George W. Bush advocated repeatedly our need to go on living our lives, walking about freely, and carrying out the tasks of living, working, and shopping that preceded the many terrorist attacks the world has come to know as, more or less, weekly events. In addition, however, President Bush and others have advocated that we all remain vigilant. We are told that if we see a suspect package on a bus or airplane or at the Boston Marathon, or if we notice a suitcase left alone at an airport, we should immediately leave the area, warn others, and contact the police. Schools have since developed zero-tolerance rules requiring that if a student is heard speaking of violence toward himself or others, he must immediately be removed from the school and not reinstated until an expert deems him safe to return.

Mathematicians use an intuitive construction that combines the probability of a negative outcome multiplied by the result of that negative outcome. For example, if the probability of losing a certain wager is 1 percent and would result in their losing $10, most people would feel comfortable taking that risk. The risk in mathematical terms? One percent x $10 or 10 cents. However, if the probability is the same and the loss would result in losing a $200,000 home, it's time to buy insurance! There, the risk is 1 percent x $200,000 or $2,000, which is more than the cost of an insurance policy to recoup such losses, making it, so to speak, a reasonable expenditure to buy the insurance. Having said that, I feel that our risk calculation involves considerably more than whether it is a reasonable expenditure to buy the insurance; the loss of a home for most people would be devastating.

Conclusion

Donald Trump has displayed, frequently, all six of the characteristics that I and many other mental health professionals associate with severe character pathology. I cannot say with certainty what diagnostic box, if any, he fits—not, indeed, before and without careful examination and testing, as those who support the Goldwater rule avow. Some of my colleagues, citing the duty to warn others of possibly imminent danger, are comfortable assigning Mr. Trump in this category or some other condition from the American Psychiatric Association's *Diagnostic and Statistical Manual* (DSM-V); I am not comfortable doing so. Still, I strongly agree with the likelihood that these fit the preponderance of people who behave as President Trump does. This doubt is equally present when I'm reporting to the appropriate social service agency my sense that there is a likelihood that a certain child is being molested or that one of my patients may be planning to shoot his wife's lover. I needn't be certain if the outcome is potentially dire. When the outcome is possibly devastating, even if the probability that it will occur is relatively small, the clinician and perhaps every citizen is *duty-bound to warn.*

In becoming president and commander in chief of the most powerful armed forces on earth, Trump is armed to the teeth and has openly spoken about the wonder he experiences, though we simultaneously maintain this nuclear firepower, that we have a reluctance to use it. He displays all the signs of a seriously personality-disordered person and has repeatedly spoken of using violence. And the outcome? The outcome, if he is indeed as ill as some sizable portion of the mental health professional community suspects, could well be potentially devastating to a significant percentage of humanity.

Back to me: I believe that my ethical duty to warn is unquestionable, as is my ethical responsibility to work within the confines of the law to have Mr. Trump psychologically and psychiatrically examined—or, in the absence of his willingness to do so, to have him removed from office.

Indeed, I am in good company. The policeman who meets a driver armed and talking crazy is ethically bound to disarm that driver. The shopper or passenger on a city bus or marathon route who sees an unattended package lying about is responsible for taking action. The coffee-drinking Starbucks customer, as well as the psychotherapist in her office, who is confronted by a gun-toting, crazy-talking person has the citizen's responsibility either to disarm that person or to arrange to have it done. How much less can I or any other mental health professional be ethically bound by a duty to warn and by the biblical proscription not to stand idly by as others are placed in potential danger (Leviticus 19:16)? This assuredly applies to a possibly unfit-to-serve president who is in possession of the U.S. nuclear codes.

Howard H. Covitz, Ph.D., A.B.P.P., has combined the practice of psychoanalysis in the suburbs of Philadelphia with a variety of other interests. He has taught university-level mathematics, psychology, and biblical characterology (1968–2011), was a training analyst at the Institute for Psychoanalytic Studies and the Institute for Psychoanalytic Psychotherapies, and its director (1986–98). He also ran a school for disturbed inner-city adolescents in the 1970s. His Oedipal Paradigms in Collision *(1998, reissued in 2016) was nominated for the Gradiva Book of the Year Award. His connectedness to his wife, grown children, and grandchildren motivates his writing and thinking.*

References

American Psychiatric Association. 2013. *Diagnostic and Statistical Manual of Mental Disorders*. 5th ed. Arlington, VA: American Psychiatric Association.

Covitz, Howard. 2016. *Oedipal Paradigms in Collision: A Centennial Emendation of a Piece of Freudian Canon (1897–1997)*. 1988. Repr. New York: Object Relations Institute Press.

Freud, Sigmund, Walter John Herbert Sprott, and James Strachey. 1933. *New Introductory Lectures on Psycho-Analysis.* Vol. 22. New York: Norton.

Freud, Sigmund. 1955. *The Standard Edition of the Complete Psychological Works of Sigmund Freud*, vol. 24. London: Hogarth.

NEW OPPORTUNITIES FOR THERAPY IN THE AGE OF TRUMP*

WILLIAM J. DOHERTY, PH.D.

The boundary between the personal and public has ruptured in the age of Trump. A fixed, hard boundary was of course a fiction—we are always influenced by what's going on in society, and our personal actions affect the whole. Yet, before Trump, we therapists who felt comfortable in the mainstream of a democratic society could assume that our therapist "hat" and our citizen "hat" were separate. In our therapist role, we told ourselves, we were professional healers; as citizens, we followed public issues, supported candidates, and cast votes. The main crossover was our advocacy for better mental health policies and reimbursement.

Feminist, ethnic minority, and LGBT therapists have argued for decades against this personal/political split in the therapy world—witness the big literature on therapy and social justice. But that perspective was relegated to the sidelines of the therapy world, confined to situations in which the clients were part of an oppressed minority. For the most part, psychotherapy marched along with its traditional

* Portions of this essay were adapted with permission from his article "Therapy in the Age of Trump," in *The Psychotherapy Networker* (May–June 2017): 34–35.

focus on the intrapsychic and interpersonal realms—in part, I think, because many of us assumed that we and our clients had personal lives adequately buffered from public turmoil and stress. Yes, occasionally an event such as 9/11 burst that bubble, but it soon re-formed.

After the election of Donald Trump in November 2016, however, the bubble did not return. Many of our clients across social classes and racial groups are distressed by what's happening to the country and are living with current anxiety, worries for the future, and the reactivation of past fears. This is occurring both for people immediately at risk, such as immigrants, and for those less personally vulnerable who are watching the rise of hate, the disregard for the truth, and the flouting of core democratic values such as a free press and respect for the rule of law. What's more, we have a president whose public behavior represents the triumph of the antitherapeutic—a lionizing of the unexamined life where personal insecurities are boldly projected onto the world and where self-serving beliefs become public facts.

In the face of these challenges, a number of professions are facing a paradigm crisis: How do they go forward with business as usual when the democratic foundations of their work are being threatened? As an example, consider the soul-searching among journalists now: they are having to call out systematic lying, not just reporting the shading of the truth or one take on the facts versus another.

For psychotherapists, the challenge is to integrate our roles as therapists and citizens so that we can help our clients do the same. This has to begin with the "self of the therapist"—how do our personal lives intersect with our professional practice? Nearly every therapist I know is feeling personal stress and is dealing with clients whose reactions range from reliving experiences of being bullied to fears of deportation to a sense that the arc of the moral universe no longer seems to bend inevitably toward justice. We're seeing families and friendships fracture along political lines. I do know some therapists who are glad that Trump ascended to the presidency, but they, too, are concerned with the polarization in the country and the tearing of the social fabric.

This is bigger than Trump and the November 2016 election. It's the culmination of at least two decades of increasing divisiveness in our culture and in politics, where those who differ are seen as dangerous enemies, not just misguided opponents. So how do we respond as therapists and citizens to the impact of Trump in the context of these broader trends? How do we handle our personal reactivity to these events? The starting point is to acknowledge that we need new ways to think about ourselves and our clients as members of the broader public (i.e., citizens), and not just as providers and consumers of services.

Expanding the Frame of Psychotherapy in the Age of Trump and Beyond

Clearly, we have to help our clients deal with the Trump Effect in their lives. Yet, the challenges are bigger, just as Trump represents larger trends. If our approach to therapy is to go beyond helping clients deal with the impact of this one president, we need new conceptual categories for what we address in our work. I'd like to introduce two: public stress and political stress. I define them in this way:

- *Public stress* refers to challenges for personal and relational well-being stemming from forces in neighborhood, the community, and local institutions (such as schools and the police), as well as forces in the larger political, economic, cultural, and historical environment.

- *Political stress* (a type of public stress) refers to how the words, actions, and policies of government bodies, elected officials, and candidates for public office create challenges for personal and relational well-being.

Using the language of public and political stress allows therapists to expand beyond our traditional intrapsychic and microsocial frames while still paying attention to the personal: how our clients are thinking, feeling, and acting in the face of stress.

This broader thinking about our clients' lives can be reflected in the questions we ask at intake. Every profession communicates its area of interest in its intake forms. For example, medicine is dominated by biological disease–based questions. Mental health professionals ask mainly about psychological symptoms and interpersonal functioning. I've developed two intake questions to signal my interest in the public lives of my clients. The first asks about public stress and the second about clients' engagement in their world.

1. Sometimes people in counseling feel stress from events and forces in their community, the nation, or the world. If that's true for you, I encourage you to briefly let me know. (Otherwise, just skip this section.) Here's what is causing me stress:_____.

2. Sometimes people in counseling have commitments to groups or causes outside their family and close social world. If that's true for you, could you briefly write down what those commitments are for you? (Otherwise, just leave this section blank).

I've found that these intake questions provide door openers to conversations about the public realm in clients' lives—both how they are affected and how they engage as citizens. And then there are other door openers at the outset of sessions. One is to inquire whether clients are following what's going on in the political world right now, and if so, how it's affecting them. The result is that many clients open up about Trump-related anxieties and relationship strains they hadn't previously shared, probably because they had thought the therapy room was supposed to be a politics-free zone—as we ourselves may have believed.

Another way to signal openness to discussing public/political stress is an open letter placed in the waiting room. Here's an example of such a letter:

Dear Clients,
We're living in troubled times. I feel it, and most people I know feel it. I'm
writing this note to let you know that I'm open to talking about some-
thing not always brought up in therapy: how what's going on in the pub-
lic and political world is affecting you and your relationships, and how
you're coping.

- *After a divisive presidential election, a lot of people are upset and*
  feeling discouraged by the political infighting in this country.
- *There's great uncertainty about what the upcoming years will*
  look like. Some people are feeling alarmed, insecure, and threat-
  ened, while others feel hopeful that necessary change will happen.
  And those two kinds of people are often at odds with one another.
- *I see both liberal and conservative members of our community*
  feeling as if their values are no longer acceptable in the public
  arena—or to some of their friends and family.

The list could go on. For now, consider yourself invited to bring
your concerns about the public world into our conversations in therapy. No expectation or requirement that you do so, of course—just if
you think it might be helpful.

I'm here to listen, support you, and help you figure out how to
manage today's stresses while living a life that's in keeping with your
personal and community values.

Once clients open up, we can help them cope with political stress
just as we do any other kind of stress: through buffering methods
such as reducing exposure to the 24/7 news cycle, refusing to be
baited by people who just want to goad them, and self-care efforts.
The other kind of coping, active coping, is about helping clients enact
their civic values in the world via action steps such as getting better
informed through reputable sources, donating to causes they support, volunteering to help others, getting politically active, or (as one
client decided) being kinder in public to society's "others." And
when clients are having powerful, dysregulated emotional responses

to the political situation, we can help them unpack how it connects to their personal journeys.

I see our job as helping clients avoid the twin dangers of being either numb/reactive or agitated/reactive in the face of political stress. The middle is where we're aiming, for ourselves and our clients: being grounded/responsive, where we're in touch with our feelings and can act thoughtfully according to our values. Therapy like this can be an incubator for an empowered citizenry in a democracy in which we're neither victims nor flamethrowers.

The Citizen Therapist in the Larger World

Donald Trump has done me the favor of helping me better see the connection between psychotherapy and democracy. In fact, there is a close connection between the personal agency focus of psychotherapy and the work of democracy understood not just as an electoral system but as a collective agency for building a shared life in community: We the (responsible) People. In our offices, we promote the kind of personal agency that's necessary for a self-governing, democratic people, a people whose worlds are public as well as private. In other words, we are growing citizens of democracies. And therapy needs the larger system of democracy in order to thrive. (I've trained non-American therapists who went home to dictatorial systems that greatly inhibited what they could encourage their clients to say and do in their social world.)

Still, to truly fulfill the potential of our professional role in a democracy, we have to be active outside our offices. I feel passionately that we're healers with something important to offer our neighbors and communities. Here's a short definition of the concept of the citizen therapist: A citizen therapist works with people in the office and the community on coping productively with public stress and becoming active agents of their personal and civic lives. Citizen-therapist work is not separate from the traditional practice of psychological and interpersonal healing—it's integrated with it.

As an example of citizen-therapist work in today's toxic public environment, I've been doing depolarization workshops with "Red" and "Blue" Americans. One stands out in particular: thirteen hours over a December weekend in rural Ohio with eleven Hillary supporters and ten Trump supporters. The goal was to learn if people could better understand their differences (beyond stereotypes) to see if there were common values, and to share, if possible, something hopeful with their community and the larger world. For me, it was like couples' therapy with twenty-one people—intense, painful, illuminating, and ultimately gratifying. After a second, equally successful weekend in southern Ohio, a new action-for-depolarization group was formed of Red and Blue citizens, a chapter of a national organization called Better Angels. I've also developed a series of different kinds of workshops and trainings, offered through Better Angels, that therapists can learn to conduct in their local communities.

The age of Trump calls therapists beyond the personal/public split, a blind spot that has kept us from engaging in comprehensive care for people who bring to us their whole selves, private and public, intimate and civic. It's an invitation to expand and enrich the work we do for our clients and communities.

William J. Doherty, Ph.D., is a professor of family social science and director of the Minnesota Couples on the Brink project and the Citizen Professional Center at the University of Minnesota. In May 2016, he authored the Citizen Therapist Manifesto Against Trumpism, *which was signed by more than 3,800 therapists. After the election, he founded Citizen Therapists for Democracy (www.citizentherapists.com). He is a senior fellow with Better Angels, an organization devoted to depolarizing America at the grassroots level. He helped pioneer the area of medical family therapy, and in 2017 he received the American Family Therapy Academy Lifetime Achievement Award.*

PART 3

THE TRUMP EFFECT

TRAUMA, TIME, TRUTH, AND TRUMP

How a President Freezes Healing and Promotes Crisis

BETTY P. TENG, M.F.A., L.M.S.W.

In the days following the November 8, 2016, election of Donald Trump as president of the United States—the most powerful leadership position in the world—many individuals, particularly those targeted by Trump's rageful expressions of xenophobia, racism, sexism, and Islamophobia, experienced the event as traumatic, without quite knowing why. "I feel like I did after 9/11," said one colleague. "I am in shock," reported a patient. "I don't know what to think."

Throughout the next weeks, patients and colleagues alike told me that the very idea of a President Trump left them feeling exposed, vulnerable, and helpless. "I have four out of six identity markers Trump will target: Arab, gay, immigrant, and woman," commented one patient. "I don't feel safe walking around anymore." One woman who was conflicted about whether to report her rape decided she would not. "How could it matter anymore?" she asked. "No one would believe me now." Another survivor was more blunt: "We elected a rapist to the presidency," referring to the accusations of sexual assault (Crockett and Nelson 2017) that several women brought against him, to no consequence. A colleague who treated New Yorkers in the months following the 9/11 terrorist attacks on the World Trade

Center said the reactions he has seen in his patients to Trump's election and presidency are far worse. "The difference is, the attacks of 9/11 were finite and enacted by an outside source," he observed. "Trump was elected by those among us, and his aggression feels incessant and never ending."

These reactions were also my own. I, too, was in shock; sitting with patients, I struggled to focus. I was prone to spontaneous tears. When asked, I found it difficult to summon the words to explain my distress. I recognized these responses as symptoms of traumatic shock, the possible harbingers of PTSD—posttraumatic stress disorder—which is commonly experienced by traumatized patients.

I am a psychotherapist—specifically, a trauma therapist who treats at a major hospital in New York City adult survivors of sexual assault, domestic violence, and childhood sexual abuse. My job is to have some clinical understanding of trauma and how it impacts individuals and knowing how to treat its subjugating effects. Yet, I was baffled. How could a nonviolent event such as the peaceful election of a president generate a trauma response? Whatever one's political leanings, one could not equate Trump's win with an actual physical attack or a natural catastrophe.

Or could one?

The American Psychological Association defines *trauma* as "an emotional response to a terrible event like an accident, rape, or natural disaster." And for many people—especially, but not confined to, those in groups that Trump targeted during his campaign—his election and now his presidency are truly terrible, even disastrous, events.

Indeed, in the months since November, psychotherapists nationwide have reported an unprecedented focus on politics in their sessions, and a surge in new patients (Gold 2017) seeking help with the high anxiety and stress they feel in reaction to Trump's steady stream of extreme tweets and impulsive actions. Indeed, from the confusion and worry caused by his disastrous immigration travel ban; his irrational accusations that President Obama wiretapped Trump Tower;

and his sudden military actions against Syria and North Korea, President Trump appears more concerned with drawing attention to his power through creating crises rather than resolving them.

It is inevitable that such destabilizing behavior in one who holds the most powerful leadership position in the world will heighten anxiety and fear in not only the previously traumatized, but the untraumatized as well. Media pundits and clinicians have coined terms such as *post-election stress disorder* (Gold 2017), *post-Trump stress disorder* (Pierre 2016), and *headline stress disorder* (Stosny 2017) to draw parallels between the anxiety reactions suffered by increasing numbers of concerned Americans and the symptoms of PTSD. If what we read about is true—and I will return to this, as Trump and his top advisers have also shaken our notions of truth and fact—PTSD-like symptoms of insomnia, lack of focus, hypervigilance, irritability, and volatility now afflict not only combat veterans, first responders, and survivors of rape, violent crime, natural disaster, torture, and abuse, but many of the rest of us as well.

Again, as a trauma therapist, I puzzle over this correlation of symptoms in greater numbers of the general American populace to PTSD, where the source of trauma is not a physical attack or a natural catastrophe, but the incessant barrage of aggressive words and daily reports of the erratic conduct of a powerful, narcissistic, and attention-seeking world leader. There is much debate over whether post-Trump stress disorder is "real" or just another example of how "snowflake liberals," goaded on by a "hysterical" left-leaning media, overinflate their suffering. There are questions about whether this trivializes the suffering of "true" trauma survivors, who have experienced "real" attacks and harm.

From a clinical perspective, however, such debates at best distract and at worst shame us away from a more thorough consideration of the root causes of this unique phenomenon: how the election and actions of a president such as Donald Trump could cause a large swath of American citizens to feel traumatized or retraumatized. It is important to remember that Trump's ascendance to the White

House is unprecedented and incongruous. We are in uncharted territory. How a New York City real estate magnate and reality television celebrity who had no previous legal, legislative, government, or foreign policy experience could become president of the United States is a circumstance many still find difficult to comprehend. If we agree that the skills of a U.S. president are as crucial as that of a heart surgeon—whose professional judgment and expertise can mean life or death for his patients—then it is terrifying to see that the American body politic has, in Donald Trump, a cardiac surgeon who has never set foot inside an operating room. He is a doctor who has no knowledge of, and arguably no interest in, the inner workings of the American government's heart. It therefore makes sense that his lack of qualifications and his insensitivity to the complexities and impact of his role would inspire great anxiety, if not even panic, in those of us whose lives depend on his care—regardless of political affiliation or trauma history.

For those previously traumatized, however, Trump is even more triggering. Such individuals may experience his volatile, retaliatory, and unilateral behavior as mirroring that of the abusive parent, the wanton bully, the authoritarian teacher, or the sexually aggressive boss who subjugated them in the past. Because a trauma survivor's brain often exists in a heightened state of hyperarousal, Trump's daily outrages deliver unnecessary neurobiological overstimulation, narrowing a survivor's "window of tolerance," or cognitive space for calm, linear thinking. Such individuals are thus more likely to feel more anxious or even to fall out of their "window of tolerance" into panic attacks, flashbacks, and dissociation. And when we consider who is particularly vulnerable to such heightened anxiety, the numbers of Americans who hold one form of trauma or another are greater than we may think. According to Harvard trauma expert Dr. Bessel van der Kolk (2014):

Research by the Centers for Disease Control and Prevention
has shown that one in five Americans was sexually molested

as a child; one in four was beat by a parent to the point of a mark being left on their body; and one in three couples engages in physical violence. A quarter of us grew up with alcoholic relatives, and one out of eight witnessed their mother being beaten or hit.

When we consider how many Americans experience, personally or intergenerationally, the traumas of slavery, immigration, war, natural disaster, and genocide, we start to understand on another level how it is that Donald Trump, a wholly unqualified president who neglects history, highlights divisions, and makes impulsive decisions, would foment unrest in us all.

Trauma, Time, Truth, and Trump

Thus, President Trump is a destabilizing force that stirs some of us to the point where we experience him as a psycho-socio-political tornado. In fact, the debate over whether post-Trump stress disorder is "real," and if it is as serious as PTSD, is itself a kind of trauma response. Queries voiced among Americans in response to Trump's election and after his first one hundred days in office—"Is this real?"; "This is not serious, or is it?"; and "I don't know what happened, but I can't move on"—mirror those asked by many of my patients after they begin treatment. They grapple with experiences that are paradoxically too upsetting to consider and too overwhelming to deny. When a U.S. president inspires such internal confusion among the citizens he has been elected to serve, this bears serious consideration. Is Donald Trump causing a trauma epidemic?

From my perspective as a trauma therapist, I highlight two key components of trauma (time and truth) to illuminate how Trump impacts so many of us in a traumatogenic way. In so doing, I aim not only to validate the trauma responses many have had to this president, but also to point out how we can minimize Trump's effect on us. If we know how trauma is constructed, we can do something with its component parts to lessen its effect. In this way, we can prevent ourselves from becoming overwhelmed and immobilized by anger or anxiety in the face of Trump's erratic and vindictive behavior.

Time and Trauma

Media ecologist and cultural studies professor Jade E. Davis (2014) considers how online digital media reflects and shapes our perceptions of historical or current events. In her breakdown of the phenomenon, Davis states that "trauma can exist only in the post-tense," after survivors have been able to find words to describe the horrific event. This is to say, our ability to consider trauma is always contingent on time.

Davis's assertion that trauma is "located in the narrative and accessible through testimony and witnessing" reflects a cornerstone of our work in trauma therapy. A main objective of treatment is to provide the traumatized individual with a sense of safety so she can relate her story, trusting in the fact that her therapist has the tolerance and compassion to bear witness to the survivor's pain, fear, and shame. This relieves the deep isolation that plagues the traumatized. Van der Kolk (2014) agrees:

> This is one of the most profound experiences we can have, and such resonance, in which hitherto unspoken words can be discovered, uttered, and received, is fundamental to healing the isolation of trauma. Communicating fully is the opposite of being traumatized.

In trauma therapy as in daily life, "communicating fully," be it with oneself or another, takes skill, care, and time. Mental reflection relies on our having the space and time to take an experience in and to sift through its various parts, in order to engage in dialogue with oneself and others. This is how we orient ourselves to our experiences, our opinions, and our values; this is how we verify our realities. This is how we *think*.

When we are traumatized, our capacity to think and communicate can become so compromised that we need extra support. Neurobiologically, traumatic experiences silence the speech centers of the brain (van der Kolk 2014), rendering us literally speechless. When a survivor has no time or ability to find the words to tell her side of the story in a traumatic situation, Davis defines this as *crisis*. She describes crisis as a closed and sealed circle representing a situation inaccessible to time and witnessing—that is, a circumstance that lacks space for perspective, one that is subsequently isolated from exchange, change, and growth (Davis 2014).

The following diagram (Davis 2014) illustrates the difference between trauma and crisis:

SOCIETY AT LARGE

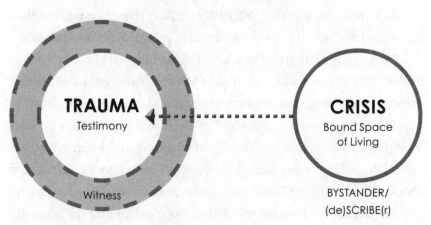

Illustration courtesy of Jade E. Davis

Trauma refers to a response to a disastrous event that exists in language and time. In Davis's illustration, it has a porous, dashed-line boundary because a traumatic narrative is a testimony that allows others to bear witness and enter the experience of the traumatized. It is open, not closed. By listening, a witness helps contain the trauma, as represented by the outer dashed-line circle. In the exchange between a traumatized patient and her witness, shifts in the traumatic narrative naturally occur, and growth results. This narrative eventually moves to a fully mourned space, freeing the patient from being controlled by heightened anxiety and triggers that prompt flashbacks and panic attacks.

By contrast, "Crises are histories that exist in closed circles . . . there are no testimonies and no witnesses . . . People in crisis become bounded, out of place and out of time" (Davis 2014). In Davis's diagram, crisis is illustrated by a sealed circle. It shows that within its nonporous boundary, events are cut off from time and language, and therefore inaccessible. Without the crucial perspective that time and language afford, a disastrous experience can neither be thought about nor shared, nor mourned. Possible witnesses can only be helpless bystanders, unable to hear or respond to those imprisoned within. Individuals in crisis remain stuck in place; there can be no growth or letting go. Their internal chaos remains the same because there are no words to make sense of it. Without language, there is only mindless action and reaction, a cycle driven by fear, panic, and dissociation.

This is the state that President Trump keeps us in. He does so by flooding media outlets, both old and new, with myriad vindictive tweets, defensive press conferences, and sudden firings. Context is key; if Trump were not president of the United States, his ravings would simply be those of an arrogant, unmindful, loudmouthed reality TV celebrity who compulsively seeks attention by cultivating shock and outrage on both ends of the political spectrum. The "no press is bad press" boorishness of his actions would find traction only on reality TV and in tabloid and gossip pages that, before the 2015–2016 election cycle, were the main sites trafficking in Trump's baldly self-promotional broadcasts. While it is beyond the scope of this essay to delve into the social, economic, political, and demographic circumstances that allowed Trump to morph from entertainment persona to leader of the free world, it is important to note aspects of our current technological climate, which combine with Trump's now-central role as U.S. president and his narcissistically compulsive personality, to keep the American public fixated on his toxic behavior and stuck in a state of chaotic, meaningless crisis.

Our ever-increasing use of the Internet demands that we process new information at the speed of the supercomputers that drive it. As Brown University digital media scholar Wendy Chun (2016) observes, "[T]here is an unrelenting stream of updates that demand response, from ever-updating Twitter.com feeds to exploding inboxes. The lack of time to respond, brought about by the inhumanly clocked time of our computers that renders the new old, coupled with the demand for response, makes the Internet compelling."

"I think, therefore I am," Descartes's Enlightenment-era definition of human existence, has become, in the twenty-first century, "I *post*, therefore I am." Compelling as this is, there is a falseness to this promise. This is marked by the exhaustion we experience when we spend too much time online. For the insomnia-stricken among my trauma patients, I recommend removal of screen time at least an hour before bedtime; Web-surfing scatters attention and overstimulates the brain. Moreover, backlit screens have been proven to block the brain's production of melatonin, a natural sleep-promoting hormone. For the traumatized, whose neurobiological systems are already in a state of hyperarousal, heightened anxiety and sleep disturbance narrow their "windows of tolerance." This makes finding calm even more challenging and hinders healing significantly.

We are not machines; feeding our quest for knowledge and defining our existences online delivers a synthetic fulfillment that is fleeting and unsustainable. Seeking such satisfaction via the Internet is like trying to quench thirst by sipping water from a fire hose. By drinking from the Internet's fire hose, we not only end up still thirsty, but we may get seriously hurt in the process. Because this onslaught of information disallows us from taking the time to truly consider any of it, we open ourselves to believing dangerous and unchecked falsehoods. Both Chun and Stanford University election law scholar Nathaniel Persily (2017) warn of the alarming political consequences of our collective inability to think or verify the truth of what is broadcast online. As Chun (2016) observes, "The Internet . . . has been formulated as the exact opposite of Barlow's dream (of an unregulated space for a free marketplace of ideas): a nationalist machine that spreads rumors and lies."

While Chun points to the Internet's potential for fostering the seeds of nationalist propaganda, Persily asks, "Can Democracy survive the Internet?" in the very title of his recent paper. By analyzing the 2016 digital campaign for U.S. president, he orients us to what today's Internet amplifies: social media retweets, false news shares, bot-driven articles, and troll-inspired critiques that reflect and stir reactivity rather than disseminate the truth: "What the Internet uniquely privileges above all else is the type of campaign message that appeals to outrage or otherwise grabs attention. The politics of never-ending spectacles cannot be healthy for a democracy. Nor can a porousness to outside influences that undercuts the sovereignty of a nation's elections. Democracy depends on both the ability and the will of voters to base their political judgments on facts."

Persily highlights the maladaptive match between Trump, a spectacle-driven reality TV persona, and our current technological age. The pairing of online media sites that rely on page views to maximize advertising dollars with Trump's factually thin but impossible-to-ignore shock effect ravings has resulted in his effortlessly infecting media outlets primed to spread his viral-ready broadcasts. His success at capitalizing on the mass market use and influence of social media is something that social and political scientists, digital media scholars, campaign experts, journalists, and government officials are scrambling to understand. As Persily observes, "For Trump, his assets included his fame, following, and skill in navigating the new media landscape. He also figured out that incendiary language could command media attention or shift the narrative. These combined strategies allowed him to garner roughly $2 billion worth of free media during the primaries, and probably a comparable amount during the general-election campaign."

Trump's immense talent for grabbing attention and turning it into material wealth and power, makes him, first and foremost, a master of marketing. What Chun and Persily point out is that in the Internet era, the filterless, open, and interactive nature of online media channels promotes the spread of rumors and spectacle because information traffics too quickly to favor the nuances and subtleties of truth. In a climate where the "new" becomes "old" (Chun 2016) in a matter of moments, where the mobile devices of dissemination are literally in our hands at all times, it is too easy and compelling to immediately spread what feels alarming or outrageous to our audiences of social media "friends," who are just a click away.

Trauma and Truth

Looking through the lens of trauma treatment, it is of particular concern that we find ourselves in a perfect storm where we have, as our U.S. president, a narcissist fixed on broadcasting his own unilateral and inconsistent versions of reality in a climate driven by Internet media channels that produce information so quickly that they privilege falsehoods over truth. It is a tenet of trauma therapy to validate our patients' truths—that is, their experiences of their subjugation. Without it, the work of healing cannot progress. Being believed and not having one's experience denied are crucial to anyone who has seen unspeakable horrors or who has been subjugated by another through torture, rape, or physical or sexual abuse. Such events turn one's world upside down, and a cornerstone of our work is to help a patient stabilize herself by affirming the truth of what her experience was. Only then can we build, with words, a narrative of the event so that the patient can make sense of and communicate to herself and others what happened. She is thus able to move out of her isolation and shame to recruit witnesses to help her bear such a painful burden. This allows the patient to move her experience from crisis, or wordless reactivity; to trauma, a narrative of pain; to history, a story about the past. With time to validate truths and make meaning out of chaos, a patient can reduce her panic attacks, flashbacks, and dissociation. Rather than being caught in a cycle of meaningless crisis, she can regain stability, increase her sense of calm, and move on with her life. Again, as trauma expert van der Kolk (2014) put it, "Communicating fully is the opposite of being traumatized."

Thus, it is traumatizing to have, in the White House, a president and an administration intent on confounding "full communication" by manipulating the truth to serve their own ends. As Columbia University psychoanalyst Joel Whitebook points out (2017), according to Trump and his team, there is only one reality—Donald Trump's:

> Armed with the weaponized resources of social media, Trump has radicalized this strategy in a way that aims to subvert our relation to reality in general. To assert that there are "alternative facts," as his adviser Kellyanne Conway did, is to assert that there is an alternative, delusional, reality in which those "facts" and opinions most convenient in supporting Trump's policies and worldview hold sway. Whether we accept the reality that Trump and his supporters seek to impose on us, or reject it, it is an important and ever-present source of the specific confusion and anxiety that Trumpism evokes.

When a world leader as powerful as the president of the United States insists on there being "alternative facts" derived from a reality only he knows, this is alarming and destabilizing for us all. Democracy and the rule of law are threatened without an agreement between government and its citizens on the objectivity of truth and reality. A breakdown in this agreement puts the definition of truth and reality into the hands of those with the most social, political, and/ or economic power. In history, this has supported the severe wrongdoings of institutions intent more on preserving their power than on protecting individual rights. The sexual molestation of children by priests in the Catholic Church represents a stark and long-standing example of an institution that insisted on its own truth and reality rather than those of abused innocents. To hold on to power, Catholic Church leaders permitted the ongoing sexual abuse of society's most vulnerable, the very individuals they had a holy mandate to protect.

In trauma therapy, we see the corrosive long-term effects upon the human spirit when an individual's truth and reality are denied, particularly when those individuals grapple with traumas that take away their sense of subjectivity and self-efficacy. In his constant attempts to redefine the truth against the wrongdoings he has enacted, Donald Trump behaves like an aggressive perpetrator who fundamentally has no respect for the rights and subjectivities of those in American society who disagree with him. He shows this through his insistence on overpowering and shaming individuals who will not bend to his opinion or his will. From my stance as a trauma therapist, it is heartbreaking to see the damage Donald Trump is wreaking upon American society. It is a perpetration, creating deep wounds from which, I fear, it will already take us years to heal.

Conclusion

When the U.S. presidency, a position that already occupies the focus of global attention, is held by an extreme individual such as Donald Trump, his dramatic and inconsistent behavior captures all media attention. This constant coverage becomes a compulsive fixation for us all. For those of us who have been previously subjugated, this kind of exposure is particularly overstimulating and blocks us from recruiting the tools so necessary for healing from trauma. We are prevented from taking time to use language to validate truths and create meaning through narratives of those experiences. Without adequate time to process what shocks or destabilizes us, we cannot make sense of what happened; nor can we communicate our horrors to others. This robs all of the opportunity to humanize the subjugating effects of terror, abuse, and attack or to lift the isolation and shame that accompany them.

Moreover, the unfortunate symbiosis of our president's narcissistic, attention-hungry outrageousness with our Internet era's insatiable appetite for spectacle has resulted in a flood of incendiary news and information that none of us, whether previously traumatized or not, has the time or mental space to process. Yet, we gorge ourselves on such toxic infotainment with a niggling sense of impending doom.

As *New Yorker* editor in chief David Remnick said of White House press secretary Sean Spicer's unusually high ratings for press briefings: "Undoubtedly, some people watch Spicer to be entertained. But there's another reason his ratings are high: we watch because we're worried" (Remnick 2017).

Indeed, we are worried. Due to Trump and his administration's constant and volatile shifts in mood, communication, and representations of basic truths, far more Americans now possess narrower "windows of tolerance" in managing stress. As president, Trump has created an epidemic of heightened anxiety. By denying us access to time and calling our perceptions of truth into question, he shuts down our ability to reflect, causes us to doubt reality, and thus encourages reactivity and stress, keeping us in a difficult-to-sustain state of crisis.

It is hard to predict how tenable this is for us, as individuals or as a society. Uncertain times call for collective strength and stability, and such disempowerment is detrimental to our individual and national mental health. We can, however, use this deeper understanding of trauma, and of its elements of time and truth, to promote measured thought instead of reactive freezing, panic, or avoidance. We can be aware of the propensity for new media outlets to privilege emotionally stimulating falsehoods over measured and nuanced facts. We can unplug ourselves and take time simply to enjoy the act of thinking freely. It is a privilege we still enjoy in the United States, and it will be the skill we need to prevent us from careening toward crisis, as it seems Donald Trump would have us do.

Betty P. Teng, M.F.A., L.M.S.W., is a trauma therapist in the Office of Victims Services of a major hospital in Lower Manhattan. A graduate of Yale College; UCLA's School of Theater, Film, and Television; and NYU's Silver School of Social Work, Ms. Teng is in psychoanalytic training and practices at the Institute for Contemporary Psychotherapy. She is also an award-winning screenwriter and editor whose credits include films by Ang Lee, Robert Altman, and Mike Nichols.

References

Chun, Wendy. 2016. *Updating to Remain the Same: Habitual New Media.*
Cambridge, MA: MIT Press.

Crockett, Emily, and Libby Nelson. 2017. "Sexual Assault Allegations
Against Donald Trump: 15 Women Say He Groped, Kissed, or Assaulted Them." *Vox.* www.vox.com/2016/10/12/13265206/trump
-accusations-sexual-assault.

Davis, Jade E. 2014. "The Catholic Schoolgirl and the Wet Nurse: On the
Ecology of Oppression, Trauma and Crisis." *Decolonization: Indigeneity,
Education, and Society* 3 (1): 143–58.

Gold, Jenny. 2017. "'Post-Election Stress Disorder' Strikes on Both Sides."
CNN, February 20. www.cnn.com/2017/02/20/health/post-election
-stress-partner/index.html.

Persily, Nathaniel. 2017. "Can Democracy Survive the Internet?" *Journal of
Democracy* 28 (2): 63–76.

Pierre, Joe. 2016. "Understanding Post-Trump Stress Disorder" *Psychology
Today*, November 10. www.psychologytoday.com/blog/psych-unseen
/201611/understanding-post-trump-stress-disorder.

Remnick, David. 2017. "The Presidency and the Press." *The New Yorker*
weekly e-mail newsletter, May 14.

Stosny, Steven. 2017. "He Once Called It 'Election Stress Disorder.' Now the
Therapist Says We're Suffering from This." *Washington Post*, February 6. www.washingtonpost.com/news/inspired-life/wp/2017/02/06
/suffering-from-headline-stress-disorder-since-trumps-win-youre
-definitely-not-alone/.

Van der Kolk, Bessel A. 2014. *The Body Keeps the Score.* New York: Penguin
Books.

Whitebook, Joel. 2017. "Trump's Method, Our Madness." *New York Times*,
March 20. www.nytimes.com/2017/03/20/opinion/trumps-method
-our-madness.html.

TRUMP ANXIETY DISORDER

The Trump Effect on the Mental Health of Half the Nation and Special Populations

JENNIFER CONTARINO PANNING, PSY.D.

Two thousand sixteen marked a period of intense uncertainty and upheaval leading up to the contentious American presidential election on November 8, 2016, between Donald J. Trump and Hillary R. Clinton. Despite the vast majority of polls (Silver 2016) indicating that Hillary Clinton's odds of winning the election were 70–95 percent, and many individuals believing that Trump's candidacy was a farce, Trump won the presidency (although he lost the popular vote by more than 3 million votes).

This stunning result led to an unprecedented level of post-election shock, grief, and anxiety in about half the American population, many being progressive by political persuasion, but not always (American Psychological Association 2017).

This chapter will detail the pre- and post-election anxiety (dubbed "Trump anxiety disorder") widespread in the general public. However, unlike generalized anxiety symptoms, these symptoms were specific to the election of Trump and the resultant unpredictable sociopolitical climate. The role of the media, with a focus on biased and fake news reporting, is another factor in the development of these symptoms. This chapter will conclude with the author illustrating examples of this disorder from her clinical work with psychotherapy clients—most of whom are from an upper-middle-class background, intelligent, and educated.

Many of Trump's bombastic, grandiose attitudes and campaign untruths created an environment of uncertainty, with Americans feeling threatened in their personal safety; these ideologies created the perfect environmental factors for Trump's nonsupporters' anxieties to develop (Sheehy 2016). According to the "Stress in America" report, half of Americans (49 percent) endorsed that the 2016 election had been a significant stressor in their lives (American Psychological Association 2017). Many therapists were faced with the task of helping their clients manage this stress as well as the frustration of trying to "normalize" behavior that they did not feel was normal for an American president (Sheehy 2016).

It is important to differentiate generalized anxiety disorder and Trump anxiety disorder. The *Diagnostic and Statistical Manual of Mental Disorders*, 5th ed. (commonly referred to as DSM-V), is widely used among mental health professionals (American Psychiatric Association 2013). It describes generalized anxiety disorder (GAD) as characterized by excessive, uncontrollable, and often irrational worry—that is, apprehensive expectation about events or activities. This excessive worry often interferes with daily functioning, as individuals with GAD typically anticipate disaster and are overly concerned about everyday matters such as health issues, money, death, family problems, friendship problems, interpersonal relationship problems, or work difficulties. Individuals often exhibit a variety of physical symptoms, including fatigue, fidgeting, headaches, nausea, numbness in hands and feet, muscle tension, muscle aches, difficulty swallowing, excessive stomach acid buildup, stomach pain, vomiting, diarrhea, bouts of breathing difficulty, difficulty concentrating, trembling, twitching, irritability, agitation, sweating, restlessness, insomnia, hot flashes, rashes, and an inability to fully control the anxiety. These symptoms must be consistent and ongoing, persisting at least six months, for a formal diagnosis of GAD (American Psychiatric Association 2013). Generalized anxiety disorder is one of the more prevalent mood disorders in Americans; according to the National Institute of Mental Health, 3.1 percent of American adults struggle with GAD within a year, or over 7 million.

Symptoms associated with Trump anxiety disorder include: feeling a loss of control; helplessness; ruminations/worries, especially about the uncertain sociopolitical climate while Trump is in office; and a tendency toward excessive social media consumption. In fact, the polarization that this has created has caused a deep divide between families and friends of differing political beliefs. Trump's specific personality characteristics, and his use of psychological manipulation tools such as gaslighting, lying, and blaming, are described as contributing factors to Trump anxiety disorder.

Trump anxiety disorder, albeit not a formal diagnosis, differs from GAD in regard to several measures. One difference is in the duration of time for the symptoms to develop. The volatile events leading up to the 2016 election (i.e., false news reports, Comey's report questioning Clinton's ethics) were challenging in themselves, but many Americans were reassured by multiple polls (e.g., Silver 2016) predicting that Hillary Clinton would win the election in a landslide. This led to a sense of shock and disbelief after Trump was announced as president of the United States.

An additional symptom of Trump anxiety disorder is that symptoms are directly related to the uncertain sociopolitical climate. An elevated stress level when reading articles about numerous topics—the Muslim ban, the threat/promise of disbanding the Affordable Care Act, tensions between the United States and North Korea, the possibility of Russia's having interfered in the 2016 election and Russia's financial connection to Trump, the U.S./Mexican wall, immigration issues, the defunding of environmental groups such as the National Park Service and the Environmental Protection Agency, and the defunding of medical research—is strong. An individual impacted by Trump anxiety disorder may be directly impacted by one of these singular issues, have multiple concerns, or worry about the future democratic state in America given these issues. Therefore, the ruminative worry associated with an anxiety disorder is specific to these events (Clarridge 2017).

Social media have changed the way Americans are exposed to news. Internet news sites (CNN, *Huffington Post*, etc.) and social media such as Facebook and Twitter provide immediate access to news as well as to comments from other readers with differing viewpoints. Many Americans impacted by Trump anxiety disorder have admitted to an unhealthy obsession with checking news websites much more often than they previously did, and the amount of news involving Trump and his new administration has been constant, chaotic, confusing, and often overwhelming. When struggling with anxiety, many individuals, in an attempt to maintain control, will falsely assume that the more they know, the more they can be prepared. However, this tends to give them a false sense of control and, paradoxically, may increase anxiety symptoms once they realize their grip on control is not solid.

Other symptoms endorsed by many Americans post-election have included: feelings of helplessness and paralysis, an inability to focus on work or family obligations, and difficulty sleeping. Maladaptive coping strategies have included stress eating, drinking, smoking, and other ways to avoid feeling anxious.

Gaslighting, a term popularized in psychological literature over the past ten to fifteen years, describes unhealthy dynamics in a power relationship (Stern 2007). A gaslighter is "someone who desperately needs to be right in order to bolster his own sense of self and hold onto his own sense of power" (Stern 2007). Our gaslighter in chief has created anxiety for many Americans. During Trump's campaign, there were many examples of his lies, untruths, and other information that served to create doubt and to manipulate. However, gaslighting also serves to deceive someone into doubting her own perception of reality (Gibson 2017).

A February 2017 survey by the American Psychological Association (2017), "Stress in America: Coping with Change," indicated that two-thirds of Americans say they are stressed about the future of our nation. Although 76 percent of Democrats have reported stress about the future of our nation, 59 percent of Republicans have also endorsed the same stress level.

This also related to the therapists themselves. While mental health professionals were helping their clients deal with the stress of the post-election period, they were also struggling to handle and process their own feelings, which often were very similar to those of their clients.

One Psychologist's Work with Clients with Trump Anxiety Disorder

I am a licensed clinical psychologist and owner of a small group practice in Evanston, Illinois, a suburban, liberal, higher-socioeconomic-status, and educated suburb just north of the Chicago city limits. Evanston is a college town, home to Northwestern University, with much of its sixty-five thousand residents comprising professionals who work at Northwestern or at other white-collar, professional jobs. The majority of my clients are Northwestern University undergraduate and graduate students diagnosed with disorders as straightforward as adjusting to college life and struggling with identity development as well as more serious diagnoses such as major depressive disorder, bipolar disorder, eating disorders, stress, and other mood disorders (primarily anxiety-related). I should note that given the very progressive area in which I practice, I had zero Trump supporters among my caseload of clients during this time.

After the 2016 election, and most especially the week after it, the vast majority of my clients discussed and processed their feelings about the election. In fact, it was unusual when a client did *not* mention the election during this period. Most clients struggled with similar feelings of shock, sadness, worry, panic, uncertainty for the future, and anger. Some were still in shock, and many endorsed feeling as if the election results were a nightmare that they hadn't yet woken up from.

Most notably, the clients who came in the day after the election were still in disbelief. As their therapist, I concentrated on validating, normalizing, and maintaining a safe place for them to discuss their troubled feelings. We also discussed basic self-care, such as getting enough sleep, eating healthy meals, connecting with friends and family, and limiting consumption of election news stories. Certain clients were satisfied with discussing this for a short period of time and then resuming discussing their personal issues, while others struggled with daily functioning during the days and weeks after the election.

I (along with many other mental health professionals) have struggled to help clients while struggling myself with similar feelings of shock, anger, disbelief, frustration, and fear. The majority of mental health professionals tend to be liberal in their leanings (Norton 2016), which is unsurprising, given our profession's focus on social justice, health care rights, and other progressive causes. Therefore, many therapists were saddled with both helping their clients deal with their anxieties while also struggling with their own symptoms. Some of this work was comforting. Being able to help clients gave us welcome relief from the constant barrage of news stories. It also helped me not feel as helpless; being "in the trenches" with clients was a way to feel productive.

I found that clients with a loved one (usually a parent or a partner) with a personality disorder (most notably narcissistic personality disorder) were more impacted than others. Much of the work done with these individuals helps them to acknowledge the gaslighting involved in their relationship with their loved one; to identify that they are not crazy and do have sound and intact judgment regarding their impaired loved one; to acknowledge the limitations of their loved one; and to develop healthy coping strategies to cope with their loved one's erratic mood changes, blaming, and lying.

One woman, "Claire" (all names in clinical situations have been changed and placed in quotation marks where they first appear), a mother of a young child with special needs and a husband with narcissistic traits, had been referred to me by her husband because he felt that she was "going crazy" and needed professional help. Part of our work together was to help her understand the legitimacy of her husband's assessment; continue to work on her anxiety, which had been triggered by this dynamic; and to set healthier boundaries with her husband. Claire was very educated, politically liberal, and struggled with the impact of Trump's being elected. Her anxiety symptoms were exacerbated during the post-election and post-inauguration period. Her treatment focused on normalizing her feelings and encouraging her to establish control by making a difference in the ways she could. For her, this entailed volunteering, expressing appreciation to her child's teachers and other related professionals, and by calling her local congressional representatives.

Another woman, "Ida," was in her early twenties and an undergraduate student in her junior year. Ida was gifted and also extremely sensitive and inquisitive. She had struggled in therapy to make sense of her relationship with her father, who had narcissistic traits. I remember her stating after the election, "I feel like we are all in an emotionally abusive relationship with our president." She struggled with increased anxiety as well, and our work was to help ground her in what she could and could not control. She participated in several protest marches, which helped her feel less helpless. However, she struggled with minimizing her social media consumption and would often come into sessions feeling overwhelmed by the latest news.

Working in a very progressive area without one Trump supporter as a client enabled me to be honest with my clients that I was experiencing similar feelings, and that many of these feelings were universal to progressives post-election. I like to think that my clients appreciated my honesty and my ability to see a very human side to their therapist. However, many times the role of the therapist involves helping clients feel more hopeful and confident in their lives. This task proved to be quite difficult, as we therapists were left with similar feelings of helplessness and, perhaps due to our professional training, more concern given the characterological issues we saw in Trump's behavior and personality.

> *Jennifer Contarino Panning, Psy.D., is a licensed clinical psychologist and owner of Mindful Psychology Associates, a small group practice in Evanston Illinois. She received her doctorate in clinical psychology from the Chicago School of Professional Psychology in 2003, and completed training at Northern Illinois University and Northwestern University. Panning opened her private practice in 2004, and now has three psychologists and a postdoctoral fellow on staff. She specializes in the treatment of mood disorders, eating disorders, college student mental health, stress, and trauma using an integrative approach of cognitive behavioral therapy, mindfulness, and dialectical behavioral therapy, and is also trained in clinical hypnosis.*

References

American Psychiatric Association. 2013. *Diagnostic and Statistical Manual of Mental Disorders*. 5th ed. Arlington, VA: American Psychiatric Association.

American Psychological Association. 2017. "Many Americans Stressed About Future of Our Nation, New APA Stress in American Survey Reveals." APA.org, February 15. www.apa.org/news/press/releases /2017/02/stressed-nation.aspx.

Clarridge, Christine. 2017. "Mental Health Therapists See Uptick in Patients Struggling with Postelection Anxiety." March 29. www.chicagotribune .com/lifestyles/health/ct-mental-health-postelection-anxiety-20170329 -story.html.

Gibson, Caitlin. 2017. "What We Talk About When We Talk About Donald Trump' and 'Gaslighting.'" January 27. www.washingtonpost.com /lifestyle/style/what-we-talk-about-when-we-talk-about-donald-trump -and-gaslighting/2017/01/27/b02e6de4-e330-11e6-ba11-63c4b4fb5a63_ story.html.

Glinton, Sonari. 2016. "Survey Says Americans Are Getting Stressed by the Elections." October 15. www.npr.org/sections/the two-way/2016/10/15 /498033747/survey-says-Americans-are-getting-stressed-by-the -elections.

National Institute of Mental Health. "Any Anxiety Disorder Among Adults." www.nimh.nih.gov/health/statistics/prevalence/any-anxiety -disorder-among-adults.shtml.

Norton, Aaron. 2016. "The Political Beliefs of Mental Health Counselors." *In Thought* (blog), May 9. www.aaronlmhc.blogspot.com/2016/05/political -beliefs-of-mental-health-counselors.html.

Sheehy, Gail. 2016. "America's Therapists Are Worried About Trump's Effect on Your Mental Health." October 16. www.politico.com/magazine/story /2016/10/donald-trump-2016-therapists-214333.

Silver, Nate. 2016. "Election Update: Clinton Gains, and the Polls Magically Converge." November 7. https://fivethirtyeight.com/features/election -update-clinton-gains-and-the-polls-magically-converge/.

Stern, Robin. 2007. *The Gaslight Effect*. New York: Morgan Road Books.

IN RELATIONSHIP WITH AN ABUSIVE PRESIDENT

HARPER WEST, M.A., L.L.P.

As "Amelia"* describes her husband's behavior in my therapy office, it immediately strikes me as emotionally abusive, although she acts as if his behavior were completely normal.

"Justin" can be harshly critical, calling her a "fat loser" and her home-cooked meals "a disaster." If she asks even reasonable questions, he lashes out at her: "You're always so negative and critical." If she states a fact he disagrees with, he accuses her of making up "fake" stories. Despite Justin's family and financial security, he is joyless and scowls much of the time.

Amelia is mystified how the most minor disagreements seem to escalate into major arguments. I ask if Justin can apologize or admit fault. "Oh, never," she says. "He's very stubborn. It's always my fault. I call him 'Justifying Justin.'"

Their most recent argument began when she asked if he had paid a bill. He became enraged and said he had paid it. She later learned that he had not paid the bill, but he refused to apologize for the lie, the ensuing argument, or his excessive anger.

---

* This is a fictional couple.

Justin has lied so frequently that Amelia has become concerned she is "losing her mind" or has a poor memory, a belief aided by the fact that Justin accuses her of these faults. He insists that she forget his mistakes, but he brings up her mistakes repeatedly during arguments.

She describes Justin as being successful at business, very decisive, and a strong leader. She hesitates to confront him because she has learned that it leads to arguments escalating, with no resolution. She is always the one to compromise.

Amelia reports high levels of anxiety, and fears Justin's unpredictable reactions.

This couple is a composite of many cases where the pattern of abuse ranges from subtle to glaring. Not coincidentally, this couple is an analogy for the current relationship between America and a psychologically unstable, emotionally abusive president.

Domestic abusers and President Donald Trump share common personality traits because they share common human drives, emotions, and reactions. These characteristics negatively impact relationships, whether interpersonal or with an entire country, and they must be addressed for the health of those being harmed.

Renaming Narcissists

Some mental health professionals have associated Trump with a variety of diagnoses, such as narcissistic personality disorder, antisocial personality disorder, paranoid personality disorder, delusional disorder, malignant narcissist, and some form of dementia (Lenzer 2017).

Some of these labels come from the *Diagnostic and Statistical Manual* (American Psychiatric Association 2013), which numerous authors have identified as an unscientific, arbitrary categorization system that overcomplicates and falsely medicalizes emotional and behavioral problems ("DSM: A Fatal Diagnosis?" 2013; Caplan 1995; Deacon and McKay 2015; Kinderman 2014; Miller 2010; Whitaker and Cosgrove 2015).

To avoid this categorization system and to simplify and focus on the character flaw that is at the core of these personalities, I will call these types of people Other-blamers.

The cause of their behaviors is low self-worth, which leads them to have poor shame tolerance. They learned in childhood to manage feelings of inadequacy by adopting unhealthy coping mechanisms to forestall or avoid shaming experiences.

Poor shame tolerance causes behaviors associated with the just-mentioned DSM disorders, including vindictive anger, lack of insight and accountability, dishonesty, impulsivity, entitlement, paranoia, lack of remorse and empathy, self-importance, and attention-seeking. Trump is an extreme example, but "subclinical" versions of this behavior exist in millions of people, including domestic abusers.

It may be difficult to discern the low self-worth of Other-blamers because they often adopt an aggressive, dominating persona to achieve emotional self-protection. They rarely admit feelings of inadequacy because they believe this would make them vulnerable to the same abuse and control they are perpetrating.

As a psychotherapist, I see the victims of Other-blamers in my office every day. Less-severe Other-blamers cause high-conflict or estranged relationships. More-severe cases can engage in emotional and physical abuse of partners and children, criminal behavior, and addictive behaviors. I have often said we should not be diagnosing those who come into therapy but, rather, those who *caused* them to come to therapy.

Despite their toxic behavior, Other-blamers rarely voluntarily agree to therapy because of their aversion to the shaming experience of self-awareness and accountability. Yet, they are quite often the subject of the therapy of others.

Certainly, Other-blamers are aided to some degree by the deferential behaviors of individuals who employ two other types of shame management strategies: self-blaming and blame avoidance (West 2016).

Other-blamers instinctively seek out those willing to be controlled, manipulated, or intimidated. This sets up relationships with submissive people who will not challenge, correct, or blame them. Dictators throughout history have surrounded themselves with a coterie of family members and sycophants who avoid questioning the leader for fear of his angry retribution.

(For the sake of clarity, this article will refer to abusers as males, but both genders can be Other-blamers and abusers.)

Causes of Other-blamer Behavior

As children, Other-blamers were likely exposed to developmental or attachment trauma, such as abusive, shaming, rejecting, or neglectful parenting. Parents who are substance abusers or psychologically troubled often underfocus on a child's needs. Parents may have exhibited narcissistic or Other-blaming behaviors that the child models. Another possible cause is parents who were permissive or conflict avoiding and did not hold the child accountable. Parents who overfocus on achievement or behavioral compliance can also encourage a fear of failure that may bring on Other-blaming tendencies.

These experiences can cause children to feel unloved, unprotected, and inadequate. They may struggle to experience empathy for others and may develop an unhealthy hypersensitivity and overreaction to shaming experiences. While Other-blaming as a shame-management strategy may be adaptive in childhood, it causes difficulties for adult relationships at all levels, from presidential to personal.

Emotional Reactivity with Fear, Shame, and Anger

In all humans, survival fear overwhelms the deliberative, logical functioning of the cognitive brain (Pasquali 2006). Children exposed to trauma continually rehearse "fight-or-flight" reactions so that their brains become habituated to and easily hijacked by survival emotions (Anda et al. 2006). Chronic exposure to the fear response leads to anxiety-based behaviors, such as impulsivity, hyperactivity, irrationality, volatility, impetuousness, poor frustration tolerance, and poor concentration—all of which Trump exhibits on a daily basis. Trump's incoherent gibberish may be a sign of his fearful, reactive emotional state; he cannot calm his brain enough even to form a complete sentence. One must be calm to be mindful of one's thoughts, feelings, and experiences and to gain self-awareness.

Although they are adept at hiding it, Other-blamers know a lot about fear. They spend their lives in an emotional survival panic, in terror of being judged and found unworthy. They are in a mad scramble to find some way to feel better about themselves or at least to protect themselves from feeling additional shame. That shame can lead to protective anger, as recognized in the aphorism "Anger is shame's bodyguard."

For extreme Other-blamers, elevated "fight-or-flight" reactivity can lead to shame-driven rage and abusive violence. Domestic violence incidents are usually triggered when the abuser feels challenged, demeaned, or rejected by the partner. Abusers failed to learn to tolerate shame in healthy ways, so even minor or perceived slights to their weak self-worth, such as dinner not being served on time, may throw them into an uncontrollable rage.

Trump's first wife, Ivana, accused him of raping her in sworn deposition testimony, an accusation she later softened, as a part of a lucrative divorce settlement, but did not completely retract. This alleged violence fits with the personality of someone fearful of rejection and living with elevated anxiety who might be triggered into violent rage. Abusers can escalate to murder/suicide when a relationship is ending and they must face the humiliation of undeniable rejection. That some abusers will kill others or even themselves to avoid experiencing this emotion shows the power of shame.

This pattern of escalating instability is concerning when considering Trump. As the pressures of governing and of the investigations such as that of alleged collusion with Russia increase, he may be overwhelmed by fear, which will further limit his cognitive and prosocial capabilities. His behaviors may become increasingly volatile and unpredictable.

Healthy relationships require partners who are calm, thoughtful, and deliberate, not fearful and reactive. Fear-driven behaviors and a lack of insight are exactly the opposite of what we should expect of a safe, dependable partner or a leader.

Lack of Accountability

With shame and fear as the primary emotions driving Other-blamers, a lack of accountability becomes their most obvious and destructive character flaw.

They have difficulty being introspective and acknowledging the effect of their behavior. This would involve gaining insight, admitting fault, and demonstrating remorse—actions that Other-blamers find devastatingly humiliating. In therapy, I get the sense that an Other-blamer wants to put his hands to his ears and sing "la-la-la" in an attempt to avoid hearing the truth. Other-blamers do not like to be held accountable because they do not hold themselves accountable.

In general, Other-blamers do not believe they must play by the same societal or relational norms as others, which can be disorienting to partners. Trump's refusal to release his tax returns or comply with ethics regulations is clear evidence of this thought process.

Lack of accountability causes escalating arguments in couples because Other-blamers stubbornly refuse to admit fault, even if the facts are staring them squarely in the face. Or they admit fault reluctantly, but only after much lying and excuse-making. The betrayals of trust mount up, driving a wedge into the relationship.

During arguments, Other-blamers frantically attempt to manage shame by shifting blame, making excuses, or denying behavior. One wife said about her emotionally abusive husband, "During conversations, he is not really listening, because he is trying to figure out how to make it not his problem."

Domestic abusers are notorious for their lack of accountability. They can go to extremes of rationalization. One abuser noted that while he had locked his wife in the closet for hours, thrown her to the floor repeatedly, and pointed a gun at her head, he had not punched her—as if this arbitrary demarcation excused his inexcusable crimes. The Other-blamer routinely blames the victim, as if a late dinner were worth a slap in the face.

Unlike Harry Truman, who placed a sign on his Oval Office desk stating, "The Buck Stops Here," Trump appears to be completely lacking in accountability. He regularly shifts blame to others and never seems to apologize for any of his lies or mistakes. Trump's blame shifting is so predictable that he can barely make one statement without a deflection (Millbank 2017). His assertion, although false, that he does not settle lawsuits is an example of his distaste for being held responsible. Trump's tendency to ridicule facts or the opinions of others is another way of avoiding dealing with a situation honestly.

Because of their lack of accountability and resulting lack of insight, Other-blamers are highly resistant to change, leaving their partners with limited power to affect the relationship. In an interpersonal relationship, the partner can leave. Yet, as a country, we have little recourse other than faith that our democratic institutions will keep Trump in check.

Unfortunately, abusers and authoritarians such as Trump do not like laws, which are ultimately about holding people accountable. This worldview is a danger to a democracy founded on the rule of law.

In contrast, emotionally mature people can accept the boundaries others establish. When they violate expectations, they can apologize promptly and gracefully, which resolves arguments and repairs relationships. Healthy relationships require awareness of one's faults; care for one's impact on others; and an ability to handle mistakes, defeats, and criticism with equanimity.

Lack of Prosocial Emotions

An Other-blamer's inability to apologize clearly signals to others a lack of conscience and empathy. Compassion, kindness, and altruism are prosocial traits and moral behaviors that are largely innate

(Martin and Clark 1982). Yet, those described as sociopaths and narcissists (American Psychiatric Association 2013) are often noted for their lack of remorse, guilt, or empathy.

Other-blamers lack these emotional traits for several reasons. Some did not experience warm interactions in early attachment relationships with caregivers. Perhaps they learned to be hurtful toward others through experiencing or witnessing abuse. Being raised in an environment of trauma increases one's reliance on the survival responses of "fight-or-flight" and decreases access to "tend-and-befriend" responses, making one less inclined to aid others or even be aware of the needs of others.

When in distress or cornered, people often lash out, especially if they have a model of relationships that may not include safety, comfort, or love. An abuser's violent rage is an extreme version of a fear-based deficit in prosocial sentiment. An abuser may say he loves his partner and claim he would never hurt her, but his emotionally reactive behaviors speak the truth: that, when dysregulated by fear and shame, he can care only about himself.

For Other-blamers, it is their emotional struggle to protect their fragile self-image from shame that makes them lack consideration. Other-blamers become overwhelmed by their own emotional pain, so they prefer offloading it onto another, even if that means harming that person or the relationship.

Even those with less-severe Other-blaming traits end up damaging relationships because they lack an ability to attend or respond to their partner's emotions with kindness and caring. The resulting lack of emotional connection is a major reason relationships fail. In couples' therapy, it is difficult to get an Other-blamer to pay attention to his effect on his partner. Even if his wife is crying, the Other-blaming husband may sit there unmoved or, worse yet, argumentative and defensive. He is so busy protecting himself from experiencing shame and blame that he has little capacity to be warmly responsive. Certainly, abusers are harming the relationship every time they react violently.

Other-blamers often have difficulty attuning to the emotional status of others because, as one Other-blamer admitted in a rare moment of self-awareness, "I care more about being right than doing the right thing for the relationship."

And this is exactly what is happening in Trump's relationship with America. He cares far more about sheltering his fragile psyche than doing what is right for the country. Trump's lack of empathy has been on display for decades, with well-documented bigotry, greed, name-calling, intimidation, and vindictiveness.

Because he is in emotional survival mode, Trump fails to notice that his ranting press conferences or bullying tweets are destabilizing. His goal is merely to lash out so he can feel better about himself in that moment. Trump has no concern that his divisive hate speech leads many to fear for their safety and liberty. He is unconcerned about the long-term effect on the country. He is too busy being right at any cost to notice that his lies and accusations are damaging his relationship with the citizens he is leading.

Trump has no apparent moral urge to care for others or serve his constituents. He may cite "America First" slogans, but he has no real understanding of the selfless giving in true patriotism. Trump got five deferments during the Vietnam War, yet he has repeatedly verbally attacked war heroes. His policies emphasize cruelty toward the less fortunate and an abdication of caring stewardship of the earth's resources.

As is the case with most Other-blamers, the country is learning quite clearly that Trump is in it only for himself. The pervasive sense that an Other-blamer does not care about you is a betrayal and leads, rightfully, to distrust and disconnection. This type of behavior violates our primal need for mutuality and trust in relationships and is why relationships with narcissists are toxic and usually end poorly.

Depersonalizing the Victim

A lack of emotional attunement and prosocial responsiveness leads to an objectification or depersonalization of others. This distancing is an adaptive mechanism that allows Other-blamers to experience less guilt when they harm their partners.

"An abusive man has to bury his compassion in a deep hole in order to escape the profound inherent aversion that human beings have to seeing others suffer. He has to adhere tightly to his excuses and rationalizations, develop a disturbing ability to insulate himself from the pain he is causing, and learn to enjoy power and control over his female partners" (Bancroft 2002).

Trump, for decades, has made demeaning comments about women's looks and has bragged on videotape about sexually assaulting women. During the campaign, he mocked a disabled reporter.

When most pundits said Trump's behavior might improve in the White House, I predicted that his behavior would get worse. His extreme depersonalization of others will worsen as his entitlement increases with the power of his position.

"Objectification is a critical reason why an abuser tends to get worse over time. As his conscience adapts to one level of cruelty—or violence—he builds to the next. By depersonalizing his partner, the abuser protects himself from the natural human emotions of guilt and empathy, so that he can sleep at night with a clear conscience. He distances himself so far from her humanity that her feelings no longer count, or simply cease to exist" (Bancroft 2002).

It is frightening to consider that we have a president who may have lost the ability to care about the human lives he is charged with protecting.

Entitlement

Other-blamers exhibit entitlement, which is closely linked to depersonalization and a lack of accountability. Trump seems to believe he is above reproach, once stating that he could shoot someone on Fifth Avenue and not lose any voters (Johnson 2016).

Most abusers try to hide socially unacceptable traits; they are often polite to others but abusive to a partner. Sadly, Trump makes no effort to mask his verbal abuse. He feels entitled to publicly shame and demean. Name-calling with comments of "loser" and "lock her up" were a staple of his campaign. He appears unrestrained by any sense of moral propriety, which indicates a very dangerous, extreme abuser who does not even attempt to plaster over his ill will with a sociopath's charm. He cannot even pretend to be good-natured, despite all his popularity, wealth, and power.

Deception

Other-blamers lie to exaggerate achievements in an attempt to seek approval, deflect blame, and avoid accountability. They become adept at outright deception, lies of omission, twisted responses, denial, and subject changing.

Lying to others is second nature to Other-blamers because they lie to themselves constantly. To routinely shift blame to others is a massive, lifelong effort at self-deception. Other-blamers lie by rationalizing, convincing themselves that their behavior is appropriate, with the goal of avoiding hearing the truth and experiencing shame.

Author Tony Schwartz has said about Trump that "Lying is second nature to him . . . More than anyone else I have ever met, Trump has the ability to convince himself that whatever he is saying at any given moment is true, or sort of true, or at least ought to be true" (Meyer 2016).

Other-blamers and abusers lie so frequently that their partners often do not know what to believe. How can a relationship of any kind withstand the betrayal of a constant barrage of deception, excuses, and denials?

Humans have a survival-oriented need for trust in relationships: "Can I really count on you when it matters? Do you have my back?" With repeated lies, interpersonal partners (and national allies) will learn that the answer is no.

This is exactly what is causing distress for many Americans since Trump's election. They sense, correctly, that he will impulsively betray us to achieve his aims, even if it is not in the best interest of the country.

Rep. Adam Schiff, a Democrat from California, noted that Trump's constant lies may lead to a loss of trust in a leader's words that may have major international implications. "When a president of the U.S. makes claims that are proved baseless, it weakens the presidency and undermines our security and standing in the world. Presidential credibility once squandered may never be fully regained. If the president may one day assert that North Korea has placed a nuclear weapon on a ballistic missile and action is necessary, it will be an enormous problem if untrue. If true, it may be an even bigger problem if the president has lost the capacity to persuade our allies of the facts, let alone the American people" (Schiff 2017).

Other characteristics of abusive Other-blamers include:

- **Placing high value on personal loyalty, surrounding themselves with "yes men."** Trump relies almost exclusively on family members as advisers, even though none has government experience.

- **Isolating their partners and often convincing their victims that others do not have their best interests at heart.** Throughout the campaign, Trump created an "us-versus-them" mentality in his followers, belittling anyone who might weaken his hold on those followers' hearts and minds.

- **Being attracted to power and tending to misuse it.** They use an authoritarian style of speaking that gets others to doubt reality. Trump boldly repeats lies so that the truth has little opportunity to flourish.

- **Promoting an image of success.** Trump's gold-plated lifestyle and obsession with crowd sizes and vote counts provide ample evidence that protecting his delicate ego takes precedence.

Driven to Distraction: Trump's Effect on Our Psychological Health

A fundamental problem with a Trump presidency is not merely that his poorly thought-out policies may harm us. It is that his character defects will normalize immoral Other-blaming behaviors and encourage their full expression among those who may have previously been held in check by expectations of socially acceptable behavior. If the recent uptick in racial violence is an indicator, Trump has given his followers a green light to act out.

Just as the trauma of witnessing domestic violence damages children, an emotionally immature president can affect the future of our nation regarding moral behavior, cultural stability, and psychological wellness.

Other-blamers can be restrained only by prompt, calm boundary setting and an enforcement of moral and social norms. Without these influences, Other-blamers grow in boldness and their presumption of power. Other-blamers will take as much ground as they can get.

We must resist, not only to contain Trump's behaviors, but also to signal to his followers that abusive behavior is not appropriate. Unfortunately, now that millions of Other-blamers have been encouraged by Trump to misbehave, it may be impossible to get that genie back in the bottle.

In therapy, it is common to see families where a narcissist or sociopath has not been held in check—sometimes multiple generations of them—and the resulting dysfunction creates ripples of psychological trauma, including insecure attachment patterns in children, addictions, estrangement, and conflict.

Because the Other-blamer refuses to compromise or engage in fair play, it becomes "every man for himself." Family members resent having to always give so the Other-blamer can take. They resent the Other-blamer lying and refusing to agree on facts. They resent always being blamed while the Other-blamer can never admit fault. Abuse victims often experience frustration because when they try to get through to the abuser, the rules of fair play do not apply.

As a country, we are attempting to apply democratic rule of law to Trump. If Trump refuses to play by the rules, and the courts and Congress do not hold him accountable, we citizens have little recourse, which will cause us to have the sense of helpless desperation of an abused spouse.

Compromise and reciprocity are key parts of politics and healthy relationships. Other-blamers are inclined to adopt an attitude of "my way or the highway," as Trump did with his ham-handed rushing through of a replacement for the Affordable Care Act without debate. If Trump has to be right and win at all costs, and if he views discussion and compromise as losing, this offers little hope for the future of the country's relationship with him.

It is common for a jealous spouse to angrily text his wife thirty times a day, call repeatedly, and argue for hours. The effort it takes to manage the abuser causes the partner to have less time and energy for parenting, career, or self-care. In narcissistic relationships, one has little left over after the arguments. Abused partners tend to overfocus on the relationship, rather than address their own self-improvement, until the relationship is ended.

In the same way, since the 2016 election, much of the world has been in a panic, overfocused on Trump and unable to deal with much else but his foibles and follies. The world is scrambling to respond to chaos, which leaves little energy to address legitimate issues. When the Japanese prime minister visited, the discussion about Trump's bizarrely aggressive handshaking style overtook talk of trade deals or North Korea. Antarctic ice shelf breaking off? Wars, refugees, the European Union in turmoil? These issues receive inadequate attention because the world is trying to make sense of the attention-seeking distraction in the White House. This is potentially tragic for those people and issues ignored as a result of the dysfunctional relationship we have with this president.

I am experiencing this personally, as I spend much more time reading news articles, organizing rallies, writing letters, and making phone calls. This is time and energy I could be spending championing worthy causes. In fact, here I am writing about Trump's mental health when, with a different person in office, I could be working to improve the mental health care system.

This narcissistic president is doing what all narcissists do: sucking the air out of the room. When in relationship with an Other-blamer, one must spend one's time and energy arguing about the arguing, rather than living peacefully and productively. Trump will continue to have a toxic effect at the individual and global level, not just through his harmful, ill-considered policy decisions, but through increased anxiety and the diversion of attention from other issues.

A true leader or a caring spouse manages his or her behaviors and emotions in a mature, temperate way. The country will have less ability to focus on solutions to complex problems until we get rid of the Other-blamer in chief we are in relationship with. The coarsening of society and the loss of civility and empathy will likely be irreparable in the near term. We can only hope that we break up with this abusive president before he breaks up the country.

Harper West (www.HarperWest.co), M.A., L.L.P., is a licensed psychotherapist in Clarkston, Michigan. She graduated from Michigan State University with a degree in journalism and worked in corporate communications, later earning a master's degree in clinical psychology from the Michigan School of Professional Psychology. Ms. West is the developer of self-acceptance psychology, which challenges the biological model of mental disorders and offers a new paradigm that reframes emotional problems as adaptive responses to fear, trauma, shame, and lack of secure attachment. Her self-help book Pack Leader Psychology *won an Independent Book Publishers Association Ben Franklin Award for Psychology.*

References

American Psychiatric Association. 2013. *Diagnostic and Statistical Manual of Mental Disorders*. 5th ed. Arlington, VA: American Psychiatric Association.

Anda, Robert F., Vincent J. Felitti, J. Douglas Bremner, John D. Walker, Charles Whitfield, Bruce D. Perry, Shanta R. Dube, and Wayne H. Giles. 2006. "The Enduring Effects of Abuse and Related Adverse Experiences in Childhood." *European Archives of Psychiatry and Clinical Neuroscience* 256: 174–86. doi: 10.1007/s00406-005-0624-4.

Bancroft, Lundy. 2002. *Why Does He Do That? Inside the Minds of Angry and Controlling Men*. New York: Berkley Books.

Caplan, P. J. 1995. *They Say You're Crazy: How the World's Most Powerful Psychiatrists Decide Who's Normal*. Boston: Da Capo Press.

Deacon, Brett, and Dean McKay. 2015. *The Behavior Therapist, Special Issue: The Biomedical Model of Psychological Problems* 38: 7.

"DSM-5: A Fatal Diagnosis?" 2013. [Editorial.] *British Medical Journal* 346, f3256.

Johnson, Jenna. 2016. "Donald Trump: They Say I Could 'Shoot Somebody' and Still Have Support." *Washington Post*. www.washingtonpost.com /news/post-politics/wp/2016/01/23/donald-trump-i-could-shoot -somebody-and-still-have-support/?utm_term=.31d27df01dc5.

Kinderman, Peter. 2014. *A Prescription for Psychiatry: Why We Need a Whole New Approach to Mental Health and Wellbeing*. London: Palgrave Macmillan.

Lenzer, Jeanne. 2017. "Do Doctors Have a 'Duty to Warn' If They Believe a Leader Is Dangerously Mentally Ill?" *The BMJ* 356 (March 9): j1087. https://doi.org/10.1136/bmj.j1087.

Martin, Grace B., and Russell D. Clark. 1982. "Distress Crying in Neonates: Species and Peer Specificity." *Developmental Psychology* 18: 3–9. doi:10.1037 /0012-1649.18.1.3.

Meyer, Jane. 2016. "Donald Trump's Ghostwriter Tells All." *The New Yorker*, July 25. www.newyorker.com/magazine/2016/07/25/donald-trumps -ghostwriter-tells-all.

Millbank, Dana. 2017. "Personal Irresponsibility: A Concise History of Trump's Buck-Passing." *New York Times*, April 5. www.nytimes.com.

Miller, Gregory A. 2010. "Mistreating Psychology in the Decades of the Brain." *Perspectives on Psychological Science* 5: 716. doi: 10.1177/17456916 10388774.

Pasquali, Renato. 2006. "The Biological Balance Between Psychological Well-Being and Distress: A Clinician's Point of View." *Psychotherapy and Psychosomatics* 75 (2): 69–71.

Schiff, Adam. 2017. "Rep. Schiff Delivers Democratic Weekly Address on Need for an Independent Commission." March 25. www.youtube.com /watch?v=IsB5n_qVdvE.

West, Harper. 2016. *Self-Acceptance Psychology*. Rochester Hills, MI.: Wing-Path Media.

Whitaker, Robert, and Lisa Cosgrove. 2015. *Psychiatry Under the Influence: Institutional Corruption, Social Injury, and Prescriptions for Reform*. New York: Palgrave Macmillan.

BIRTHERISM AND THE DEPLOYMENT OF THE TRUMPIAN MIND-SET

LUBA KESSLER, M.D.

Donald Trump straddles the country's divide between those who cheer his ascendance to the presidency and those who are greatly disturbed by it. This intensely felt division points to the highly emotional effect he has on the nation. What is it? People have cited a variety of factors. This chapter offers a singular look at Trump's method of political insinuation through an examination of his embrace and loud propagation of the "birtherism" conspiracy. His use of it as a jumping-off platform to launch his presidential candidacy showed from the start the unmistakable signs of an unabashed bending of reality and a deployment of demagoguery to achieve his political aims.

What is birtherism? Since 2011, Donald Trump was the loudest and most persistent spokesperson for the conspiracy theory that Barack Obama was not a native U.S. citizen. In denying that Obama was a naturally born American, Trump joined the "birtherism" argument espoused by the national far-right political fringe.

It was Trump's first visible political falsehood, initiating a perversion of the political discourse that ultimately led to his election.

A false covenant with the public followed, spawning a multitude of other "alternative" realities.

This brings up disturbing questions. Why did this falsehood take root? And what are the ramifications of a presidency based on it? This chapter attempts to consider this question in light of recent history.

The first decade of the country's political history in the twenty-first century saw two profoundly transformative national events. America suffered the first and only foreign attack on its mainland since the War of 1812, on September 11, 2001. And in 2008, it elected a black man as its president, and reelected him for a second term in 2012. One event came from the outside; the other, from developments inside the country. Is there something about this convergence between the shock of the one and the internal ripples of the other? Let us examine.

The 9/11 terrorist attacks shook the country's sense of invincibility. Ever since then, the United States has been at war in foreign lands, in an effort to recover its sense of security and prowess. Our nation has always been proud of its sovereignty, its expansive Manifest Destiny at home and its voice of authority abroad. The adjustment of its post-9/11 self-image on the national and international stage has been painful. We entered the new millennium with a great deal of self-questioning. American millennials came face-to-face with ethnic and religious Otherness with an urgency unknown to previous generations. On the one hand, it widened their horizons, fueling greater interest in and openness to the world. Yet, on the other hand, life became more unsettled; the breakdown in the social and family sense of security made their entrance into this new world more susceptible to feelings of mistrust and fearfulness. The impulse to "circle the wagons" and turn inward encouraged suspicion of Others: xenophobia.

The election of Barack Obama as the U.S. president also represented a great shift in the nation's life and psychology, though of a different nature. Blacks have historically carried connotations of

Otherness in America, by the difference of their skin color and the circumstances of their arrival on the continent, compared to the majority population, which has led to persistent racism. Certainly, the election of an African American man to the highest office in the land represented a dramatic civic achievement in the country's history. It gave cause to consider the possibility that the United States may have reached a postracial consciousness.

Yet, the production of the "birtherism" movement, in this historical context, tells a different story. How so?

The questioning of the authenticity of Barack Obama's native birth is without precedent in the history of the American presidency. No other president, all of whom were white, was ever subjected to the deep offense of such a cruel falsehood. It was as if such an arrogant affront to the dignity of the president, or any man, was permissible because he was black. With such calumny, Donald Trump signaled thinly veiled bigotry. While not expressing directly an outright racist slur, his embrace of birtherism was a "dog whistle," an unmistakable call to delegitimize a black American citizen as the Other because he aspired to the presidency of the nation.

The American public takes great pride in the fact that any of its native born could become president. It has always been the aspirational ideal of this country's self-image as a place of freedom and opportunity for all. Both Barack Obama, an African American professor of constitutional law with a record of community service and the audacity of hope, and Donald Trump, a brash real estate developer with no political experience, could succeed in the quest for the highest office in the land on the strength of their appeal to the citizenry.

The bigotry of birtherism set a limit on this national aspiration. It signaled that a black person could not be truly American. Just as the election of Barack Obama thrilled the nation, imbuing us with civic pride in the seeming achievement of a postracial society, birtherism signaled that it was permissible for America, deep in its soul, to continue harboring and nursing the historic racial prejudice. It said that a black president could not be legitimate, and so the factual reality of his very birth on American soil had to be denied. In this willful distortion of fact, Donald Trump showed the essential quality of his personality: the perversion of his relationship to truth. It showed that he could and would distort and deform the truth in his quest to secure any deal he was after. Truth and reality were commodities just like any other—a matter for a transactional sale of a desired acquisition. This appears to be the hallmark of the Trumpian mind-set. Birtherism was its opening political bid.

We are living in a time of great demographic, economic, social, and political transformation at home and abroad. What it means is that the pressures from outside the national realm resonate with those within it. America's unrivaled democratic diversity, as seen in its immigrant descendants continues to evolve, just as its standing in the global transformation is adjusting anew to evolving realities, global terrorism among them. This stretches the psychological resources of the nation, and its resilience. The American citizenry meets its moment of truth under conditions of shaken security and changing identity. It becomes a matter of paramount importance to the well-being of the country, therefore, that it withstand and manage these pressures with a calm resolve based on a moral sense of decency and reason.

At such times, the nation looks to its leader to uphold its vital interests and values. It is for this reason that we celebrate those presidents who showed the capacity to meet the challenging realities of their moment in history with dignity, and appeal to what Abraham Lincoln called the "better angels of our nature." This is the reason that Lincoln stands in the American presidential pantheon with George Washington and Franklin Delano Roosevelt. Each of these men lifted the nation not with partisan transaction but with vision and moral purpose.

Donald Trump's appeal has just the opposite effect. It debases civic discourse and corrodes national unity.

Birtherism shows the essential characteristics of Donald Trump's mind-set: A self-professed ultimate dealmaker first and foremost, he pursued the presidency in an entirely transactional manner. He did not hesitate to make up falsehoods or wink at bigotry to win. In a manner similar to exploiting every available tax loophole; every feasible advantage over his debtors, contractors, and workers; every opportunity to have "special" relationships advance his deal-making aims, he made an unerring political calculation to seize the transitional moment of national insecurity. His business acumen worked brilliantly, against all odds. But his transactional win represents a profound danger to the nation because it sells out the most essential qualities of democratic values, of moral integrity, and of true inventiveness. What binds us together is the shared reality of our country's history and its present: *E pluribus unum*. "Out of many, one." The country's cherished motto cannot hold when truth is open to transactional competition from "alternative facts."

We are left with the question about what made the American public receptive to Donald Trump's promissory bid despite his falsehoods. Yes, our country is ever open to enterprising inventiveness and grand boldness. But it is not naïve. There has been too much toil, hardship, and strong civic pride in building this nation for its citizenry to surrender the habits of common sense and clearheaded pragmatism. However, this does not make America immune to the lingering effects of its own historical legacy of slavery and racism. Without a full reconciliation between that legacy and the nation's founding ideals, the significant fault line between the two will open up in times of increased strain. The startling fabrication of the birtherism movement offers a window into just such a fault line.

It does not require particular professional schooling to recognize that birtherism was a telltale sign of a preoccupation with Otherness. It is easy to grasp the sense of threat from the foreign Other in the age of terrorism and massive global migration. It is more difficult to acknowledge the persistent fear and lingering mistrust of the black Other at home in America.

We want to believe in our postracial integration and equality. We are proud of the progress we have made. The election of Barack Obama is its rightful proof. It is a lot more difficult to recognize the prejudices of an inborn and ingrown kind of stereotyping. The fact that Donald Trump could successfully use the myth of birtherism as an under-the-radar deployment of bigotry attests to its subterranean persistence.

This is not an indictment of American society. It is a call for recognition of America's historical conditions. We associate the settling of the country with white colonists. We grow up with those lessons of our history and culture. Although the labor of the Blacks was indispensable to the fledgling American economy, slavery denied them the recognition and rights of equal participation. The result was persistent discrimination, which further disenfranchised them from full civic participation, with each perpetuating the other. White and black cultural traditions came to develop their own idioms, furthering the racial divide.

It is beyond the scope of this chapter to consider the myriad ways in which racism continues to plague our national realities. It remains our challenge to right the political, civic, and interpersonal relations needed for the mutual benefit of the present and future American generations: white, black, and any Other. In order to rise to the challenge, we need the courage of truth and awareness. We need to question rationalized public policies that maintain segregation and inequality, be it at the voting booth or in judicial or police protection. We need to tune into and question habits of prejudice and bigotry. We need to probe better the stereotypes of our culture and of ourselves. Such an examination will inoculate our civic consciousness against the lies masquerading as truth. We will choose worthy leaders aware of their responsibility to represent the integrity of the nation's essential values. Birtherism shows Donald Trump not only as unworthy but as dangerous to the nation's central tenet: *E pluribus unum*. It is not negotiable.

Luba Kessler, M.D., is a psychiatrist and psychoanalyst in private practice. Born in the post-Holocaust displacement in the Ural Mountains, she has lived and received her education in the Soviet Union, Poland, Italy, and the United States. That journey included essential lessons in history, geography, culture, art, and politics. Postgraduate training and faculty appointments followed, in psychiatry at Hillside Hospital on Long Island, and in psychoanalysis at NYU Psychoanalytic Institute (now the Institute for Psychoanalytic Education, affiliated with NYU Medical School). She is editor of Issues in Education *for* The American Psychoanalyst *of the American Psychoanalytic Association.*

TRUMP'S DADDY ISSUES:

A Toxic Mix for America
STEVE WRUBLE, M.D.

As a psychiatrist, I am interested in why people are the way they are. Ultimately, the more I understand others, and my relationship to them, the better I understand myself. I am intrigued by the factors that have guided Donald Trump into the Oval Office and into the hearts, minds, and clenched fists of so many Americans. I'm especially frustrated by his having captured the attention and respect of the man I have always craved a closer relationship with—my father.

Fathers and sons have a storied history of playing off each other as they grapple with their evolving separate and shared identities. We tumble through time doing our best to make sense of all that we witness and experience. I, like Donald Trump, grew up watching and interacting with a strong, proud, and successful father. We both looked up to our fathers for guidance, but at the same time we also felt a certain competitiveness with them as we fought for our innate need for separation and individuation. The spectrum of how sons interact with their fathers is vast. The early beliefs that each has about himself will determine the path chosen to act out their drama. As much as I am disturbed by Trump's behavior, I can't help but wonder what of him is in me and vice versa. Who is this man who has captivated so much of the American electorate, and for that matter, the whole world? As a son locked into a drama with a father, can I shed light on that question?

Politically, many people in America are single-issue voters. Whether it be abortion, the economy, or foreign policy, it's that one main issue that holds sway over their vote. In my family's case, that one issue is Israel. I come from a family of Modern Orthodox Jews, and Orthodox Jewry as a group has thrown its support behind President Trump because it feels Israel will be safer under his watch. Of course, other issues are also important to Orthodox Jews, but these are usually overshadowed by concern for Israel.

About ten years ago, I made the difficult decision to let my family know that I had stopped following the many dictates that an Orthodox Jew is expected to follow. This new choice was quite freeing for me, since I had already been living this way secretly for a few years. At the same time, it was upsetting to my parents and especially my father, because Judaism is a major part of his identity. He said he was worried that this would create chaos in our family and wished, for my children's sake, that I would keep my secret to myself. On a deeper level, it felt as if he perceived it as a threat to his leadership in the family.

My decision to leave Orthodox Judaism feels connected to the evolution of my political views toward a more liberal agenda. This, at first, was uncomfortable because it was frowned upon in my community to question anything that supported the State of Israel. Donald Trump's behavior was clear and disturbing to me and overshadowed his support for Israel. However, my misgivings were not echoed in my community. My attempts to be understood by family and friends were surprisingly difficult.

Many Republicans seem to be locked in a dysfunctional relationship with Trump as a strong father figure who appears to have far less to offer than they're pining for. Yet, like myself, they are looking to their "father" in the hope that he will deliver them from what feels broken within them and the lives they are leading.

Before addressing the difficulties in my family around what it's like to see the political world so differently and yet to continue to share family events and happy occasions, I'd like to take a short drive through Donald Trump's life to show you some things that help make sense of what we're all witnessing.

There are several details that seem to shine a light on how Trump's relationship with his father, Fred Trump, may have impacted his development. Donald is the fourth of five children. His oldest sister is a circuit court judge and his oldest brother, Freddie Jr., died at the age of forty-three from complications due to alcoholism. According to a *New York Times* article (Horowitz 2016), it was apparent to those who watched Fred Trump with his children that his intensity was too much for Freddie Jr. to tolerate. As Donald watched the tragedy unfold, he stepped up and became his father's protégé in his building empire. I can only imagine that following a brother who drank himself to death didn't leave Donald much room to do anything but try and fill the void where his older brother had failed. Obviously, he was successful at this endeavor in his father's world of real estate, and the two spent many years working together until Donald moved on to captain his own company. Fred Trump could never understand why Donald wanted to take the financial risk of building in Manhattan. The elder Trump felt that the ease they enjoyed being successful in Brooklyn and Queens should have been intoxicating enough for his son. However, Donald appeared to be attracted to the bright lights of the big city and the challenge of being more successful than his father.

From the same *New York Times* article, "Trump's childhood friends have said they see in him his father's intensity, but also a constant and often palpable need to please and impress the patriarch who ruled his family with a firm hand. Even today, Donald Trump seems to bathe in his father's approval. A framed photo of Fred Trump faces him on his cluttered desk." Donald said he learned his father's values, and his killer sense of competition, by following him to building sites and watching him squeeze the most out of every dollar. In a speech to the National Association of Home Builders,

Trump said, "My father would go and pick up the extra nails and scraps, and he'd use whatever he could and recycle it in some form or sell it."

According to an article in *The Guardian* (Dean 2016), when Fred Trump died in 1999, Donald Trump gave a cheerful quote for his father's *New York Times* obituary, focusing on the way his dad had never wanted to expand into Manhattan. "It was good for me," he said. "You know, being the son of somebody, it could have been competition to me. This way, I got Manhattan all to myself!" At his father's wake, Donald stepped forward to address family, friends, and the society power brokers in the crowd. One attendee recalled Mr. Trump's unorthodox eulogy to his father, "My father taught me everything I know. And he would understand what I'm about to say," Mr. Trump announced to the room. "I'm developing a great building on Riverside Boulevard called Trump Place. It's a wonderful project." Not the warmest send-off, but it highlighted the language and sentiment that the two men shared. It was the point of their connection. When Donald's father, Fred Trump, was fifteen, he started in the building business alongside his mother due to the fact that his father died just three years earlier. At the age of fifty-three, Donald, with the death of *his* own father, was wasting no time on tears; he was moving forward in the familial quest for financial success.

Donald witnessed his father's tough negotiating style, even at home. One time, some of Donald's friends were confused as to why his wealthy father would not buy him a new baseball glove. Trump said it was because his father suspected him, correctly, of playing dumb about the high price of the glove he wanted, and of trying to get the salesman to go along with this ruse. It appears Donald learned early on that his father's frugality would leave him wanting. It also may have taught him that he needed to be sneaky at times to get what he desired.

When I was about the same age, I remember my father telling me how surprised and impressed he was that I was able to convince a salesman to refund our money and take back an expensive board game that we had already opened but didn't like. I could see in my father's face that he was enamored of my moxie. The power of a father's attention to our behavior forms a strong lock and key for that behavior to become something we depend upon in order hopefully to receive that same coveted attention again and again. Of course, I've learned the hard way that behaviors I picked up from pleasing my father don't always translate to the healthiest way to relate to others. Those habits take time and experience to break.

Fred Trump's housing projects made him wealthy and powerful. Some tenants appreciated him for his solid, well-priced apartments; others loathed him for his suspected exclusion of blacks from his properties. The famous folk singer Woody Guthrie, who wrote "This Land Is Your Land," was a tenant of Mr. Trump's Beach Haven apartments for two years. In the early 1950s, he composed two songs that address his disgust with the racist practices of Fred Trump that he witnessed. Here are some of his lyrics from the songs he wrote: "I suppose Old Man Trump knows just how much Racial Hate he stirred up in the blood-pot of human hearts when he drawed that color line here at his Eighteen hundred family project. . . . Beach Haven looks like heaven where no black ones come to roam! No, no, no! Old Man Trump! Old Beach Haven ain't my home!"

Unlike Trump, I was fortunate to watch my father come home daily from saving lives as a physician. I can only imagine how ashamed I would have felt if my father had been accused of being racist by anyone, much less a famous composer. That being said, Donald may not have given it a second thought.

The human brain can protect us from seeing and feeling what it believes may be too uncomfortable for us to tolerate. It can lead us to deny, defend, minimize, or rationalize away something that doesn't fit our worldview. Actually, as I observe President Trump's behavior, I imagine that there is a good chance he identifies with his father's aggressive business style and parenting, and is now employing that orientation to his role as president. In psychology, this is called *identification with the aggressor*. At first, it may appear counter-intuitive to identify with an aggressor who has abused his position of power to take advantage. However, our brains often use this early relationship as a template to shape our future behavior. We are attracted to the power we witness from our powerless position. We can be hungry for the same power that we originally resented or even fought against. Taking all this into consideration, President Trump's aggressive behavior seems to illuminate the part of his father that still lives on within him.

Individuals with such a history often exhibit insecurities that can lead to all kinds of compensatory behaviors. However, no matter how successful a person is at alleviating the associated anxiety, fear usually still exists unconsciously and can be uncovered at times of stress. Trump's sensitivity to being seen as weak or vulnerable along with his need to exaggerate and distort the truth are signs of his deep-seated insecurity. His confabulation protects his fragile ego. Meanwhile, his blustering becomes fodder for comedians and the media. Watching reporters try to address the "alternative facts" and Trump's impulsive tweets with his press secretary staff is comically surreal.

In simplified fashion, in order for Trump to avoid feeling the effects of his insecurities, and to feed his narcissistic needs, he appears to compensate by trying to be seen as powerful and special with the hope that he will indeed *feel* powerful and special. Only he knows the truth about how successful he is at this. The human brain has a unique ability to work in the background, using past beliefs as if we were living in the times when those beliefs were birthed. From a survivalist standpoint, our brains work off the assumption that we are safer to believe that situations will most likely repeat themselves. We don't challenge those beliefs unless something drastic occurs that overwhelms our defenses. We have learned through research on trauma survivors that early events that stimulate our fight-or-flight response have long-lasting effects. It usually directs us to create a negative belief about ourselves, which in turn leads to the counterbalancing behaviors that try to minimize the deleterious effects of those negative beliefs. Therefore, President Trump will most likely change his way of being only if reality throws him a large enough curveball to which he is unable to respond using the signature defensive measures he has grown accustomed to.

The beliefs and compensatory mechanisms that young Donald created to help steward him through the turbulent waters of his childhood are probably still in effect today. They were reinforced during his years working with his father, and later as a successful businessman. As the owner of his own company, he was able to exact control and demand loyalty in ways that he cannot as president. Transferring his strategies and expectations to the culture of government has been frustrating for him, and his responses to that frustration have been eye-opening. He doesn't appear to have the flexibility to switch gears in order to deal with the function of his job as president. His handling of FBI director James Comey is a good example. Conversations about loyalty appear to have contributed to his firing. Trump's befuddlement regarding all the fireworks that ensued makes it appear that he is either limited in understanding the impact of his behavior or insensitive to it. Either way, his leadership leaves a large segment of the population feeling insecure and fearful about what to expect next.

Fred Trump's competitiveness was quite apparent near the end of his life, when he was quoted as saying that his thrice-divorced son would never beat him in the "marital department," since he had been married to the same woman for sixty years. In addition, when Donald Trump was asked in 2016 while he was running for office what his father would have said about him running for president, he said, "He would have absolutely allowed me to have done it." Allowed?? Despite being seventy years old, Trump answered as if he were an adolescent in an oedipal battle with his father who had died seventeen years earlier.

In August of 2016, I was speaking with my father on the phone about the presidential election, and he was addressing his confusion as to why Trump was acting so erratically. This was at a time when there were several articles being written about how Trump's advisers were having difficulty getting him to stop tweeting his aggressive thoughts and feelings. I was surprised when my father asked me what my understanding as a psychiatrist was regarding Trump's behavior. Usually, my father has his own ideas about why things are the way they are and enjoys teaching me what he feels the truth is. Although I had strong feelings and ideas about why Trump was acting the way he was, my father's inquiry felt like an easy path to receiving some of the attention and respect that I continue to look for. It felt powerful and invigorating to be asked by my father what my thoughts were.

As I proceeded to describe my hypothesis of what was happening with Trump, I confidently and proudly told my father that I believed that Trump was unconsciously sabotaging his chances of winning the election because a part of him probably recognized he wasn't worthy and/or capable of being successful in that position. I went on to say that Trump appeared to be more comfortable complaining about, and fighting against, the system that he believed was conspiring against his bid to be elected. In response, my father said, "Well, whatever's going on, I wish he would just shut up because if Hillary wins, it'll be horrible for Israel." Despite giving my father what I felt was my intellectual gold, he only commented on what was important to him.

Since Trump has taken office, I have tried to engage my father, and others within my family and in the Orthodox Jewish community, about my concerns with Trump's exaggerations and lying, along with his xenophobia, all of which appear to be playing on the fears and insecurities of his support base. Almost invariably I hear, "Yeah, he's a little crazy, but he'll be better than Obama ever was," or something like, "Don't be such a bad sport. You guys lost; deal with it!" And when people were protesting peacefully around the country, I would hear, "When Obama won, we never acted this way." When I explained that it's a wonderful thing that we live in a place where we have the right to protest, my words usually fell on deaf ears. I couldn't believe that Trump's behavior was being downplayed. By questioning it, I was automatically labeled by some as having drunk the liberal Kool-Aid. Some inferred that I must believe that Israel wasn't without sin in its fight to live in peace with the Palestinians. Others accused me of wanting a socialist state. It became clear that, in parts of my family and within the wider community of Orthodox Jews, there was an "us-versus-them" mentality. It's frustrating to be told that my thoughts and clinical ideas about unfolding events are really just politically motivated.

It is especially difficult for me to be thrown into a category where family and friends wrongly assume that I must not care about Israel enough, or that I am more sympathetic to the plight of Syrian refugees than to the safety of Israelis and Americans. I try to explain that my love for Israel is separate from my feelings for anybody who is being trampled on by Trump's process. No lives should be dismissed as unimportant. All this feels surreal as I try to emphasize that any end, even Israel's security, that follows an inappropriate process is dangerously fragile and not worth depending on.

The online environment of Facebook has taken center stage as the arena of choice for many Jews to fight about politics in general and about Trump specifically. I had a "friend" on Facebook say that in continuing to attack Trump's behavior, I was forgetting the Holocaust. I was told that Trump's policies were protecting Americans by keeping "dangerous" people outside our borders. The fact that innocent people were being harmed, they said, was an unfortunate but necessary side effect. Conversely, a few Jewish patients I treat who are children of Holocaust survivors fear that another Holocaust is more likely because of Trump's policies and his association with the likes of Steve Bannon. They are afraid that those in bed with white nationalists send a message to anti-Semitic people that it is safe to act out their racist and prejudiced agendas.

I recently spent the Jewish holiday of Passover with my family at a resort where a conservative political writer had been hired to speak. My family and I attended the talk, which I assumed would be pro-Trump. I sat with my father while the speaker made clear that he was not happy with Trump and, furthermore, he felt that Trump's leadership style was dangerous. I almost laughed out loud as I watched my father's mouth drop open. During the question-and-answer session, I asked about the impact on Orthodox Jews voting for a man who has such a flawed process of leading, yet who strongly supports the State of Israel. The speaker validated my concerns by responding that the ends do not justify the means, stating emphatically, "President Trump needs to shut up and just let those he has selected for his Cabinet do their jobs and push their conservative agenda forward." Afterward, my father minimized what he had heard as if acknowledging the speaker's full message would leave him too vulnerable. In the end, I felt as if I had won a battle. Perhaps, more importantly, this situation illustrates the dance my father and I often fall into when we unknowingly work out where we stand in relationship to each other.

My father and I, like Donald and his father, are men with unique flavors of insecurity. Unwittingly, we use each other to make a case for the verdict we already believe about ourselves. Donald and I are expert at putting our fathers on pedestals while at the same time trying to knock them off in order to make room for us to have our time being seen as special. A part of us believes this will lead to feeling special, but it's fleeting. It only lasts long enough to make us keep wishing for it again and again. Unfortunately, since it's a cover for our true negative beliefs about ourselves, we often sabotage and cut short our stay on this shaky pedestal. It's a precarious perch for us. A lonely view from a place we actually don't feel we fully deserve.

On the night that Donald Trump won the election, he couldn't be found for a number of hours for comment on his momentous victory. In Leslie Stahl's *60 Minutes* interview aired three days later, he was asked where he had been during those hours. He soberly responded, "I realized this is a whole different life for me." It was as if the president-elect had never imagined actually winning. He seemed stunned that he had knocked out his formidable opponent and now would be expected to put his angry fighter persona on the shelf and go to work as the next president. Is that what he really wanted? One wonders if he even had a victory speech prepared at all.

As with all adults, Donald Trump's early development created who we are witnessing. Children need to receive love and attention in order to feel secure, but they receive only the love and attention that their parents are capable of providing. Indeed, his father's intensity left its mark on the entire family. Donald's oldest brother essentially killed himself under his father's rule. This tragedy must have played a prominent role in the formation of Donald's identity and left minimal room to rebel against his father's authority, except through competition in the realm of business success. Despite their appreciation for each other, the tension between father and son caused Donald psychological wounds that still fester. To compensate, Donald Trump puffs himself up to project a macho image that appeals to many of his followers. But it's empty, a defense against his fear of seeming weak and ineffectual like his brother. Before being elected, Trump could treat people as he wished, using his wealth and status as a means to achieve his goals. As the president of the United States, he is expected to handle issues more delicately and follow the checks and balances that make up our democratic society. Unfortunately for him and possibly the nation, his strengths that got him elected president don't ensure success in that position.

Trump's base of support saw in him the strength to be powerful in ways they didn't see in themselves and/or in past leadership. What they may not be aware of is that President Trump appears to question his own ability to deliver what they are seeking. Evidence of this can be seen in his use of lying, distortion, marginalization, and the firing of those he fears are disloyal. Our fathers did the best they could with the resources they had, and our unique connection with them helps fill the gaps where we feel deficient. Despite the moments of contention, and maybe even because of them, I feel fortunate to have a relationship with a father who continues to do his part to help our relationship become closer. I'm also grateful for the insight I've received through psychotherapy to address those parts of myself that are either stuck or confused by my past. It's unfortunate that our president has not figured out how to heal himself or at least learn how to do his job without being defensive and aggressive with those that disagree with him. I feel for the young parts of the president that are trying desperately to help him swim through rough waters despite fear of drowning. What most concerns me is whether we Americans can tread water long enough to come together and avoid being pulled under.

Steve Wruble, M.D., is an accomplished singer-songwriter and storyteller. He has won the Moth StorySLAM, and is about to have the Off-Broadway début of his solo show, Escape from Daddyland. *Dr. Wruble is also a board-certified child and adult psychiatrist in private practice in Manhattan and Ridgewood, New Jersey, at the Venn Center. He specializes in anxiety disorders, trauma, and men's psychological health. He attended medical school in his hometown of Memphis, Tennessee, and did his general psychiatry residency at Northwestern University. He did his child psychiatry fellowship at the Institute for Juvenile Research at the University of Illinois at Chicago, where he was chief fellow.*

References

Dean, Michelle. 2016. "Making the Man: To Understand Trump, Look at His Relationship with His Dad." *The Guardian*, March 26. www.theguardian .com/us-news/2016/mar/26/donald-trump-fred-trump-father-relation ship-business-real-estate-art-of-deal.

Horowitz, Jason. 2016. "Fred Trump Taught His Son the Essentials of Show-Boating Self-Promotion." *New York Times*, August 12. www.nytimes.com /2016/08/13/us/politics/fred-donald-trump-father.html?_r=0.

TRUMP AND THE AMERICAN COLLECTIVE PSYCHE*

THOMAS SINGER, M.D.

While I join those who believe that we need to question Donald Trump's psychological fitness to be president, my focus is less on individual psychopathology than on the interface between Trump and the American collective psyche. There are ways in which Trump mirrors, even amplifies, our collective attention deficit disorder, our sociopathy, and our narcissism. Therefore, this is less about diagnosing a public figure than about recognizing our own pathology.

Trump has mesmerized our national psyche like no other public figure in recent memory. There is no doubt that his appeal (his wealth, power, celebrity status, and his brash willingness to shoot from the hip) resonates powerfully with the collective psyche of many Americans, while these same qualities are repulsive to many others. The more vulgar, bullying, impulsive, and self-congratulatory Trump's behavior and rhetoric, the more some people worship him, while

---

* This chapter has been adapted from an earlier essay, "Trump and the American Selfie," in *A Clear and Present Danger: Narcissism in the Era of Donald Trump*, coedited by Steven Buser and Leonard Cruz, and from the article, "If Donald Trump Had a Selfie Stick, We'd All Be in the Picture" (billmoyers.com /story/donald-trump-selfie-americas-worst-side/).

others fervently denounce him as a grave danger to our republic. To probe the profound collective disturbance that Trump activates and symbolizes, I draw on my experience as a psychiatrist and Jungian psychoanalyst.

A Psychological Theory About Trump's Appeal: A Marriage of the Shadow, Archetypal Defenses, and the Self at the Group Level of the Psyche to Form a Cultural Complex

You don't need to be a psychologist or psychiatrist to see that Donald Trump has a problem of narcissism. Ted Cruz announced on May 3, 2016, the day of the Indiana Republican presidential primary, that Trump was "a pathological liar, utterly amoral, a narcissist at a level I don't think this country's ever seen and a serial philanderer" (Wright, Kopan, and Winchester 2016). In a series of papers and books written over the past decade, I have developed a working model of the theory of cultural complexes that may be useful for understanding Trumpism. I will be talking about the psyche of the *group*—what lives inside each of us as individual carriers of the group psyche and what lives between us in our shared group psyche. The group psyche engages with themes and conflicts that are not the same as our more personal psychological struggles.

I hypothesize a direct link between Trump's personal narcissism and the collective psyche of those American citizens who embrace his perception of America and who feel that he understands and speaks to them. This is not a political analysis. It is a psychological analysis of what we can think of as the *group psyche*, which contributes enormously to and fuels political processes. This analysis is based on the notion that there are certain psychological energies, even structures, at the level of the cultural or group psyche that are activated at times of heightened threats to the core identity of the group—what we might think of as the group Self. Three of these most important energies/structures are (1) the shadow, (2) archetypal defenses of the group Self, and (3) the group Self itself. These energies/ structures take shape around social, political, economic, geographic, and religious themes that are alive in specific contexts and with particular contents. This same type of analysis may currently apply in the Brexit crisis in Great Britain, or in the Palestinian-Israeli conflict, with very different contexts and contents in which various groups can be seen as protecting their threatened or wounded Self from being further injured by pursuing a defensive, aggressive attack against imagined or real, dangerous enemies.

What is it about Trump that acts as an irresistible magnet with ferocious attraction or repulsion? Is Trump the end product of our culture of narcissism? Is he what we get and deserve because he epitomizes the god or gods we currently worship in our mindless, consumerist, hyperindulged cult of continuous stimulation and entertainment? Here is how Christopher Hedges states it in *Empire of Illusion: The End of Literacy and the Triumph of Spectacle:*

> An image-based culture communicates through narratives, pictures, and pseudo-drama. Scandalous affairs, hurricanes, untimely deaths, train wrecks—these events play well on computer screens and television. International diplomacy, labor union negotiations, and convoluted bailout packages do not yield exciting personal narratives or stimulating images . . . Reality is complicated. Reality is boring. We are incapable or unwilling to handle its confusion . . . We become trapped in the linguistic prison of incessant repetition. We are fed words and phrases like *war on terror* or *pro-life* or *change*, and within these narrow parameters, all complex thought, ambiguity, and self-criticism vanish. (Hedges 2009)

In addition to our collective inability to sort out illusion from reality, our culture gets further hopelessly entangled with our cult of

celebrity. Hedges does not spare us the dire consequences of our intoxication with celebrity, which both fuels the split between illusion
and reality while simultaneously filling the gap between the two.

> Celebrity culture plunges us into a moral void. No one has
> any worth beyond his or her appearance, usefulness, or abil-
> ity to *succeed*. The highest achievements in a celebrity cul-
> ture are wealth, sexual conquest, and fame. It does not
> matter how these are obtained . . . We have a right, in the
> cult of the self, to get whatever we desire. We can do any-
> thing, even belittle and destroy those around us, including
> our friends, to make money, to be happy, and to become fa-
> mous. Once fame and wealth are archived, they become
> their own justification, their own morality. (Hedges 2009)

It seems clear that Trump's narcissism and his attacks on political correctness dovetail with deep needs in a significant portion of
the American population to enhance their dwindling sense of place
in America and of America's place in the world. Trump's narcissism
can be seen as a perfect compensatory mirror for the narcissistic
needs and injuries of those who support him—or, stated another way,
there is a good "fit."

With this general formulation in mind, I analyze how Trump's
presidency speaks to three highly intertwined parts of the American group psyche: (1) a woundedness at the core of the American
group Self; (2) the defenses mobilized in the groups that feel wounded,
who wish to protect against further injury to the shared group Self;
and (3) the promise or hope of a cure for the wound.

1. A Wound to the American Group Self

There is a wound at the core of the American group Self/spirit that
is deeply felt by many, especially by those who have not participated
in our nation's prosperity and by others who are relatively well off
but are keenly aware that our system of government and our way of

life are threatened at the core of our collective being. Here is a working definition of the group Self or spirit that I put forth in an earlier paper:

> The *group spirit* is the ineffable core beliefs or sense of identity that binds people together . . . that [is] known to its members through a sense of belonging, shared essential beliefs, core historical experiences of loss and revelation, deepest yearnings and ideals . . . One can begin to circle around the nature of a group's spirit by asking questions such as:
> What is most sacred to the group?
> What binds the group's members together?
>
> (Singer 2006b)

Many in our country, on the left, right, and in the center, feel that this stage in our history is less secure than earlier stages. This nervousness about our essential well-being is deeply felt by the progressive left, by the conservative right, and by all those who feel alienated and angered by the current leaders of all branches of government, whom they see as destroying the country, whether the archenemy be Donald Trump of the Republicans or Hillary Clinton of the Democrats. On the right, the threat of terrorism (Muslims), immigrants (Mexicans), the global economy (China and international trade agreements), or progressives are seen as leading us to the brink. On the left, the threats to a sense of well-being and security in our national group Self come as the result of the growing disparity in the distribution of wealth and income; the mistreatment of vulnerable minorities of different races, colors, ethnicities, sexual identities, or genders; our power relationships to other countries around the world; and of course the maltreatment of the environment.

I postulate that these threats are amplified on all sides by an even deeper, less conscious threat that I call *extinction anxiety*. Extinction anxiety exists both in the personal and group psyche and is based on the fear of the loss of supremacy by white Americans of the United States, the loss of America's place in the world as we have known it, and ultimately the destruction of the environment and the world itself. One might think of extinction anxiety as the cultural psyche's equivalent of *death anxiety* in the individual. For instance, climate change deniers on the right may be seen as denying the very real possibility of the planet's destruction as a way of defending themselves against the fear of extinction. Aligning himself with this attitude, Trump offers to dispel *extinction anxiety* by denying it is real and appointing a well-known climate change denier as head of the EPA. Denial, whether at the individual or group level, is the most primitive defense the mind employs to protect itself from psychic pain.

Here is how Joseph Epstein (2016) has described the injury to the group Self/spirit of those attracted to Trump:

> Something deeper, I believe, is rumbling behind the astounding support for Mr. Trump, a man who, apart from his large but less than pure business success, appears otherwise entirely without qualification for the presidency. I had a hint of what might be behind the support for him a few weeks ago when, on one of the major network news shows, I watched a reporter ask a woman at a Trump rally why she was supporting him. A thoroughly respectable-seeming middle-class woman, she replied without hesitation: *"I want my country back"* . . .
>
> I don't believe that this woman is a racist, or that she yearns for immigrants, gays and other minorities to be suppressed, or even that she truly expects to turn back the clock on social change in the U.S. What she wants is precisely what she says: her country back . . . [S]he couldn't any longer bear to watch the United States on the descent, hostage to progressivist ideas that bring neither contentment nor satisfaction but instead foster a state of perpetual protest and agitation, anger and tumult. So great is the frustration

of Americans who do not believe in these progressivist ideas, who see them as ultimately tearing the country apart, that they are ready to turn, in their near hopelessness, to a man of Donald Trump's patently low quality. (Epstein 2016)

The Self or group spirit of America is built on more than three hundred years of progress, success, achievement, resourcefulness, and ingenuity, accompanied by almost endless opportunity and good fortune. We love and believe in our heroic potential; our freedom and independence; our worship of height and speed, youth, newness, technology; our optimism and eternal innocence. We have enjoyed the profound resilience of the American spirit, which has shown it-self repeatedly through very difficult historical trials, including our Civil War, World War I, the Great Depression, World War II, the Viet-nam War, the 9/11 attacks, the Iraq War, the financial collapse in 2008, and other major crises, including the one we may be in now. As a country, we have been blessed in our capacity to transcend loss, failure, and the threat of defeat in the face of crisis time and again, and this has contributed to a positive vision of ourselves that has been fundamentally solid at the core for a long time. Of course, that Self-image is subject to inflation, arrogance, and a morphing into *hubris,* in which we believe in our own exceptionalism and are blind to our causing grave injury to peoples at home and abroad. It is quite possible that Trump's personal inflation, arrogance, and hu-bris represent a compensatory antidote in our group psyche that is beginning to suffer severe self-doubt about our ability to navigate a highly uncertain future—the nostalgic longing of which is perfectly articulated in the phrase "I want my country back."

2. Archetypal Defenses of the Group Self

A significant number of people in our society feel cut off from what they believe to be their inherited, natural birthright as American citi-zens. Although they would not use this language, they are suffering a wound and threat at the level of the group Self, even as they are also suffering individually. We can think of this as a narcissistic injury at the group level. I suggest that Trump has somehow intuited that injury and is playing to it, both as a self-proclaimed carrier of the group renewal and as a defender against those who would do further harm to it—be they terrorists, immigrants, Washington political insiders, the established Republican Party, Barack Obama, Hillary Clinton, James Comey, or anyone else who gets in Trump's way.

Trump's Embrace of the Shadow of Political Correctness

Trump's particular political genius in the 2016 presidential election cycle was to launch his campaign with an attack on political correctness. With incredible manipulative skill, Trump's call to arms, "Get 'em outta here!" made its first appearance at his rallies, when he urged the faithful in his crowds to get rid of protesters. "Get 'em outta here!" also seems to be his pledge to rid the country of Mexicans, Muslims, and other groups that are being portrayed as dangerous threats to the American Way of Life.

Trump's strategy has been shrewd. He sensed that *political correctness* could be the trigger word and target for unleashing potent levels of shadow energies that have been accumulating in the cultural unconscious of the group psyche. He rode a huge wave of pent-up resentment, racism, and hatred long enough to crush all opponents and become the president of the United States. The notion of a trigger word activating a complex goes back to Jung's early word-association tests, in which certain words detonated powerful emotions contained within personal complexes—such as the mother or father complex. Skillful politicians can trigger cultural or group complexes by a collective word association process that then takes on a life of its own.

Trump is at his best when he is at his most awful: his willingness to be politically incorrect became a sign, to many, of his "truth-telling." Amid a most dangerous battle between the "alternative facts" of the alt-right and "fake news" came an outpouring of the paranoia and hostility embedded in the cultural complex of those who loathe "the deep state." Collective emotion is the only truth that matters. A group caught up in a cultural complex has highly selective memory—if any historical memory at all—and chooses only those historical and contemporary *facts* that validate their preexisting opinion. Evidence of this is that no matter what Trump does or how many lies he tells, his base remains steadfast in its support of him, as the polls tell us.

This kind of shadow energy is available for exploitation if a group that previously saw itself as having a solid place in American society (such as white middle-class Americans in the Rust Belt or coal miners in West Virginia) finds itself marginalized and drifting downward, both socially and economically. How easy it is for such a group to see recent immigrants to this country as stealing the American dream from them.

Here is how George Orwell, in *1984*, imagined the exploitation of those most subject to intoxication with an authoritarian leader like Trump:

> In a way, the world-view of the Party imposed itself most successfully on people incapable of understanding it. They could be made to accept the most flagrant violations of reality, because they never fully grasped the enormity of what was demanded of them . . . They simply swallowed everything.

Donald Trump uncovered a huge sinkhole of dark, raw emotions in the national psyche for all of us to see. Rage, hatred, envy, and fear surfaced in a forgotten, despairing, growing white underclass who had little reason to believe that the future would hold the promise of a brighter, life-affirming purpose. Trump tapped into the negative feelings that many Americans have about all the things we are supposed to be compassionate about—ethnic, racial, gender, and religious differences. *What a relief*, so many must have thought, to hear a politician speak their unspoken resentments and express their rage. Trump tapped into the dirty little secret of their loathing of various minorities, even though we may all be minorities now. Trump's formula for repairing these deep wounds had him chanting around the country the hopeful mantra of making better "deals." Once the complex takes over the narrative or the narrative gives voice to the complex's core, facts simply become irrelevant. Inevitably, this leads to the kind of terrifying *1984* scenario in which

> The Ministry of Peace concerns itself with war, the Ministry of Truth with lies, the Ministry of Love with torture, and the Ministry of Plenty with starvation. These contradictions are not accidental, nor do they result from ordinary hypocrisy: they are deliberate exercises in doublethink . . . If human equality is to be forever averted—if the High, as we have called them, are to keep their places permanently—then the prevailing mental condition must be controlled insanity.

Trump's Cabinet appointments strongly suggest that this is what is happening in our own country. The job of each new Cabinet leader is to reverse or dismantle the very reason for which his or her department exists.

Unholy Marriage of Shadow, Archetypal Defenses of the Group Self, and the Group Self

What makes Trump's unleashing of the shadow in the American psyche even more dangerous is that these energies become linked or even identical with what I call *archetypal defenses* of the group spirit:

> When this part of the collective psyche is activated, the most primitive psychological forces come alive for the purpose of defending the group and its collective spirit or Self. I capitalize *Self* because I want to make it clear that it is not just

the persona or ego identity of the group that is under attack but something at an even deeper level of the collective psyche which one might think of as the spiritual home or *god* of the group. The tribal spirit of the clan or of the nation often lies dormant or in the background, but when it is threatened, the defenses mobilized to protect it are ferocious and impersonal. The mobilization of such potent, archaic defenses is fueled by raw collective emotion and rather simplistic, formulaic ideas and/or beliefs [that] dictate how the group will think, feel, react, and behave. (Singer 2006b)

These activated archetypal defenses of the group spirit find concrete expression in forms as varied as the unrest of divided populations over the legal status of foreign immigrants in countries around the world; the threatened development of nuclear weapons by nation-states such as Iran or North Korea; the deployment of suicide bombers by terrorist groups; or the launching of massive military expeditions by world powers. And these same kinds of archetypal defenses come alive in all sorts of skirmishes between diverse groups of people who perceive their most sacred values in jeopardy—the LBGTQ community, blacks, Latinos, white men, women, the Christian right in the United States, Jews around the world, the Muslim Brotherhood throughout the Middle East. The list of groups threatened at the core of their being or at the level of the group Self seems endless (Singer 2006b). What makes Trump's narcissism so dangerous in its mix of shadow (his attacks on all sorts of groups of people) and Self elements (his self-aggrandizing, inflated sense of himself and those for whom he pretends to speak) is that it plays to the unholy marriage of Self and the aggressive, hateful, and violent elements in the collective psyche.

Trump's example gives permission for shadowy thoughts, feelings, and actions on behalf of the Self. This underlying group dynamic explains the comparison of Trump to Hitler. Evoking an archaic image of the German Self, Hitler mobilized the most shadowy forces in modern history in the so-called service of that Self-image, which centered on the supremacy of the Aryan race—first the Brownshirts, then the Gestapo, SS, and other forces of the Third Reich, including its highly efficient bureaucracy. Trump seems to be toying with the collective shadow, encouraging its acting out in the name of the Self. It is hard to imagine Trump leading the United States in the same direction that Hitler led Germany—I certainly hope I don't live to regret writing these words!—but the dynamic is still terrifying. From a Jungian perspective, when the shadowy defenses of the group spirit and the group Self closely align, there is great danger of violence, tyranny, and absolutism—especially with an authoritarian leader and a citizenry responsive to authoritarianism.

3. Curing the Wounded Self of America: Trump's "Selfie" and America's "Selfie"

The third and final component of this intertwined triad of forces in the group psyche is Trump's implicit promise of providing a cure for the wound at the level of the group Self. This is where his narcissism is most prominent and most dangerous. The unconscious equation can be stated as follows: "I am the Greatness to which America may once again aspire. By identifying with how great I am, you can rekindle your wounded American dream and make yourself and America great again." Or even more bluntly: "I have achieved the American dream; I am the American dream; I am the incarnation of the Self that the country aspires to." This, of course, is a massive inflation. Trump's identification of his personal being with the Self of America is his source of demagogic appeal. He is encouraging those who have lost a foothold in the American dream to place their trust in him as a mirror of their own potential—a potential that he has already achieved. Trump's book *The Art of the Deal* characterizes his magnetic appeal:

> I play to people's fantasies. People may not always think big
> themselves, but they can still get very excited by those who

do. That's why a little hyperbole never hurts. People want to believe that something is the biggest and the greatest and the most spectacular. I call it truthful hyperbole. (Fisher and Hobson 2016; Trump with Schwartz 1987)

Trump has managed to cultivate and catch the projection of a powerful and successful person who, by virtue of his alleged business acumen and ability to negotiate, is able to make things happen for his own betterment—though rarely for the betterment of others, despite his false claims of giving generously to charities and creating untold jobs. "You, too, can be like me: aggressive, successful, big, powerful," he is saying. This is the narcissism of Trump joining with the injured narcissism of those Americans who have seen their chances for well-being and security rapidly slip away. Trump celebrates the materialistic, power version of the American dream—of the big man who has made himself rich and powerful through the strength of his personality. He is free to speak his own mind and to pursue, without limits, his own self-aggrandizing goals that he equates with those of America.

The negative aspects of Trump's narcissism strike those who are repelled by him both at home and abroad as a symbolic mirror of everything negative about a culture of narcissism. For many, he has become the very embodiment of everything bad about America: a self-promoting brand; an arrogant bully bursting with hubris; gross insensitivity to others' needs; possession by consumerism and greed; and entitlement in good fortune, which we have come to believe is our natural due. These are core characteristics of an American cultural complex that betrays that best Self or spirit on which the nation and its constitution were founded. Trump's narcissism is a perfect mirror of our national and even personal narcissism.

Ultimately, I believe that the Trump phenomenon is less about Trump than about us—about who we are as a people: the elephant in the room turns out to be "We the People of the United States." How terrifying to think that our politics and our lives today have gotten horribly confused with reality TV, social media, computer and cell phone technology, and their infinite capacity to turn reality into illusion, Self into narcissism.

Conclusion: Groping the American Psyche and Psychic Contagion

There are so many potentially destructive consequences of the emerging Trump presidency—on the climate, on minorities, on immigrants, on women's rights, on the integrity of the Constitution, and on our relationships with China, Russia, Syria, Iran, North Korea, and even our own allies. But one of the most disturbing thoughts about the Trump presidency is that he has taken up residence not just in the White House but in the psyches of each and every one of us. We are going to have to live with him rattling around inside us, all of us at the mercy of his impulsive and bullying whims, as he lashes out at whatever gets under his skin in the moment with uninformed, inflammatory barbs. The way a president lives inside each of us can feel like a very personal and intimate affair. Those who identify with Trump and love the way he needles the "elites" whom they fear, envy, and despise may relish the fact that he lives inside us as a tormentor. Trump is well versed in brutally toying with his enemies, who include women, professionals, the media, the educated classes, and minorities—to mention just a few.

What most frightens me about Trump is his masterful skill at invading and groping the national psyche. Many tired of the Clintons' taking up permanent residence in our national psyche. Trump will soon put the Clintons to shame in his capacity to dwell in and stink up our collective inner space, like the proverbial houseguest who overstays his welcome. And many of us never invited Trump into our psychic houses in the first place. That is perhaps why the image that has stayed with me the most from the national disgrace that was our election process in 2016 is that of the woman who came forward to tell her story of allegedly being sexually harassed by Trump (Legaspi 2016).

Some years ago, she was given an upgrade to first class on a plane and found herself sitting next to "the Donald." In no time at all, she says, he was literally groping her all over—breasts and below. She describes the physicality of the assault as akin to being entangled in the tentacles of an octopus, and she was barely able to free herself and retreat to economy class.

It now feels as though we have all been groped by the tentacles of Trump's octopus-like psyche, which has invaded our own and threatens to tighten its squeeze for several years. To put it as vulgarly as Trump himself might: Trump has grabbed the American psyche by the "pussy."

As we slowly collect ourselves after the devastating and unexpected tsunami of Trump winning the presidency and the rollercoaster ride of his early days as president, many are finding renewed energy and commitment to challenge his shadowy agenda in new and creative ways. I hope that in a deep resurgence of activism to reclaim our most cherished and threatened American values, we will resist our tendency to cocoon ourselves in a self-righteous, arrogant bubble of narcissistic ideals, even in the name of being "progressive."

Thomas Singer, M.D., is a psychiatrist and Jungian psychoanalyst practicing in San Francisco. In addition to private practice, he has served on Social Security's Hearing and Appeals Mental Impairment Disability team. His interests include studying the relationships among myth, politics, and psyche in The Vision Thing *and the* Ancient Greece, Modern Psyche *series. He is the editor of a series of books exploring cultural complexes, including* Placing Psyche, Listening to Latin America, Europe's Many Souls, The Cultural Complex, *and a book in preparation on Asia. He is the current president of National ARAS, an archive of symbolic imagery that has created* The Book of Symbols.

References

Epstein, Joseph. 2016. "Why Trumpkins Want Their Country Back." *Wall Street Journal*, June 10. www.wsj.com/articles/why-trumpkins-want -their-country-back-1465596987.

Fisher, Marc, and Will Hobson. 2016. "Donald Trump Masqueraded as Publicist to Brag About Himself." *Washington Post*, May 13. www .washingtonpost.com/politics/donald-trump-alter-ego-barron/2016/05 /12/02ac99ec-16fe-11e6-aa55-670cabef46e0_story.html?hpid=hp_rhp -top-table-main_no-name%3Ahomepage%2Fstory.

Hedges, Chris. 2009. *Empire of Illusion: The End of Literacy and the Triumph of Spectacle*. New York: Nation Books.

Legaspi, Althea. 2016. "Woman Says Trump Groped Her on Plane: 'It Was an Assault.'" *Rolling Stone*, October 13. www.rollingstone.com/politics /news/woman-says-she-was-groped-by-trump-on-plane-it-was-an -assault-w444700.

MacWilliams, Matthew. 2016. "The One Weird Trait That Predicts Whether You're a Trump Supporter." *Politico*, January 17. www.politico.com /magazine/story/2016/01/donald-trump-2016-authoritarian-213533.

Orwell, George. 1949. *1984*. Repr. New York: Houghton Mifflin Harcourt, 1983.

Singer, Thomas. 2006a. "The Cultural Complex: A Statement of the Theory and Its Application." *Psychotherapy and Politics International* 4 (3): 197–212. doi: 10.1002/ppi.110.

———. 2006b. "Unconscious Forces Shaping International Conflicts: Archetypal Defenses of the Group Spirit from Revolutionary America to Confrontation in the Middle East." *The San Francisco Jung Institute Library Journal* 25 (4): 6–28.

Trump, Donald, with Tony Schwartz. 1987. *The Art of the Deal*. New York: Random House.

Wright, David, Tal Kopan, and Julia Winchester. 2016. "Cruz Unloads with Epic Takedown of 'Pathological Liar,' 'Narcissist' Donald Trump." CNN Politics, May 3. www.cnn.com/2016/05/03/politics/donald -trump-rafael-cruz-indiana/.

WHO GOES TRUMP?

Tyranny as a Triumph of Narcissism

ELIZABETH MIKA, M.A., L.C.P.C.

Tyrannies are three-legged beasts. They encroach upon our world in a steady creep more often than overcome it in a violent takeover, which may be one reason they are not always easy to spot before it is too late to do much about them. Their necessary components, those three wobbly legs, are: the tyrant, his supporters (the people), and the society at large that provides a ripe ground for the collusion between them. Political scientists call it "the toxic triangle" (Hughes 2017).

The force binding all three is narcissism. It animates the beast while, paradoxically and not, eating it alive, bringing its downfall in due time. This force and its influences, which knit the beast into such a powerful and destructive entity, remain invisible to us for reasons that are clearly hinted at but somehow continue to evade our individual and collective comprehension. They make sure we don't recognize the tyranny's marching boots, which can be heard from miles away and months away, until they show up on our doorstep, and that's despite the fact that this very same process has repeated itself countless times in history.

We have known who tyrants are and how tyrannies form since antiquity, and this knowledge has been supported by the ever-growing tragic evidence of the tyrannies' effects on humanity. Yet, despite making promises to ourselves and one another to "Never forget," we seem not to remember or not to know, always with devastating consequences. Our forgetting stems partly from miseducation (Giroux 2014) and partly from denial. It gives us clues to the kind of work (psychological, social, political, and economic) that we must do if we are to avoid the self-destruction promised by tyrannies today.

Let's take a look at tyranny's components and their interactions.

The Tyrant

Tyrants come in different shapes and sizes, and depending on perspective, various writers stress similarities or differences among them (Newell 2016). This paper will not delve into those classifications but, rather, attempt to simplify and maybe even illuminate their most salient common features.

Although the terms *dictator* and *tyrant* are used interchangeably, it makes sense perhaps to stress that not all dictators are tyrants. Tyrants are dictators gone bad. A leader may start as a seemingly benevolent dictator but turn into a tyrant as his reign progresses, becoming ruthlessly destructive with time, something we have seen repeatedly in history.

All tyrants share several essential features: they are predominantly men with a specific character defect, narcissistic psychopathy (a.k.a. malignant narcissism). This defect manifests in a severely impaired or absent conscience and an insatiable drive for power and adulation that masks the conscience deficits. It forms the core of attraction between him and his followers, the essence of what is seen as his "charisma." In his seminal paper on "Antisocial Personality Disorder and Pathological Narcissism in Prolonged Conflicts and Wars of the 21st Century" (2015), Frederick Burkle observes that narcissism augments and intensifies the pathological features of a psychopathic character structure, making those endowed with it especially dangerous, not in the least because of their ability to use manipulative charm and a pretense of human ideals to pursue their distinctly primitive goals. We talk about the chief feature of narcissistic psychopathy, the impairment of conscience, and its destructive consequences in "The Unbearable Lightness of Being a Narcissist" (Mika and Burkle 2016).

Impulsive, sensation-seeking, and incapable of experiencing empathy or guilt, a narcissistic psychopath treats other people as objects of need fulfillment and wish fulfillment. This makes it easy for him to use and abuse them, in his personal relationships and in large-scale actions, without compunction. His lack of conscience renders him blind to higher human values, which allows him to disregard them entirely or treat them instrumentally as means to his ends, the same way he treats people.

This dangerous character defect, however, serves him well in the pursuit of power, money, and adulation. Not having the inhibitions and scruples imposed by empathy and conscience, he can easily lie, cheat, manipulate, destroy, and kill if he wants to—or, when powerful enough, order others to do it for him.

The characteristics indicative of narcissistic psychopathy are observable already in childhood. Biographies of tyrants (Fromm 1973; Miller 1990; Newell 2016) note the early manifestations of vanity, sensation-seeking, and impulsivity often accompanied by poor self-control, aggression and callousness, manipulativeness, and a strong competitive drive and desire to dominate coexistent with a lack of empathy and conscience. Plato remarked on the "spirited" character of a future tyrant showing the above-mentioned symptoms already in his youth.

Another common, but not universal, biographical finding is a history of childhood abuse. Here, however, accounts vary; for example, while some, like Miller (1990), stress Hitler's purported severe abuse at the hands of his stepfather, others (Fromm 1973; Newell 2016) note that his childhood was uneventful in this respect. Biographies can be incomplete or tendentious, intentionally and not, and so it is not always possible to verify the truth. It is impossible to rule out narcissistic upbringing as being involved in raising a future tyrant—

creating a narcissistic injury that shapes the child's life and sets him on a path of "repairing" it through a ruthless and often sadistic pursuit of power and adulation—even when there is no evidence of overt abuse and/or neglect in his biographical data.

While the exact causes of this character defect are a matter of speculation, their possible origins offer intriguing possibilities explaining their clinical manifestations. For example, a narcissistic injury in the first years of a child's life could possibly impair development of the object constancy capacity. This results in an inability to grasp and adhere to the solidity of facts and, consequently, in a disregard for the truth and other human values, the understanding of which comprises a large part of our conscience. The narcissistic psychopath's propensity to lie, whether on purpose to achieve a specific result or, seemingly effortlessly, to invent a universe of "alternative facts" that just happen to affirm his grandiose and guiltless image of himself, could be a result of that impaired object constancy capacity.

His lack of empathy, whether resulting from an inborn cause or narcissistic/authoritarian upbringing, would further (or separately) limit development of his conscience and influence not only the child's socioemotional development but also his cognitive capacities, resulting in what Burkle (2016) calls being smart but not bright. Dąbrowski (1996) termed this as one-sided development, where intelligence and certain cognitive skills develop more or less normally but one's emotional growth remains stunted. The capacity for emotional development is crucial, as this is the only kind of growth possible throughout our lifespan: expanding and deepening our conscience, and spurring us to learning and meaningful change.

Whether the developmental arrest typical for this form of pathology is inborn, acquired, or a combination of both nature and nurture, it results in the narrow and inflexible character structure, with intelligence subsumed under primitive drives (for power, sex, and adulation).

As Dąbrowski (1986, trans. E. Mika) writes:

A psychopath is emotionally rigid and narrow. He has strong ambitions and significant talents, but they remain narrow and under the influence of primitive drives. He does not experience inner conflicts, but instead he creates external ones. He is not capable of empathy, and so he strives to gain control over others, or, before he can gain dominance, he submits to the control of others. He is usually deaf and blind to the problems of others, to their development and developmental difficulties. He relentlessly realizes his own goals. A psychopath exists on the level of *primary integration* and is emotionally stunted.

We can distinguish "small" and "big" psychopaths. We find the big ones among the most notorious world criminals, and among aggressive tyrants and dictators (e.g., Nero, Hitler) who do not hesitate to sacrifice others for their own goals. For a big psychopath, a person and a social group do not have any moral value. To him, rules of justice do not exist. Genocide or concentration camps are not a moral problem for him, but a means to an end.

Small psychopaths are miniatures of the big ones. In general, they submit to big psychopaths in the right circumstances. A small psychopath looks for opportunities to realize his own interests and to satisfy his desire to wreak havoc in society. A psychopath thinks that laws are to be broken and that they do not apply to him. He uses any circumstances to secure his position, money, and fortune, regardless of the consequences for others, without any consideration for ethical norms. Psychopaths do not know how to emotionally compare themselves with others, they cannot emotionally understand others, and they lack an empathic attitude.

The individual distinctions between "small" and "big" psychopaths, a.k.a. tyrants, appear to lie predominantly in the level of their narcissism, observed by Burkle (2015), but also in the presence of some socially approved skills, an ability to modulate and/or mask their aggressive impulses and deeds, as well as life opportunities and luck. A narcissistic psychopath without sufficiently developed self-control or advantageous life opportunities may turn into a mass killer whose crimes will land him in prison before his grandiose dreams of power and domination come to fruition.

Narcissistic psychopaths turned tyrants possess the right combination of manipulativeness, self-control, and intelligence to convince others to support them long enough to put their grandiose ideas to work on a large scale. They also appear to possess skills that are seen as charisma, the most frequent of which is the ability to deliver public speeches that inspire others to follow them. More often than not, however, this "charisma" is simply their ability to tell others what they want to hear (i.e., to lie), to make them go along with whatever scheme they've concocted for the moment. Their glibness is something that easily fools normal people, who do not understand the kind of pathology that results from a missing conscience.

Once in positions of power, tyrants can fully unleash their sadism under the cloak of perverted ideals, which they peddle as a cover for their primitive drives. Instead of turning into common criminals condemned by society, they become oppressors and/or murderers of thousands or millions, with their atrocities always justified in their own minds and those of their supporters. This is why Pol Pot could say without hesitation: "[Y]ou can look at me. Am I a savage person? My conscience is clear" (Mydans 1997), even though he was directly responsible for the deaths of millions of his compatriots.

Tyrants identify with other tyrants and find inspiration in their successes, while remaining oblivious to their failures. They recognize and respect power as much as they are envious of and despise its wielders. The greater and more ruthless the living or historical tyrant, the bigger an inspiration he is for aspiring ones. His disdain for morality and law and his unbridled aggression in pursuit of power appeal to the tyrant in the making and form a template for his behavior, showing him what is possible.

On the eve of invading Poland in 1939, Hitler, after issuing orders to "mercilessly and without pity" annihilate "every man, woman, and child of Polish ethnicity and language," spoke admiringly of one such role model: "Genghis Khan had sent millions of women and children to their deaths, and did so consciously and with a happy heart. History sees in him only the great founder of states." Then he exhorted his subordinates in Poland to "be hard, spare nothing, act faster, and more brutally than the others"—and they eagerly obliged (Gellately 2007).

The upcoming tyrant dreams of becoming as great as and preferably greater than his favorite tyrannical role models; and if those role models are alive, the tyrant-in-the-making can be expected to curry favor with the existing ones while plotting their demise and besting them in the tyrants' world rankings. To accomplish this, though, he must obtain a position of ultimate power within his own nation first.

This brings us to the second leg of the tyrannical beast . . .

The Tyrant's Supporters

The process through which the tyrant gains popularity and power usually baffles the outside observers and historians looking at it from the perspective of time, as its main ingredient, narcissism, somehow remains invisible to both participants and observers.

The tyrant's narcissism is the main attractor of his followers, who project their hopes and dreams onto him. The more grandiose his sense of his own self and his promises to his fans, the greater their attraction and the stronger their support. As Plato wrote in *The Republic*, "The people have always some champion whom they set over them and nurse into greatness."

Through the process of identification, the tyrant's followers absorb his omnipotence and glory and imagine themselves as powerful as he is, the winners in the game of life. This identification heals the followers' narcissistic wounds, but also tends to shut down their reason and conscience, allowing them to engage in immoral and criminal behaviors with a sense of impunity engendered by this identification. Without the support of his narcissistic followers, who see in the tyrant a reflection and vindication of their long-nursed dreams of glory, the tyrant would remain a middling nobody.

The interplay of grandiose hopes and expectations between the tyrant-in-the-making and his supporters that suffuses him with power and helps propel him to a position of political authority is an example of narcissistic collusion: a meshing of mutually compatible narcissistic needs. The people see in him their long-awaited savior and a father substitute, hinting at the narcissistic abuse implicated in the authoritarian upbringing that demands obedience and worship of the all-powerful parental figure. In their faith and unquestioning admiration, he in turn receives a ready line of narcissistic supply, thousands of mirrors reflecting his greatness.

Describing the narcissistic collusion between the tyrant and his supporters, Erich Fromm (1980) stressed the elements of submission to and identification with the strongman:

> The highly narcissistic group is eager to have a leader with whom it can identify itself. The leader is then admired by the group which projects its narcissism onto him. In the very act of submission to the powerful leader, which is in depth an act of symbiosis and identification, the narcissism of the individual is transferred onto the leader. The greater the leader, the greater the follower. Personalities who as individuals are particularly narcissistic are the most qualified to fulfill this function. The narcissism of the leader who is convinced of his greatness, and who has no doubts, is precisely what attracts the narcissism of those who submit to him. The half-insane leader is often the most successful one until his lack of objective judgment, his rage reaction in consequence to any setback, his need to keep up the image of

omnipotence may provoke him to make mistakes which lead to his destruction. But there are always gifted half-psychotics at hand to satisfy the demands of a narcissistic mass.

Jerrold Post (2015) underscored the authoritarian parenting aspect of that identification when discussing Hitler Youth:

Especially for the Hitler Youth Movement, which was at the forefront of Hitler's support, Hitler's externalizing hate-mongering rhetoric was a comforting and inspiring message, and Hitler provided the strong inspiring father figure that these children could not find within their own families. But, in rebelling against their own families, they submitted uncritically to Hitler's authoritarian leadership. Importantly, Adolf Hitler's unleashing of the demons of war was turning the passive humiliation of defeat [in World War I] into the active experience of redemptive action.

The narcissistic mixture of elevated expectations, resentments, and desire for revenge on specific targets and/or society in general for not meeting those expectations is what sociologist Michael Kimmel (2013) called aggrieved entitlement. Although Kimmel talked specifically about white American men in the twenty-first century, some form of aggrieved entitlement has been driving tyrants and their supporters, as well as organized and "lone wolf" terrorists, the world over since time immemorial.

The tyrant makes many good-sounding—but also openly unrealistic, bordering on delusional—promises to his supporters, and usually has no intention or ability to fulfill most of them (if any). He holds his supporters in contempt, as he does "weaker" human beings in general, and uses them only as props in his domination- and adulation-oriented schemes.

The narcissistic collusion between the tyrant and his supporters is also driven by the latter's need for revenge, for the tyrant is always chosen to perform this psychically restorative function: to avenge the humiliations (narcissistic wounds) of his followers and punish those who inflicted them.

However, as the wounds often date to the supporters' personal ancient past and more often than not are perceived rather than real, the choice of the object of this vengeful punishment is not based on reality. Rather, it is based on the displacement and projection characteristic of the scapegoating process that becomes an inextricable part of the narcissistic collusion between the tyrant and his followers.

The scapegoating designates the Others as an object upon which the narcissistic revenge will be inflicted. The Others always represent the split-off, devalued, and repressed parts of the narcissistic individual's own psyche, which are projected onto them. These projections are shared and augmented through a narcissism of small differences (Freud 1991), which allows us to focus on and enlarge insignificant differences between ourselves and the Others in order to solidify our negative projections and justify our contempt and aggression toward them.

The tyrant and his followers typically choose as vessels for their negative projections and aggression the members of society who are not just different but weaker. The tyrant fuels that aggression in order to solidify his power but also to deflect it from himself, shield his own narcissism, and repair his own narcissistic injuries dating to his childhood. The figure of the narcissistic parental abuser/tyrant is protected through the scapegoating and the return to the authoritarian, order- and obedience-based mode of social functioning promised by the tyrant, as he himself assumes the mantle of father-protector and directs his own and his supporters' aggression onto the Others, who have nothing to do with those supporters' real and perceived wounds.

The tyrant's own narcissism hints at the level of woundedness in his supporters. The greater their narcissistic injury, the more grandiose the leader required to repair it. While his grandiosity appears grotesque to non-narcissistic people who do not share his agenda, to his followers he represents all their denied and thwarted greatness, which now, under his rule, will finally flourish. Hitler's bizarre dream of a Thousand-Year Reich spread upon the world did not seem at all preposterous or dangerous to so many Germans suffering from the pain, humiliation, and privations inflicted upon them by the fiasco of World War I, just as Stalin's vision of communism as dictatorship of the working class taking over the world did not appear strange or dangerous to his beleaguered followers. Narcissism is blind to itself.

The natural consequence of scapegoating that stems from the projections of the narcissist's devalued parts of himself is dehumanization of the Others, which then justifies all kinds of atrocities perpetrated on them. The ease with which this attitude spreads in narcissistic groups is frightening, and indicative of a narcissistic rage that fuels it, a rage focused on purging, psychically and physically, all that is weak and undesirable from the narcissists' inner and external worlds.

That rage, along with dreams of glory, is what makes the bond between the tyrant and his followers so strong that it remains impervious to reality. It also makes the tyrant's rule easier, as he does not have to exert himself much to infect his followers with contempt for the dehumanized Others and incite aggression against them. In fact, the tyrant's permission for such aggression appears to be a large part of his appeal to his blood- and revenge-thirsty followers.

The tyrant's and his followers' projections always reveal much about their own pathology. In his private notes about Jews in Nazi-occupied Poland, Hitler's propaganda minister, Joseph Goebbels, wrote that they were "not people anymore" but "beasts of prey equipped with a cold intellect" (Gellately 2007), the latter description obviously more applicable to Goebbels and the Nazis themselves than their victims (who, it must be stressed, were observed by Goebbels in captivity, under dehumanizing conditions of ghetto life).

Once we dehumanize the Others and imbue them with a murderous motivation directed at us, we can easily rationalize any act of violence we perpetrate upon them as self-defense. And so, removing en masse and without mercy those "beasts of prey" became one of the main goals of the Nazis, who believed that Jews, Poles, Gypsies, and other non-Aryans threatened their existence. The fear, whether genuine or faked, stemming from this false belief was used as a sufficient justification for mass murder on a scale unseen previously in the modern world.

It must be noted that the tyrant's supporters and especially sycophants within his closest circle tend to share his character defect. The sycophantic echo chamber around the tyrant magnifies but also hides his pathology. His surrogates usually serve as ego substitutes to his rampaging id, and are responsible for introducing and implementing his destructive plans in ways that would seem rational and acceptable to the public.

Their role becomes more important with time, as he psychologically decompensates, which inevitably happens to narcissistic psychopaths in positions of ultimate power. As his paranoia, grandiosity, and impulsivity grow, his aides, family members, and surrogates, fearful for their positions and often their lives, scramble to preserve an image of his "normalcy" and greatness for public consumption to the very end. Their loyalty can be fierce and undying, unlike that of the tyrant himself.

The Society

Tyrants do not arise in a vacuum, just as tyranny does not spring on the world unannounced. It takes years of cultivation of special conditions in a society for a tyranny to take over. Those conditions invariably include a growing and unbearably oppressive economic and social inequality ignored by the elites who benefit from it, at least for a time; fear, moral confusion, and chaos that come from that deepening inequality; a breakdown of social norms; and growing disregard for the humanity of a large portion of the population and for

higher values. In effect, we could see that the pre-tyrannical societies, whether nominally democratic or based on other forms of political organization, exhibit signs of a narcissistic pathology writ large.
Those involve the inevitable split into their grandiose and devalued
parts, including those of the society's self-image, and a denial of their
shadow, which is projected outward onto Others.

Oppressive, dehumanizing (narcissistic) systems, like narcissists
themselves, cultivate their delusions of superiority on the basis of that
internal, unseen, and unspoken split between the grandiose blame-
less I/Us and the devalued, inferior Others. The Others become re-
positories of the narcissists' repressed vices, just as the tyrant is the
vessel for their grandiose beliefs about themselves.

Another narcissistic aspect of such societies is the growing and
ruthless competition, jealousy, and aggression within its borders, but
also directed externally toward other nations in a scapegoating mechanism that is meant to prevent an internal breakdown of a society
by redirecting its narcissistic rage onto external objects. Oftentimes,
these vulnerable societies reel from some form of a narcissistic injury, such as the humiliation of a lost war, international sanctions, or
treaties perceived as unfair, as Germany did after the Treaty of Ver-
sailles after World War I.

None of these processes is openly acknowledged or even noticed
by the members of the society, save by a few typically ignored Cas-
sandras. Just as individual narcissists are incapable of experiencing
guilt, taking responsibility for their vices, or making genuine efforts
to set things right in their lives, narcissistic societies also persist in
their self-destructive blindness. While the chaos and discord brew
in the underclasses, the elites, ensconced in their narcissistic bubbles,
remain oblivious to the suffering of their fellow citizens and the fate
it portends for the nation.

Fritz Stern (2005) has said that "German moderates and German
elites underestimated Hitler, assuming that most people would not
succumb to his Manichean unreason; they did not think that his
hatred and mendacity could be taken seriously." Hitler was seen by

many as a bombastic but harmless buffoon, while many others, including members of clergy, intellectual elites, and the wealthy were nevertheless mesmerized by his grand visions of Germany's future glory, and eagerly supported his agenda.

Narcissism of the elites makes them as well blind to the encroaching tyranny. It is a convenient—and yes, narcissistic—myth that only the dispossessed and uninformed would support the tyrant. It is not the economic or educational status that determines such susceptibility, but one's narcissism, and that cuts across socioeconomic strata. Dorothy Thompson describes it brilliantly in her 1941 essay, "Who Goes Nazi?," in which she identifies those threads of frustrated grandiosity, resentments, and hatreds in the well-heeled individuals' characters that make them fall for tyrannical ideologies and movements. She also observes those who would naturally resist the toxic pull of Nazism, noting their humility and depth.

Stern (2005) quotes a letter from philosopher and Nobel Prize–winning physicist Carl Friedrich von Weizsäcker, who confessed to him "that he had never believed in Nazi ideology but that he had been tempted by the movement, which seemed to him then like 'the outpouring of the Holy Spirit.' On reflection, he thought that National Socialism had been part of a process that the National Socialists themselves had not understood. He may well have been right. The Nazis did not realize that they were part of a historic process in which resentment against a disenchanted secular world found deliverance in the ecstatic escape of unreason."

Note that the process that the Nazis themselves had not understood is the very narcissistic collusion, a near-psychotic infection with this virus of grandiosity and rage on a mass scale. It is rarely grasped, not even from the perspective of time, as our blindness makes it impossible to acknowledge it, which renders our narcissism the last taboo in a world that has dispensed with taboos. Our denial and social amnesia further entrench our incomprehension and ensure that history repeats itself.

Part of our forgetting involves distortions of historical and psychological facts. Safely removed, time- and distance-wise, from the latest tyranny-caused mayhem, we tend to imagine tyrants as instantly recognizable evil beings and tyrannies as something exotic enough never to happen to us. But as history and experience demonstrate, power-hungry narcissistic psychopaths do not look different from normal people; and if they stand out, it is often for socially approved reasons: their resolve, charisma, decisiveness, and ability to inspire others.

No tyrant comes to power on the platform of genocidal tyranny, even though such ideas may be brewing already in the recesses of his mind. Each and every one of them promises to bring back law and order, create better economic conditions for the people, and restore the nation's glory.

These empty promises—for the tyrant has little desire and even less ability to fulfill them—are always tied together with the thread of scapegoating Others, a necessary component that channels the narcissistic rage outward and increases the society's cohesion. But the tyrant sows discord and division among his own peoples as well. He cannot help it: pitting people against one another satisfies his irrepressible sadistic urge and makes it easier for him to dominate and control them.

The tyrant shows up in a society that is already weakened by disorder, blind to it, and unable and/or unwilling to take corrective measures that would prevent a tyrannical takeover. Once he and his sycophantic cabal assume power, they deepen and widen the disorder, dismantling and changing the society's norms, institutions, and laws to fully reflect their own pathology.

Andrew Łobaczewski (2007) discusses at length the formation and progression of *pathocracies*, political and other systems run by characterologically impaired individuals, predominantly psychopaths and narcissists. He describes how pathocracies change the society by the introduction of *paralogisms*, ways of distorting reality and truth; and *paramoralisms*, methods of perverting moral values. Under tyranny, paralogisms and paramoralisms are unleashed on a large scale through various propagandist means that include repetition of flat-out lies, accompanied by denials and obfuscations served through the increasingly centralized and controlled media. Fortified by magical thinking and contempt for reason, these distortions lead to the creation of the kind of absurdist unreality well known to people raised in authoritarian regimes, where up is down and black is white, and where what one knows to be true may have nothing to do with the officially sanctioned version of the truth.

We can see the tyrant's own pathology influencing every area of a society's functioning, from politics through culture and social mores to science and technology. What is being seen, said, and studied, and what's ignored and silenced, depends on the tyrant's whims, and soon enough the society itself and its ideology are structured in ways that meet his pathological needs for power and adulation. The implementation of this ideology is usually a gradual process, one that is eventually reinforced by the use of violence against persistent objectors.

As freedom of speech, the press, and assembly disappears and the tyrant's destructive "reforms" take hold, an ethos of the New Man, an ideal of a human being compatible with the disordered ideology, is forced upon the populace.

This New Man is a dehumanized caricature of a human person, usually exemplifying the tyrant's distorted views and thus meeting his pathological needs, mainly for dominance and adulation. He—we will use the male pronoun, but there is of course a compatible version of the New Woman to go with the New Man—is wholly devoted to the Cause and the Leader (which, in tyrannies, are often one and the same, an ultimate expression of the tyrant's narcissism) and acts in prescribed ways meant to demonstrate this devotion in his life. Hero worship and utmost loyalty become parts of the New Man's prescribed behavior, reinforced by new laws and norms, but also by individuals who eagerly cooperate with the authoritarian rules by spying on and denouncing their fellow citizens' ideologically improper behavior.

Our human propensity to submit to inhumane rules established by pathological authority cannot be overestimated. We have plenty of historical and contemporary evidence for it, as well as experimental data (Milgram 1974). An approving nod from an authority figure, no matter how insignificant or even real, can easily absolve us of responsibility in our minds and override any scruples imposed by our conscience, proving its perplexing malleability.

The ease with which many so-called normal people shut down their conscience makes them not very different from functional psychopaths. This disturbing fact of human life is something the tyrant counts on when he establishes his reign. He knows that he can expect loyalty from his followers and successfully demand it from the majority of society. And those unwilling to follow his dictates and/or actively opposing them will be eliminated.

The New Man's thoughts must of course change, too, to better aid his transformation. Thus, the criteria of mental normalcy and pathology also are redefined, and psychology and psychiatry, like other branches of social science, are co-opted to serve the regime. What's considered normal, both in the sense of statistical norm and mental health, is in fact pathological, and mental health, defined as the capacity for multilevel and multidimensional development, is pathologized.

The ease with which the tyrannical ideology spreads is always greater than we want to imagine. Our narcissistic blindness makes it impossible for us to believe that it could happen here and that we, too, could be as susceptible to it as any other human beings in history.

Tyranny feeds on the irrationality of narcissistic myths and magical thinking, even though its ideology may be disguised as hyper-rationalism, as was the case with communism. In this, it very much resembles the narcissistically psychopathic character of the tyrant himself: solipsistic, withdrawn from reality, and full of grandiose and paranoid beliefs impervious to the corrective influences of objective facts.

These pathological factors ensure that eventually the tyrant's reign collapses. The inherent and violent irrationality, bereft of internal brakes that stem from a conscience, and unchecked by external forces, is the main reason tyrants and their regimes are doomed to fail (Glad 2002). Their growing malignancy (corruption, aggression, and oppression) provokes opposition, which eventually brings the tyranny down, but not until its pillaging and violent reign create much human suffering. The reset of a society's mores that follows the tragic aftermath of a tyrannical rule usually leads to a greater appreciation for the importance of universal human values (equality, justice, truth, and compassion), but if care is not taken to implement these values in consistent practice, our narcissistic tendencies creep in and lead to social disorder, making us susceptible to tyranny again. Given our growing potential for self-destruction, the stakes go up with every tyrannical turn.

Conclusion

Narcissism is as much a character problem as it is an error in our thinking. Seeing oneself as "above" is the general attitude of a narcissist toward the world, and the error of the tyrant and his followers. This error appears to grip many so-called civilized human societies, and is especially pronounced in those where inequality grows despite any official sloganeering to the contrary. Our narcissism is what gives rise to inequality, and inequality fuels our narcissism. The resultant suffering and despair, along with a desire for revenge, are among the necessary conditions for the emergence of tyranny.

As Burkle (2015) observes, we are seeing a resurgence of tyrannical leaders around the globe, even in nations that supposedly have learned the lessons of tyrannies past in the most painful ways. It is a sign of our pressing need to reckon with our collective shadow.

If we as a species are to flourish and prosper, we need to understand that our urgent and necessary task is to transcend and dismantle our narcissism, both individual and collective.

Elizabeth Mika, M.A., L.C.P.C., of Gifted Resources in Northern Illinois (in the Chicago area), received her degree in clinical psychology from Adam Mickiewicz University in Poznan, Poland. She specializes in assessment and counseling of gifted children and adults. Her professional interests include creativity and mental health, learning differences and learning styles, multiple exceptionalities, and emotional and moral development.

References

Burkle, Frederick M. 2015. "Antisocial Personality Disorder and Pathological Narcissism in Prolonged Conflicts and Wars of the 21st Century." *Disaster Medicine and Public Health Preparedness* 1 (October): 1–11.

Burkle, Frederick M., and Dan Hanfling. 2016. "When Being Smart Is Not Enough: Narcissism in U.S. Polity." March 2. http://hir.harvard.edu /article/?a=12701.

Dąbrowski, Kazimierz. 1986. *Trud istnienia*. Warszawa: Wiedza Powszechna.

———. 1996. *W poszukiwaniu zdrowia psychicznego*. Warszawa: Wydawnictwo Naukowe PWN.

Dąbrowski, Kazimierz, Andrew Kawczak, and Janina Sochanska. 1973. *The Dynamics of Concepts*. London: Gryf Publications.

Freud, Sigmund. 1991. *Civilization, Society, and Religion*. Canada: Penguin Freud Library, p. 12.

Fromm, Erich. 1973. *The Anatomy of Human Destructiveness*. New York: Holt, Rinehart and Winston.

———. 1980. *The Heart of Man*. New York, Evanston, and London: Harper and Row.

Gellately, Robert. 2007. *Lenin, Stalin and Hitler: The Age of Social Catastrophe*. New York: Alfred A. Knopf.

Giroux, Henry A. 2014. *The Violence of Organized Forgetting: Thinking Beyond America's Disimagination Machine*. San Francisco, CA: City Lights Publishers.

Glad, Betty. 2002. "Why Tyrants Go Too Far: Malignant Narcissism and Absolute Power." *Political Psychology* 23, no. 1 (March): 1–37.

Hughes, Ian. 2017. "The Solution to Democracy's Crisis Is More Democracy."

DisorderedWorld.com. https://disorderedworld.com/2017/05/04/the
-solution-to-democracys-crisis-is-more-democracy/.

Kimmel, Michael. 2013. *Angry White Men: American Masculinity at the End of an Era*. New York: Nation Books.

Łobaczewski, Andrew M. 2007. *Political Ponerology: A Science on the Nature of Evil Adjusted for Political Purposes*. Grande Prairie, AB, Canada: Red Pill Press.

Mika, Elizabeth, and Frederick M. Burkle. 2016. "The Unbearable Lightness of Being a Narcissist." *Medium*, May 13. https://medium.com/@Elamika/the-unbearable-lightness-of-being-a-narcissist-251ec901dae7.

Milgram, Stanley. 1974. *Obedience to Authority: An Experimental View*. New York: Harper and Row.

Miller, Alice. 1990. *For Your Own Good: Hidden Cruelty in Child-Rearing and the Roots of Violence*. New York: Noonday Press.

Mydans, Seth. 1997. "In an Interview, Pol Pot Declares His Conscience Is Clear." *New York Times*, October 23. www.nytimes.com/1997/10/23/world/in-an-interview-pol-pot-declares-his-conscience-is-clear.html.

Newell, Waller R. 2016. *Tyrants: A History of Power, Injustice and Terror*. New York: Cambridge University Press.

Plato, Grube, G. M. A., and C. D. C. Reeve, eds. 1992. *Republic*. Indianapolis, IN: Hackett Pub. Co.

Post, Jerrold. 2015. *Narcissism and Politics*. New York: Cambridge University Press.

Stern, Fritz. 2005. "Reflection: Lessons from German History." *Foreign Affairs* (May–June). www.foreignaffairs.com/articles/europe/2005-05-01/reflection-lessons-german-history.

Thompson, Dorothy. 1941. "Who Goes Nazi?" *Harper's Magazine*, August. https://harpers.org/archive/1941/08/who-goes-nazi/.

THE LONELINESS OF FATEFUL DECISIONS

Social Contexts and Psychological Vulnerability

EDWIN B. FISHER, PH.D.

At nine o'clock, Tuesday morning, October 16, 1962, the special assistant for national security entered the living quarters of the White House with startling news: "Mr. President, there is now hard photographic evidence that the Russians have offensive missiles in Cuba" (Neustadt and Allison 1971). During the next thirteen days of the Cuban Missile Crisis,* the world faced a horrible threat. Fewer than one in five U.S. citizens alive today is old enough to remember well the experience of those events, but the sense of possible doom was profound. Sitting in Mr. Capasso's eleventh-grade History class, I thought that we all might not be there in a day or two. Spy satellite photos showed that the Soviet Union was within weeks or perhaps days of finishing the installation of missiles in Cuba capable of reaching major U.S. East Coast cities. As this is being written, many are calling the possibility of North Korea possessing operational nuclear-armed rockets capable of reaching U.S. West Coast cities within

---

* This name for the crisis will be used for ease of communication, although it has been rightly criticized as reflecting a U.S.-centric view of the world.

several years the greatest threat we face. Imagine if we were in the same position as in 1962: "Our military experts advised that these missiles could be in operation within a week" (Kennedy 1971).*

In reacting to the threat, President Kennedy brought together the "best and the brightest," to borrow David Halberstam's term for the Kennedy Cabinet and advisers (Halberstam 1972). They included the secretaries of state and defense, the UN ambassador, other senior policy advisers, the Joint Chiefs of Staff, and the president's highly trusted brother Robert, the attorney general. They debated daily over the period, considering varied alternatives. There was only one problem with this "best" and "brightest" advice. They disagreed. Indeed, they disagreed sharply. President Kennedy was left to make the decision. As President George W. Bush put it, President Kennedy was "the decider."

That the most powerful person in the world can be isolated and lonely in making fateful decisions dramatizes the importance of classic questions. How does the individual shape her/his world, and how does that world shape the individual? Research makes clear, for example, the fundamental value of social connections, that their absence is as lethal as smoking cigarettes (Holt-Lunstad, Smith, and Layton 2010; House, Landis, and Umberson 1988). So, too, the varied group of individuals who advised President Kennedy clearly influenced his perspectives and choices. On the other hand, President Kennedy shaped the variety of perspectives of that group of advisers.

This chapter examines two major themes. First, it examines the interplay among social contexts and individual characteristics as they were apparent in and around President Kennedy in 1962. The

---

* Much of the history of the October 1962 crisis has been drawn from Robert Kennedy's 1971 memoir of those events, *Thirteen Days: A Memoir of the Cuban Missile Crisis* (New York: W. W. Norton, 1971). Unless otherwise noted, quotations are from that source.

strategies, personal characteristics, and social settings that surrounded the president during those thirteen days pose important questions for our current evaluation of President Trump. The second theme is an emphasis on the patterns of behavior that result from that interplay of person and context. Emerging through that interplay, it is those behavior patterns themselves, not speculations about either their interpersonal or personal sources, that provide us confidence in a leader's ability to make fateful, lonely decisions.

The 1962 Crisis

Many of the Joint Chiefs of Staff felt that air strikes and an invasion were clearly necessary. In arguments that sound very current in 2017, they argued that the incursion of Soviet missiles into our hemisphere could not be allowed to stand, that a line needed to be drawn, and that clear and decisive action was required. Others argued that there was little reason to respond aggressively. Secretary of Defense McNamara articulated one of the strongest arguments for a modest response, pointing out that nuclear warheads would kill just as many people whether they came from Cuba or somewhere else. Others encouraged diplomacy and working with the Soviets. Complicating this strategy was the fact that the Soviet foreign minister had clearly lied to President Kennedy in denying the existence of the missiles after the president already had the satellite photos showing their installation.

In the end, President Kennedy chose a firm response, but one that did not include a direct attack in Cuba. He established a naval quarantine that would not allow any ships carrying munitions to enter waters around Cuba. Soviet ships were on their way and not turning back. What would happen if they challenged the quarantine? In written exchanges, two messages were received from the Soviets. One clearly reflected the hard-liners in the Kremlin. A second, apparently written by Premier Khrushchev himself, was far more conciliatory. In an important model of wise negotiation, President Kennedy ignored the belligerent message and responded to the conciliatory one. At almost the literal eleventh hour, 10:25 a.m. on Wednesday, October 24, a message came from the field: "Mr. President, we have a preliminary report which seems to indicate that some of the Russian ships have stopped dead in the water . . . or have turned back toward the Soviet Union." The world breathed.

President Kennedy's Strategies

Especially striking in his brother Robert's recounting of those thirteen days (Kennedy 1971), President Kennedy was determined to consider the position of the antagonists, Premier Khrushchev and the other Soviet leaders. Recognizing strong militarist forces in Moscow, Kennedy realized that "We don't want to push him to a precipitous action . . . I don't want to put him in a corner from which he cannot escape." From their previous communications, he recognized that Khrushchev also did not want war and agreed that a nuclear war would doom the planet. In a letter reflecting a remarkably personal dimension of their relationship, Khrushchev wrote to Kennedy during the height of the tensions:

> I have participated in two wars and know that war ends when it has rolled through cities and villages, everywhere sowing death and destruction . . . Armaments bring only disasters . . . they are an enforced loss of human energy, and what is more are for the destruction of man himself. If people do not show wisdom, then in the final analysis they will come to a clash, like blind moles, and then reciprocal extermination will begin . . .
>
> . . . Mr. President, we and you ought not to pull on the ends of the rope in which you have tied the knot of war, because the more the two of us pull, the tighter the knot will be tied. And a moment may come when that knot will be tied so tight that even he who tied it will not have the strength to untie it . . . Consequently, if there is no intention to tighten that knot, and thereby to doom the world to the catastrophe

of thermonuclear war, then let us not only relax the forces pulling on the ends of the rope, let us take measures to untie that knot. We are ready for this.

President Kennedy's understanding of the other person's point of view extended to his own advisers as well as international adversaries. In his memoir, Robert Kennedy noted that after the Russians agreed on Sunday, October 28, to withdraw their missiles from Cuba, "it was suggested by one high military adviser that we attack Monday in any case. Another felt that we had in some way been betrayed." He goes on: "President Kennedy was disturbed by this inability to look beyond the limited military field. When we talked about this later, he said we had to remember that they were trained to fight and to wage war—that was their life."

President Kennedy also cultivated allies. He recognized that a stand-off with the Soviet Union without allies would put the United States in a very weak position. He worked with the Organization of American States to gain endorsement of the U.S. position and was successful in its turning out to be unanimous. He cultivated European allies and gained a strong endorsement—"It is exactly what I would have done"—from President Charles de Gaulle, the assertively nationalist leader of France and its greatest World War II hero.

In cultivating his allies, President Kennedy was highly aware of the importance of his and the United States' credibility. He was careful throughout the crisis to communicate honestly, with neither hyperbole nor minimization, about the facts on the ground and the U.S. response.

Finally, President Kennedy was a cagy negotiator. In the course of negotiations, Premier Khrushchev raised a counterdemand that the United States remove its own Jupiter rockets from Turkey. This was especially frustrating because President Kennedy had previously recognized their obsolescence and very modest strategic value and so, sometime before the Cuban Missile Crisis, had directed that they be removed. Now he was clearly willing to meet this demand of the

Soviets, but not publicly and not at the same time as the removal of the rockets from Cuba. So, he promised their removal in the months ahead and, fortunately for us all, had cultivated enough good faith with Premier Khrushchev that this unsecured promise was accepted.

Illustrative of his broad reading, President Kennedy had found much of this negotiating stance in a book he had reviewed in 1960, *Deterrent or Defense*, by the British military analyst Basil Liddell Hart: "Keep strong, if possible. In any case, keep cool. Have unlimited patience. Never corner an opponent and always assist him to save his face. Put yourself in his shoes—so as to see things through his eyes. Avoid self-righteousness like the devil—nothing is so self-blinding." Kennedy's habits of mind, organization, administration, and leadership have been accorded substantial responsibility for the avoidance of catastrophe in 1962.

Taking advantage perhaps of a time of more common bipartisanship, Kennedy sought counsel from a wide group, including Republicans such as John McCloy, a former U.S. ambassador to the United Nations, and Dean Acheson, secretary of state under President Truman and a highly opinionated authority in foreign affairs. His own secretary of defense, Robert McNamara, had been a Republican and a CEO of the Ford Motor Company. Even though he was secretary of the treasury, President Kennedy included Douglas Dillon, for whose wisdom he had great respect. Dillon had also been President Eisenhower's undersecretary of state. In addition to the highly respected "old hands" of McCloy, Acheson, and Secretary of State Dean Rusk, he included much younger individuals as well. McGeorge Bundy, a former Republican, had already been dean of the Harvard faculty when, at forty-one, he became special assistant for national security in 1961. Clearly, Robert Kennedy was a close, most trusted and apparently constant confidant, but beyond his brother, President Kennedy cultivated a broad and varied group of advisers, not an inner circle of three or four. President Kennedy was thoughtful not only in assembling these divergent views but also in cultivating them, such as by having his advisers meet without him so that his presence would not tilt opinions in his direction or stifle free exchange.

Actions such as those of President Kennedy are often attributed to the "great man," to the remarkable or praiseworthy characteristics of the individual. President Kennedy's actions in the Cuban Missile Crisis reflect his wisdom and skills but also the social relationships that surrounded him. That he took a hand in constructing and managing these relationships points to an important dialectic between the individual and the social, but diminishes neither.

Social Networks and Support

Many studies document the impacts of social relationships. One of the most provocative found that social connections with spouse, parents, family members, coworkers, groups or organizations protect against the "common cold" (Cohen et al. 1997). What was most important about this finding, however, was that it was not just the *number* of social connections that protected against symptoms such as a runny nose, but also their *variety*. Having many versus fewer friends was not protective, but having a variety of types of relationships with family, friends, etc. resulted in fewer symptoms following exposure to a cold virus. Similarly, the *variety* of social connections predicted death among older adults in a more recent study (Steptoe et al. 2013).

Why should the variety of social connections matter? One answer comes from work many years ago by the anthropologist Erving Goffman, in his study of "asylums" such as prisons and mental hospitals. Goffman observed that inmates or patients in such institutions have but one social role. The patient hospitalized in a psychiatric facility is seen by all (professionals and staff, family members, former acquaintances, and even other patients) as a patient with a mental illness, not as a spouse, child, friend, or coworker (Goffman 1961). Being stuck in one role limits our ability to buffer the stressors of daily life. This is because we often cope with stressors in one setting by complaining, getting advice, or simply seeking solace in another. We complain about our coworkers to our spouses and complain about our spouses, children, and/or in-laws with our coworkers or close friends. For the hospitalized schizophrenic patient, however, this is not possible. As all come to see her/him as schizophrenic, all complaints to or about family, friends, hospital staff, doctors, etc. are taken as expressions of schizophrenia, and thereby invalidated. The individual is isolated in only one role from which she or he cannot escape.

The importance of not being locked in one role, even as the all-powerful president, is reflected in a current book on the office of White House chief of staff (Whipple 2017). A recurrent theme is the importance of the chief of staff being the one person who can tell the president he cannot do something. President Carter's initial decision not to have a chief of staff and then appointing one who was not an effective manager is suggested as a major cause for problems in his administration. Turning to President Trump, doubts about his trust in his chief of staff are frequently cited as key to problems in the execution of his plans during the early days of his administration.

Applying Goffman's observations to the president of the United States is ironic. Goffman developed these ideas in observing and trying to understand the challenges of those stripped not only of their multiple roles but also of their independence and freedom. But the observation may also apply to those who become isolated in a single social role amid privilege. A concern one might raise about President Trump is his apparent choice always to be "the Donald." Consider, for example, his making Mar-a-Lago an extension of the White House. Rather than preserving it as a place to which he can get away and separate himself at least somewhat from his role as president, he chose to go there weekly during the first months of his administration and to "bring his work home with him," including his official visitors, such as President Xi Jinping of China.

A final important feature of social connections points also to the importance of varied perspectives. In examining how groups adopt innovations, sociologist and communication theorist Everett Rogers noted the importance of tight-knit, cohesive networks in quickly and effectively acting to implement a good idea (Rogers and Kincaid 1981). But where do the good ideas come from? One source of good ideas was observed to be "weak ties." One member of a tightly knit group might have a connection to someone in another village, a sister-in-law who is a lawyer, or a job that takes him periodically to the "big city." Such weak ties, not intimate or especially important in day-to-day activities, nevertheless provide exposure to innovations. The combination of new ideas plus a cohesive network to implement them provides the idea for and the execution of innovation.

The variety, provision of multiple roles, and availability of weak ties in social networks seem to fit well the social setting in which President Kennedy worked through the Cuban Missile Crisis. The variety of connections was clear. An important feature of his network was Kennedy's preserving of his relationship with his brother, through which he could complain about his group of advisers, perhaps, but also seek an outside perspective in making sense of the advice he was getting. He also read widely and drew on that reading in his thinking. Barbara Tuchman's *The Guns of August*, detailing how European leaders miscalculated and slid into World War I, was much in Kennedy's mind. As noted, President Kennedy maintained "weak ties" with those with varied viewpoints through his wide reading, intellectual curiosity, and openness to a wide range of views.

Turning to President Trump's social connections, an April 2017 article in the *New York Times* noted a "group of advisers—from family, real estate, media, finance and politics, and all outside the White House gates—many of whom he consults at least once a week" (Haberman and Thrush 2017). They include nine millionaires or billionaires (Thomas Barrack, Carl Icahn, Robert Kraft, Richard LeFrak, Rupert Murdoch, David Perlmutter, Steven Roth, Phil Ruffin, and Steve Schwarzman); the conservative television cable news host Sean Hannity; the conservative political strategists Corey Lewandowski and Roger Stone; Republican politicians Chris Christie, Newt Gingrich, and Paul Ryan; a financial lawyer, Sheri Dillon; President Trump's sons; and his wife. Although the article says that President Trump "needs to test ideas with a wide range of people," those in whom he confides are described as "mostly white, male and older" and were chosen based "on two crucial measures: personal success and loyalty to him."

A somewhat more critical characterization of President Trump's circle of relationships emerges through a recent article in *The New Yorker*, by Evan Osnos: "He inhabits a closed world that one adviser recently described to me as 'Fortress Trump.' Rarely venturing beyond the White House and Mar-a-Lago, he measures his fortunes through reports from friends, staff, and a feast of television coverage of himself."

Quoting Jerry Taylor, "the president of the Niskanen Center, a libertarian think tank," Osnos describes how "he is governing as if he is the President of a Third World country: power is held by family and incompetent loyalists whose main calling card is the fact that Donald Trump can trust them, not whether they have any expertise."

As the noted constitutional lawyer Lawrence Tribe (2017) has put it, "He only wants loyalists." Later, Osnos notes that:

> it's not clear how fully Trump apprehends the threats to his presidency. Unlike previous Republican Administrations, Fortress Trump contains no party elder with the stature to check the President's decisions. "There is no one around him who has the ability to restrain any of his impulses, on any issue ever, for any reason," Steve Schmidt, a veteran Republican consultant said.

Of greatest concern, Osnos (2017) reports that

> Trump's insulation from unwelcome information appears to be growing as his challenges mount. His longtime friend Christopher Ruddy, the C.E.O. of Newsmax Media . . . noticed that some of Trump's associates are unwilling to give

him news that will upset him . . . Ruddy went on. "I already
sense that a lot of people don't want to give him bad news
about things. I've already been approached by several people that say, "He's got to hear this. Could you tell him?"

Psychopathology

Although no firm conclusions should be ventured or considered possible without detailed, firsthand knowledge or examination of President Trump, categorizations of him that have been suggested have
included narcissism, psychopathic deviance, and attention deficit/
hyperactivity disorder (ADHD). Despite the impossibility of a conclusion, discussion of which one of these may best fit the president
has been lively. The assumption that there should be one best diagnosis, however, is at odds with important trends in how we view psychopathology in general. In fact, 50 percent of those qualifying for
one diagnosis meet criteria for an additional diagnosis (Kessler et al.
2011). Thus, the inability to reach agreement among speculative
diagnoses of the president's mental status may well reflect that *several* diagnoses may be pertinent. What is important is not a specific
diagnosis but, rather, understanding the behavior patterns that raise
concerns about mental status and that affect policy decisions and
public welfare.

In addition to overlap among the categories, there is increasing
recognition that the diagnostic categories of the DSM-V, the *Diagnostic and Statistical Manual* of the American Psychiatric Association
(American Psychiatric Association 2013), are themselves flawed.
For example, a diagnosis of major depressive disorder requires
(a) either dysphoria or anhedonia (diminished ability to feel pleasure); (b) four of seven symptoms, such as insomnia, fatigue, decreased concentration/indecisiveness; and (c) the presence of these
most of the day and nearly every day for at least two weeks (Ritschel
et al. 2013). That means that one person with dysphoria and symptoms one through four and another with anhedonia and symptoms
four through seven both meet criteria for the same disorder, even

though they have only one feature in common. Similar problems exist with other diagnostic categories, each judged by the presence or absence of sufficient numbers of symptoms or characteristics from a longer list of possible symptoms or features.

A recent approach to categorizing psychopathology that has been promoted by the National Institute of Mental Health focuses on individuals' strengths or deficits in more discrete categories of psychological function rather than the broad categories of DSM-V. Among these, for example, are acute threat or fear, potential threat or anxiety, sustained threat (such as in PTSD), loss, working memory, cognitive control, affiliation/attachment, social communication, perception/ understanding of self and understanding of others, arousal, and biological rhythms (Kozak and Cuthbert 2016). The theme of this approach is that individual functions or groups of functions might account for patterns of aberrant behavior. In the case of President Trump, acute threat, cognitive control, affiliation/attachment, social communication, perception/understanding of both self and others, arousal, and biological rhythms are all functions that may be pertinent to a number of the concerns that have been raised about his behavior. From such a perspective, the issue is not which of such a group of psychological functions might be primary, but how they interact to lead to troublesome patterns of behavior that, in the case of the president, have substantial societal implications. So, an inability to identify "whether it's basically perceptions of self or perceptions of others" is of little concern. Rather, recognizing the confluence of deficits in these functions as they build an alarming pattern of behavior becomes the basis for sounding an alarm.

If we are to focus on more specific behavior patterns that raise concerns about the mental fitness of President Trump, we still have an outstanding question. How do we judge that a particular characteristic is abnormal, pathological, or indicative of compromised mental fitness? The field of psychopathology and abnormal psychology has long wrestled with this question. When does a quirk or a distinctive personal style become the object of clinical concern and the basis for encouraging the individual to recognize her/himself as having a problem or, even, qualifying for loss of rights or enforced hospital commitment? Among the criteria that have often been proposed for identifying pathology are: resistance to change or to normal social pressure; an almost automatic repetitiveness; disregard for consequences or an inability to adjust behavior according to consequences; harmfulness to self or others; negative impacts on relationships, work, or key interests; and distortions of reality that are frequent, disruptive, and go beyond normal variation in judgments and perceptions. The criteria for identifying psychopathology might be applied to judging the fitness of the president to exercise his power.

For example, what is striking is the persistence of some of his behavior in spite of strong disconfirmation, such as in his arguments about why Hillary Clinton won the popular vote, the size of his inaugural crowd, or the assertion that President Obama had wire-tapped him and his colleagues during the election campaign. So, too, he seems not to notice the harmfulness of his behavior, such as in his contradictory and self-indicting comments about the firing of former FBI director James Comey. He also appears to deny or ignore the aggressiveness of his behavior, as in his admonition to "beat the crap out of him" (referring to a protester being removed from a campaign rally) or in the Twitter threat to Comey about the possible existence of recordings of their conversations. Remarkably, these patterns persist despite their negative characteristics receiving broad attention and even though they may place President Trump in jeopardy of criminal charges or impeachment.

Another approach to making the judgment that behavior is a problem lies in the criminal law for judging innocence by virtue of insanity. In most jurisdictions, the criteria for innocence are an inability to appreciate the criminality of one's actions and to conform one's behavior to the requirements of the law. Whether this is by virtue of schizophrenia or depression or personality disorder or some other posited diagnosis is not critical. What is determinative is the inability to follow the law and understand how it applies to one's own behavior. Clearly, many of the instances observed and widely remarked upon with regard to President Trump would suggest an inability on his part to recognize how his behavior is at odds with applicable laws, including the U.S. Constitution. In his disparaging comments about judicial decisions, and in his ad hominem attacks on a judge who presides over one of the cases in which he is a defendant, and in the comments indicating that he asked Comey about investigations of him during a conversation about Comey's tenure as FBI director, President Trump manifests an apparent lack of recognition of how his behavior is at odds with law, the Constitution, and important precedents for the conduct of his office.

The judgment of "innocent by virtue of insanity" is a legal decision, a finding of innocence, not a finding of psychopathology. Expert opinion about possible pathology may be pertinent to the finding but is not determinative. This suggests considering the judgment of fitness for office as not a medical or psychiatric or psychological question but as a legal and political judgment. As James Gilligan noted at the Yale conference, "It's not whether [President Trump] is mentally ill or not. It's whether he's dangerous or not" (Milligan 2017; Osnos 2017; and Gilligan's essay in this book, "The Issue Is Dangerousness, Not Mental Illness"). Research and clinical knowledge about mental health may be helpful in making the judgment of dangerousness, but they do not themselves determine the decision. Abraham Lincoln apparently suffered serious depression, but few would say it compromised his ability to serve. Yet, the observations of experts in mental health and psychopathology suggest real liabilities in President Trump's behavior. The question remains, however: does it matter?

One answer to that final question has recently been posed by strong voices on the conservative side of the political spectrum. Under the title "Trump Has a Dangerous Disability," George Will wrote in the *Washington Post*, on May 3, 2017:

It is urgent for Americans to think and speak clearly about President Trump's inability to do either [i.e., think and speak clearly]. This seems to be not a mere disinclination but a disability. It is not merely the result of intellectual sloth but of an untrained mind bereft of information and married to stratospheric self-confidence . . .

His fathomless lack of interest in America's path to the present and his limitless gullibility leave him susceptible to being blown about by gusts of factoids that cling like lint to a disorderly mind.

Americans have placed vast military power at the discretion of this mind, a presidential discretion that is largely immune to restraint by the Madisonian system of institutional checks and balances.

Writing two days later, on May 5, 2017, also in the *Washington Post*, Charles Krauthammer articulated further the psychological dimensions of President Trump's fitness to serve:

And this is not to deny the insanity, incoherence and sheer weirdness emanating daily from the White House . . .

Loud and bombastic. A charlatan. Nothing behind the screen—other than the institutional chaos that defines his White House and the psychic chaos that governs his ever-changing mind . . .

Krauthammer goes on to describe what he considers to be a blunder of threatening to make South Korea pay for a defensive missile system and to renegotiate trade agreements. He asserts that this blunder forces

lingering fears about Trump. Especially because it was an unforced error. What happens in an externally caused crisis? Then, there is no hiding, no cushioning, no guard-rail. It's the wisdom and understanding of one man versus whatever the world has thrown up against us. However normalized this presidency may be day to day, in such a moment all bets are off.

What happens when the red phone rings at 3 in the morning?

The Social, the Personal, and the President

Our culture tends to put the social and the personal in opposition. Echoing the tradition of the "self-made man," or Governor Romney's campaigning about "job creators," President Trump himself has bristled at suggestions that his business accomplishments are not wholly of his own doing. Consider, too, the scorn of many for Hillary Clinton's book title *It Takes a Village*, and contrast that title with Nancy Reagan's admonition to "Just say 'no.'" But a major trend in social and behavioral science of the past decades is toward an integration of the development and behavior of the individual with the contexts of culture, community, family, neighborhood (e.g., Fisher 2008). Among numerous examples, living in a neighborhood with only fast-food outlets and no supermarkets raises one's chances of being obese far more than living in a neighborhood with only supermarkets, even after controlling for important factors such as education, ethnicity, and income (Morland, Diez Roux, and Wing 2006). Similarly, after controlling for other characteristics, community violence is associated with numbers of individuals with asthma and with the frequency of their problems with the disease (Wright et al. 2004; Sternthal et al. 2010). Thus, our social and community contexts have real impacts on our behavior and health. Key, however, to this perspective is recognition of the reciprocal nature of influence; just as the community may influence the family, so the family may influence the community, and the individual may influence both.

The interaction of the personal and the contextual can be seen in President Trump's often-alleged narcissism and heightened sensitivity to personal insult. A common effect of these is an erosion of social connections as slights lead to aggressive responses that drive others away. The contrast with President Kennedy's assembly of advisers during the Cuban Missile Crisis is not between one who is socially well connected and one who is socially isolated. President Trump clearly has a number of friends and social contacts. How his personal characteristics may limit the nature and variety of the advice he receives, however, may be a major difference. According to Robert Kennedy's memoir, if President Kennedy became aware that some with alternative views had been excluded from meetings, he would often "enlarge the meetings to include other options . . . President Kennedy wanted people who raised questions, who criticized, on whose judgment he could rely, who presented an intelligent point of view regardless of their rank or viewpoint."

The apparent extent of President Trump's narcissism has drawn increasing attention. In varied meetings and interviews, his preoccupation with and exaggeration of the size of his Electoral College victory, his claims that voter fraud accounted for Secretary Clinton's popular vote margin of over 3 million, and his claims about the size of the crowd at his inauguration have been remarkable. Central to narcissism is the self-referential defense. In response to strong condemnation of his sharing highly classified intelligence information with Russian foreign minister Lavrov and Russian ambassador Kislyak, his first tweet read, "As President I wanted to share with Russia . . . which I have the absolute right to do, facts pertaining . . ." Noteworthy is the primacy in the tweet of his role "as President" and his "absolute right." Closely related, too, is the attention to power. Commenting on the choices to disclose top-secret information to the Russians, to be the first to congratulate President Erdogan for a disputed election victory that shrank democratic processes in Turkey, and to praise and invite to the White House President Duterte, widely blamed for thousands of extrajudicial killings in the Philippines, political commentator and journalist Eugene Robinson (2017) summarized it well: "He conflates power with virtue."

Reflecting the interplay of personal and social, narcissistic concerns for self and a preoccupation with power may initially shape and limit those invited to the narcissistic leader's social network. Sensitivity to slights and angry reactions to them may further erode it. Those left tend to be indulgent of the individual and to persist for other gains. Either way, the advice and counsel they provide are liable to be guided by their motives for persisting. Also, those who remain are likely to be constrained lest ill-considered words create a rift that distances them and compromises the gains they anticipate. A disturbing feature of this kind of dynamic is that it tends to feed on itself. The more the individual selects those who flatter him and avoid confrontation, and the more those who have affronted and been castigated fall away, the narrower and more homogenous his network becomes, further flattering the individual but eventually becoming a thin precipice. President Nixon, drunk and reportedly conversing with the pictures on the walls, and praying with Henry Kissinger during his last nights in office, comes to mind.

The shrinking of the network to those most loyal in spite of affronts and exploitative treatment applies to the relationships of the office of the president with national and international allies. A number of commentators have suggested that Republicans in the House of Representatives who voted for a new health care bill in early May 2017 would have given President Trump an opportunity to claim an accomplishment around the end of his first one hundred days in office, while giving themselves major problems in their reelection campaigns in 2018. So, too, much has been written about the international importance of trust in the president's words. Especially as his own and his advisers' descriptions of the firing of FBI director Comey have collided, and after his sharing of highly classified intelligence information with the Russian foreign minister and ambassador to the United States, writers have questioned the ability of President Trump to draw allies together in a major crisis if they are untrusting of his assurances or his characterizations of events. Writing in 1967, Robert Kennedy anticipated much of this concern:

[H]ow important it was to be respected around the world, how vital it was to have allies and friends. Now, five years later, I discern a feeling of isolationism in Congress and through the country, a feeling that we are too involved with other nations, a resentment of the fact that we do not have greater support in Vietnam, an impression that our AID program is useless and our alliances dangerous. I think it would be well to think back to those days in October, 1962.

Kennedy goes on to recount the importance of the support from the Organization of American States, the NATO allies, and critical countries in Africa (Guinea and Senegal), from which Russian planes might have delivered arms to Cuba, circumventing the quarantine. The trust and affirmation of all of these "changed our position from that of an outlaw acting in violation of international law into a country acting in accordance with . . . allies."

The narcissism that is central to the shrinking networks of those who seek blind loyalty and flattery in their relationships leads also to a preoccupation with the credit and praise received. President Trump's preoccupation with his election or the size of his inaugural crowd contrasts sharply with President Kennedy's stance at the end of the thirteen days:

After it was finished, he made no statement attempting to take credit for himself or for the Administration for what had occurred. He instructed all members of the Ex Comm and government that no interview should be given, no statement made, which would claim any kind of victory. He respected Khrushchev for properly determining what was in his own country's interest and what was in the interest of mankind. If it was a triumph, it was a triumph for the next generation and not for any particular government or people.

A fitting end to this chapter draws on the concluding words of Robert Kennedy's *Thirteen Days*: "At the outbreak of the First World War the ex-Chancellor of Germany, Prince von Bülow, said to his successor, 'How did it all happen?' 'Ah, if only we knew,' was the reply." Delicate are the dynamics and nuanced are the judgments that may keep the world safe or plunge it into the abyss. We are currently led by a man broadly flawed in his own person and supported by a truncated set of advisers. As the breadth and "vigor"—to use a word JFK favored—of advice sought by Kennedy in 1962 contrasts with that reported to surround President Trump, so the personal characteristics of President Trump leave us alarmed over the prospect of his narrowing further his network of advisers, leaving him few on whom to rely. The impulsive, ill-considered, narcissistic, reckless, and apparently intentional lies, threats, and bravado not only damage the country but may leave the president even more isolated. That President Trump might ever occupy the loneliness of deciding about a potentially catastrophic course of action is rightly our most urgent and greatest fear.

Coda

Apart from the contrasts drawn here, several similarities in their backgrounds and personal characteristics almost make Presidents Kennedy and Trump something of a natural experiment. Both of their fathers were highly successful in business, men who sometimes worked on both sides of the border of legality. Both were born to privilege. Both went to "the best schools." Both, apparently, were "womanizers," but also apparently cared much for their families. These similarities, along with the many contrasts in their behavior, point to the uncertainty in our understanding of all these matters. That uncertainty, however, leads us back to the wisdom of focusing on the actual behavior in question. Wisdom from the fields of psychology and medicine can illuminate our understanding of these problems, their social and personal sources, and the likelihood that they may change or be tempered by events, but judgment of them rests with us all.

Edwin B. Fisher, Ph.D., is a clinical psychologist and a professor in the Department of Health Behavior in the Gillings School of Global Public Health at the University of North Carolina at Chapel Hill. He is a past president of the Society of Behavioral Medicine and editor of Principles and Concepts of Behavioral Medicine: A Global Handbook *(Springer, 2017). In addition to community and peer support in health and health care, asthma, cancer, diabetes, smoking cessation, and weight management, he has written on concepts of psychopathology, including depression and schizophrenia, and on the relationships between mental illness and physical disease.*

Acknowledgments

Thanks to Rebecka Rutledge Fisher, Ruth Salvaggio, Kathryn Skol, Barbara and Richard Vanecko, and to the editor, Bandy Lee, for their helpful comments on a preliminary draft.

References

American Psychiatric Association. 2013. *Diagnostic and Statistical Manual of Mental Disorders.* 5th ed. Arlington, VA: American Psychiatric Association.

Cohen, S., W. J. Doyle, D. P. Skoner, B. S. Rabin, and J. M. Gwaltney. 1997. "Social Ties and Susceptibility to the Common Cold." *Journal of the American Medical Association* 277 (24): 1940–44.

Fisher, E. B. 2008. "The Importance of Context in Understanding Behavior and Promoting Health." *Annals of Behavioral Medicine* 35 (1): 3–18.

Goffman, E. 1961. *Asylums.* New York: Doubleday.

Haberman, M., and G. Thrush. 2017. "Trump Reaches Beyond West Wing for Counsel." *New York Times*, April 22.

Halberstam, D. 1972. *The Best and the Brightest.* New York: Random House.

Holt-Lunstad, J., T. B. Smith, and J. B. Layton. 2010. "Social Relationships and Mortality Risk: A Meta-Analytic Review." *PLOS Medicine* 7 (7): e1000316. doi: 10.1371/journal.pmed.1000316.

House, J. S., K. R. Landis, and D. Umberson. 1988. "Social Relationships and Health." *Science* 241: 540–44.

Kennedy, R. F. 1971. *Thirteen Days: A Memoir of the Cuban Missile Crisis.* New York: W. W. Norton.

Kessler, R. C., J. Ormel, M. Petukhova, K. A. McLaughlin, J. G. Green, L. J. Russo, D. J. Stein, A. M. Zaslavsky, S. Aguilar-Gaxiola, J. Alonso, L. Andrade, C. Benjet, G. de Girolamo, R. de Graaf, K. Demyttenaere, J. Fayyad, J. M. Haro, Cy Hu, A. Karam, S. Lee, J. P. Lepine, H. Matchsinger, C. Mihaescu-Pintia, J. Posada-Villa, R. Sagar, and T. B. Ustun. 2011. "Development of Lifetime Comorbidity in the World Health Organization World Mental Health Surveys." *Archives of General Psychiatry* 68 (1): 90–100. doi: 10.1001/archgenpsychiatry.2010.180.

Kozak, M. J., and B. N. Cuthbert. 2016. "The NIMH Research Domain Criteria Initiative: Background, Issues, and Pragmatics." *Psychophysiology* 53 (3): 286–97. doi: 10.1111/psyp.12518.

Milligan, S. 2017. "An Ethical Dilemma. Donald Trump's Presidency Has Some in the Mental Health Community Re-evaluating Their Role." *US News & World Report*, April 21.

Morland, K., A. V. Diez Roux, and S. Wing. 2006. "Supermarkets, Other Food Stores, and Obesity: The Atherosclerosis Risk in Communities Study." *American Journal of Preventive Medicine* 30 (4): 333–39.

Neustadt, R. E., and G. T. Allison. 1971. "Afterword." In Robert F. Kennedy, *Thirteen Days: A Memoir of the Cuban Missile Crisis.* New York: W. W. Norton.

Osnos, E. 2017. "Endgames: What Would It Take to Cut Short Trump's Presidency?" *The New Yorker*, May 8, pp. 34–45.

Ritschel, L. A., C. F. Gillespie, E. O. Arnarson, and W. E. Craighead. 2013. "Major Depressive Disorder." *Psychopathology: History, Diagnosis, and Empirical Foundations.* Ed. by W. E. Craighead, D. J. Miklowitz, and L. W. Craighead. Hoboken, NJ: Wiley, pp. 285–333.

Robinson, E. 2017. *Morning Joe.* MSNBC, May 16.

Rogers, E. M., and D. L. Kincaid. 1981. *Communication Networks: Toward a New Paradigm for Research*. New York: Free Press.

Steptoe, A., A. Shankar, P. Demakakos, and J. Wardle. 2013. "Social Isolation, Loneliness, and All-Cause Mortality in Older Men and Women." *Proceedings of the National Academy of Sciences USA* 110 (15): 5797–801. doi: 10.1073/pnas.1219686110.

Sternthal, M. J., H. J. Jun, F. Earls, and R. J. Wright. 2010. "Community Violence and Urban Childhood Asthma: A Multilevel Analysis." *European Respiratory Journal* 36 (6): 1400–9. doi: 10.1183/09031936.00003010.

Tribe, Lawrence. 2017. On *Last Word with Lawrence O'Donnell*. MSNBC, May 11.

Whipple, Chris. 2017. *The Gatekeepers*. New York: Penguin Random House.

Wright, R. J., H. Mitchell, C. M. Visness, S. Cohen, J. Stout, R. Evans, and D. R. Gold. 2004. "Community Violence and Asthma Morbidity: The Inner-City Asthma Study." *American Journal of Public Health* 94 (4): 625–32.

HE'S GOT THE WORLD IN HIS HANDS AND HIS FINGER ON THE TRIGGER

The Twenty-Fifth Amendment Solution

NANETTE GARTRELL, M.D., AND DEE MOSBACHER, M.D., PH.D.

In 1994, President Jimmy Carter lamented the fact that we have no way of ensuring that the person entrusted with the nuclear arsenal is mentally and physically capable of fulfilling that responsibility (Carter 1994). Throughout U.S. history, presidents have suffered from serious psychiatric or medical conditions, most of which were unknown to the public. A review of U.S. presidential office holders from 1776 to 1974 revealed that 49 percent of the thirty-seven presidents met criteria that suggested psychiatric disorders (Davidson, Connor, and Swartz 2006). For example, Presidents Pierce and Lincoln had symptoms of depression (Davidson, Connor, and Swartz 2006); Nixon and Johnson, paranoia (Glaister 2008; Goodwin 1988), and Reagan, dementia (Berisha et al. 2015). President Wilson experienced a massive stroke that resulted in severely impaired cognitive functioning (Weinstein 1981). Although military personnel who are responsible for relaying nuclear orders must undergo rigorous mental health and medical evaluations that assess psychological, financial, and medical fitness for duty (Osnos 2017;

Colón-Francia and Fortner 2014), there is no such requirement for their commander in chief.

Over the course of the U.S. 2016 presidential campaign, it became increasingly apparent that Donald Trump's inability or unwillingness to distinguish fact from fiction (Barbaro 2016), wanton disregard for the rule of law (Kendall 2016), intolerance of perspectives different from his own (DelReal and Gearan 2016), rageful responses to criticism (Sebastian 2016), lack of impulse control ("Transcript" 2016), and sweeping condemnations of entire populations (Reilly 2016) rendered him temperamentally unsuitable to be in command of the nuclear arsenal. When Mr. Trump became the president-elect, we, as psychiatrists, had grave concerns about his mental stability and fitness for office. Despite the claim by gastroenterologist Dr. Harold Bornstein that Mr. Trump "will be the healthiest individual ever elected to the presidency" (Schecter, Francescani, and Connor 2016), there is no evidence that Mr. Trump has ever received psychological testing or a neuropsychiatric examination. In fact, there is no evidence that any prior president completed such an evaluation before assuming the duties of office.

On November 10, 2016, we received a call from our psychiatrist friend and colleague Judith Herman, M.D., who shared our concerns about Mr. Trump's grandiose, belligerent, and unpredictable behavior. She proposed that we send a private letter to President Obama outlining our observations, and recommending an impartial psychiatric evaluation of the president-elect. We agreed that such an assessment was warranted as a matter of national security. Dr. Herman offered to draft the letter. Each of us took responsibility for contacting colleagues who might be interested in cosigning.

The three of us have been allies since the early 1980s. As members of the Harvard Medical School faculty, Dr. Herman collaborated with Dr. Gartrell on national studies of sexually abusive physicians, and on mental health projects for the American Psychiatric Association. We knew that we could count on one another to be efficient and ethical.

At the end of November, the letter was sent to President Obama, stating that Mr. Trump's "widely reported symptoms of mental instability—including grandiosity, impulsivity, hypersensitivity to slights or criticism, and an apparent inability to distinguish fantasy from reality—lead us to question his fitness for the immense responsibilities of the office" (Greene 2016). We also strongly recommended that the president-elect receive a "full medical and neuropsychiatric evaluation by an impartial team of investigators."

We heard nothing from the White House. On December 16, Drs. Gartrell and Mosbacher were contacted by a journalist asking if we knew of any mental health professionals who would be willing to comment on Mr. Trump's psychiatric conditions. The three of us decided that we were willing to take the step of sharing our letter, in the interest of placing our recommendation in the public discourse. The journalist asked our permission to circulate the letter, and the next thing we knew, it was published in the *Huffington Post* (Greene 2016). It went viral (Pasha-Robinson 2016). The coverage seemed to reflect a sense of foreboding that Mr. Trump's erratic behavior represented a danger to the world order (Pasha-Robinson 2016; "Grave Concerns" 2016). We declined all requests for further comment, since most journalists wanted us to specify psychiatric diagnoses for the president-elect, even though we had not personally evaluated him.

Gloria Steinem posted the *Huffington Post* article on her Facebook page, and contacted JH to brainstorm about who in the government could implement our recommendation. Robin Morgan suggested that we convey our letter to Gen. Joseph Dunford, chairman of the Joint Chiefs of Staff, and reminded us of the series of events that transpired during the final days of the Nixon administration. Because President Nixon was drinking heavily and threatening war (Davidson, Connor, and Swartz 2006), the secretary of defense, James Schlesinger, instructed the military not to act on orders from the White House to deploy nuclear weapons unless authorized by Schlesinger or the secretary of state, Henry Kissinger (McFadden 2014). Robin Morgan thought that it would be useful for Chairman Dunford and the

Joint Chiefs to be apprised of this history, because of Mr. Trump's imminent access to the nuclear arsenal. Drs. Gartrell and Mosbacher contacted colleagues to obtain Chairman Dunford's official e-mail address. On January 3, we sent our letter to Chairman Dunford, with the subject line: "An urgent matter of national security."

A week later, Dr. Gartrell met a woman who worked in government intelligence. Dr. Gartrell inquired if she would be willing to convey our recommendation to other professionals at the agency. The woman agreed to distribute our letter among key individuals who shared our views about Mr. Trump's mental instability.

As Inauguration Day grew closer, Dr. Gartrell, Dr. Mosbacher, Dr. Herman, Gloria Steinem, and Robin Morgan decided to send our letter to members of Congress whom we know personally or to whom we had access. We also agreed to publicize our recommendation whenever there was an opportunity. Dr. Mosbacher called House Minority Leader Nancy Pelosi and sent our letter to her. Gloria Steinem conveyed our letter to Sen. Chuck Schumer, and Dr. Mosbacher discussed our recommendation with Sen. Elizabeth Warren. At the Women's March on Washington, Gloria Steinem quoted our recommendation during her speech ("Voices of the Women's March" 2017). Robin Morgan read our letter during her Women's Media Center Live radio show (Morgan 2017a), and quoted it in her blog (Morgan 2017b).

Since being sworn in, Mr. Trump's impulsive, belligerent, careless, and irresponsible behavior has become even more apparent:

- He has angry outbursts when facts conflict with his fantasies (Wagner 2017). The day after the inauguration, he lashed out at the media for contradicting his claim that there were "a million, a million and a half people" on the Mall listening to his speech (Zaru 2017).

- His opposition to the press borders on paranoia (Page 2017). He screams at the television when his ties to Russia are mentioned

(Pasha-Robinson 2017). He calls the media "the enemy of the people" (Siddiqui 2017).

- He deflects the blame for failed operations, such as the air strike
  he authorized in Yemen that killed thirty civilians and a U.S. Navy
  SEAL (Schmitt and Sanger 2017; Ware 2017).

- He makes false and unsubstantiated claims that are easily disputed, asserting, for instance, that the Yemen action yielded significant intelligence (McFadden et al. 2017), and accusing President
  Obama of spying on Trump Tower (Stefansky 2017).

- He discredits other branches of the government. After issuing an
  executive order banning immigration from seven Muslim-majority
  countries, Mr. Trump sought to delegitimize the decisions of federal courts that imposed a halt to the ban, and used demeaning
  language to dishonor the judiciary (e.g., referring to James Robart
  as a "so-called judge") (Forster and Dearden 2017).

- He praises authoritarian leaders of other countries. Mr. Trump ad-
  mires despots Vladimir Putin, Kim Jong-un, and Rodrigo Duterte
  (*New York Times* Editorial Board 2017; Pengelly 2017), and invited
  Abdel Fatah al-Sissi and Recep Tayyip Erdogan to the White House
  (Nakamura 2017; DeYoung 2017).

- He deflects attention from Russia's interference in the 2016 election.
  After firing the director of the FBI during its criminal investigation into collaboration between Russian intelligence and the Trump
  campaign, Mr. Trump met with Putin's senior diplomat and revealed highly classified intelligence (Miller and Jaffe 2017).

- He is indifferent to the limits of presidential powers and fails to
  understand the duties of the office. He could not answer the simple

question "What are the top three functions of the United States government?" (Brown 2016).

- He provokes North Korea with casual references to impending military actions. Mr. Trump claimed that an "armada" was steaming toward North Korea as a "show of force," resulting in a defensive response from Kim Jong-un, whose state news agency called Mr. Trump's bluff "a reckless act of aggression to aggravate tension in the region" (Sampathkumar 2017).

All in all, Mr. Trump's hostile, impulsive, provocative, suspicious, and erratic conduct poses a grave threat to our national security.

The Twenty-Fifth Amendment to the U.S. Constitution addresses presidential disability and succession (Cornell University Law School, 2017). Section 4 of this amendment has never been invoked to evaluate whether a standing president is fit to serve. We (Drs. Gartrell and Mosbacher) call on Congress to act now within these provisions to create an independent, impartial panel of investigators to evaluate Mr. Trump's fitness to fulfill the duties of the presidency. We urge Congress to pass legislation to ensure that future presidential and vice-presidential candidates are evaluated by this professional panel before the general election, and that the sitting president and vice president be assessed on an annual basis. We also recommend that panel members receive all medical and mental health reports on the president and vice president, with the authorization to request any additional evaluations that the panel deems necessary.

Our specific recommendations are as follows:

- Under Section 4 of the Twenty-Fifth Amendment to the U.S. Constitution, Congress should immediately constitute an independent, nonpartisan panel of mental health and medical experts to evaluate Mr. Trump's capability to fulfill the responsibilities of the presidency.

- The panel should consist of three neuropsychiatrists (one clinical, one academic, and one military), one clinical psychologist, one neurologist, and two internists.

- Panel members should be nominated by the nonpartisan, nongovernmental National Academy of Medicine (Abrams 1999).

- The experts should serve six-year terms, with a provision that one member per year be rotated off and replaced (Abrams 1999).

- Congress should enact legislation to authorize this panel to perform comprehensive mental health and medical evaluations of the president and vice president on an annual basis. This legislation should require the panel to evaluate all future presidential and vice-presidential candidates. The panel should also be empowered to conduct emergency evaluations should there be an acute change in the mental or physical health of the president or vice president.

- The evaluations should be strictly confidential unless the panel determines that the mental health or medical condition of the president or vice president renders her/him incapable of fulfilling the duties of office.

Congress must act immediately. The nuclear arsenal rests in the hands of a president who shows symptoms of serious mental instability. This is an urgent matter of national security. We call on our elected officials to heed the warnings of thousands of mental health professionals who have requested an independent, impartial neuropsychiatric evaluation of Mr. Trump. The world as we know it could cease to exist with a 3:00 a.m. nuclear tweet.

Nanette Gartrell, M.D., is a psychiatrist, researcher, and writer who was formerly on the faculties of Harvard Medical School and the University of California, San Francisco. Her forty-seven years of scientific investigations have focused primarily on sexual minority parent families. In the 1980s and '90s, Dr. Gartrell was the principal investigator of groundbreaking investigations into sexual misconduct by physicians that led to a clean-up of professional ethics codes and the criminalization of boundary violations. The Nanette K. Gartrell Papers are archived at the Sophia Smith Collection, Smith College.

Dee Mosbacher, M.D., Ph.D., is a psychiatrist and Academy Award–nominated documentary filmmaker who was formerly on the faculty of the University of California, San Francisco. As a public-sector psychiatrist, Dr. Mosbacher specialized in the treatment of patients with severe mental illness. She served as San Mateo County's medical director for mental health and was senior psychiatrist at San Francisco's Progress Foundation. The Diane (Dee) Mosbacher and Woman Vision Papers are archived at the Sophia Smith Collection, Smith College. Dr. Mosbacher's films are also contained within the Smithsonian National Museum of American History collection.

Acknowledgments

We thank Esther D. Rothblum, Ph.D.; Madelyn Kahn, M.D.; Judith Herman, M.D.; Robin Morgan; Gloria Steinem; Mary Eichbauer, Ph.D.; Nate Gartrell; Marny Hall, Ph.D.; Kathryn Lee, M.D; and Patricia Speier, M.D., for their assistance in the preparation of this chapter.

References

Abrams, Herbert L. 1999. "Can the Twenty-Fifth Amendment Deal with a Disabled President? Preventing Future White House Cover-Ups." *Presidential Studies Quarterly* 29: 115–33.

Barbaro, Michael. 2016. "Donald Trump Clung to 'Birther' Lie for Years, and Still Isn't Apologetic." *New York Times*, September 16. www.nytimes.com/2016/09/17/us/politics/donald-trump-obama-birther.html?_r=1.

Berisha, Visar, Shuai Wang, Amy LaCross, and Julie Liss. 2015. "Tracking Discourse Complexity Preceding Alzheimer's Disease Diagnosis: A Case Study Comparing the Press Conferences of Presidents Ronald Reagan and George Herbert Walker Bush." *Journal of Alzheimer's Disease* 45: 959–63.

Brown, Lara. 2016. "Government Stumps Trump." *U.S. News & World Report*, March 31. www.usnews.com/opinion/blogs/opinion-blog/articles /2016-03-31/donald-trump-doesnt-understand-the-us-political-system -or-government.

Carter, Jimmy. 1994. "Presidential Disability and the Twenty-Fifth Amendment: A President's Perspective." *JAMA* 272: 1698.

Colón-Francia, Angelita, and Joel Fortner. 2014. "Air Force Improves Its Personnel Reliability Program." *U.S. Air Force News,* February 27. www .af.mil/News/Article-Display/Article/473435/af-improves-its-personnel -reliability-program/.

Cornell University Law School. 2017. "U.S. Constitution 25th Amendment." www.law.cornell.edu/constitution/amendmentxxv.

Davidson, Jonathan R. T., Kathryn M. Connor, and Marvin Swartz. 2006. "Mental Illness in U.S. Presidents Between 1776 and 1974: A Review of Biographical Sources." *Journal of Nervous and Mental Disease* 194: 47–51.

DelReal, Joseph A., and Anne Gearan. 2016. "Trump Stirs Outrage After He Lashes Out at the Muslim Parents of a Dead U.S. Soldier." *Washington Post*, July 30. www.washingtonpost.com/politics/backlash-for-trump -after-he-lashes-out-at-the-muslim-parents-of-a-dead-us-soldier/2016 /07/30/34b0aad4-5671-11e6-88eb-7dda4e2f2aec_story.html?utm_term= .b5ffdee05a40.

DeYoung, Karen. 2017. "U.S.-Turkish Relations Deeply Strained Ahead of Erdogan's Visit to White House." *Washington Post*, May 14. www .washingtonpost.com/world/national-security/us-turkish-relations -deeply-strained-ahead-of-erdogans-visit-to-white-house/2017/05/14 /40797a5c-3736-11e7-b412-62beef8121f7_story.html?utm_term= .58cb9d1f490f.

Forster, Katie, and Lizzie Dearden. 2017. "Donald Trump Calls Judge's

Suspension of Immigration Ban 'Ridiculous' and Says It Will Be Overturned." *Independent*, February 4. www.independent.co.uk/news /world/americas/donald-trump-muslim-ban-judge-suspended-reacts -big-trouble-tweet-immigration-bob-ferguson-a7562671.html.

Glaister, Dan. 2008. "Recordings Reveal Richard Nixon's Paranoia." *Guardian*, December 3. www.theguardian.com/world/2008/dec/03/richard -nixon-tapes.

Goodwin, Richard N. 1988. "President Lyndon Johnson: The War Within." *New York Times*, August 21. www.nytimes.com/1988/08/21/magazine /president-lyndon-johnson-the-war-within.html?pagewanted=all.

"'Grave Concerns' About Trump's Mental Stability: Top U.S. Professors." 2016. *Times of India*, December 20. http://timesofindia.indiatimes.com /world/us/grave-concerns-about-trumps-mental-stability-top-us -professors/articleshow/56076603.cms.

Greene, Richard. 2016. "Is Donald Trump Mentally Ill? 3 Professors of Psychiatry Ask President Obama to Conduct 'A Full Medical and Neuropsychiatric Evaluation.'" *Huffington Post*, December 17. www .huffingtonpost.com/richard-greene/is-donald-trump-mentally_b _13693174.html.

Kendall, Brent. 2016. "Trump Says Judge's Mexican Heritage Presents 'Absolute Conflict.'" *Wall Street Journal*, June 3. www.wsj.com/articles /donald-trump-keeps-up-attacks-on-judge-gonzalo-curiel-1464911442.

McFadden, Cynthia, William M. Arkin, Ken Dilanian, and Robert Windrem. 2017. "Yemen SEAL Raid Has Yielded No Significant Intelligence: Officials." NBC News, February 28. www.nbcnews.com/news /investigations/yemen-seal-raid-yielded-no-significant-intelligence -say-officials-n726451.

McFadden, Robert D. 2014. "James R. Schlesinger, Willful Aide to Three Presidents, Is Dead at 85." *New York Times*, March 27. www.nytimes .com/2014/03/28/us/politics/james-r-schlesinger-cold-war-hard-liner -dies-at-85.html.

Miller, Greg, and Greg Jaffe. 2017. "Trump Revealed Highly Classified Information to Russian Foreign Minister and Ambassador." *Washington Post*, May 15. www.washingtonpost.com/world/national-security

/trump-revealed-highly-classified-information-to-russian-foreign
-minister-and-ambassador/2017/05/15/530c172a-3960-11e7-9e48
-c4f199710b69_story.html?utm_term=.495bc0f95d9d.

Morgan, Robin. 2017a. "Women's Media Center Live with Robin Morgan. WMC Live #197: Farai Chideya." February 19. http://wmclive.com /wmc-live-197-farai-chideya-original-airdate-2192017.

———. 2017b. "20 Feb: The Real Story." *Robin Morgan* (blog). February 20. www.robinmorgan.net/blog/the-real-story/.

Nakamura, David. 2017. "Trump Welcomes Egypt's Sissi to White House in Reversal of U.S. Policy." *Washington Post*, April 3. www.washington post.com/politics/trump-welcomes-egypts-sissi-to-white-house-in -reversal-of-us-policy/2017/04/03/36b5e312-188b-11e7-bcc2 -7d1a0973e7b2_story.html?utm_term=.8edadf26503f.

New York Times Editorial Board. 2017. "Donald Trump Embraces Another Despot." *New York Times*, May 1. www.nytimes.com/2017/05/01 /opinion/donald-trump-embraces-rodrigo-duterte.html?_r=0.

Osnos, Evan. 2017. "How Trump Could Get Fired." *The New Yorker*, May 8. www.newyorker.com/magazine/2017/05/08/how-trump-could-get -fired.

Page, Clarence. 2017. "What's Next for Trump's War Against the Free Press?" *Chicago Tribune*, February 21. www.chicagotribune.com/news/opinion /page/ct-trump-media-war-fake-news-perspec-0222-20170221-column .html.

Pasha-Robinson, Lucy. 2016. "Harvard Professor Says There Are 'Grave Concerns' About Donald Trump's Mental Stability." *Independent*, December 18. www.independent.co.uk/news/world/americas/us -elections/harvard-professors-us-president-barack-obama-grave -concern-donald-trump-mental-stability-a7482586.html.

———. 2017. "Donald Trump 'Has Been Screaming at the Television About Russia Links Investigation,' Says White House Adviser." *Independent*, May 10. www.independent.co.uk/news/world/americas/donald -trump-russia-links-scream-television-james-comey-fired-fbi-director -investigation-white-house-a7727516.html.

Pengelly, Martin. 2017. "North Korea: Trump Keeps Options Open Against

'Smart Cookie' Kim Jong-un." *Guardian*, April 30. www.theguardian.com
/us-news/2017/apr/30/trump-vague-possible-us-strike-north-korea
-chess-game.

Reilly, Katie. 2016. "Here Are All the Times Donald Trump Insulted Mexico."
Time, August 31. http://time.com/4473972/donald-trump-mexico-meeting
-insult/.

Sampathkumar, Mythili. 2017. "'Armada' Trump Claimed Was Deployed to
North Korea Actually Heading to Australia." *Independent*, April 19.
www.independent.co.uk/news/world/americas/us-politics/donald
-trump-north-korea-aircraft-carrier-sailing-opposite-direction
-warning-a7689961.html.

Schecter, Anna R., Chris Francescani, and Tracy Connor. 2016. "Trump
Doctor Who Wrote Whole Health Letter in Just 5 Minutes as Limo
Waited." NBC News, August 26. www.nbcnews.com/news/us-news
/trump-doctor-wrote-health-letter-just-5-minutes-limo-waited-n638526.

Schmitt, Eric, and David E. Sanger. 2017. "Raid in Yemen: Risky from the Start
and Costly in the End." *New York Times*, February 1. www.nytimes.com
/2017/02/01/world/middleeast/donald-trump-yemen-commando-raid
-questions.html.

Sebastian, Michael. 2016. "Here's How Presidents and Candidates Who
Aren't Donald Trump Respond to Protesters." *Esquire*, March 15. www
.esquire.com/news-politics/news/a43020/heres-how-presidents-and
-candidates-who-arent-donald-trump-respond-to-protesters/.

Siddiqui, Sabrina. 2017. "Trump Press Ban: BBC, CNN and Guardian
Denied Access to Briefing." *Guardian*, February 25. www.theguardian
.com/us-news/2017/feb/24/media-blocked-white-house-briefing-sean
-spicer.

Stefansky, Emma. 2017. "Trump Refuses to Apologize, Drags Germany into
Absurd Wiretapping Lie." *Vanity Fair*, March 18. Accessed May 11, 2017.
www.vanityfair.com/news/2017/03/trump-refuses-to-apologize-drags
-germany-into-wiretapping-lie.

"Transcript: Donald Trump's Taped Comments About Women." 2016. *New
York Times*, October 8. www.nytimes.com/2016/10/08/us/donald
-trump-tape-transcript.html?_r=0.

"Voices of the Women's March: Angela Davis, Gloria Steinem, Madonna, Alicia Keys, Janet Mock, and More." 2017. *Democracy Now*, January 23. www.democracynow.org/2017/1/23/voices_of_the_womens_march _angela.

Wagner, Alex. 2017. "Trump vs. the Very Fake News Media." *The Atlantic*, February 17. www.theatlantic.com/politics/archive/2017/02/trump-vs -the-very-fake-news-media/516561/.

Ware, Doug G. 2017. "Trump Deflects Blame for Yemen Raid That Killed U.S. Navy SEAL." UPI, February 28. www.upi.com/Top_News/US/2017 /02/28/Trump-deflects-blame-for-Yemen-raid-that-killed-US-Navy-SEAL /3241488319168/.

Weinstein, Edwin A. 1981. *Woodrow Wilson: A Medical and Psychological Biography*. Princeton, NJ: Princeton University Press.

Zaru, Deena. 2017. "It Took FOIA for Park Service to Release Photos of Obama, Trump Inauguration Crowd Sizes." CNN Politics, March 7. www.cnn.com/2017/03/07/politics/national-park-service-inauguration -crowd-size-photos/.

PART 4

SOCIOCULTURAL CONSEQUENCES

PERSISTENT ENSLAVEMENT SYSTEMIC TRAUMA: THE DELETERIOUS IMPACT OF TRUMP'S RHETORIC ON BLACK AND BROWN PEOPLE

KEVIN WASHINGTON, PH.D.

Rhetoric can be a powerful shaper of culture, especially when it is from a president. Donald Trump's rhetoric appeals through a promise of restoration ("Make America Great Again"), nativism ("Build a Wall"), and nationalism ("America First") that will deliver his supporters from a rigged system and myriad threats. This orientation is dangerous because it pivots on a handful of goals unaccompanied by factual practicability (deport "criminal aliens," bring back jobs, cut taxes, insure everyone at lower cost while delivering high-quality care) (Jamieson and Taussig 2017). He entices through emotion, while his hearkening back to the greatness of the past rarely reveals when the country was great, what was laudable about it, or who was responsible for its past glory, with the one notable exception of Trump's nostalgia for the harsher punishments meted out to protesters "in the good old days" (Parker 2016). If he has any ideology, it is White supremacy. A way to enforce this ideology is through engagement in White terrorism, which fits his psychological disposition. His language, considered to be a dog whistle to proponents of White supremacy, is a violent alarm of terror to African Americans and other marginalized racial, ethnic, and cultural groups.

Although his verbiage has been dehumanizing, marginalizing, and disenfranchising for all Nonwhite people, reminiscent of a time when the physical enslavement of African people was the standard of the day, some suggest that his language is innocuous to those who understand what being American really means. However, for persons of African ancestry, a return to the past means that said population returns to being dehumanized, under servitude, brutally worked, and beaten from can-to-can't (from the time one can see the sun to the time when one cannot see the sun). Language that speaks of returning to the past, therefore, is grossly disruptive to the psyche of persons of African descent because they can recall conditions of horror being meted out by Whites who sought to enjoy their position of privilege at the expense of traumatizing others. More generally, his language is psychologically challenging for many Americans—White and those of Nonwhite racial, ethnic, cultural, and linguistic groups.

The term "Trump Anxiety Disorder" (TAD) has been advanced in order to capture the feelings associated with the forty-fifth president's derogatory rhetoric and erratic behaviors as experienced by Whites. Jennifer Panning, Psy.D., described this condition in an earlier chapter of this volume to capture the psychological response of many to the election of the forty-fifth president of the United States. TAD has become associated with the anxiety felt by those classified as White: Americans in general are experiencing record levels of stress and anxiety since the current presidency. It should stand to reason that persons of African descent will have deeper visceral responses to the language of the forty-fifth president of the United States.

His discourse becomes the most unnerving when he describes Nonwhite people. He has referred to African countries and those countries heavily populated by those of African ancestry as most undesirable places to live in or in which to conduct business. He has disparaged inner-city (urban) areas or Black-populated regions within the United States as being places that are crime-ridden. He has asserted that Muslim-majority countries or countries that are closely associated with the religion of Islam are terrorist countries. When running for president of the United States, he stated that Mexico does not send its best people, but rather they send people with lots of problems. He stated, "They are bringing those problems with them. They are bringing drugs and crime. They're rapists." He added that he assumed some of them are good, suggesting that most of them were bad people, and only some of them might be good.

What is absent from this discourse is the fact that England sent its undesirables to inhabit the land now known as the United States; that religious crusades were used to persecute people in the name of Christianity; and that this land was stolen by violence from the ancestors of Native or Indigenous people of what is now called North America. Also, a missing portion of the discourse is the fact that once excommunicated from Europe, the European Americans engaged in the human trafficking of the inhabitants of Africa and forced them to endure the backbreaking toil of agriculture, animal husbandry, and the other labor upon which the economy of the United States was established. Additionally, Whites raped African women and separated African families for their convenience. They practiced terrorism that brutalized African people through abuse, beatings, and mob lynching. If one were to apply a Freudian lens to his xenophobic statements or behavior to the widespread nature of White (European) rape, pillaging, violent procuring, and religious persecution, then it would suggest that the forty-fifth United States president is employing an ego-defense mechanism called "projection." Projection is defined as the unconscious attribution of one's own unwanted, undesirable, or unacceptable feelings, thought, behaviors, or beliefs onto another person or group.

The forty-fifth president of the United States utilizes language that dehumanizes persons of African descent as well as those classified as "the cultural other" (Ani, 1994) when he refers to them as "dogs," questioning their intellectual abilities while suggesting that they have innate criminal tendencies. This can be seen in the statement that he made to California lawmakers in May 2018 about allegedly criminal Mexicans immigrating to the United States. In this statement he assumes that they are all affiliated with the MS-13 organization (a gang). He stated: "We have people coming to this country . . . You wouldn't believe how bad these people are. These aren't people. These are animals. . . . It's crazy" (Martelle 2018). The forty-fifth president of the United States asserts that all non-European immigrants are mostly of questionable character and of lower intelligence and should not be allowed to enter into the United States. Defamation of character is a critical aspect of destroying a person.

His rhetoric toward Black men and Black women is particularly toxic to the psyche of said group. When he addressed the behaviors of some NFL football players who elected to kneel on one knee during the playing of the U.S. national anthem, "The Star-Spangled Banner," in response to the police brutality that Black males encounter within the United States, he attacked the Black community, since many of the players taking a knee were Black males. He framed the behavior as not honoring the U.S. flag. The matter that Colin Kaepernick, a former NFL quarterback, initiated was really about the racism found in the country and celebrated in the anthem of Francis Scott Key, a supporter of African enslavement in the United States. The degree to which the forty-fifth U.S. president subverted the position of Mr. Kaepernick and to which other so-called Whites missed the issue(s) of concern is another contributing factor to the psychological duress experienced by persons of African ancestry. Whites' convenient repackaging of matters of race to mean something about being un-American in an effort to neutralize the voices of Black people adds frustration to the subjugation. When oppressed people speak out against their oppression, they are villainized and called derogatory names—by the forty-fifth president of the United States himself.

The forty-fifth president called the players' mothers dogs when he stated that the football team owners should tell those "sons of bitches" to stand for the anthem and play football or be fired. Referring to Black women as female dogs is consistent for him, as is seen in his statement about his African American former employee, Omarosa Manigault-Newman:

"When you give a crazed, crying lowlife a break, and give her a job at the White House, I guess it just didn't work out. Good work by General Kelly for quickly firing that dog." All of his language is unsettling for many persons of African descent and too reminiscent of the most violent factions of Western/European ideology.

It is difficult to miss the racist implementation of the intelligence quotient (IQ) by Lewis Terman and other behavioral scientists for the purpose of discriminating against immigrants and instituting sterilization laws for undesirable populations such as those of African descent. In June 2018, the forty-fifth U.S. president stated the African American Congresswoman Maxine Waters was "an extraordinarily low IQ person" because she challenged U.S. White House officials on their immigration policies (Cummings 2018). When questioned about his policies, he consistently retaliates with the common cultural rhetoric that advances White supremacy. Don Lemon, an African American CNN news anchor, conducted an interview with African American basketball player LeBron James in August 2018 about a school that James opened for at-risk children. James stated that the forty-fifth U.S. president was using athletics to divide the country. It apparently infuriated the forty-fifth president, who retorted: "LeBron James was just interviewed by the dumbest man on television, Don Lemon," Mr. Trump wrote. "He made LeBron look smart, which isn't easy to do. I like Mike!" (Stewart 2018). The response is most juvenile but is consistent with the pseudoscientific rhetoric of racist ideology that was used to promote the violence of slavery and colonialism. This ideology has been the source of much pain and suffering for Black people in America. It brings to remembrance the trauma of the past, which could be associated with the forty-fifth president's statements suggesting that the aim is to make America "hate" again and again.

Psychic Trauma

New research reveals the inheritability of trauma (Dias and Ressler 2014), and the idea of *transgenerational trauma* and its treatment is worthy of consideration, given the historical aspects of the trauma that persons of African descent encounter, coupled with the ongoing aspects of trauma as exemplified societally in the language of the forty-fifth president, police brutality, and marches by White supremacist or terrorist groups like those in Charlottesville, Virginia, and Pikeville, Kentucky, in 2017 and the Washington, D.C., rally in 2018.

Posttraumatic stress disorder (PTSD) is a misnomer for African Americans, because the prefix "post" would suggest that the trauma is finished. When an entire group or a culture has ongoing trauma in the United States, whether it be police brutality, poor health care services, environmental racism, food deserts, or the pipeline-to-prison process, it is not clear that it should be described as PTSD. Psychological and historical researcher Joy DeGruy advances Post Traumatic Slave Syndrome (PTSS), which is a theory that states that African Americans sustained traumatic psychological and emotional injury as a direct result of slavery and continue to be injured by trauma caused by the larger society's policies of inequality, racism, and oppression. Whereas it contextualizes the trauma experienced by persons of African descent, the "post" traumatic aspect of the descriptor implies that one is beyond the trauma. This is not the case.

For the unrelenting trauma that persons of African descent continue to experience, we propose the concept of "Persistent Enslavement Systemic Trauma." "Persistent" suggests that, although physical slavery is past, enslavement takes on many forms, and the mental form is more violent in many ways than the physical form. However, the mental period of enslavement represents a different season of the trauma process and requires a unique approach to healing. Here, we desire to acknowledge the physical-psycho-spiritual assaults of the African enslavement process, because they were easily identifiable and most instrumental in solidifying the stronghold of the mental enslavement structures that repeat the physical brutality. Here, the primary purpose of the physical brutality is to cause psychic/spiritual disruption, and it is "systemic" in terms of targeting an entire group of people on all levels of existence. Therefore we see the post physical enslavement as closer to Persistent Enslavement Systemic Trauma (PEST). It is this disruption that we seek to highlight and repair.

This concept is newer but closely related to the term South African psychologist Gill Straker has proposed: "continuous traumatic stress" (CTS). CTS is distinct from PTSD, in that it is continuous in the context of the political violence and state oppression of South Africa in the 1980s (Eagle, Gillian, and Kaminer 2013). Others have advanced the thought of multiple occurrences of trauma, in terms of Complex PTSD (Herman 1992) and developmental trauma disorder (van der Kolk 2005) to capture the psychological impact of prolonged abuse within the context of a relationship with a perpetrator. Collective or historical trauma (Eyerman 2001) and identity trauma (Kira 2001) are constructs that reflect traumas resulting from the targeting of specific groups of people, rather than individuals. The emerging question is: What does one call the convergence of all of these within one person? Such is the case for Black and many brown people within the United States.

While this section has focused on the African American experience, it is important to note that we are developing once again a contemporary version of slavery with other races and nationalities throughout the world. Further, other ethnic groups such as Muslims are suffering from displacement in the Middle East due to violent American foreign policy interventions. Hence, while the African experience is specific, there are universal lessons to be gleaned.

Mental Health Intervention Imperative
The psychological needs of ethnically, culturally, racially, and linguistically diverse populations including African Americans will never be met until we address the dynamics surrounding their individual

and cultural experiences. Social, political, economic, and community violence have a huge impact on the emotional and psychological well-being of many diverse families. Racism, economic disenfranchisement, and various forms of discrimination are acts of psychological violence that often manifest only momentarily in physical violence. These negative occurrences often cause or accompany incidents of personal violation.

Psychologist Robert Carter described race-based trauma as emotional, psychological, and physical reactions to personal experiences with racial harassment and/or discrimination that cause pain (Carter 2007). They include the following:

- **Racial Discrimination** *Avoidant*: barring access, exclusion, withholding, deception
- **Racial Harassment** *Hostile*: physical, interpersonal, and verbal assaults, stereotyped
- **Discriminatory Harassment** *Aversive hostility*: White flight, isolation, denial of promotion, questions of qualifications.

Nonwhite populations encounter substantial stress caused by several different experiences (e.g., cultural, individual, and institutional) of racism. Whereas racial discrimination and posttraumatic symptoms and race-based traumatic stress are relatively new areas of research, they have been long understood in the lived experiences of Black people.

Trauma and Black People

Prevalence rates for PTSD (again, a misnomer) among Blacks are reported as the highest among all ethnicities, at 8.7 percent (Roberts et al. 2011). One explanation for why rates for PTSD are higher among African Americans is due to the differential exposure to trauma inducing events. The lingua franca used by the forty-fifth president brings to remembrance the trauma of African ancestors. The exposure to the African American experience in the United States, the collective memory of what their ancestors have experienced, and how African Americans continue to be mistreated can itself be a potential risk factor for developing PTSD or PEST.

Healing and Repair

Understanding the worldview of persons of African descent is critical to healing the psycho-spiritual disruption and the ancillary, lingering psychological effects of what has been called the transatlantic slave trade encountered by African people in America and throughout the African diaspora as well as continental Africans. A culturally relevant psychology of healing is necessary. Such a distinct psychology of healing will be consistent with the unique psychology of Africans, be they African Americans, diasporic Africans, or continental Africans, as it will in general be sensitive to the essence and ethos of "Africanness."

This brand of psychology would be based on the African cultural continuum between African/Black people in America and abroad (Akbar 1996; Myers 1988; Nobles 2015). The current African cultural expression has been a major source of strength for the survival of African people in the midst of the aforementioned forces of European ideology (Herskovits 1958). African/Black psychology acknowledges that the ideological core of African people is consistent across tribes, societies, countries, and other arbitrary borders (Nobles 2015; Washington 2010). The anchoring element of this African/Black psychology is the African philosophical system of life (Mbiti 1970; Myers 1988; Nobles 2015; Ojelade et al., 2014). The key components of this African psychology are that Spirit is ever present, all is connected, family is sacred, and the community is essential (Mukuka 2013). Historical and contemporary survival and the thriving of persons of African descent has been and continues to be found within the essence of the collective identity and communal survival thrust of the African worldview (Myers and Speight 2010).

In South Africa, the philosophy of *ubuntu* (the Zulu word that speaks to the idea of profound humanity within a communal context; *ubu* refers to being while *ntu* alludes to universal life force) is the name for the ideology that one is a part of a distinct community and one is to remain accountable to that community. *Ubuntu* psychotherapy is advanced and worthy of consideration (Washington 2010) when treating persons of African descent. Ubuntu psychotherapy is about restoring a sense of connectedness and wholeness within a people that feels alienated and disconnected. It can therefore be extrapolated to permeate all cultures and communities of alienation. The *ubuntu* ideology will continue to disrupt the cultural rhetoric of racism, ethnic hatred, and oppression by promoting collective identity and communal accountability.

Kevin Washington (Mwata Kairi), Ph.D., is a licensed, African-centered psychologist in Florida and in the District of Columbia. He has taught at several colleges nationally and internationally. He is the immediate past president of the Association of Black Psychologists and is head of the Sociology and Psychology Department at Grambling State University. He examines cultural and historical trauma of people who are impacted by Persistent Enslavement Systemic Trauma (PEST). As the founder of ubuntu psychotherapy, he advances culturally responsible, trauma-informed mental health interventions for Black men and boys as well as Black Families. NewsOne, Essence, Black Entertainment Television (BET) News, Vocal Point, and many other organizations have sought his expertise.

References

Akbar, Na'im. 1996. *Breaking the Chains of Psychological Slavery*. Tallahassee: Mind Production & Associates.

Alegría, Margarita, Lisa R. Fortuna, Julia Y. Lin, L. Frances Norris, Shan Gao, David T. Takeuchi, James S. Jackson, Patrick E. Shrout, and Anne Valentine. 2013. "Prevalence, Risk, and Correlates of Posttraumatic

Stress Disorder Across Ethnic and Racial Minority Groups in the US." *Medical Care* 51 (12): 1114.

Ani, Marimba. 1994. *Yurugu: An African-Centered Critique of European Cultural Thought and Behavior.* Trenton, NJ: Africa World Press.

Bryant-Davis, Thema. 2007. "Healing Requires Recognition: The Case for Race-Based Traumatic Stress." *Counseling Psychologist* 35 (1): 135–43.

Carter, Robert T. 2007. "Racism and Psychological and Emotional Injury: Recognizing and Assessing Race-Based Traumatic Stress." *Counseling Psychologist* 35 (1): 13–105.

Cummings, W. 2018. "Trump Slams 'Low IQ' Rep. Maxine Waters Who Called for Harassment of White House Officials." *USA Today.* June 25. https://www.usatoday.com/story/news/politics/onpolitics/2018/06/25/maxine-waters-trump-exchange/732505002/.

DeGruy, Joy. (2005). *Post Traumatic Slave Syndrome: America's Legacy of Enduring Injury and Healing.* Portland, OR: Joy DeGruy Publications.

Dias, Brian G., and Kerry J. Ressler. 2014. "Parental Olfactory Experience Influences Behavior and Neural Structure in Subsequent Generations." *Nature Neuroscience* 17 (1): 89–96.

Eagle, Gillian, and Debra Kaminer. 2013. "Continuous Traumatic Stress: Expanding the Lexicon of Traumatic Stress." *Peace and Conflict* 19 (2): 85.

Eyerman, Ron. 2001. *Cultural Trauma: Slavery and the Formation of African American Identity.* Cambridge, UK: Cambridge University Press.

Herman, J. L. (1992). "Complex PTSD: A syndrome in Survivors of Prolonged and Repeated Trauma." *Journal of Traumatic Stress,* 5 (3), 377–91.

Herskovits, Melville J. 1958. *The Myth of the Negro Past.* Boston: Beacon.

Jamieson, Kathleen Hall, and Doron Taussig. 2017. "Disruption, Demonization, Deliverance, and Norm Destruction." *Political Science Quarterly* 132 (4): 619–50.

Kambon, Kobi. 1998. *African/Black Psychology in the American Context: An African-Centered Perspective.* Tallahassee: Nubian Nation.

Kira, I. (2001). "A Taxonomy of Trauma and Trauma Assessment." *Traumatology: An International Journal*, 2, 1–14.

Kira, Ibrahim A., Mounir H. Fawzi, and Mohab M. Fawzi. 2013. "The Dynamics of Cumulative Trauma and Trauma Types in Adult Patients with Psychiatric Disorders." *Traumatology* 19 (3): 179–95.

Martelle, Scott. 2018. "About Those Immigrants Trump Referred to as 'Animals.'" *Los Angeles Times*. May 17. http://www.latimes.com/opinion/la-ol -enter-the-fray-about-those-immigrants-trump-referred-to-1526569123 -htmlstory.html.

Mbiti, John S. 1970. *African Religions and Philosophy*. Portsmouth, NH: Heinemann.

Mukuka, Richard. 2013. "Ubuntu in SM Kapwepwe's 'Shalapo Canicandala': Insights for Afrocentric Psychology." *Journal of Black Studies* 44 (2): 137–57.

Myers, Linda James. 1988. *Understanding an Afrocentric World View: Introduction to an Optimal Psychology*. Dubuque: Kendall/Hunt Publishing Company.

Myers, Linda James, and Suzette L. Speight. 2010. "Reframing Mental Health and Psychological Well-Being Among Persons of African Descent." *The Journal of Pan African Studies* 3 (8): 66–82.

Nobles, Wade W. 2015. "From Black Psychology to Sakhu Djaer: Implications for the Further Development of a Pan African Black Psychology." *Journal of Black Psychology* 41 (5): 399–414.

Nuttman-Shwartz, Orit, and Yael Shoval-Zuckerman. 2016. "Continuous Traumatic Situations in the Face of Ongoing Political Violence: The Relationship Between CTS and PTSD." *Trauma, Violence, & Abuse* 17 (5): 562–70.

Ojelade, Ifetayo I., Kenja McCray, Joel Meyers, and Jeffrey Ashby. 2014. "Use of Indigenous African Healing Practices as a Mental Health Intervention." *Journal of Black Psychology* 40 (6): 491–519.

Parker, Ashley. 2016. "In 'Good Old Days,' Donald Trump Says, Campaign Protesters Got More Than Just an Escort Out," *New York Times*. February 27. https://www.nytimes.com/politics/first-draft/2016/02/27/in-good

-old-days-donald-trump-says-campaign-protesters-got-more-than
-just-an- escort-out/.

Pieterse, Alex L., Robert T. Carter, Sarah A. Evans, and Rebecca A. Walter. 2010. "An Exploratory Examination of the Associations Among Racial and Ethnic Discrimination, Racial Climate, and Trauma-Related Symptoms in a College Student Population." *Journal of Counseling Psychology* 57 (3): 255–63.

Roberts, Andrea L., Stephen E. Gilman, Joshua Breslau, Naomi Breslau, and Karestan C. Koenen. 2011. "Race/Ethnic Differences in Exposure to Traumatic Events, Development of Post-Traumatic Stress Disorder, and Treatment-Seeking for Post-Traumatic Stress Disorder in the United States." *Psychological Medicine* 41 (1): 71–83.

Stewart, Emily. 2018. "Trump Is Insulting LeBron James's Intelligence—and Don Lemon's—on Twitter." *Vox*. August 4. https://www.vox.com/2018/8/4/17650982/trump-lebron-james-tweet-don-lemon.

Van der Kolk, Bessel A. 2005. "Developmental Trauma Disorder: Toward a Rational Diagnosis for Children with Complex Trauma Histories." *Psychiatric Annals* 35 (5): 401–8.

Washington, Kevin. 2010. "Zulu Traditional Healing, Afrikan Worldview and the Practice of Ubuntu: Deep Thought for Afrikan/Black Psychology." *The Journal of Pan African Studies* 3 (8): 24–39.

TRAUMATIC CONSEQUENCES FOR IMMIGRANT POPULATIONS IN THE UNITED STATES

ROSA MARIA BRAMBLE, L.C.S.W.

"Give me your tired, your poor,
Your huddled masses yearning to breathe free,
The wretched refuse of your teeming shore.
Send these, the homeless, tempest-tost to me,
I lift my lamp beside the golden door!"

—"The New Colossus," Emma Lazarus

The day prior to the 2016 presidential election, I sat down with a family seeking support for their immigration case. Their fear was palpable when they disclosed, "If Donald Trump wins the presidency, we don't know what will happen to our family." The children were twelve- and nine-year-old U.S.-born citizens, but their parents were undocumented. They sought support in cancellation of removal, a form of relief from deportation. If rejected, the parents could be forced to return to their country for up to ten years. There was a state of genuine panic, with tears in the parents' eyes. They feared that if Trump won the presidential election, they would surely be deported. The family felt uncertain; their future was unpredictable and out of their control.

I have worked for more than fifteen years with immigrants, asylum seekers, and refugees, providing psychotherapy and community-based services. My parents inspire my work, as they fled a political upheaval in Venezuela to seek stability, employment, and educational opportunities for their family. I dedicated myself to serving individuals seeking refuge from violence and persecution based on their political, religious beliefs, ethnic, and sexual identity. During the past eighteen months of the current presidential administration, my practice has become more intense, and my training in trauma-informed psychotherapy indispensable. In this chapter, I share my clinical observations with the families and individuals I have served. I also offer insights regarding implications for particular groups, including asylum seekers, DACA recipients, children, families, and mental health providers.

Immigrants have always faced challenges in the United States. From job discrimination in the 1930s and Japanese internment during World War II to anti-Muslim sentiments following the September 11, 2001, terrorist attacks, our country has constantly struggled with systemic, institutional, and personal discrimination. The 2016 presidential campaign brought along a new wave of anti-immigrant rhetoric, giving a national voice to those who felt similarly. The president won on a platform of discrimination, including against Latino and specifically Mexican undocumented immigrants. Their lives became threatened because the campaign cast undocumented immigrants as criminals and rapists who were taking jobs and burdening the U.S. economy. The contrary is true: undocumented immigrants commit lower rates of crime and contribute heavily to the American economy. Trump's victory signified the explicit endorsement of discriminatory sentiments that directly hurt our clients.

As countless therapists across the United States have experienced, the 2016 presidential election instilled a new level of anxiety in our clients. Through our practice, we gain a window into the abuse, torture, and exclusion an individual suffers solely due to their identity and circumstances. We bear witness to the worst of human experiences. Despite their profound trauma, my clients demonstrate incredible resilience, remarkably transforming their suffering into purpose when given the chance to live freely and safely. For thousands of refugees and asylum seekers, the United States no longer offers this.

Within the first forty-eight hours after the presidential election, I was asked to address the alarming fear and terror emerging in the Latino undocumented community to my clients and to the radio audience on Radio WADO, the most listened-to radio station in the Latino community nationwide. I talked about how we can conceptualize these fears from a trauma-informed perspective, a framework developed by world-renowned psychiatrist Judith Herman (1997). Trauma can be defined as witnessing or experiencing an immediate threat to an individual, whether physically, mentally, or emotionally. Traumatic events shatter our reality, and we perceive our environment as unsafe. The presidential campaign, election, inauguration, rhetoric, and consequent anti-immigrant policies served as cumulative stressors to an already vulnerable community. I discussed posttraumatic stress and the prevalent phrase, "Post-Trump Traumatic Stress" (similar to the "Trump Anxiety Disorder" described earlier in this book). Undocumented immigrants were experiencing symptoms classically consistent with traumatic stress: anxiety, uncertainty, fear of their surroundings, hypervigilance, and nightmares.

One woman sought supportive counseling and an evaluation to support her spouse's immigration case and prevent deportation. She was emotionally distressed at having to provide for her young children without her husband's presence. Her children were visibly shaken and anxious. Like their parents, they were watching the news and were fearful of what could happen to their family. As in the aftermath of a traumatic event, the family was trying to understand their situation and how they could restore their safety. Although legal clinics and other resources have been established, the perceived lack of safety and traumatic stress persists. I utilized trauma-informed therapy and disaster mental health techniques to help the family understand what they were experiencing. These strategies emphasized remaining grounded and engaging in regular daily activities when experiencing traumatic events that affect one's life and community.

Despite my attempts to make sense of this new reality, the perception of threats to immigrants' survival became very real in their day-to-day lives. The fear of their surroundings was amplified due to the criminalization of the border sanctions in sanctuary cities. The twelve million undocumented clients living in the United States were already living under the radar, but the current administration gave the Immigration and Customs Enforcement (ICE) an aggressive mandate to find and deport them. They feared being separated from their loved ones and from the land that had become their home. ICE's threat became very real, even in New York City, a "sanctuary city" and safe haven for millions of undocumented immigrants. One of my clients fell and was injured in a Queens train station because someone suddenly yelled that ICE agents were approaching the area. There were terror and panic everywhere. Even immigrants with legal status experienced the terror of being separated from their loved ones, detained, and criminalized, based solely on their appearance. Lawful permanent residents rushed to become U.S. citizens, as it was the only protection against deportation.

My daily commute passes through avenues where day laborers abound, waiting for and seeking daily work. After the inauguration, the streets were suddenly absent of workers under this spell of fear and silence. Queens, which is considered one of the most diverse areas in the world, visibly experienced the fear. People were out less, and storeowners reported that business was down. The eeriness of the silence following the inauguration felt similar to days after the collectively traumatic terrorist attacks of September 11, 2001. In this case, the Latino immigrant community was specifically targeted and left in fear. Communities that have faced ostracism also experienced vulnerability. One of my clients, a son of holocaust survivors, feared an increase of attacks on the Jewish community.

Consequent Traumatic Events

The week of January 27, 2017, was one of the most difficult in my professional career. On that day, an executive order was signed, blocking entry from seven countries in the Middle East and Africa. This "travel ban" raised fear and terror not just among refugees and asylum seekers from the selected regions considered a "threat to national security," but also for all immigrants. They received a clear message: "You are not welcome, and you are no longer safe." It represented deliberate action and the fulfillment of the anti-immigrant rhetoric that had persisted. While the travel ban has been revised due to numerous acts of protest, advocacy, and court decisions, the Trump administration instantly set the tone of their administration: the United States is not open to refugees, asylum seekers, or other immigrants. The new asylum guidelines, effective in February 2017, now raise the bar for claimants to demonstrate a preponderance of evidence to establish credible fear. Asylum seekers, already suffering disproportionately from PTSD, are now required to divulge their story to the asylum officer and relive their trauma. With the new guidelines, the officer is instructed to be more skeptical. If the officer determines an inconsistency in their story, the claim will be more easily denied, and the claimant will be deported. New guidance directs asylum officers to begin considering illegal entry to the United States a factor that they may count against an individual's application for asylum.

A "Zero Tolerance" policy was put into effect in 2005 in order to penalize illegal entry into the United States (American Immigration Council 2018). The current administration has enhanced this policy to send adults charged with illegally crossing the border directly to federal court. Their children would be sent to the Department of Health and Human Services' Office of Refugee Resettlement, which works with shelters or relatives in the United States. From April to May 2018, approximately 2,654 children had been separated from their parents and detained. Under enormous social and political pressure, President Trump signed an executive order to reverse this policy on June 20, 2018 (Shear, Goodnough, and Haberman 2018). Nevertheless, other immigration challenges persist. Current immigration policies still restrict the number of refugees to 30,000 per year (Davis 2018) and dictate how usage of public benefits may hinder immigrants' capacity to obtain documented status. These changes clearly disregard the poor, the tired, and those yearning to be free.

Seeking Asylum

I think of the hundreds of people I have worked with in the LGBT community who are persecuted because of sexual orientation, women who have undergone female genital mutilation, and men and women who are tortured because of their political opinions. I reflect on conversations with a Chinese client who was tortured because of her religious practices. I remember a lesbian client who was sexually abused as a teenager in South America because the male perpetrator said, "I'll show you what you need," and I wonder about a young man from El Salvador who was discriminated against because of his indigenous identity and also had to flee gang recruitment attempts. They were able to find a home and a future in the United States. Would these clients be heard now? Would they be accepted, or would they be told to go back to their country because they are unwelcome here? How could they start healing?

I think of the Venezuelans I have assisted, who are living in the United States while their country is experiencing a humanitarian crisis. They would benefit from the Temporary Protective Status (TPS), a protective status for individuals who are unable to return to their country because of an environmental disaster or extraordinary conditions. The program that allowed thousands of individuals from different countries to work legally and to build their lives is now threatened to end. Will humanitarian relief no longer be part of our national tapestry?

Herman (1997) writes about the stages of trauma recovery: safety and stabilization, coming to terms with traumatic memories and events, and integration and moving forward. For asylum seekers, asylum approval is the first stage of starting a new life. They can begin living fulfilling lives when there is safety, where identity-based threats no longer exist.

My client Zoila fled Ecuador after facing many years of gender-based violence. Zoila was born a product of rape. Due to poverty, Zoila worked and lived with different relatives who sexually assaulted her as well. Childhood sexual abuse placed her at risk for adult interpersonal violence. She felt loved and protected by an older man who made her feel safe. Over time, he became physically abusive to the point that her bruises and shame kept her indoors. He also forced her to work long hours to support him, and she did, with the hope that he would change. Zoila made several unsuccessful attempts to flee to other parts of the country and finally made the traumatic journey through Central America to the United States, fighting for her own survival. When she arrived at the Arizona border, she asked for asylum. She crossed the border without inspection and was charged with a misdemeanor.

New York has many pro bono attorneys who generously work with immigrants. Zoila's attorney contracted me to meet with her, explaining that Zoila's emotional distress could impact her ability to convey her experiences to the judge. In asylum proceedings, the client's narrative is their evidence. If there are inconsistencies, the individual's credibility is questioned, and they risk losing their case.

Through psychoeducation of trauma techniques, including grounding and breathing exercises, I helped Zoila regulate her emotions and understand the legal process. She soon became comfortable enough to tell her story. The first thing she said was, "Had I known that I would have to tell my story of violence, I would not have left." This profound statement demonstrates the severity of abuse she had endured—she avoided the topic because it was so painful. After we worked together and recognized her trauma, Zoila was able to present her case and find a path toward healing in the United States.

Deferred Action for Childhood Arrivals (DACA)

September 5, 2017, was another traumatic day for the immigrant communities across the United States. The current immigration policy known as Deferred Action for Childhood Arrivals (DACA) affected 800,000 young adults who arrived to the United States as minors and were able to seek education and employment opportunities; they are called "Dreamers." There was disbelief that President Trump would go as far to end the program, since he said, "We are going to deal with DACA with heart. . . . I love these kids" (2017). However, this nation of immigrants was shocked when the executive administration announced that Dreamers would not receive an extension. These individuals who arrived as children, often not knowing any other country as their home, would become illegal overnight and subject to deportation. That same evening, the Hispanic Federation held an informational day in response to the end of DACA. I was asked to be available to meet with families and to address their mental health needs. I met with twelve Dreamers and their families. There was initial silence in the room, but as we went around by way of introduction, each Dreamer shared their story of sudden fear, hopelessness, and disappointment. There were tears due to uncertainty of the future and a lack of safety in what they had known as their home. Creating a space for shared experience and support is what we felt we could provide, and Dreamers and their families were invited to attend the walk in Washington, D.C. Academic institutions all over the nation took action to support DACA recipients, often modifying their policies to protect and support their students. The activism that took place all over the country led to stopping the legislation to end DACA. Nevertheless, there continues to be a state of uncertainty for these individuals, many of whom have gone on to college, earned graduate degrees, led productive lives, and undoubtedly contributed to the growth and betterment of the United States.

Children and Families

In supporting family unity for many years, I have included children in the evaluation process. They often share how their mom takes care of them, that "she's my best friend," or that their dad "cooks for me and takes me to school." However, since the presidential campaign and especially after Trump's election, the demeanor of these children has changed. Like their parents, they watch the news and are fearful of what could happen to their family. Even their body postures of lowered, hunched-over shoulders communicate a sense of defeat, fear, and powerlessness. Their speech is despondent, their gazes lowered and hopeless. Their acute fear of parental deportation is often manifested in an inability to focus in school and a fear that their mom and dad may not be there when they return home.

One woman sought counseling for her two children in support of her spouse's immigration case and to prevent deportation. The two children stayed very close together on the couch. We spoke about how the family spends time together. After developing rapport and trust ("confianza" in Spanish), I asked each child if they knew why we were talking, and they did. They immediately started crying, sharing what it would be like if their dad were not with them. It was the most difficult part of the session. Unlike interviews with children in previous years, this was the first time these emotions were accompanied with genuine fear. Their fear and love moved me, and I could not hold back my own tears. After observing so many children with acute anxiety and traumatic stress, I thought of an intervention that would be empowering and directly related to their parents' immigration case. I had the two siblings write letters as a way of expressing their feelings but also of providing a sense of control in their surroundings. The next week, the children walked in with intention, their postures a bit straighter. They were eager to read their letters and grateful to know that their letters would be part of their parent's immigration packet. They shared:

> From what I have heard in the news, I want my Dad and Mom and the rest of my family to be together because it makes me real sad how Donald Trump is separating a lot of families. My family means a lot to me, and I feel like everyone in my family plays an important role that keeps us together. What I think of our new president is that he was

misunderstood by someone, and now he decides to take his aggression out on innocent people. This is what I feel is going on in my family, community, and country.

They were given a chance to voice their fears, even citing politico-societal forces that overwhelmed their thoughts. Writing letters fostered an internal locus of control and served as a force for empowerment.

Children witness and internalize the lack of compassion apparent in our country; this has policy, developmental, and real-life consequences. Having parents of mixed status who are undergoing immigration proceedings affects children deeply. Approximately 5.5 million children in the United States, including 4.5 million U.S.-born citizens, have at least one parent who is an unauthorized immigrant (Pew Research Center 2018). Parents have lived and worked here for many years, but because they entered the country without inspection, overstayed their visas, or did not have access to resources and assistance, they remain undocumented. Parents facing removal must frequently make the decision whether to take their children with them or leave their children in the United States in the care of another parent, relative, or friend, often determining that it is in their child's best interest for the child to remain in the United States. Consequently, family separation brings about further trauma to children. The thought that children could relocate to their parent's home country is equally traumatizing, because "reverse forced migration" is not in the family's best interest. Immigration policies and practices directly traumatize everyone in the family, threatening their sense of safety and stability.

Recent research has demonstrated that in the immediate aftermath of parental deportation, the consequences for the children and families included feelings of abandonment, symptoms of trauma, fear, isolation, and depression (Brabeck and Xu 2010). In his book *Forgotten Citizens: Deportation, Children, and the Making of American Exiles and Orphans*, Dr. Luis Zayas describes how parental removal places children at increased risk of developing psychological problems (2015). Many children are experiencing acute anxiety and traumatic stress. Re-experiencing trauma leads to symptoms such as nightmares, excitation, attention problems, excessive vigilance, numbing, withdrawal from caretakers, and play constriction. Review of school records indicates that these children's grades are lower, they isolate from peers, and they dissociate, whereby the traumatic stress they are experiencing disrupts their daily functioning. One client's four-year-old child shared traumatic memories of her father's detention and fears it will happen again. These immigration challenges have additional impacts on pregnancy and adverse birth outcomes (Novak et al. 2017). Mothers frequently experience perinatal and postnatal mood disorders, while infants may experience toxic stress and neurodevelopmental deficits in utero. Clearly, these experiences deplete a child's inner resources, limit their worldview, and predispose them to future medical and psychological conditions that may last a lifetime.

Despite attempts to rebuild a sense of normalcy, more systemic solutions addressing the underlying concerns must be addressed. Immigration raids, detention, and deportations are realistic and frequent possibilities. We do a disservice to children when we allow this fear and uncertainty to interfere with their natural curiosity, growth, family stability, and wellness. The administration's immigration policies have traumatic effects and have interwoven anxiety, depression, anger, and insecurity into the daily lives of American children and families.

Looking Forward

As a forensic mental health professional consulting with legal bodies that determine whether or not an asylum case is valid, I have the privilege of working with interdisciplinary teams to advocate for our clients. Our work has become more complicated, and clients are facing unprecedented challenges. Undocumented immigrants and asylum seekers are experiencing great levels of traumatic stress, despair, and isolation. In the face of terror, they disconnect. We need immigration policies that allow balance, respecting the pre-migratory trauma that immigrants bring with them as they seek safety and support in a new, unknown country. We cannot penalize families and children out of fear and racism. In 2017, Kamal Amakrane, former political director of the United Nations General Assembly, stated, "What we are experiencing today is not a crisis of immigration but a crisis of compassion." He added, "Let's be clear: the action taken today isn't required legally. It's a political decision and a moral question."

Our profession teaches us to bring hope where there is despair. Currently, the very existence of millions of immigrants, asylum seekers, refugees, and DACA recipients is threatened. We must do more. We can no longer be bystanders in the face of human trauma and vulnerability. We need to advocate for the development of a comprehensive immigration policy that is realistic and compassionate. Clinical professionals are now challenged to take on an even more proactive role with clients. Our role as mental health professionals and citizens must be reimagined to restore hope through advocacy, voting, and exercising our voices. We have a duty to move beyond our comfort zones to protect our clients and the public's health. We must advocate for human rights, human dignity, and the right to be human.

Rosa Maria Bramble (Caballero), L.C.S.W., is a bilingual practitioner with a private practice in clinical and forensic psychosocial services in New York City. She conducts psychosocial evaluations and provides expert testimony in immigration cases. Bramble provides posttraumatic stress disorder treatment utilizing sensorimotor psychotherapy, eye movement desensitization and reprocessing (EMDR), the Internal Family Systems (IFS) model, and Coherent Breathing. As a lecturer at Columbia University School of Social Work and a consultant, she trains students and service providers on trauma-informed service delivery. She founded Borders of Hope to increase trauma awareness in Latino immigrant communities.

References

Ms. Bramble expresses appreciation to Charles Sanky for his contributions to this chapter.

American Immigration Council. 2018. Prosecuting Migrants for Coming to the United States.

Brabeck, Kalina, and Qingwen Xu. 2010. "The Impact of Detention and Deportation on Latino Immigrant Children and Families: A Quantitative Exploration." *Hispanic Journal of Behavioral Sciences* 32 (3), 341–61.

Davis, Julie Hirschfeld. (2018). "Trump to Cap Refugees Allowed into the U.S. at 30,000, a Record Low." *New York Times,* September 17.

Flores, Antonio. 2017. "Facts on U.S. Latinos: Statistical Portrait of Hispanics in the United States, 2015." Pew Research Center Hispanic Trends, September 18.

Herman, Judith Lewis. 1997. *Trauma and Recovery.* New York: BasicBooks.

Hirschfeld Davis, Julie. 2018. "Trump to Cap Refugees Allowed into U.S. at 30,000, a Record Low." *New York Times.* September 17.

Novak, Nicole L., Arline T. Geronimus, and Aresha M. Martinez-Cardoso. 2017. "Change in Birth Outcomes Among Infants Born to Latina Mothers After a Major Immigration Raid." *International Journal of Epidemiology* 46 (3): 839–49.

Pew Research Center. (2018). "U.S. Unauthorized Immigrant Total Dips to Lowest Level in a Decade." November 27.

Shear, Michael D., Abby Goodnough, and Maggie Haberman. 2018. "Trump Retreats on Separating Families, but Thousands May Remain Apart." *New York Times.* June 20.

White House. (2017). "Remarks by President Trump in Press Conference." February 16. www.whitehouse.gov/briefings-statements/remarks -president-trump-press-conference.

Zayas, Luis H. 2015. *Forgotten Citizens: Deportation, Children, and the Making of American Exiles and Orphans.* Oxford and New York: Oxford University Press.

TO TRUMP, SOME LIVES MATTER

ELLYN URAM KASCHAK, PH.D.

The year is 2018. It is a century since women won the vote in 1920 with the passage of the Nineteenth Amendment. Not until 1965 did the Voting Rights Act of 1965 secure the same for all racial minorities (United States Department of Justice 2017). It is only fifty years since women have won the right to conditional control of our own bodies by decision of the Supreme Court in the case of *Roe v. Wade* in 1973. We women are in clear danger of losing all the rights we have had to struggle to assert. Meanwhile white men, under this administration, retain their rights and acquire even more.

At the inception of feminist psychotherapy, we therapists decided to listen respectfully to women's stories and to consider them within the social context rather than to dismiss them as internal pathology as had been done previously. These were not all fantasies, desires, or delusions as Freud and others had believed, but abuse that had happened to more women than we could have imagined. The stories poured out, and we ourselves were stunned at what we had discovered.

The more I heard, the more I began to develop the idea that mental illness was a result of wounds more than of illness, that madness and being angry (mad) were related by more than etymology.

In the first class I taught in feminist therapy in Berkeley in 1973, every student told her own story of being locked in a back ward for asking for a divorce or an abortion, for accusing a husband of infidelity. The men owned us. After a lifetime of struggle for equality, we seem to be turning back to that time. The struggle for equality for women is far from over.

When posttraumatic stress disorder (PTSD) was first being considered as an addition to the DSM, I wrote that the "P" and the "D" should be removed for those who were not returning from Vietnam after removing themselves from the battlefield of the official war that the Vietnamese call the American War (Kaschak 1992). For women, people with disabilities, queer people, and people of color, the stress never becomes post. We learn to live with it in various ways, none of them having to do with being healthy or happy. We adjust. We protest. We carry on.

As for the "D," in my opinion, there is nothing disordered about these reactions to perpetual danger. They are the most natural responses of functional human beings, and we must listen to them. Women and other marginalized groups were and still are frightened, shamed, and angry. I would have preferred post, acute, or chronic traumatic injury.

If I pass someone who is lying in the street bleeding, it makes a crucial difference if that person has hemophilia or was stabbed. Whether I can save his life depends on my making the correct determination. Trauma is the result of an attack and is an injury (Herman 1992; Herman 2015). Many women in the United States and in most other countries have been disrespected or abused, sexually assaulted or raped.

A great deal of progress has occurred in neuroscience imaging since we discovered trauma (Edelman and Tononi 2001; Kandel 2018). These discoveries and techniques will eventually lead to more effective treatment. Both talk therapy and medication are useful, often in combination, and both are biological treatments (Kandel 2018). I consider talk therapy to be based in physics as well. A profound exchange of energy occurs. Nevertheless, as for many injuries, scars can last a lifetime and memories are deeply embedded in various locations inside and outside the brain (Kaschak 2015). They can be triggered internally or by context.

Tragically, we seem to be returning to a time that we thought we had left behind. Black men are being killed in the streets and in the presumed privacy of their own apartments for the crime of being in a black male body. Women are being sexually assaulted with equivalent impunity for the crime of being in a female body. Indigenous people are being murdered for trying to defend their own land from being stolen from them. And now, innocent children are being kept in cages, separated temporarily or permanently from their mothers, at a cost to the American taxpayer and a boon to Donald Trump and his cronies of $775 per each of the 1,500 children for a gross profit of $1,162,500 a day. Quite a sum, and all you have to do to earn it is to destroy the lives of thousands of vulnerable refugees trying to run from the danger of Central American gangs. If there is no safety for these people, there is no safety for any of us. These mothers and children are being brutally and irrevocably traumatized. "Stress" is too small a word to contain the horrors of this situation. Perhaps "terror" fits better for this never-ending war against women and others, but I would minimally use anxiety and not stress as a descriptor.

At the very same time that impoverished and terrified Central American mothers are being forcibly separated from their children, pregnant white Russian women are waiting in the luxury of high-priced Trump properties in Florida, paying as much as $100,000 (McFadden et al. 2018) to have their babies born on American soil.

As an alternative to assessing illness only, I devised an instrument I call the Mattering Map (Kaschak 1992, 2013). We use it to assess injury or illness contextually and to be compatible with the brain mapping that is occurring as technology permits. The human brain is a pattern detector and designed to search for or create meaning or mattering. If it spontaneously creates meanings that are too idiosyncratic, mental health professionals call this "illness." If it creates idiosyncratic meanings from experience, we must call these "injuries."

I developed the Mattering Map, which asks everyone in treatment to begin by describing in words or pictures a map of what has the most meaning in their particular situation. This includes the issues of context and thus indicates that the skin serves only as the most porous of boundaries (Kaschak 1992). We begin with a list of categories that other subjects have declared to matter as a start. There is no demand to use them all, but many do. These categories are:

Gender
Race
Ethnicity
Culture
Language
Class
Ecology-Environment, Physical Health, Biology, Neurology
Family
Interpersonal other than family
Religious-Spiritual
Written and Electronic Media. Level of literacy
Other Institutions, e.g., school, work
Age, Life cycle
Political Beliefs
Group Memberships
Education
Sexual Orientation
Substance-Use and Abuse
Violence
Finances
Power

The Mattering Map can be drawn at the beginning or end of each therapy session. It can be drawn on transparencies for easy comparison. It can be used in a variety of circumstances and I have used it in my classes on gender and peace. Many of my international students have gone on to use this tool in their own countries, working with women, refugees, and LGBT+ people.

This map can morph at any moment with the words of a therapist or a new insight or an effective chemical intervention. It may morph for some of you right now as you are reading these words. The theory underlying this tool can be found in my earlier publications (Kaschak 2010), as well as in Rebecca Goldstein's 1983 novel *The Mind-Body Problem*.

Black, brown, and white women fought for the rights that we do have. No one wanted us to be equal citizens but ourselves. The battles were as long and fierce as what men call the official wars, those between men and other men (of late some women are in the armed forces). The unofficial wars are conducted on the streets and in the homes of our own country every day, and those are the wars against women, people of color, and those who do not practice heteronormative sexuality. Women who are sexually assaulted are two to three times more likely to develop PTSD than men who enter and then leave combat (Olff 2017). Perhaps this is because women live our entire lives on the field of combat. For us it is everywhere and an attack cannot be anticipated, nor are we supplied with tanks and guns and encouraged to use them. Instead we are humiliated and further traumatized if we come forward.

From attacking health care and undermining women's legal rights to elevating out-of-touch, regressive nominees to key positions, in spite of sexual assault allegations, Trump reveals his fundamental scorn for the myriad challenges women face and how they are interrelated. When taken together, these actions reveal an aggressive assault on women's rights and women's psychological health. We must do far more than marching, and mental health professionals are not exempt from this demand. It becomes no longer a partisan issue, but a fight for our very health and survival. As psychologists and psychiatrists, we cannot sit by silently and patch up the victims of

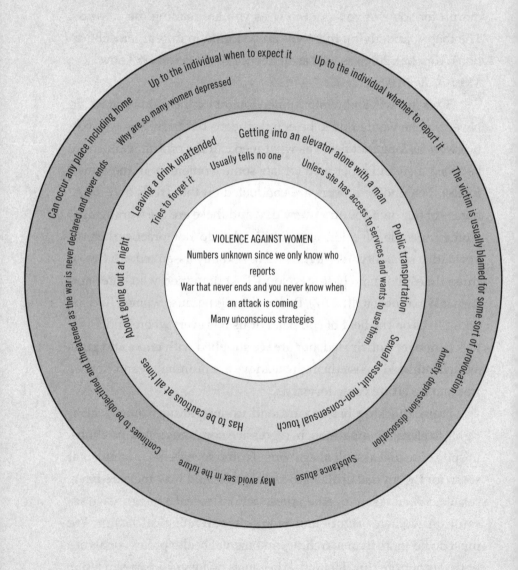

VIOLENCE AGAINST WOMEN
Numbers unknown since we only know who reports
War that never ends and you never know when an attack is coming
Many unconscious strategies

Up to the individual when to expect it
Up to the individual whether to report it
Why are so many women depressed
Can occur any place including home
Leaving a drink unattended
Getting into an elevator alone with a man
Usually tells no one
Tries to forget it
Unless she has access to services and wants to use them
About going out at night
The war is never declared and never ends
The victim is usually blamed for some sort of provocation
Public transportation
Sexual assault, non-consensual touch
Has to be cautious at all times
Continues to be objectified and threatened as the war is never declared and never ends
May avoid sex in the future
Substance abuse
Anxiety, depression, dissociation

DECLARED OR OFFICIAL WARS

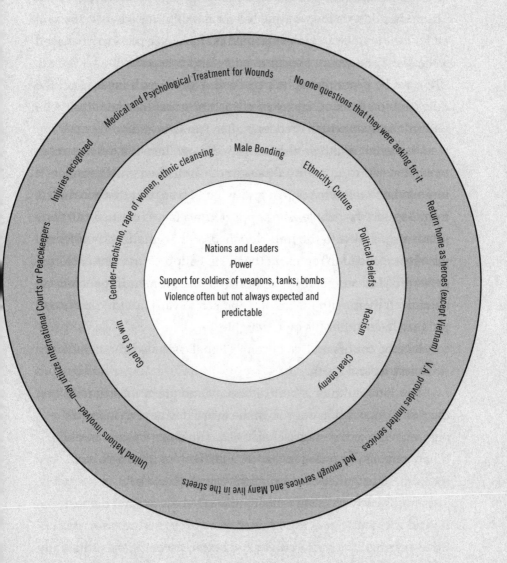

Medical and Psychological Treatment for Wounds

No one questions that they were asking for it

Injuries recognized

Male Bonding

Gender-machismo, rape of women, ethnic cleansing

Ethnicity, Culture

Political Beliefs

Racism

Clear enemy

Goal is to win

Nations and Leaders
Power
Support for soldiers of weapons, tanks, bombs
Violence often but not always expected and
predictable

United Nations involved—may utilize International Courts or Peacekeepers

Not enough services and Many live in the streets

V.A. provides limited services

Return home as heroes (except Vietnam)

assault and terror. We must speak up. We have a duty to warn and a duty to create as much safety as possible to prevent the injuries. *We have a moral code.*

Trump has harmed so many people in so many ways that it is impossible to focus on gender outside the context of ethnicity, sexual orientation, race, and other factors. In my opinion, the worst thing that Trump has done is to lower the bar for morality, for what can be said and done in public and in private. What if a female president behaved as he does? She would appear to be psychotic to most of us (Kaschak 2015). Yet he is not the worst part of the story, which involves all the duly elected officials who are protecting him and the supporters who will still be filled with hatred long after Trump is gone.

As mental health professionals, we know there is a difference between delusion and reality, illness and health. Gaslighting renders it impossible to tell what is real and what is fake, and that is Trump's forte. He sold the people who support him a fake elixir to fix all their problems. He lied to the impoverished or marginalized white people. He pretended to represent them. He whipped them into a frenzy of hatred. He ridiculed his opponents and women in general. He demeaned them with his grabby and schoolyard bullying ways. He publicly lusted after his own daughter.

It is the confusion that becomes lethal, as it also gives rise to assault, injury, and death.

Toxic masculinity is both abundant and precarious and built on the shaky foundation of every male every day having to prove he is not a woman or a girl (Kaschak 1992). The worst thing a boy in the schoolyard can be called is "a girl": that they "throw like a girl," "cry like a girl," or are "being a pussy." Being called "gay" is, arguably, just another way of doing this. It's meant to be cruel and demeaning. It is no accident. Speaking of women as prey in a superior and entitled manner, the more vulgar the better, accomplishes this daily requirement.

Recently discovered mirror neurons and other neurological structures appear to be somewhat responsible for emotional contagion (Kohler et al. 2002; Kandel 2018) along with the rapid transmission of opinions. Hatred and shaming have spread like wildfire in the Trump administration. It can easily be ignited once learned, and that is a major component of what is occurring in our streets and in our social networks. Everyone is arguing. Everyone is right. There is no room for compromise. The din is deafening.

What has changed that has permitted this vulgar display of white male power? Obviously it is the recent successes of previously degraded groups, including women, people of color, and LGBT+ people, in feeling more confident in exercising the rights they already had, but didn't dare act on. And the insult to everything Trump stands for from a successful, respectful, intelligent, and feminist black president, whom he tried to destroy with the endless "birther" movement. He had greater success with his lies about Hillary, arguably the most qualified and well-prepared candidate for the presidency in history. He ridiculed and criminalized her, applying his best skills to get his supporters to chant "Lock her up." The power of group psychology and a united and rhythmic chant on the human psyche is well-known.

Who wants a highly qualified, brilliant, experienced woman to be president? That would be too threatening. She was sabotaged at every turn by white men, some white women, and many young people. Feminist psychology tells us that Hillary could only be wrong, too aggressive or too passive, too young or too old, too feminine or too masculine, too intelligent or not intelligent enough. Only the open advocacy by several beautiful, admired, and successful celebrities has permitted some fifty years of social justice work to be publicly acknowledged and supported, along with the #MeToo movement, to become a matter of dueling celebrities. This movement must grow and continue through the classes and ethnicities.

The citizens working for improvement, the women and men of conscience, the people of color, the people with disabilities, the LGBT+ people, and the concerned professionals are able to unite and restore health to our nation. Many women have been motivated to run for

office, and if the country is restored or bettered, it will be largely because women are strong enough when united to have defeated these
men of less wholesome intent.

Efforts at creative resistance are under way to restore our country to decency and health. Our first job is to clean up the toxic mess
left by these men so it cannot spread. We must do that together.
Mental health professionals need to support women and men of
conscience, able and disabled, queer and straight, black, white, and
brown. It is our moral, professional, and humanitarian obligation.
Mental health professionals have to work overtime to educate the
populace, to produce books such as this and tools such as the Mattering Map, and possibly to emphasize more group work and group
support than is usual. Many women must begin therapy individually to even realize that they have this power, but, at some crucial
point, we should be meeting in groups to reduce shame and isolation, while increasing the strength there is in numbers. This administration is actually helping to pull back the veil that has hidden
corruption, racism, misogyny, and schemes to replace education with
prison and awareness with poor cognitive reasoning among disad-
vantaged groups, in this way diminishing the power of the people.

When we speak of mental health, I would suggest that we remember physical and environmental context. For example, the health
of the mind and the brain are linked. It has recently been discovered
that the immune system and the gastrointestinal system play a major role in mental health via their connections to the brain (Dantzer
et al. 2008). Women have to enter into situations of potential danger
every day. The simple sound of a man's footsteps behind you at night
or an elevator with only a woman and one man are part of the battlefield for women. We can be hypervigilant all the time, but this kind
of stressful trigger to the brain is not mental health. We can go out
only in the daytime, but this is not mental health. We can learn to
fight; we can go out accompanied by a man. These are all battlefield
strategies of the undeclared wars.

As mental health professionals, we can and must speak out, as there is an epidemic of violence, misogyny, and racism in our land and it is our profession that can most clearly recognize it. We are treating it every day if we practice psychotherapy. We must sound the warning and provide the treatment, but we must do more inside the confines of private offices, such as acknowledging and helping to remove the veil of lies, and we must speak up outside the private offices, while carefully considering our own professional and personal ethics. That is our part in halting the epidemic.

Right now, some of us need to rest and recuperate to get ready for the next battle. When each of us can, it is time to get up and continue the struggle. We need to remember not to take out our anger and grief on ourselves or each other. We are on the same side of the undeclared wars, and together we are stronger. If they did not want to conquer us, they would not be trying to divide us. Women, people of color, LGBT+ people, and others must join forces and stand tall and together right at the center of our own Mattering Map. And the experts, the mental health professionals, must lead the way when we can and support you as we can because it matters.

Ellyn Uram Kaschak, Ph.D., is one of the founders of feminist psychology. She has been on the faculties of San Jose State University since 1974 and the Universidad Nacional and the University for Peace, both in Costa Rica, and was editor of the Journal of Women and Therapy *from 1996 to 2017. Kaschak is the past chair of the Feminist Therapy Institute and a fellow of five APA Divisions. She received awards for her two groundbreaking books,* Engendered Lives: A New Psychology of Women's Experience *(1992) and* Sight Unseen: Gender and Race Through Blind Eyes *(2015), as well as numerous other awards, including the Lifetime Achievement Award of the Division on LGBT Issues and the Distinguished Career Award of the Association for Women in Psychology.*

References

Cardin, Maria S. 2018. "Gender Equality in Trump's America." *ARI* 38 (English version).

Dantzer, R., J. C. O'Connor, G. G. Freund, R. W. Johnson, and K. W. Kelley. 2008. "From Inflammation to Sickness and Depression." *Nature Reviews Neuroscience.* 9 (1): 46–56.

Edelman G. (2001). "Consciousness: The Remembered Present." Annals of the New York Academy of Science. Wiley Online Library.

Herman, Judith. 2015. *Trauma and Recovery.* New York: Basic Books.

Kandel, Eric. 2018. *The Disordered Mind: What Unusual Brains Tell Us About Ourselves.* New York: Farrar, Straus & Giroux.

Kaschak, Ellyn. 1992. *Engendered Lives: A New Psychology of Women's Experience.* New York: Basic Books.

———. 2010. "The Mattering Map: Morphing and Multiplicity." In *Feminist Therapy in the 21st Century,* ed. by C. Bruns and E. Kaschak. Abingdon-on-Thames: Taylor & Francis.

———. 2013. "The Mattering Map: Confluence and Influence." *Psychology of Women Quarterly,* 37:4.

———. 2015. *Sight Unseen: Gender and Race through Blind Eyes,* New York: Columbia University Press.

Kohler, E., C. Keysers, M. A. Umilta, L. Fogassi, V. Gallese, and G. Rizzolatti. 2002. "Hearing Sounds, Understanding Actions: Action Representation in Mirror Neurons." *Science* 297 (5582): 846–48.

McFadden, Cynthia, Sarah Fitzpatrick, Tracy Connor, and Anna Schecter. 2018. "Birth Tourism Brings Russian Baby Boom to Miami." *NBC News,* January 9. https://www.nbcnews.com/news/us-news/birth-tourism -brings-russian-baby-boom-miami-n836121.

Olff, Miranda. 2017. "Sex and Gender Differences in Post-Traumatic Stress Disorder: An Update." *European Journal of Psychotraumatology.* 8 (S4): 1351204.

Prochazkova, E., and M. E. Kret. 2017. "Connecting Minds and Sharing Emotions Through Mimicry." *Neuroscience and Biobehavioral Reviews.* 80 (September): 99–114.

United States Department of Justice. 2017. *History of Federal Voting Rights Laws.* Washington, DC: United States Department of Justice. https:// www.justice.gov/crt/history-federal-voting-rights-laws.

THE CHARISMATIC LEADER-FOLLOWER RELATIONSHIP AND TRUMP'S BASE*

JERROLD M. POST, M.D.

One of the remarkable features of the Trump psycho-political phenomenon is the durability of the base. One would think that the most extreme of his impulsive behaviors and extremist language would severely injure his popularity, yet polls continue to reflect 43–48 percent support. I have written about the political psychology of the tie between leaders and followers before. The sense of grandiose omnipotence of the leader is especially appealing to his or her needy followers. In contrast to "reparative charismatics" who heal their nation's wounds, a hallmark of destructive charismatic leaders is absolutist, polarizing rhetoric, drawing their followers together against the outside enemy. I distinguish the psychologically healthy follower

_____

* This chapter has been adapted from an earlier essay, "Narcissism and the Charismatic Leader-Follower Relationship," in *Leaders and Their Followers in a Dangerous World: The Psychology of Political Behavior* by Dr. Post, and a chapter in Dr. Post's forthcoming book on Donald Trump, *The Quintessential Narcissist*.

rendered temporarily needy by societal stress from the mirror-hungry follower who only feels whole when merged with the idealized other.

The victory of the Islamic Revolution in Iran did not fulfill Ayatollah Khomeini's messianic aspirations. Still driven by dreams of glory, the aged ayatollah relentlessly pursued his greater goal of one "united Islamic Nation" under his guidance (Zonis 1985). The fundamental political, economic, and social changes and the violence and havoc that the revolution unleashed are vivid testimony to the powerful forces that can be mobilized by charismatic leader-follower relationships. Osama bin Laden similarly forged a powerful bond with his alienated followers, resulting in the powerful events of September 11, 2001. The Islamic revolution, the radical Islamic terrorism of al Qaeda, and now the Trump presidency are pointed reminders that such relationships continue to play an important, and often determining, role in world affairs.

I speak not of charismatic leaders but rather of charismatic leader-follower relationships. I will be elaborating the political psychology of this tie between leaders and followers, attempting to identify crucial aspects of the psychology of the leader that like a key, fit and unlock certain aspects of the psychology of their followers. In delineating this lock-and-key relationship, I will draw on emerging understandings of the psychology of narcissism.

When Max Weber (1922) first introduced the concept of charismatic authority, he addressed the psychology of the followers, but only in a cursory fashion. He considered the determinant of the relationship between the charismatic leader and his followers to be the compelling forcefulness of the leader's personality, in the face of which the followers were essentially choiceless and felt compelled to follow. Irvine Schiffer (1973) has observed that later commentators on the phenomenon of charismatic authority have also focused disproportionately on the magnetism of the leader, failing to make the fundamental observation that all leaders—especially charismatic leaders—are at heart the creation of their followers. It emphasized the psychological qualities of the followers that render them susceptible to the force of the charismatic leader and lead to collective regression, drawing attention to narcissistically wounded individuals and the charismatic leader-follower relationships.

The relationship between Trump and his hard-line followers represents a charismatic leader-follower relationship, whereby aspects of the leader's psychology unlock, like a key, aspects of his followers' psychology. A strong hypothesis concerning the psychology of followers of charismatic leaders, which is discussed in my book, *Narcissism and Politics: Dreams of Glory* (2014), is that "in times of crisis, individuals regress to a state of delegated omnipotence and demand a leader who will rescue them, take care of them."

When Max Weber first explored the *charismatic* phenomenon, he focused his attention on charismatic leaders and the forcefulness of their personalities. He had little to say about the followers. In her study of charismatic leaders, *The Spellbinders* (1984), Ruth Ann Willner has observed that the concept of charisma has been much abused and watered down since Weber (1922) first introduced it. The media indeed often use charisma as synonymous with popular appeal, whereas Weber defined charismatic authority as a personal authority deriving from "devotion to the specific sanctity, heroism or exemplary character of an individual person and of the normative patterns or order revealed or ordained by him." To operationalize the concept, Willner surveyed the vast literature bearing on charismatic leadership. She emerges with the definition: charismatic leadership is a relationship between a leader and a group of followers that has the following four characteristics in common:

1. The leader is perceived by the followers as somehow superhuman;
2. The followers blindly believe the leader's statements;
3. The followers unconditionally comply with the leader's directives for action;
4. The followers give the leader unqualified emotional support.

But as noted in my review of Willner's book, these are not characteristics of leaders, but of followers! They relate to a perception, belief, or response of the followers. Willner dismisses as interesting but unproven hypotheses that say that "in times of crisis, individuals regress to a state of delegated omnipotence and demand a leader (who will rescue them, take care of them)" and that "individuals susceptible to (the hypnotic attraction of) charismatic leadership have themselves fragmented or weak ego structures." Willner also dismisses as interesting but unproven Schiffer's (1973) pathbreaking explorations of charisma, in which he trenchantly observed that "the leader is the creation of his followers." In an extended footnote, Willner's discussion of Schiffer shares the distinguished company of Sigmund Freud and Erik Erikson.

In my judgment, there is indeed powerful support for these hypotheses. Clinical work with individuals with narcissistic pathology, the detailed studies of individuals who join charismatic religious groups, and psychodynamic observations of group phenomena all provide persuasive support for these hypotheses concerning the psychological makeup and responses of individuals susceptible to charismatic leadership—the lock of the follower for the key of the leader. Formation of the "wounded self" results in two personality patterns that have particular implications for our study of charismatic relationships.

There are two vicissitudes of the "wounded self": the "mirror-hungry personality" and the "ideal-hungry personality." I would suggest that these are the templates for the complementary portions of the charismatic leader-follower relationship: the leader and the follower. The first is the "mirror-hungry" personality. Trump has a mirror-hungry leader personality, which feeds on the adoration of his followers in the charismatic leader-follower relationship he has with his base. This personality pattern results from the "injured self," whose grandiose façade feeds on confirming and admiring responses to counteract their inner sense of worthlessness and lack of self-esteem. To nourish their famished self, the individual feels compelled to display himself in order to evoke the attention of others. However, no matter how much positive attention they receive, they are never satisfied, consistently seeking new audiences from whom they can receive the continuing attention and recognition they crave. It is this constant need for new and more attention that led the high-profile businessman Trump to continuously seek a prominent celebrity status, eventually culminating in his hit TV reality game show *The Apprentice* beginning in 2004. However, the attention he received from this show could not satisfy him, causing him to seek a new audience by running for president of the United States.

Central to the mirror-hungry leader's ability to elicit the admiration they require is their ability to convey a sense of grandeur, omnipotence, and strength. Leaders such as Trump who convey this sense of grandiose omnipotence are attractive to individuals seeking idealized sources of strength because they convey a sense of conviction and certainty to those who are consumed by doubt and uncertainty. This was evident in Trump's support from mostly white rural and working-class voters, among whom Trump's motto to "make American great again" had a strong resonance. Despite his lack of any concrete policy, his tweets concerning "JOBS, JOBS, JOBS" had resonated with many of his followers, especially those who are struggling and feel abandoned by the last administration.

Mirror-hungry charismatic leaders are drawn to large crowds, where the roar of admiration becomes music to their ears. It was evident during the election how much Trump thrived on followers shouting his name at the large rallies. This is why even after the election ended, he has continued to hold giant rallies across the country, because he continues to need expressions of admiration from his followers as compensation for his insecurity and self-doubt.

It is also important to note that these rallies have been vital for his supporters as well. There is a quality of mutual intoxication for both sides, whereby Trump reassures his followers, who in turn reassure him of his self-worth.

During the election campaign, Trump was able to tap into the already existing rhetoric of the white supremacist alt-right in the United States. His comments against foreigners, Latinos, Muslims, African Americans, women, and a number of other groups fit into the existing rhetoric of a number of alt-right parties.

It was comments such as these that led to widespread support among the alt-right, including the Ku Klux Klan. Trump has received support from a number of high-ranking KKK members, including former Imperial Wizard David Duke and current spokeswoman for the Knights Party, Rachel Pendergraft. On November 2, 2016, Pendergraft tweeted, "KKK's official newspaper supports Donald Trump for president." The KKK continues to support Trump through their radio program, *White Resistance News*, where the two hosts (including Pendergraft) also bash anyone who opposes Trump. After the press conference following Charlottesville, after Trump became publicly pro–Neo Nazi and pro–white supremacy, David Duke, the former Grand Wizard of the KKK, publicly thanked him. After the fatal riot between white supremacists and those protesting their actions, Trump did not disavow the white supremacist extremism but stated, "There are fine people on both sides," which won him widespread opprobrium.

The second type is the "ideal-hungry" personality. These individuals can experience themselves as worthwhile only so long as they can relate to individuals whom they can admire for their prestige, power, beauty, intelligence, or moral stature. The hypnotic pull of the charismatic leader is compelling for the ideal-hungry follower. The wounded follower feels incomplete by himself and seeks to attach himself to an ideal other. Thus, there is a powerful, almost chemical attraction between the mirror-hungry charismatic leader and the ideal-hungry charismatic follower. And if Trump thrives on the adoring mirroring response of his followers, he provides for them a sense of completeness. Incomplete unto themselves, they have an enduring need to attach themselves to an idealized other.

I wish to emphasize that I assuredly am by no means implying that all those who voted for Donald Trump are narcissistically wounded individuals. The phenomenon of the charismatic leader-follower relationship is surely too complex to lend itself to a single overarching psychological model. One of the remarkable aspects of the Trump phenomenon is the stability and psychological power of his followership. But in trying to understand the resilience of Trump's followership and the core of his base, I am suggesting that Trump's political personality is particularly appealing to wounded individuals seeking an externalizing leadership and that Trump is particularly talented in appealing to individuals who are seeking a heroic rescuer. I believe elements of the narcissistic transferences just described are present in all charismatic leader-follower relationships, and in some charismatic leader-follower relationships they are crucial determinants.

At moments of societal crisis, otherwise mature and psychologically healthy individuals may temporarily come to feel overwhelmed and in need of a strong and self-assured leader, a heroic rescuer. Consider how the overwhelmed British people during the blitz responded to the remarkable charismatic leadership of Winston Churchill. Yet after the war was over, when the British people no longer needed a rescuer and returned to their customary self-sufficiency, they cast Churchill in the dustbin of history. When Trump assured West Virginia that coal mining would be returning, he was sending a rescuing message to a socioeconomic bloc that was temporarily overwhelmed and needed a powerful rescuer.

Central to the mirror-hungry leaders' ability to elicit the admiration they need is their ability to convey a sense of grandeur, omnipotence, and strength. These individuals who have had feelings of grandiose omnipotence awakened within them are particularly attractive to individuals seeking idealized sources of strength. So profound is the inner doubt that a wall of dogmatic certainty is necessary to ward it off. For them, preserving grandiose feelings of strength and omniscience does not allow for expressions of weakness and doubt. The mechanism of splitting, to which we referred earlier, is of central importance in maintaining their illusion.

There is the me and the not me, good versus evil, strength versus weakness. Analysis of the speeches of charismatic leaders repeatedly reveals such all-or-nothing polar absolutism. Ayatollah Khomeini identified the United States as "the great Satan." Although it is a common political tactic to attempt to unify the populace against an outside enemy, the rhetoric of polarization is most effective when, as in the case of Hitler, *they* are absolutely believed to be the source of the problem, *they* are evil, and to eliminate *them* is to eliminate *our* problems. Phyllis Greenacre observed that in order to be effectively charismatic it is a great asset to possess paranoid conviction. Although there is no necessary relation between charisma and paranoia, when the two are linked some of the most fearful excesses of human violence in history have occurred (Robins 1984).

A leader's posture of total certainty is very attractive to one besieged by doubt. Indeed, this posture is necessary to ward off the inner doubt of the leader, too. In one of his last essays, Kohut (1984) began to consider implications of self-psychology for group psychology and historical phenomena. He summarized the characteristics of the individual who is especially suitable to become the admired omnipotent model, observing that "certain types of narcissistically fixated persons (even bordering on the paranoid) . . . display an apparently unshakeable self-confidence and voice their opinions with absolute certainty. . . . Such individuals' maintenance of their self-esteem depends on the incessant use of certain mental functions . . . they are continually judging others—usually pointing up the moral flaws in other people's personality and behavior—and, without shame or hesitation, they set themselves up as the guides and leaders and gods of those who are in need of guidance, of leadership, and of a target for their reverence." Indeed, the degree of moral righteousness is often quite extraordinary. Kohut goes on to observe that the psychological equilibrium of such charismatic leaders is of "an all or nothing type: there are no survival potentialites between the extremes of utter firmness and strength on the one hand, and utter destruction on the other."

It is important to reemphasize that such individuals have disowned and projected on the environment all of the unacceptable weaknesses and imperfections within themselves. For the charismatic leader with paranoid characteristics who is projecting inner aggression, the rhetoric becomes the basis for justifying attacking the outside enemy.

There is a quality of mutual intoxication in the leader's reassuring his followers who in turn reassure him. This is powerfully in evidence at Trump's rallies.

Observers of the mesmerizing effect of Hitler on his followers at the mass rallies have likened him to a hypnotist who placed his entire audience into a trance. Even those present at the rallies who did not understand German have described themselves as coming under his hypnotic sway. And most striking of all, it is also autohypnosis, as Hitler himself apparently entered a trance state, mesmerized by the enraptured responses of his mesmerized followers. But the power of the hypnotist ultimately depends upon the eagerness of their subjects to yield to their authority, to cede control of their autonomy, to surrender their will to the hypnotist's authority.

Even in the quietest of times, charismatic leader-follower relationships develop. What are the characteristics of the ideal-hungry followers? Damage to the self-concept during early childhood development leaves the individual permanently psychologically scarred, with an enduring need to attach himself to a powerful, caring other. Incomplete unto themselves, such individuals can only feel whole when in relationship, attached, or merged with this idealized other. The charismatic leader comes to the psychological rescue of the ideal-hungry followers. Taking on heroic proportions and representing what the followers wish to be, he protects them from confronting themselves and their fundamental inadequacy and alienation. The leader's success becomes the follower's success, a succor to their self-esteem. Galanter's (1978) studies of charismatic religious groups confirm the hypothesis that narcissistically wounded individuals are especially attracted to charismatic leader-follower relationships. For the Unification Church, the more lonely and isolated the individuals were before joining, the more apt they were to affiliate themselves and stay through the entire recruitment process. They tended to suspend individual judgment and follow unquestioningly the dictates of the leader. Moreover, the more psychological relief that was experienced on joining, the less likely the individual was to question the leader's requirement for actions and behavior that ran counter to their socialization.

The dependency group turns to an omnipotent leader for security. Acting as if they do not have independent minds of their own, the members blindly seek directions and follow orders unquestioningly. In the pairing group, the members act as if the goal of the group is to bring forth a messiah, someone who will save them. There is an air of optimism and hope that a new world is around the corner. And the fear-based, "fight-or-flight" group organizes itself in relationship to a perceived outside threat. The group itself is idealized as part of a polarizing mechanism, while the outside group is regularly seen as malevolent in motivation. The threatening outside world is at once a threat to the existence of the group, and also the justification for its existence.

For alienated and marginal individuals, who tend to externalize the source of their own failures—for the narcissistically wounded ideal-hungry individuals (Kohut 1977, 1978)—the psychological attractiveness of these states is overwhelming. When one is besieged by fear and doubt, it is extremely attractive to be able to suspend individual judgment and repose one's faith in the leadership of someone who conveys with conviction and certainty that he has the answers, that he knows the way, be it Reverend Moon or Reverend Jim Jones, Osama bin Laden, Adolf Hitler, or Ayatollah Khomeini. Particularly through skillful use of rhetoric, he persuades his needy audience: "Follow me and I will take care of you. Together we can make a new beginning and create a new society. The fault is not within us but out there, and the only barrier to the happiness, peace, and prosperity we deserve is the outside enemy out to destroy us."

A bonus for the potential follower lured by the siren song of the leader's strength and conviction comes from the promise, "Join my followers and you will no longer be alone." These followers draw strength from sharing their allegiance with others; the identity of follower becomes a badge of honor, a statement of membership in a collective self. In having merged themselves with the collective other, the success of the followers becomes *their* success.

For isolated individuals with damaged self-esteem and weak ego boundaries, the sense of "we" creates and imparts a coherent sense of identity. For such individuals, the self and the "we" are fused so that the self is experienced *as* the relationship. They tend to merge themselves with the group. The group becomes idealized and the standards of the group, as articulated by the leader and his disciples, take over and become the norm. This helps explain the startling degree to which individuals can suspend their own standards and judgment and participate in the most violent of actions when under the sway of the psychology of the group if persuaded that the cause of the group is served by their actions. Even that most basic of human needs—the drive for self-preservation—can be suspended in the service of the group, as was horrifyingly evidenced by the phenomenon of Jonestown.

The base will continue to be the core of Trump's support as long as the externalizing rhetoric and solutions Trump supplies continue to provide solace to his wounded followers. While two-thirds of Americans polled by CNN opposed Trump's family separation policy, 58 percent of self-identified Republicans supported it. Importantly, the percentage of the electorate identified as Republicans in Gallop polls is shrinking, from 32.7 percent before the election to 28.6 percent recently. But the solidity of the Trump base will continue to provide a reliable floor of support for President Trump.

Jerrold M. Post, M.D., is Professor of Psychiatry, Political Psychology, and International Affairs and Director of the Political Psychology Program at George Washington University. Dr. Post had a twenty-one-year career with the Central Intelligence Agency, where he founded and directed the Center for the Analysis of Personality and Political Behavior. He is the recipient of numerous awards and coauthor of When Illness Strikes the Leader *(1993) and* Political Paranoia *(1997). He is author of* The Psychological Assessment of Political Leaders *(2003) and* Leaders and Their Followers in a Dangerous World *(2004). After the invasion of Kuwait, Dr. Post's profile of Saddam Hussein was featured prominently in the media. His forthcoming book,* The Quintessential Narcissist, *will be on Donald Trump.*

References

Galanter, M. 1978. "The 'Relief Effect': A Sociobiological Model for Neurotic Distress and Large Group Therapy." *American Journal of Psychiatry* 135 (5): 588–91.

Kohut, Heinz. 1977. *The Restoration of the Self.* New York: International Universities Press.

———. 1978. *The Search for the Self.* New York: International Universities Press.

———. 1984. *How Does Psychoanalysis Cure?* Chicago: University of Chicago Press.

Post, Jerrold M. 2014. *Narcissism and Politics: Dreams of Glory.* Cambridge, UK: Cambridge University Press.

Robins, Robert S. 1984. "Paranoia and Charisma." Paper presented to the annual meeting of the International Society of Political Psychology, Toronto, Canada.

Schiffer, Irvine. 1973. *Charisma.* Toronto: University of Toronto Press.

Weber, Max. 1922. *The Sociology of Religion.* Boston: Beacon Press, 1963.

Willner, Ann Ruth 1984. *The Spellbinders.* New Haven: Yale University Press.

Zonis, Marvin. 1985. Shi'ite Political Activism in the Arab World. Draft manuscript, available from the author, Middle East Institute, University of Chicago.

PART 5

HUMANITY'S PERPETUATION AND SURVIVAL

THE MYTH OF NUCLEAR WAR

JAMES R. MERIKANGAS, M.D.,* WITH TARANNUM M. LATEEF, M.D.

"Some say the world will end in fire, Some say in ice."

—Robert Frost

As it turns out, both opinions are correct. I am a neuropsychiatrist with forty-eight years of experience treating patients with neurological and psychiatric problems. I have observed many signs of emotional and intellectual disturbance in Donald Trump and have urged that he undergo a fitness evaluation. I have also been present at a nuclear explosion and seen the ravages of war firsthand. For that reason, I feel compelled to write this chapter to inform readers that someone like Donald Trump should never have his finger on the button—because the world is already close enough to the brink of annihilation.

In 1941, I was an infant evacuated from the American military base on the Philippine island fortress Corregidor along with General MacArthur, the year the Japanese bombed Pearl Harbor. My father

---

* Dr. Merikangas clarifies that this chapter reveals no classified information and represents his own opinions only, and not those of the Department of Justice where he is a contractor, or the George Washington University School of Medicine where he is a Clinical Professor.

was a doctor who commanded a hospital in Europe during World War II. I lived in Germany after the war, where I saw the massive destruction of cities from the deliberate bombing of civilians.

Therefore, as a child I was informed of the horrors of war. I went to college on a full-tuition scholarship courtesy of the Naval Reserve Officers Training Corps, and after graduation, with a degree in physics, I attended the U.S. Navy Guided Missile School and served as a nuclear weapon loading officer aboard an aircraft carrier in the Pacific.

Standing on the flight deck of my ship on July 9, 1962, I witnessed a 1.4-megaton hydrogen bomb explosion 250 miles above Johnston Island in the Pacific, our last aboveground test of a special weapon. This bomb was five thousand times more powerful than the one dropped on Nagasaki, Japan, at the end of World War II. The blast was seen as far away as Hawaii, nine hundred miles away. The electromagnetic pulse blacked out radio communication over the entire Pacific area and knocked out three hundred streetlights in Hawaii. The aural green light that the nuclear particles generated illuminated the darkening sky for ninety minutes (*Wikipedia*, "Starfish Prime"). I was awestruck in the silence of an explosion in outer space and imagined what would happen if that bomb were closer to the surface of the earth. That same year, I was in the Formosa Straits during the Cuban Missile Crisis. My ship was standing by with our attack jets loaded with nuclear bombs. We were ready to eliminate China because they were communists, even though Russia was the protagonist. Fortunately, Nikita Khrushchev backed down under the threat of nuclear annihilation.

Now each of our fighter-bomber aircraft carries more explosive power than all the bombs dropped in World War II. Our aircraft carrying nuclear weapons are ready to take off or are flying around ready to destroy their designated targets. Our ICBM silos and Polaris-equipped submarines are ready to launch on command. One bomb could eliminate a city such as New York, Washington, or Moscow. We have thousands of such bombs, and Russia, China, India, Pakistan, the UK, France, and North Korea have theirs. Israel is said to have nuclear weapons, but they may be content to have people think they do. They never signed the nonproliferation treaty and have never agreed to inspections. The United States gave them aircraft capable of delivering bombs and allowed fissionable uranium or plutonium to be "stolen" from a plant in Apollo in 1965 Pennsylvania. The threat of a Masada-like suicide by Israel if it is invaded or bombed is frighteningly real. Iran does not have nuclear weapons. South Africa had six warheads but dismantled them when apartheid ended. Ukraine, Belarus, and Kazakhstan had weapons but gave them up with the fall of the Iron Curtain. In any case, there are more than enough nuclear bombs to destroy civilization.

The Federation of American Scientists estimates there are 14,000 nuclear weapons presently, down from 70,000 at the height of the Cold War. One need not have cruise missiles, planes, or ICBMs to deliver a bomb. Any container ship could sail into a harbor and wipe out a city with no one knowing where it came from. Renewed investments by China, Russia, India, and Pakistan have raised alarms even as North Korea's nuclear weapons program has advanced. In his 2018 State of the Union address, President Trump said North Korea's pursuit of nuclear weapons threatens our mainland. Every country now striving to acquire nuclear weapons is doing it because they can be threatened by the countries that have them. Only the possibility of retaliation in kind prevents the conquest of smaller nations.

My colleague Dr. Tara Lateef who, like myself, consults at the National Institute of Mental Health, gives a sobering account of living under the threat of nuclear war in India. India detonated a nuclear device in 1974. In 1998 Pakistan detonated six nuclear devices. From 1946 to 2012 India received $65 billion in U.S. foreign aid, less than $1 billion in military aid, while Pakistan received $45 billion in economic aid and about $13 billion in military aid. By contrast Israel, in addition to $65 billion in economic assistance, received $134 billion in military aid. Israel on a per capita basis received one hundred times as much as India.

Dr. Lateef, having immigrated as an eighteen-year-old from India for freedom of speech, gender equality, the right to speak one's own mind regardless of familial approval, social class, or caste rank, believing she could rely on hard work instead of family name and individual strength rather than social connection, always believed she had reached a better place and a more evolved society. That is until 2016. The unprincipled politicians and corruption that ravaged her country of birth did not seem that far away anymore. America's stature as a rational thought leader and peacekeeper seemed to become a distant memory.

She was terrified at what our president's mental derangement could mean for the prospects of nuclear war in South Asia and the Indian subcontinent. The presence of nuclear weapons in South Asia has long been a matter of intense international concern, especially in light of India and Pakistan's long, tortured, and bloody rivalry. The partition of the British colony of India in 1947 into India and Pakistan was a bloodbath of Hindu-Muslim violence, killing about 1 million people and displacing about 15 million, with the two new nations vowing to keep the fires of their animosity burning. Amid this tense relationship, the two nations refused to accede to the international nonproliferation regime. In more recent years, both New Delhi and Islamabad have demonstrated glimmers of rational engagement and minuscule steps toward peace (Zhou 2016). It is in this precarious balance that one would most welcome America's diplomacy and leadership, but instead we find ourselves with a leader who can recklessly rant and ally himself with nationalist parties in either country if its stance meets his own personal approval. It is terrifying to know that it is not just U.S. citizens who have to endure the president's erratic behavior but in fact he can endanger the lives of millions on foreign shores where nuclear weapons are barely contained and are at the mercy of often corrupt leaders.

After a nuclear war the land will be too radioactive to occupy, and the water will become undrinkable. In the darkness of nuclear winter, no crops will grow.

World War II ended the humanitarian rules of war that were intended to limit fighting to soldiers and sailors, sparing the lives of civilians and noncombatants (Geneva and Hague Conventions). Bombing factories and the means of production inevitably led to the bombing of population centers in order to weaken and demoralize the enemy. In February 1945, Dresden, Germany, was firebombed, and in March of 1945 American firebombs incinerated 100,000 citizens of Tokyo. In August 1945, the United States dropped atomic bombs on Hiroshima and Nagasaki. The twenty-one-kiloton atomic bomb that obliterated Nagasaki, a city of half a million people, resulted in the death of about 100,000 innocent men, women, and children, but killed only 150 soldiers. One unforgettable exhibit in the Atom Bomb Museum in Nagasaki, Japan, is a human hand fused into the glass of a Coke bottle, melted by the awesome heat of the blast. The flash of an atomic explosion is silent. A wave of heat and radiation vaporizes and incinerates, then the explosive blast wave hits and destroys structures and everything standing. The cloud of radioactive dust that follows will spread through the atmosphere over the earth to poison unintended targets for thousands of years (Military 2018).

Nuclear weapons have no tactical use other than mass murder. There is no such thing as a "surgical strike," or a "punch in the nose," when it comes to nuclear weapons. The idea that one man, no matter how intelligent or reasonable, could unilaterally unleash a doomsday device is itself insane. During the Cold War, President Dwight Eisenhower, formerly the general who had commanded Allied Forces to win the war in Europe, and others, introduced the plan of "Massive Retaliation," or mutually assured destruction, in response to a nuclear attack on our country or our allies in NATO. This plan was intended to deter a nuclear war, but unfortunately it has increased the risk. Initially the "no first strike" policy was proclaimed, stating nuclear weapons would only be used for self-defense. Unfortunately, that was a fiction. Another fiction was the idea that only the president could launch a nuclear attack with the codes contained in the briefcase carried by a military officer everywhere he goes. That iconic "football" is what can send the signal to the aircraft, underground silos, and Polaris-bearing submarines to launch thousands of warheads to cities all over Russia and China. Not just military bases and launch sites, but cities full of civilians would be decimated. Half the population of Russia and China would die instantly, and half of the survivors would die slowly from radiation and famine (Ellsberg 2017). In reality, the authority to start a nuclear war has been delegated to officers down the line in case Washington is wiped out before the signal can be sent, or if communication links and confirmation codes cannot be obtained. Unfortunately, our weapons systems can be hacked, according to the Government Accountability Office in a classified report sent to Congress (GAO 2018). Perhaps some hacker can launch our nuclear arsenal for us.

To make matters worse, the Department of Defense has subtly ended the "no first strike" policy and now advocates the use of smaller (as large as those that eliminated Hiroshima and Nagasaki) nuclear weapons, not in retaliation, but instead of conventional weapons (Office of the Secretary of Defense 2018). A "small" nuclear weapon can still incinerate an entire city and all its inhabitants.

On October 21, 2018, President Trump announced his intention to abandon the Intermediate-Range Nuclear Forces Treaty that President Reagan signed with Russia at the end of the Cold War in 1987. This will allow the development of ground-launched missiles with a range of 310 to 3,400 miles to threaten Russia from anywhere in Europe, assuring a buildup of Russian nuclear missiles to counter our threat (BBC 2018).

The president, who has the ultimate responsibility for the use of the most devastating weapons in the history of the world, and who has the sole capability to murder millions of people in an instant, has received only a simple ten-minute cognitive screen. This, despite the overwhelming evidence for the need to evaluate his neuropsychiatric condition as a seventy-two-year-old man who has demonstrated a clear deterioration in his mental state. Continual observation of his speech and behavior on video recordings and his incessant tweets provide ample data that cause concern as well as giving us moment-by-moment updates on his condition. Some of his observed behaviors have been his attacks on the truth and the press. Attacks on the press can be related to an assault on reality—often a sign of mental breakdown.

Coupled with his increasingly erratic tweets, plus incendiary lies and rants at rallies packed with select supporters, these add to the evidence of mental disturbance that demands neuropsychiatric evaluation. The consensus of several thousands of mental health professionals (dangerouscase.org) is that the nuclear launch codes should not be in the hands of someone who is likely to have a mental impairment. As a hands-on neurological examination with psychological tests is unlikely to be agreed to, at the very least a screen for drugs could be accomplished in a noninvasive manner, a procedure that is commonplace for other high-risk occupations. Likely substances that are associated with pressured and disinhibited speech include stimulants like amphetamines or cocaine, or even excessive caffeine (Diet Coke). The Twenty-Fifth Amendment to the Constitution provides the method to remove from office a president who is "unfit," but the definition and the process cannot prevent a madman from starting a war.

According to the Nuclear Weapon Personnel Reliability Program (PRP, May 25, 1993), the Department of Defense has established reasonable procedures and precautions to ensure that personnel who may cause the arming or release of a nuclear weapon are evaluated and monitored on a continuing basis. These procedures mandate: "Only those personnel who have demonstrated the highest degree of individual reliability for allegiance, trustworthiness, conduct, behavior, and responsibility shall be allowed to perform duties associated with nuclear weapons, and they shall be continuously evaluated for adherence to PRP standards." The president receives no such evaluation.

Although the president has the authority to order a nuclear strike, there are safeguards, a chain of command that is required to act, which is not the same as a simple push of a button. During the Cold War there were false alerts that missiles were on their way, but cooler heads checked and verified that these were mistakes, and no retaliation was ordered. It has been suggested that responsible officers who are ordered to launch a strike may refuse on the grounds that genocide is immoral. The Nuremberg trials of Nazi generals for genocide eliminated the "I was only following orders" defense, but we cannot depend on our own officers to ignore a psychotic order to end life on earth.

The Uniform Code of Military Justice requires that lawful orders must be obeyed, with no exception for individual moral judgments, and there will be no time for philosophical arguments (Powers 2018).

"You shall not bear false witness." (Exodus 20:16)

It is common knowledge that President Trump frequently says things that are not true. He may simply be a sociopath with no regard for the truth, who lies for his own advantage, but these are not lies if he thinks what he says is true. A lie is a conscious act. We don't know if his declarations are lies or the result of a serious brain dysfunction. Sometimes these statements are one-off utterances; sometimes they are repetitive statements, such as "witch hunt" and "fake news." Many of his false statements are presented as facts that are easily shown to be misstatements of historical or statistical truths. There is a question if these falsehoods are the result of global ignorance, wishful thinking, or deliberate attempts to deceive. If he thinks what he says is true, it is confabulation, which is not a lie but a delusion. If it is simple ignorance, it is a sign of a seriously defective memory to make such frequent erroneous statements. If it is a deliberate lie, it is a sign of blatant psychopathy and criminal behavior by someone who thinks people will simply believe him because they are also ignorant or too lazy to check what the real facts may be. Only a competent neuropsychiatric examination could determine the cause of his frequent false statements.

Despite being obviously and provably wrong, attacking true statements as "fake news" has been a successful tactic by numerous known and unknown agents. This attack on reality requires investigation, as it may be more than simple psychopathy or narcissistic personality disorder. Several types of more serious psychiatric and neurological disorders may result in pathological lying. One ominous explanation for pathological lying is a neurological condition such as frontotemporal dementia, behavioral variant, or another degenerative brain disease, like a form of Korsakoff syndrome. Persons with those diseases have lost the ability to learn or form new memories, while being unaware of their own shortcomings. Otherwise his lies may simply be a skillful tactic to destroy confidence in the "mainline media." The most successful liar in history, Adolf Hitler, said, "The most brilliant propagandist technique will yield no success unless one fundamental principle is borne in mind constantly and with unflagging attention. It must confine itself to a few points and repeat them over and over. Here, as so often in this world, persistence is the first and most important requirement for success" (Hitler 1971, p. 184). Certainly, this tactic, although not always consciously mimicking Hitler, is familiar, as exemplified by the charge of "Fake News." Hitler's minister of propaganda, Joseph Goebbels, said, "If you repeat a lie often enough, people will believe it, and you will even come to believe it yourself" (Goebbels 1946). Hundreds of books have been written in an attempt to explain Hitler. The short version is that Hitler may have had measles encephalitis as a child, resulting in his damaged personality, and later abused amphetamines and showed signs of dementia as a result of Parkinson's disease. His "Fake News" was promulgated by ranting radio speeches that were required listening; ours are shorter snippets on social media and talk TV. Aeschylus said, "In war, the truth is the first casualty."

Numerous experts showed alarm that the president did not undergo a proper mental health evaluation during his routine physical exam. At that time, his White House treating doctor performed an inappropriate and inadequate ten-minute cognitive screen to give the false reassurance to a worried public that his boss and commander in chief was mentally "fit for duty." The doctor has now been removed from service as the president's physician, but his sham "mental health exam" has not been replaced. We also learned that Trump's only other disclosed medical report was self-dictated. Many have questioned the president's ability to perceive reality separately from his own thoughts, feelings, and needs, and therefore his capacity to make sound, rational decisions that serve the interests of the nation or of security.

When someone is gravely ill, it may not take a physician to recognize that the person is unwell. But in an emergency, the layperson can stand by, while the health professional cannot. In an emergency, medical professionals have no choice but to take the affected person as a patient. We must treat, according to our code of ethics. This is because we have taken a pledge to save lives first and foremost. The president is not above the law, and he is certainly not above human psychology. He has already shown a predilection for violence: verbal abuse, boasting of sexual assaults, incitement to violence in public settings, endorsement of violence in speeches and in action, and even recently threatening North Korea with "total decimation." This is without counting the escalation of global dangers by launching a trade war, emboldening despots through admiration, and re-creating a culture of nuclear proliferation and war in ways that are predictable from his mental impairments. These are not policy as much as a pattern of an inability to perceive reality outside of his thoughts, feelings, and needs, and a propensity to attack if questioned or even slightly criticized.

Those who pretend that we are in the realm of politics when we are really in the realm of psychopathology make the situation even more dangerous, because they will not be prepared while the future of the planet and the human race are at stake.

Can the United States give attention to mental health matters where it is due? For one, many experts and nonexperts have called for a thorough mental health examination of the president. What they received, instead, was a White House emergency room physician's administration of a cognitive screen. Given the observable signs, a full neuropsychiatric examination and a battery of neuropsychological tests of executive function of the frontal and temporal lobes of the brain, including imaging with MRI and PET scans, is called for. Even more importantly, a capacity evaluation of the ability to make sound, logical decisions, based on real situations and consequences, would ensure a bare minimal level of functioning in the office of commander in chief. These tests are based on the objective, established medical criteria that are applied to military personnel handling nuclear weapons. They would not decide who may or may not become president, but rather safeguard that those in the office are capable of carrying out the function for which the people elected them—including their protection from unnecessary war. President Donald Trump has at his command the ability to end life on earth, to bring about doomsday on a whim or an impulse of anger. He has threatened nuclear war with North Korea and questioned why we have not used nuclear weapons in Afghanistan. He has shown the lack of impulse control we neurologists and psychiatrists observe every day in our brain-damaged and mentally ill patients. Whether his continuous irresponsible tweets and false statements are a deliberate attempt to deceive or the result of a deranged mind is a moot point. The cause does not matter; the dangerousness is of a degree that must be stopped for the good of mankind.

James R. Merikangas, M.D., is a neuropsychiatrist, cofounder of the American Neuropsychiatric Association, and former president of the American Academy of Clinical Psychiatrists. He is a graduate of the Johns Hopkins University School of Medicine and trained in both neurology and psychiatry at Yale. Dr. Merikangas established the EEG laboratory at the Western Psychiatric Clinic of the University of Pittsburgh, where he also established the neurodiagnostic clinic and directed the psychiatric emergency room. Currently he is Clinical Professor of Psychiatry and Behavioral Science at the George Washington University School of Health Sciences and a research consultant at the National Institute of Mental Health.

Tarannum M. Lateef, M.D., is a physician and researcher. A native of Chennai, India, Dr. Lateef immigrated to the United States at age seventeen in pursuit of higher education. She completed her medical schooling at Northwestern University, interned at Georgetown University, and did her fellowship at the Children's National Medical Center. She is a faculty member at the George Washington University School of Medicine and works at both Children's National Health System and Pediatric Specialists of Virginia. Dr. Lateef's research interests include the epidemiology of childhood neurologic disorders and their intersection with mental health problems.

Acknowledgment

Thanks go to Roland Brandel, former legal officer aboard the USS *Kitty Hawk* (CVA-63) for opinions about the duty to follow orders.

References

Aeschylus, 525-456 B. www.quotationspage.com/quote/28750.html.

BBC News. 2018. "Donald Trump: US Will Build Up Nuclear Arsenal." October 22. www.bbc.com/news/world-us-canada-45946930.

Ellsberg, Daniel. 2017. *The Doomsday Machine.* New York: Bloomsbury.

Goebbels, Joseph. 1946. Quoted in: "Publications Relating to Various Aspects of Communism (1946)," by United States Congress, House Committee on Un-American Activities, Issues 1–15, p. 19.

Hitler, Adolf. 197125. "War Propaganda." *Mein Kampf.* Boston: Houghton Mifflin.

Military. (2018). http://military.wikia.com/wiki/Effects_of_nuclear _explosions.

Office of the Secretary of Defense. 2018. *Nuclear Posture Review*. February. https://media.defense.gov/2018/Feb/02/2001872886/-1/-1/1/2018 -NUCLEAR-POSTURE-REVIEW-FINAL-REPORT.PDF.

OTA. 1979. The Effects of Nuclear War, Office of Technology Assessment, #PB-396946, U S Government Printing office. May.

Powers, Rod. 2018. "What to Know About Obeying an Unlawful Military Order." *The Balance Careers*. September 14. www.thebalancecareers.com /military-orders-3332819.

PRP. 1993. https://fas.org/nuke/guide/usa/doctrine/dod/dodd-5210_42 .htm. May 25.

Starfish Prime. 1962. Defense Atomic Support Agency. Project Officer's Interim Report: STARFISH Prime. Report ADA955694. August.

USMJ. 2018. Uniform Code of Military Justice, Article 92, U.S. Government Printing office, p. 283.

Wikipedia. "Starfish Prime." https://en.wikipedia.org/wiki/Starfish_Prime.

Zhou, Steven. 2016. "India and Pakistan's Nuclear Rivalry." *Islamic Monthly*. February 16. www.theislamicmonthly.com/india-and-pakistans -nuclear-rivalry/.

THE AGE OF THANATOS: ENVIRONMENTAL CONSEQUENCES OF THE TRUMP PRESIDENCY

LISE VAN SUSTEREN, M.D., AND H. STEVEN MOFFIC, M.D.

Introduction

In 1980, recognizing the grievous threat to humanity from nuclear weapons, four doctors, including a psychiatrist, came together to create the International Physicians for the Prevention of Nuclear War. Representing thousands of physicians around the world, and recognized for having translated the risks of nuclear weapons into everyday language, in 1985 the group was awarded the Nobel Peace Prize. Now two members of that group, cofounding psychiatrist Dr. Eric Chivian and psychiatrist Robert Jay Lifton, are warning again: climate change, with the power to devastate the world, presents every bit the threat to humanity that nuclear weapons once did (Chivian 2014; Lifton 2017).

Indeed, a new volume on the subject fatalistically suggests that we may already have reached a tipping point—with no return to health possible (Vollmann 2018). Using psychiatric terms, the current trajectory is described as a collective trend toward self-inflicted harm and suicidality.

The science is in. The overwhelming consensus is that human behavior is the cause of the current worldwide destabilization of the climate from global warming. Human reliance on fossil fuels since the dawn of the industrial era and the "co-morbid" denial of our predicament are the causes. Our physical and mental health hang in the balance.

The Role of Psychiatry

Psychiatrists recognize the power of words, and we recognize that our voices, collectively, can be leveraged to address the danger and the urgency with which we need to act.

The American Psychiatric Association has made a statement of concern in this position statement on Mental Health and Climate Change:

> The American Psychiatric Association (APA) recognizes that climate change poses a threat to public health, including mental health. Those with mental health disorders are disproportionately impacted by the consequences of climate change. APA recognizes and commits to support and collaborate with patients, communities, and other healthcare organizations engaged in efforts to mitigate the adverse health and mental health effects of climate change (American Psychiatric Association 2017).

The American Association of Community Psychiatrists, especially recognizing the disproportionate risks of global warming and environmental toxins to the poor and underserved, released a position statement that even predated that of the APA: "The American Association of Community Psychiatrists (AACP) recognizes that climate change poses significant threats to public health in general and to mental health in particular" (Moran 2017).

Following the more informal Psychiatrists for Environmental Action and Knowledge (PEAK) formed by Dr. Moffic, the new Climate Psychiatry Alliance (CPA) has as its mission statement: "The mission of the CPA is to inform the profession and the public about the urgent risks of climate change and the profound impacts on mental health and well-being caused by climate disruption."

Psychiatrists understand that human beings have multiple psychological defenses to protect us from the anxiety of problems. A most prominent one is denial, conscious or unconscious, which can be of benefit or harm (Gorman and Gorman 2016). Denial can spread from individuals to groups and in the other direction via social contagion. Political leaders can have a profound effect on climate change attitudes (Kousser and Tranter 2018).

We know that we are also hardwired to react well to acute disaster, but not to long-term and slowly developing catastrophes. Neutral-sounding words and phrases can lower our assessment of risk and stand in the way of taking action. Those who are knowledgeable and realistic about conditions advocate for the use of terms such as "climate instability" and "global overheating" because these terms heighten our perception of the actual peril and are therefore more likely to move us to take action.

In September 2018, the UN Secretary-General António Guterres said, "We face a direct existential threat: If we do not change course by 2020, we risk . . . runaway climate change with disastrous consequences for people and all the natural systems that sustain us. . . . I am appealing for leadership—from politicians, from business and scientists, and from the public everywhere. . . . We stand at an existential crossroad. If we are to take the right path—the only sensible path—we will have to muster the full force of human ingenuity" (Guterres 2018).

As the harms threatening our survival from climate change continue to escalate, the pleas for action become more anguished. And yet here in the United States at the time of this writing, the path is anything but sensible, and the dangers unspool by the hour.

With our understanding of the nature of leadership and how groups work, we know the dangers of charismatic and problematically narcissistic leaders who can sway a public who feels their needs are threatened. We also understand how climate trauma can lead to lifelong consequences and can design health care systems that help promote health and resilience in response to these challenges. But while we can help, only political leaders can address the cause: inaction or insufficient action on climate. As the world waits for leadership on the climate crisis we are mindful that America, once the beacon of hope, is not only failing at this, but providing an excuse for others to fail as well. Meanwhile the process lies in tatters, and the risks accelerate.

What are these processes and risks?

The Risks of Climate Change

Ever since climate change became a societal concern, various risks have been identified. Because of the competition for resources, it is increasing international conflict between countries, a potential catalyst even increasing the risk of nuclear war. It is already known to increase violence when the temperature rises in already hot climates. In Syria, the increased heat and consequent drought were significant contributors to the recent civil war.

Climate instability has disrupted finely balanced ecosystems, with the result that the living world is now under assault. Animals and plants are going extinct at a rate a thousand times the norm. Besides being critical to our own health and to that of our planet, many of those at-risk species carry a treasure trove of health benefits for humans that may be lost (Chivian and Bernstein 2008).

All citizens are not affected equally. Those who have done the least to cause the climate crisis will be hurt the most: the poor. This includes those in undeveloped countries, as well as the poor and minorities in richer countries.

Given the embrace of relevant principles of medical ethics, the psychiatric community can add value to the discussion of leadership (American Psychiatric Association 2013). These principles pertain mainly to clinicians, but they have been adapted to administrators and leaders (Moffic 2004). Perhaps if psychiatrists were more involved in discussing and consulting on societal problems like the environment, they could contribute to a better world (Lee 2017; Moffic and Sabin 2015).

Models of Leadership

Given that the challenge of climate is ongoing, pinpointing the kind of leadership that will be needed is critical. While many theories of leadership exist, and presidential traits that are associated with success include some that might not be easy to deal with "up close," including what scholars call "fearless dominance," one trait stands out as essential in times of turmoil: an outsized passion to do good. What also stands out is the conviction that America's greatness should be defined by our country's capacity to look beyond our self-interest (Kearns 2018). Given that the climate crisis is a global issue, and the United States contributes to it disproportionately, rather than politically withdrawing, leadership that looks outward to inspire global cooperation is called for.

When the last ice age regressed some 12,000 years ago, a new geological era emerged. With its more stable climate and warmer weather, the new period, the Holocene Era, allowed civilization to flourish. Until recently and on a vast timescale, Nature created the conditions that characterize geological eras. For the first time and on a vastly compressed timescale, it is the hand of humans creating conditions that characterize a geological era. This new era is called "the Anthropocene" after the Greek word "Anthropos" for "man." Millions of years of research and development performed by nature are now being upended by its most audacious and destructive offspring: humans.

The Trump Presidency's Seven Selected Blows to Climate Security

The Paris climate accords brought the world together to hold emissions of greenhouse gasses to a level that would cause temperatures to rise no more than 2° C. The world celebrated these first steps at a global agreement to restore climate safety. But on June 1, 2017, calling climate change a hoax, in a statement made in the Rose Garden

Donald Trump officially withdrew the United States from the Paris climate accords. The United States is now the only country not to have signed the accords.

Unveiled by Obama in June 2014, the Clean Power Plan outlined nationwide, state-by-state carbon-emission reductions, with each state responsible for putting into action its own formula about how to reach federally mandated targets. In March 2017, Donald Trump signed a sweeping Executive Order instructing the EPA to begin the process of unraveling the Clean Power Plan, with states essentially free to do what they wanted—reduce their commitments, write their own regulations, or take no action at all.

Subsidies to the fossil-fuel industry have kept coal, oil, and gas artificially cheap. Not counted, however, are "the social costs of carbon." These costs include the billions of dollars in costs for cleanup, repairs, and rebuilding after more intense and more frequent extreme weather events; the physical, social, and emotional costs from the injuries, deaths, and disruption of community life, work, school, and recreation; and other burdens and costs as communities try to adapt to changing circumstances. When we add up these costs, the true subsidy to the fossil-fuel industry is in the hundreds of billions (Kretzmann 2017; Leahy 2017). In June 2017, Trump rolled back regulations and infused funds to the industry, and the United States went from being a leader in ending subsidies to ranking last among the G7.

Included in the functioning of FERC or the Federal Energy Regulatory Commission is permitting for the building of fossil-fuel infrastructure, notably pipelines. Critics call FERC an "industry rubber stamp" (Horn 2017). During the Trump administration, four people have been nominated to be commissioners of the five-member leadership at FERC, and three are strong supporters of the expansion of the fossil-fuel industry (Manning 2018).

In 2012, the Obama administration rolled out its proposal for fuel-efficiency standards. By 2025 all cars and light trucks would be required to go from an average efficiency of 25 mpg to 54 mpg, cutting greenhouse gas emissions in half. In August 2018, deferring to oil and gas interests, the Trump administration halted progress on fuel-efficiency standards, since no matter what "we do" the planet will be heating up 7° F "anyway" (Eilperin 2018).

Exposure to mercury can be exceedingly harmful to human health. In the unborn and young children, it is especially damaging to brain development, with the potential to impair cognitive abilities: thinking, reasoning, understanding, visual and auditory processing, memory, attention, language, and fine motor skills and visual spatial skills. In December 2011, the EPA announced limits were being placed on the amount of mercury pollution that power plants would be allowed to emit. While additional costs would be incurred to accomplish this, the health co-benefits—that is, the savings in health care costs from not having to treat people who were made to get sick from mercury poisoning—would more than offset the added expense. In September 2018, the Trump administration pushed to eliminate consideration of the co-benefits, setting the stage to then make the claim that the additional costs to comply with mercury regulations would not be "worth it" (Davenport 2018a and 2018b).

The EPA used to lead in presenting the work of first-rate experts to inform leaders of science-based information to drive policy. Now, thousands of documents related to climate change have been removed from government websites. Before resigning for ethics violations Director Scott Pruitt made this a priority at the EPA. Now, individuals backed by industry are expected to take over control of the boards (Kaufman 2017; Waldman 2017). The office of the science adviser at the EPA and the Advisory Committee on Climate Change and Natural Resource Science at the Department of the Interior have been eliminated, and the head of children's health at the EPA has been put on administrative leave with no explanation (Gustin 2018).

Andrew Wheeler, the current head of the EPA, is a former coal lobbyist. His former boss, Robert E. Murray of Murray Energy Company, contributed $300,000 to Donald Trump's inauguration. Shortly after Trump's inauguration, Murray specifically asked Energy Secretary Rick Perry to roll back mercury-emission regulations, and delivered a sixteen-point "Action Plan" to Vice President Pence calling for, among other actions, withdrawal from the Paris accords, elimination of the Clean Power Plan, scaling back mine safety laws, and cutting the staff of the EPA in "at least" half. Most of the items have been fulfilled (Protess 2018). The top leader in EPA's air-quality division, who will be weighing in on the decision, is William Wehrum. In his private legal practice, Wehrum represented mining companies, oil refineries, chemical companies, and coal plants that sought to weaken air pollution rules that limited harmful emissions (Davenport 2018).

Dark Times

Global warming is driving an increase in the frequency and intensity of extreme weather events—fires, storms, floods. When the place you call home is burned down, blown away, flooded, when you lose your possessions, maybe your pets, your livelihood, and see injuries, illness, and death, the mix of fear, anger, sorrow, and trauma can easily send us to a breaking point. Mental health professionals are seeing a full range of psychiatric disorders emerge: major depression, anxiety, PTSD, a rise in drug and alcohol abuse. Family stress leads to domestic violence, including child abuse. Increasingly, mental health professionals are hearing about anticipatory anxiety: "pre-traumatic stress disorder," akin to PTSD, from people who can't get thoughts of future climate trauma out of their minds. "Climate anxiety" describes a general state of worry about conditions. Solastalgia (Albrecht et al. 2007) is a newly coined term to describe the sadness and feeling of alienation that comes from seeing treasured lands forever damaged or degraded.

In his classical psychoanalytic studies, Freud described the human drive or instinct for life, Eros—for the Greek god of love—and its opposite force, a "death drive" toward self-destruction that writers later labeled Thanatos, after the Greek god of darkness and death.

As the impacts of climate change grow more apparent, the scientific consensus is that we are on a path inconsistent with our survival while government leaders chillingly intensify the resisting and denying. A more accurate term for our era might be the terrifying "Age of Thanatos."

Conclusions and Recommendations

The Founding Fathers of the United States knew the mixed blessings of the citizens' role in a democracy. Especially because the public is prone to irrational decisions and psychological denial, it needs leaders that are rational and realistic. Moreover, because the climate crisis is both an acute and a chronic one, leaders who accept established science and are committed to promoting remedies consistent with the science and evolving conditions are essential. As the world rapidly approaches tipping points, leaders who not only reach out to other countries and their leaders but who have the emotional intelligence to inspire them to dig deeper, try harder, and work faster will become not only the profile of a good president but the sine qua non of our survival.

The loss of American leadership (ceded to China) on climate change brings its own distinct dangers—to us personally and to democracy here in the U.S., and around the world. Everyone is vulnerable to the ravages of climate change, but as conditions worsen and the cumulative toll rises, it is children who will be hurt the most. Already many "climate aware" young people are saying they will not have children because of the carbon footprint of adding another person to the planet but also because of the chaos they anticipate. Some admit to hoping for a pandemic, to reduce the "offending species," and to having conversations about "rational suicide." Fury is growing toward a government that is turning a blind eye to their futures.

They are asking:

Where will we be safe?

Who will take care of us?

When we act in ways that put people in harm's way there is a name for it: it's called aggression. Direct, indirect, conscious, unconscious, . . . individual or collective, . . . it's still aggression.

Given the potential role of psychiatrists in understanding the risks of climate change as well as the character of successful leaders in times of crisis, effective psychiatric involvement in these discussions is more important than ever. Whether in the USA, Canada, Russia, India, Great Britain, or other countries, psychiatrists and other mental health professionals have unique skills to call out not only the problems of climate change but the remedies that awaken people to take action. Just as climate policy must be cross-country, so too do professional collaborations (Hayes et al. 2018). In this case, our "patients" are not only those with perceived individual mental illness, but also leaders needing certain psychological traits, because we cannot expect to have healthy people on an unhealthy planet. Our presence is needed on the media that the public views and hears, because it is the very earth itself that is suffering.

Lise Van Susteren, M.D., a general and forensic psychiatrist in Washington, D.C., is an expert on the physical and mental health impacts of climate change. She has served as a consultant to the U.S. government profiling world leaders, as Clinical Professor of Psychiatry at Georgetown University, and as a community organizer on climate issues. She presents frequently on climate issues, and coauthored "The Psychological Effects of Climate Warming on the U.S.: And Why the U.S. Mental Health System Is Not Prepared." After graduating from the University of Paris, she practiced medicine in West Africa, and at community health centers and homeless shelters.

H. Steven Moffic, over his fifty-year career, has been an award-winning psychiatrist, with a one-time designation of "Hero of Public Psychiatry" from the assembly of the American Psychiatric Association (APA). In 2016, he received the Administrative Psychiatry Award from the APA and the American Association of

Psychiatric Administrators (AAPA). A climate activist for a dozen years, he founded the informal Psychiatrists for Environmental Action and Knowledge (PEAK), which then developed into the formal Climate Psychiatry Alliance (CPA). His upcoming book is on another overlapping challenge for politics and psychiatry: Islamophobia. He is a graduate of Yale School of Medicine, which helped to cement the need to courageously follow his convictions.

References

Albrecht, Glenn, et al. 2007. "Solastalgia: The Distress Caused by Environmental Change." *Australas Psychiatry*, Suppl. 15: S95–98.

American Psychiatric Association. 2013. Principles of Medical Ethics with Annotations Especially Applicable to Psychiatry. www.psychiatry.org/psychiatrists/ethics.

American Psychiatric Association. 2017. Mental Health and Climate Change.

Chivian, Eric. 2014. "Why Doctors and Their Organizations Must Help Tackle Climate Change." *BMJ* 348:g2407. https://doi.org/10/1136/bmj.g2407.

Chivian, Eric, and Aaron Bernstein A. (eds). 2008. *Sustaining Life: How Human Health Depends on Biodiversity*. Oxford and New York: Oxford University Press.

Davenport, Coral. 2018a. "Trump Administration Prepares a Major Weakening of Mercury Emissions Rules." *New York Times*, September 30. https://www.nytimes.com/2018/09/30/climate/epa-trump-mercury-rule.html.

Davenport, Coral. 2018b. "EPA Places the Head of Its Office of Children's Health on Leave." *New York Times*, September 26. https://www.nytimes.com/2018/09/26/climate/epa-etzel-children-health-program.html.

Eilperin, Juliet. 2018. "Trump Administration Sees a 7-Degree Rise in Global Temperatures by 2100." *Washington Post*, September 28. https://www.washingtonpost.com/national/health-science/trump-administration-sees-a-7-degree-rise-in-global-temperatures-by-2100

/2018/09/27/b9c6fada-bb45-11e8-bdc0-90f81cc58c5d_story.html?utm
_term=.0bf8b0278c64.

Gorman, Sara E., and Jack M. Gorman. 2016. *Denying to the Grave: Why We
Ignore the Facts That Will Save Us*. London and New York: Oxford
University Press.

Gustin, Georgina. 2018. "Trump Administration Deserts Science Advisory
Boards Across Agencies." *InsideClimate News*. https://insideclimate
news.org/news/18012018/science-climate-change-advisory-board-epa
-interior-trump-administration.

Guterres, António. 2018. "World's Fate Is in Our Hands." UN Secretary-General
(UN Headquarters New York, September 2018).

Hayes, K., et al. 2018. "Climate Change and Mental Health: Risks, Impacts
and Priority Actions." *International Journal of Mental Health Systems* 12
(28). https://doi.org/10.1186/s13033-018-0210-6.

Horn, Steven. 2017. "FERC, Which Rejected 2 Gas Pipelines Out of 400 Since
1999, to Review Approval Policy." DeSmog, December. https://www
.desmogblog.com/2017/12/26/ferc-2-gas-pipelines-denied-400
-approved-1999-rule.

Kaufman, Alexander. 2017. "EPA Replaced Its Top Science Advisers Without Telling Them." *Huffington Post*, January 11. https://www
.huffingtonpost.co.uk/entry/epa-science-advisers-replaced_us_59fa
2b75e4b0b0c7fa37bd17.

Kearns, D. 2018. *Leadership: In Turbulent Times*. New York: Simon and Schuster.

Kousser, Thad, and Bruce Tranter. 2018. "The Influence of Political Leaders
on Climate Change Attitudes." *Global Environmental Change* 50 (May):
100–9.

Kretzmann, Steven. 2017. "Trumps Energy Plan." Oil Change International.
https://www.cbo.gov/system/files/115th-congress-2017-2018/reports
/52521-energytestimony.pdf.

Leahy, Stephen. 2017. "Hidden Costs of Climate Change." *National Geographic*.
https://news.nationalgeographic.com/2017/09/climate-change-costs
-us-economy-billions-report/9/27/17).

Lee, Bandy X. (ed). 2017. *The Dangerous Case of Donald Trump: 27 Psychiatrists and Mental Health Experts Assess a President*. New York: Thomas Dunne Books.

Lifton, Robert Jay. (2017). *The Climate Swerve: Reflections on Mind, Hope, and Survival*. New York: New Press.

Manning, Tim. 2018. "FERC Failing to Consider Climate Impacts in Gas Pipeline Approvals." Environmental and Energy Study Institute. https://www.eesi.org/articles/view/ferc-failing-to-consider-climate -impacts-in-gas-pipeline-approvals.

Moffic, H. Steven. 2004. "Ethical Principles for Psychiatric Administrators." *Psychiatric Administrator* 77 (4): 447–51.

Moffic, H. Steven, and James Sabin. 2015. "Ethical Leadership for Psychiatry." In *The Oxford Handbook of Psychiatric Ethics*, Volume 2 ed. by John Z. Sadler, K. W. M. Fulford, and Werdie van Staden. London and New York: Oxford University Press.

Moran, Mark. 2017. "AACP Approves Position Statement on Climate Change." *PsychiatryOnline*, March 9. https://doi.org/10.1176/appi.pn.2017.3b5.

Protess, Ben. 2018. "He Leaked a Photo of Rick Perry Hugging a Coal Executive. Then He Lost His Job." *New York Times*, January 17. https:// www.nytimes.com/2018/01/17/business/rick-perry-energy-photogra pher.html.

Van Vugt, Mark, and Anjana Ahuja. 2011. *Naturally Selected: The Evolutionary Science of Leadership*. New York: HarperCollins.

Vollmann, William T. 2018. *No Immediate Danger: Volume One and Two of Carbon Ideologies*. New York: Viking.

Waldman, Scott. 2017. "Climate Web Pages Erased and Obscured Under Trump." *Climatewire/Scientific American*, January 10, 2018. https://www .scientificamerican.com/article/climate-web-pages-erased-and-obscured -under-trump/.

THE GOLDWATER RULE AND THE SILENCE OF AMERICAN PSYCHIATRY*

A 2017 Symposium

NASSIR GHAEMI, M.D., M.P.H.

At the 2017 annual meeting of the American Psychiatric Association (APA), I helped organize a symposium on the Goldwater rule, the 1973 statement in the APA's Ethics Guidelines that has come to be seen as prohibiting any commentary on any public figure by any APA member psychiatrist. This symposium included two former APA presidents, a former head of CIA psychiatry, and a psychiatrist-philosopher. The audience in attendance exceeded the allotted space and, in conversation with the panel, the allotted time.

Paul Appelbaum, M.D., former president of the American Psychiatric Association, Professor of Psychiatry, Medicine, and Law at Columbia University, and a well-known international expert in forensic psychiatry, was the initial speaker. Dr. Appelbaum reviewed

---

* This chapter has been adapted from an earlier essay, "The Goldwater Rule and Presidential Mental Health: Pros and Cons," in *Medscape* (www.medscape .com/viewarticle/881006).

the history of the Goldwater rule, the rationale for its introduction, its evolution, and reasons for its continued support (Appelbaum 2017).

Briefly, the process began in the 1964 presidential election, when Republican candidate Barry Goldwater was opposed by many who feared that he was a warmonger and might trigger a nuclear war. Goldwater's famous convention acceptance speech ("extremism in the defense of liberty is no vice") alarmed some even more. The publisher of *Fact* magazine sent a poll to thousands of psychiatrists, about two-thirds of whom either didn't respond or stated that they felt Goldwater was normal psychiatrically (Martin-Joy 2015). About one-third diagnosed Goldwater with a range of ills, though, including schizophrenia. The magazine published a cover story stating that over a thousand psychiatrists believed that Goldwater was mentally ill and unfit to be president. After the election Goldwater sued the magazine for libel and won his case.

In 1973, the APA prepared an ethics guideline in which it stated that psychiatrists should be active in society but a specific caveat was inserted stating that APA member psychiatrists should not offer a diagnosis or professional opinion on a public figure where two criteria hold: a) consent was not obtained by that person and b) they were not personally examined. Thus, no professional comment should be given based on publicly available information where those two criteria were not met.

Dr. Appelbaum emphasized the problem that in every election cycle, every four years for over four decades, psychiatrists regularly have opinions about candidates, often on the right wing (like Trump and Bush), sometimes on the left (like Clinton). Dr. Appelbaum argued that such professional opinions always, without exception, follow the political preferences of said psychiatrists. He noted that psychiatrists will offer differing opinions on diagnoses—such as attention deficit disorder, sociopathy, narcissism, and bipolar disorder—about the same person. When many diagnoses are offered, he stated, one can conclude that they are all wrong.

In this setting of a cacophony of politically driven opinions,

Dr. Appelbaum argued that it is irresponsible for psychiatrists to give professional opinions about public figures, and the Goldwater rule is thus justified.

The second speaker was Jerrold M. Post, M.D., professor of psychiatry, political psychology, and international relations at George Washington University, and, for over two decades, a top psychiatrist at the Central Intelligence Agency. Dr. Post described how in the early 1990s, he had contributed to a political profile of Saddam Hussein during the Persian Gulf War. An article in the *New York Times* about his work led to a letter from an APA official raising concerns that Dr. Post's work was unethical, breaking the Goldwater rule. Dr. Post described how his entire career had involved psychological and psychiatric assessments of political leaders whom he had never examined personally and whose consent he had not obtained (Post 2002). Yet such work was important for national security and the political interests of the United States, work for which he has been recognized professionally by the psychiatric profession and by the U.S. government. Yet he has felt constrained by the Goldwater rule at times to the point where he felt morally torn. He gave an example of how during the standoff in 1993 with the religious extremist David Koresh, Dr. Post was interviewed on television, and he felt unable to state what he really thought, namely that Koresh has certain messianic traits that might lead to a mass killing, which is what happened. Instead, the FBI was being advised by a nonpsychiatrist mental health professional who had judged that Koresh was "sociopathic," and could be intimidated into submission (as with loud noise and music), an error fatal for many in the Koresh compound. Over the years, Dr. Post has wondered whether his silence, driven by concern about the Goldwater rule, might have contributed to false FBI judgments, leading to more deaths than might have occurred otherwise. Dr. Post felt that the Goldwater rule was too strict and needed to be revised and more limited in its scope.

It should be noted that in March 2017, the APA ethics committee put out an elaboration on the Goldwater rule (APA 2017), mainly as a result of growing concern about the current U.S. president, in which an exception was provided for political profiling under the authorization of the government, as in Dr. Post's work. An exception was provided also for forensic profiling with a court order, and for psychohistory for deceased public figures. The APA claimed, though, that these scenarios were exceptional and uncommon and did not change the main basis for the Goldwater rule, namely that in the majority of cases, psychiatrists need to directly examine a patient and obtain that patient's consent before offering a professional opinion. Further, the March 2017 statement expanded the limitation of the Goldwater rule beyond making an actual diagnosis; it stated that any kind of professional opinion—even commenting on the behavior of another person, even without making a diagnostic judgment—was impermissible.

The third speaker, Dr. Claire Pouncey, took up some of these specific claims of the APA ethics committee. Dr. Pouncey is immediate past president of the Association for the Advancement of Philosophy and Psychiatry. She is a practicing psychiatrist in Philadelphia and has a Ph.D. in philosophy as well (Kroll and Pouncey 2016). A central point she made is that ethics is not just about "rules"; it is not about do's and don'ts. Sometimes this is the case. It is accepted that it is and should be a rule that psychiatrists should not have sex with their patients. But that kind of red-line unethical controversy is uncommon. Most ethical decisions are nuanced; they involve contrasting values, differing outcomes, conflicting opinions. There is rarely a clear right or wrong decision. In most cases, human beings have to make ethical judgments in a complex way. A simple rule doesn't work. This is called "moral agency."

Dr. Pouncey argued that the psychiatrist members of the APA deserve some respect and trust from their main professional organization. They should be allowed to exert their moral agency and make their own judgments about whether to comment, how, and on what grounds, regarding public figures. The claim that any commentary on public figures is unethical is questionable on moral grounds, because ethics doesn't work that way. Instead of telling psychiatrists what they can and cannot do on this matter, it would make more sense to talk about the moral aspects of the problem, to discuss when one could or should discuss public figures, and for what purposes. This approach would be more respectful of the moral agency of psychiatrists, rather than setting the APA up as the sole arbiter of morality. It is understandable that some behavior is reprehensible and deserves clear prohibition, such as sex with patients. But a psychiatric discussion of public figures is not a behavior of that ilk.

I was the fourth speaker, and I made two initial points based on prior statements in the panel.

I made the initial point that emphasis on the need for consent and direct examination does not reflect current psychiatric diagnostic practice, as explained below, but rather reflects *psychotherapy* practice, which was central to psychiatry in the 1960s/1970s, and which continues to be important, but which differs from the process of psychiatric *diagnosis*.

Second, I argued that the claim that without the Goldwater rule there would be an anarchy of psychiatric opinions entails certain relativistic/nihilistic assumptions about psychiatry. If we accept the perspective that we should say nothing in public because psychiatrists have different views (e.g., bipolar disorder versus attention deficit disorder versus sociopathy versus narcissism), all of which are wrong, then we must admit that psychiatrists just don't know what they're talking about. Thus they should say nothing. The APA surely doesn't want to admit such complete ignorance. If so, the APA would be accepting the basic critique of anti-psychiatry groups, namely that there is no truth to psychiatric diagnoses.

This postmodern perspective, if used as a basis for the complete and universal censorship of the Goldwater rule, itself contradicts the ethics of science, which involves the free discussion of competing hypotheses with the confidence that eventually the truth—which is corrected error—will emerge. Science involves refutation of false hypotheses, not censorship of them.

I then turned to my main remarks, which involved approaching the problem of the Goldwater rule from two perspectives: a) its claimed rationale in the March 2017 APA ethics committee statement and b) insights from the field of psychohistory.

The March 2017 APA statement claimed three reasons to support the Goldwater rule: consent, standards of diagnosis, and stigma. The view that consent is part of standard clinical practice is undermined, I said, by common emergency room practice, where patients often are seen who are brought by the police, or friends, or the public, often against their will. It is common for psychiatric evaluation and diagnosis to happen without the consent of the patient in the emergency room. So this is not an uncommon practice, contrary to the Goldwater rule. Regarding standards of diagnosis, a direct examination of the patient commonly is not required or useful in psychiatric practice. In schizophrenia and mania, half of the patients deny their symptoms. In hypomania, it's even worse: two-thirds deny their symptoms (Ghaemi and Rosenquist 2004). This lack of insight is a central feature of the two most common serious psychiatric conditions—schizophrenia and bipolar illness. In these settings, the direct examination is uninformative and *trumped* by collateral information, from friends or family or others, just as is the case in the evaluation of a public figure. Again, this aspect of standard psychiatric diagnosis is common and contradicts the Goldwater rule. The nonspecificity of the mental status examination, in contrast to "direct" examination in the rest of medicine, was emphasized also, and hence contradicts the claim that "direct examination" is essential to making a psychiatric diagnosis.

Regarding stigma, I discussed the positive benefits of mania and depression, proven in a number of scientific studies, with mania enhancing creativity and resilience, and depression enhancing empathy and realism. In *A First-Rate Madness* (Ghaemi 2011), I showed how these symptoms and leadership traits were present in some of our greatest political, military, and business leaders. These leaders included, among others, Abraham Lincoln and Winston Churchill, who had severe depressive episodes, as well as Franklin Roosevelt and John Kennedy, who had mild manic symptoms as part of their personality (hyperthymic temperament). Mania is a state of being sped up in one's thoughts, feelings, and behavior, and it's often associated with creativity and productivity. But the flip side is that it can predispose a person to impulsivity and reckless behavior as well, especially if the symptoms become severe, even temporarily.

I described how publicly known and confirmed knowledge about Donald Trump is consistent with manic symptoms: distractibility, decreased need for sleep, high physical and sexual energy, talkativeness, and elevated self-esteem. These symptoms are constant, and part of his personality, as with hyperthymic temperament. As with the other leaders mentioned above, there are some benefits to these manic traits, such as his creativity in his business life as well as his presidential campaign. And there are some drawbacks, such as his apparent sexual impulsivity in his personal life and the possibility of impulsively dangerous decision-making in his political life.

Thus, making a diagnosis of such persons does not stigmatize them necessarily; in fact, it can and should be the reverse: it reduces stigma by showing the benefits of some psychiatric conditions. The Goldwater rule in fact is stigmatizing, because it assumes that psychiatric diagnosis is bad, harmful, and pejorative.

Finally, I emphasized that public figures give up some privacy rights if they seek to be elected officials, such as presidents. In a democracy, a leader is elected based on the consent of the governed. The governed cannot consent fully if they are uninformed or if key information about their leaders is hidden from them. This is accepted widely now regarding all medical diseases, except psychiatric conditions, because the Goldwater rule is stigmatizing and contradicts the claims of wishing parity between medical and psychiatric illnesses. Woodrow Wilson had a stroke in office; it is accepted now that the public had a right to know, instead of the knowledge being hidden, leading to de facto governance by the first lady (Owen 2008).

I described two other key cases with psychiatric aspects. John

Kennedy had Addison's disease, hidden from the public during his election campaigns, which produced severe depression at times and required steroid treatment. I documented in *A First-Rate Madness* (Ghaemi 2011) that Kennedy abused testosterone injections for two of his three presidential years, times when his leadership was erratic and his judgments often wrong. An intervention by the White House physician Adm. George Burkley led to a massive reduction in Kennedy's steroid abuse, just before a close call with nuclear war in the Cuban Missile Crisis. Adolf Hitler had bipolar illness, in my view, proven based on documentation I've provided, and received intravenous amphetamine, daily from 1937 until his death, for his severe depressive states, which worsened his manic states. Dr. Karl Bonhoeffer, chair of the main psychiatric hospital in Berlin and father of the great Nazi resistance leader Dietrich Bonhoeffer, plotted with generals in 1937 to arrest Hitler, declare him insane, and lock him in an asylum (Sifton and Stern 2013). Would Bonhoeffer's planned action have broken the Goldwater rule? Is it unethical, equivalent to having sex with one's patients?

In sum, my view was that the public also has a right to know about the psychiatric conditions of their leaders, just as it does regarding medical illnesses, because psychiatric diagnoses affect leadership, not just for ill but also for good. I argued for allowing discussion of public figures with scientifically valid diagnoses (such as bipolar illness in contrast to "narcissistic personality disorder") (Skodol, Bender, and Morey 2014) and without specific political intentions, but rather to contribute to public discussion in a scientifically sound and morally responsible manner.

The final speaker was the discussant Dr. Paul Summergrad, recent president of the American Psychiatric Association and chairman of the department of psychiatry at Tufts Medical Center. He agreed with Dr. Appelbaum and noted that the Constitution allows for the creation of a body of experts to examine the physical and mental fitness of the president, if needed. He noted that the Goldwater rule is not a general mechanism of censure for psychiatrists, but is, rather, a policy of the APA, applicable only to APA members. Any psychiatrist is free to comment on public figures as they like, irrespective of the Goldwater rule, as long as they are not members of the APA, or if they wish to drop that membership. There are no larger legal or licensing implications that would come into play.

In an extensive discussion that followed, some members of the audience expressed concern about an anarchy of opinion that might follow if there was no Goldwater rule, and some felt that discussion should be limited to political experts, such as Dr. Post. Dr. Allen Dyer, who was part of the APA Ethics committee that passed the original 1973 language, emphasized that the concept was never meant to be a "rule" but rather a "caveat" given in the setting of allowing for a role for psychiatrists as citizens in social and political life. This perspective contrasted with Dr. Appelbaum's view that a rule is not a rule if it can be broken.

Update: One Year Later

A year after this symposium, there has been no movement within the APA to change the Goldwater rule. Some prominent APA members have resigned in protest, but most leading psychiatrists, including those who oppose the rule, have not taken such steps. I put forward a formal proposal to ask the ethics committee to make small changes in the ethics guideline, changing the language from one of obligation ("must") to recommendation ("may"). This proposal was rejected. Instead the mainstream view of the APA remains that the Goldwater rule should remain as is, and that it should be strengthened even more, as in the March 2017 update.

In short, the mainstream American psychiatric profession has retreated even further from engagement with society.

A number of observers have proposed variations on a simple proposal that could break the logjam of the Goldwater rule (Warraich 2016). A solution could begin as follows: All political leaders would be required to give full financial and medical disclosure during their campaigns. They should reveal their taxes in full and submit to an independent medical board, including psychiatrists, which will review their medical records, examine the candidate, and release a full medical and psychiatric report to the voters. Privacy claims are misplaced. These leaders can order thousands to their deaths. They should make themselves known to those who they wish to command. In a democracy, this is a fair request. Any psychiatric diagnoses obtained should be open to fair-minded, scientifically based discussion by experts on those conditions.

These changes will avoid the pitfalls that led to the Goldwater rule and will protect American society from leaders who have something to hide. Further, it will allow for psychiatric conditions to come out from the shadows of prejudice, to be appreciated in the light of day for their benefits, and not just their risks.

If it fails to drop its current quietist self-censorship, American psychiatry runs the risk of following the lead of Soviet psychiatry. In the USSR, dissidents were hospitalized psychiatrically, diagnosed with schizophrenia (after all, it was delusional to reject communism), and even treated with antipsychotic medications (Van Voren 2010). This approach isn't likely in a democracy. The errors in America will be of omission.

American psychiatry stays on the sidelines, while a president criticizes his opponents as "crazy" and "nuts," fleeing from the professional obligation to fight prejudice against mental illness, even if—especially if—it comes from the president of the United States. American psychiatry stays on the sidelines, while a leader with an authoritarian bent shows empathy to his political base and enmity to those who are different. Neo-Nazi demonstrations occur and aren't condemned. Nonwhite nations are ridiculed with profanity, Muslims are denigrated, Hispanic immigrants are vilified. Allegations of sexual infidelity and harassment are ignored or discredited. Some nations and leaders are embraced, and others rejected and isolated, with questionable rationale. The risk of military conflict in some affected regions, like the Middle East, rises. Still, the psychiatric profession—which has much to offer to public discussion about xenophobia, the social psychology of sexism, and the harms of war and violence—remains silent.

American psychiatry is quiet when it needs to speak. It thereby commits the sin considered the worst of all sins by a different kind of president, John Kennedy, who, in a paraphrase from Dante's *Inferno*, often remarked: "The hottest places in Hell are reserved for those who in time of moral crisis preserve their neutrality" (John F. Kennedy Presidential Library 2018).

Nassir Ghaemi, M.D., M.P.H., is Professor of Psychiatry at Tufts Medical Center in Boston, and Lecturer on Psychiatry at Harvard Medical School. He is the author of A First-Rate Madness: Uncovering the Links Between Leadership and Mental Illness, *a New York Times bestseller (2011), about a half dozen other books, and more than two hundred scientific articles and book chapters. Since October 2017, he also has been employed as a director of Early Drug Discovery Research in Translational Medicine and Neuroscience at Novartis Institutes for Biomedical Research in Cambridge, Massachusetts. The views expressed here are solely his own, and do not reflect those of his employers.*

References

American Psychiatric Association. 2017. "APA Reaffirms Support for Goldwater Rule." https://www.psychiatry.org/newsroom/news-releases/apa-reaffirms-support-for-goldwater-rule, accessed October 21, 2018.

Appelbaum, Paul S. 2017. "Reflections on the Goldwater Rule." *Journal of the American Academy of Psychiatry and the Law* 45 (2): 228–32.

Ghaemi, Nassir. 2011. *A First-Rate Madness.* New York: Penguin.

Ghaemi, Nassir, and Klara J. Rosenquist. 2004. "Insight in Mood Disorders: An Empirical and Conceptual Review." In Amador, Xavier F. and David, Anthony S. (eds.) *Insight and Psychosis.* Oxford and New York: Oxford University Press, pp. 101–18.

John F. Kennedy Presidential Library and Museum. 2018. "John F. Kennedy's Favorite Quotations: Dante's Inferno." https://www.jfklibrary.org /Research/Research-Aids/Ready-Reference/JFK-Fast-Facts/Dante.aspx, accessed October 21, 2018.

Kroll, Jerome, and Claire Pouncey. 2016. "The Ethics of APA's Goldwater Rule." *Journal of the American Academy of Psychiatry and the Law,* 44 (2): 226–35.

Martin-Joy, John. 2015. "Goldwater v. Ginzburg." *American Journal of Psychiatry* 172 (8): 729–30.

Owen, David. 2008. *In Sickness and in Power.* New York: Praeger.

Post, Jerrold M. 2002. "Ethical Considerations in Psychiatric Profiling of Political Figures." *The Psychiatric Clinics of North America* 25 (3): 635–46, viii.

Skodol, A. E., D. S. Bender, and L. C. Morey. 2014. "Narcissistic Personality Disorder in DSM-5." *Personality Disorders* 5(4): 422–27.

Sifton, Elisabeth, and Fritz Stern. 2013. *No Ordinary Men: Dietrich Bonhoeffer and Hans von Dohnanyi.* New York: New York Review of Books.

Van Voren, Robert. 2010. "Abuse of Psychiatry for Political Purposes in the USSR: A Case-Study and Personal Account of the Efforts to Bring Them to an End." In Helmchen, Hanfried, and Santorius, Norman, eds. *Ethics in Psychiatry: European Contributions.* New York: Springer, pp. 489–507.

Warraich, Haider. 2016. "Let Nonpartisan Doctors Examine Candidates and Records, Reporting to the Public." *New York Times,* September 15.

IS THE COMMANDER IN CHIEF FIT TO SERVE?*

A Nonpartisan Test that Marries U.S. Army Leadership Standards with Psychoanalytic Theory

PRUDENCE GOURGUECHON, M.D.

In the early months of Donald Trump's presidency, the shock of his erratic, unprecedented behavior led to a great deal of attention being paid to the Twenty-Fifth Amendment to the Constitution. That's the measure, ratified in 1967, that allows for removal of the president in the event that he is "unable to discharge the powers and duties" of the office.

As the other chapters in this book attest, many mental health professionals at the time were grappling with the issue of Trump's mental stability as well as conflicts related to the ethics of speaking out publicly about it.

What is less frequently discussed is the specific language of the Twenty-Fifth Amendment. What does "ability to discharge the powers and duties of the office" mean, exactly? If the vice president and

---

* This chapter has been adapted from an earlier essay, "Is Trump Mentally Fit to Be President? Let's Consult the Army's Field Manual on Leadership," in the *Los Angeles Times*.

the Cabinet were, at some point, motivated to make this determination, what standard would they use to do it?

I believe we need a rational, thorough, and coherent definition of the mental capacities required to carry out "the powers and duties" of the presidency.

Although there are volumes devoted to outlining criteria for psychiatric disorders, there is surprisingly little psychiatric literature defining mental *capacity*, and even less on the particular abilities required for serving in positions of great responsibility. Despite the thousands of articles and books written on leadership, primarily in the business arena, I found only one source where the capacities necessary for strategic leadership are clearly and comprehensively laid out: the U.S. Army's *Field Manual 6-22 Leader Development* (Headquarters, Department of the Army 2015).

The Army's field manual on leadership is an extraordinarily rich document, founded in sound psychological research and psychiatric theory, as well as military values and practice. It articulates the core faculties that Army leaders need in order to fulfill their jobs. The principles in the Army manual are strikingly congruent with the capacities known as "ego functions" in psychoanalysis and "executive functions" in developmental psychology.

Essentially, ego functions and executive functions are the higher-level mental capacities that enable us to perform as responsible adults who can fulfill our commitments to ourselves and our communities. They are the fundamental traits and abilities that allow us to plan, learn, connect, control ourselves, wait, anticipate consequences of actions, monitor and modulate our emotions and impulses, take responsibility for our behavior, and so on. Pretty much everything we expect of a mature, high-functioning, healthy adult.

Assessing the president's capacity using the principles spelled out in the military manual serves a valuable social/political function. Rather than relying on psychiatric or psychoanalytic expertise—mine or any other clinician's—to suggest what constitutes "ability to carry out duties," the unassailable standards of the U.S. Army are more usable and consequential. They are inherently apolitical and are distanced from the fraught question of whether one is diagnosing public figures. And the psychology underlying them is sound.

Additionally, these standards emphasize functioning and behavior rather than the presence or absence of psychopathology. A now well-known study (Davidson et al. 2006) reviewing the incidence of mental illness in U.S. presidents found that 49 percent of presidents met criteria for a psychiatric disorder. This study has even been cited by some conservative critics in their attacks on psychiatrists who have publicly commented on Donald Trump. In fact, the cases of Abraham Lincoln and Winston Churchill, both of whom are thought to have suffered major affective disorders, are evidence that psychiatric diagnoses are not incompatible with great leadership. Lack of character, discipline, and ability to think, however, are unequivocally incompatible with responsible leadership.

The manual's 135 dense pages can be distilled into five crucial qualities:

Trust

According to the Army, trust is fundamental to the functioning of a team or alliance in any setting: "Leaders shape the ethical climate of their organization while developing the trust and relationships that enable proper leadership." A leader who is deficient in the capacity for trust makes little effort to support others, may be isolated and aloof, may be apathetic about discrimination, allows distrustful behaviors to persist among team members, makes unrealistic promises, and focuses on self-promotion.

Discipline and Self-Control

The manual requires that a leader demonstrate control over his behavior and align his behavior with core Army values: "Loyalty, duty, respect, selfless service, honor, integrity, and personal courage." The disciplined leader does not have emotional outbursts or act impulsively, and he maintains composure in stressful or adverse situations.

Without discipline and self-control, a leader may not be able to resist temptation, to stay focused despite distractions, to avoid impulsive action or to think before jumping to a conclusion. The leader who fails to demonstrate discipline reacts "viscerally or angrily when receiving bad news or conflicting information," and he "allows personal emotions to drive decisions or guide responses to emotionally charged situations."

In psychiatry, we talk about "filters"—neurologic braking systems that enable us to appropriately inhibit our speech and actions even when disturbing thoughts or powerful emotions are present. Discipline and self-control require that an individual has a robust working filter, so that he doesn't say or do everything that comes to mind.

Judgment and Critical Thinking

These are complex, high-level mental functions that include the abilities to discriminate, assess, plan, decide, anticipate, prioritize, and compare. A leader with the capacity for critical thinking "seeks to obtain the most thorough and accurate understanding possible," the manual says, and he anticipates "first, second and third consequences of multiple courses of action." A leader deficient in judgment and strategic thinking demonstrates rigid and inflexible thinking.

Self-Awareness

Self-awareness requires the capacity to reflect and an interest in doing so. "Self-aware leaders know themselves, including their traits, feelings, and behaviors," the manual says. "They employ self-understanding and recognize their effect on others." When a leader lacks self-awareness, the manual notes, he "unfairly blames subordinates when failures are experienced" and "rejects or lacks interest in feedback."

Empathy

Perhaps surprisingly, the field manual repeatedly stresses the importance of empathy as an essential attribute for Army leadership. A good leader "demonstrates an understanding of another person's point of view" and "identifies with others' feelings and emotions." The manual's description of inadequacy in this area: "Shows a lack of concern for others' emotional distress" and "displays an inability to take another's perspective."

The Army field manual amounts to a guide for the Twenty-Fifth Amendment. Whether a president's Cabinet would ever actually invoke that amendment is another matter. There is, however, at least one historical precedent. The journalists Jane Mayer and Doyle McManus tell the dramatic story in their 1988 book, *Landslide: The Unmaking of the President, 1984–1988.*

Before he started his job as President Reagan's third chief of staff, in early 1987, Howard Baker asked an aide, James Cannon, to put together a report on the state of the White House. Cannon then interviewed White House staff, including top aides working for the outgoing chief of staff, Donald Regan. On March 1, the day before Baker took over, Cannon presented him with a memo expressing grave concern that Reagan might not be sufficiently competent to perform his duties. Reagan was inattentive and disinterested, the outgoing staff had said, staying home to watch movies and television instead of going to work. "Consider the possibility that section four of the 25th Amendment might be applied," Cannon wrote.

After reading the memo, Baker arranged a group observation of Reagan for the following day. On March 2, Baker, Cannon, and two others—Reagan's chief counsel, Arthur B. Culvahouse Jr., and his communications director, Tom Griscom—scrutinized the president, first at a Cabinet meeting, then at a luncheon. They found nothing amiss. The president seemed to be his usual genial, engaged self. Baker decided, presumably with relief, that Reagan was not incapacitated or disabled and they could all go on with their business.

Much has changed since the Reagan era, of course. Because of Trump's Twitter habits and other features of the contemporary media landscape, far more data about his behavior are available to everyone—to citizens, journalists, Cabinet members, and members of

Congress. And we are all free to compare that observable behavior to the list of traits deemed critical for leadership by the U.S. Army.

I purposefully refrain from offering my own detailed assessment of Donald Trump vis-à-vis these five criteria. I want everyone, from Vice President Mike Pence to any citizen, to make his or her own determination. However, my personal assessment is that Trump fails on all five criteria, and there are numerous examples of his behavior to support that determination. Trump is capable of demonstrating failure regarding all of the five necessary leadership capacities in a tweet or two alone.

Here's just one example. In June 2017, Trump posted two tweets about *Morning Joe* talk show hosts Joe Scarborough and Mika Brzezinski, referring to "Psycho Joe" and "Low IQ Mika," adding that Ms. Brzezinski was "bleeding badly from a facelift." In that pair of tweets alone, Trump demonstrated his failure regarding all of the five necessary leadership capacities.

I reviewed the five-point checklist with Dr. Richard Rupp, a political scientist with extensive knowledge of twentieth-century American presidents, particularly Richard Nixon. We informally "rated" Richard Nixon, George W. Bush, Bill Clinton, and Ronald Reagan according to the five criteria. Even the most obviously impaired of these presidents, Richard Nixon, scored positively on at least two or three of the criteria.

Many people argued with me that the chance of the Twenty-Fifth Amendment being invoked is far-fetched and that therefore focusing on its language is irrelevant. My answer is that this evaluation tool is intended, in a sense, as a thought experiment, designed to stimulate conversation and, ideally, to trouble people.

But the possibility may not be as remote as some thought. On September 21, 2018, the *New York Times* reported that Deputy Attorney General Rod Rosenstein had, the previous year, "discussed recruiting Cabinet members to invoke the Twenty-Fifth Amendment to remove Mr. Trump from office for being unfit." According to the *Times*, Rosenstein's concern arose in the aftermath of Trump's firing of FBI director

James Comey, his revealing classified intelligence in meetings with Russians at the White House, and reports that Trump had previously requested Comey's loyalty. The *Times'* sources were anonymous Department of Justice and FBI officials who had attended a meeting with Rosenstein when those concerns were allegedly raised. Rosenstein's response to the *Times'* story was "The *New York Times'* story is inaccurate and factually incorrect," and he refused to comment further.

What are the consequences for the military if they can't trust the commander in chief to meet the military's own standards for leadership capacity? I posed that question to retired Lt. General Mark Hertling, a military, national security, and intelligence analyst for CNN who has addressed various comments made by the president in the past. Hertling is also an expert in the Army leadership model, currently using it as a tool to teach leadership in the private sector, particularly for health care leaders.

General Hertling told me, "It is an accepted concept in military leadership for those in position of authority to continuously attempt to build trust with those who serve. If leaders like the commander in chief don't continuously build that trust through their words and actions, it may eventually have a deleterious effect."

He emphasized that the central issue is that "there are consequences when he asks us to do illegal or unethical things."

On March 7, 2016, Hertling appeared on CNN (CNN New Day 2016) and responded to then candidate Trump's claim, in a recent debate, that the military would follow his orders to torture suspected terrorists or murder their families, actions that are considered war crimes. (Trump later reversed course and said he wouldn't violate international laws.)

Hertling said, in this CNN appearance, "Mr. Trump said he was going to order the military to do this and they will—quote—'They will do what I tell them to do, they're not going to refuse me, if I say do it they're going to do it.'"

"It's toxic leadership," he went on. "And someone needs to remind Mr. Trump that the military is not palace guards. They take an oath to defend the Constitution of the United States against all enemies foreign and domestic."

I have no pretension to position myself as an expert on military leadership, though it has long deeply impressed me, as I will explain below. In developing this leadership model that allows any concerned person to check off whether the president has the necessary competencies of character and cognitive ability to carry out his duties, my aim was not to depict "military leadership lite" but rather to create a tool for *civilians* that relied on a politically unassailable source.

I had originally wanted to include "truthfulness and capacity for reality testing" in the model. Reality testing is the ability to distinguish one's inner mental world from objective reality. We all have wishes, fantasies, and emotionally driven thoughts and impressions. Adult functioning depends on the ability to distinguish between what we know to be objectively true from what we wish or fear were true. I felt there were serious questions about Mr. Trump's capacity for distinguishing objective reality from his fantasies and wishes. There has also been well-documented, frightening evidence that he does not tell the truth. However, I chose not to include this additional core capacity in my model because it was not part of the military manual and therefore rested on a different domain of intellectual authority. It occurred to me that the absence of attention to the requirement for honesty in the Army manual might well be because the capacity to be truthful and know the difference between fantasy and reality is a bedrock given, and therefore it wouldn't occur to the framers of the Army's leadership guide to mention it.

Retrospectively, as I thought about the process I went through in developing this model, I realized my interest in the culture of military leadership has a long history. As a young college student in 1969–1970, I spent months shadowing and demonstrating with the veterans who comprised a small activist group, the New Haven, Connecticut, chapter of Vietnam Veterans Against the War. The iron discipline, mutual trust, strategic thinking, self-awareness, and empathy I observed in those intense, dedicated, and traumatized young Marines recently returned from Vietnam made an indelible impression on me. I couldn't have put the elements of their strength into words at the time, but I am glad I am able to do so now. If the reader would indulge me, I would like to dedicate this chapter to them.

Prudence Gourguechon, M.D., is a past president of the American Psychoanalytic Association (APsaA). Following a thirty-five-year career as a psychiatrist and psychoanalyst, she currently works as a consultant on the psychology of business, advising executives on leader assessment and the psychological underpinnings of business relationships and decisions. With a long-standing interest in bridging the civilian-military cultural divide, she founded APsaA's Service Members and Veterans Initiative and spearheaded a successful effort to include military history in the AMA's CPT Code's guide to social history. A Forbes.com senior contributor on leadership strategy, she can be contacted through her website, www.invantageadvising.com.

References

CNN New Day. March 7, 2016. https://www.youtube.com/watch ?v=jhDWtNu2YDA&feature=youtube.

Davidson, Jonathan R. T., Kathryn M. Conner, and Marvin Swartz. 2006. "Mental Illness in U.S. Presidents Between 1776 and 1974: A Review of Biographical Sources." *Journal of Nervous and Mental Disease* 194 (1): 47–51.

Headquarters, Department of the Army. 2015. *Field Manual No. 6-22 Leader Development.* http://www.milsci.ucsb.edu/sites/secure.lsit.ucsb.edu .mili.d7/files/sitefiles/fm6_22.pdf.

DISORDERED MINDS

Democracy as a Defense Against
Dangerous Personalities

IAN HUGHES, PH.D.

Path to Pathocracy

While dangerousness is not dependent on a specific disorder, research in psychology shows clearly that there is a sizable number of people in every society on earth whose psychological makeup renders them dangerous. Sociopathy, narcissistic personality disorder, and paranoid personality disorder, for example, make it impossible for such persons to feel empathy for others, to view others as anything other than objects to be used or threats to be eliminated, and for whom the concept of equality is impossible to conceive. Given this reality, it is time to acknowledge the role this minority is currently playing in undermining democracy and to take urgent steps to minimize their malign influence.

People with dangerous disorders represent a risk to society when they act alone. This is seen, for example, in the high proportion of homicides that are carried out by sociopaths. A much greater danger arises, however, when those with dangerous personality disorders act together. A key to understanding the danger that people with these disorders pose, therefore, is to understand how individual disorders become mass pathology.

Tragically, there are many instances of this "descent into pathocracy" to illustrate how a pathological minority can come to control an entire society (Lobaczewski 2009). These tragic examples include Hitler's Germany, Stalin's Russia, Mao's China, and Cambodia under Pol Pot.

An exploration of the dynamics of these regimes reveals two common themes. First, the rise to power of toxic leaders results from what political scientists call the "toxic triangle" (Padilla, Hogan, and Kaiser 2007). The role that people with dangerous disorders play in mass political violence cannot be explained simply by the personality of individual leaders alone. Instead the rise of dangerous leaders requires all three elements of a "toxic triangle" comprising destructive leaders, susceptible followers, and conducive environments. Stalin, Mao, Hitler, and Pol Pot all rose to power not simply as isolated individuals, but as a member of pathological parties that facilitated their rise. In each case, not only did many of those close to each tyrant also suffer from dangerous disorders, but people with such disorders played key roles, right down to the village level, in violently securing the pathological group's hold on power. In all of these cases, economic insecurity, social disintegration, and mass disaffection with existing structures of power formed the third crucial side of the toxic triangle, the conducive environment, that allowed each of these pathological leaders to come to power.

A second common feature of these regimes is the terrifying wastelands that psychologically disordered leaders produce when their pathology becomes manifest in the world. The death factories of Nazi Germany, the mass prison system of Stalin's gulag, the millions of victims of Mao's famine, and the mass murders of Cambodia's killing fields are all terrifying manifestations of the pathology of the leaders who willed them. Auschwitz in Poland and the Choeung Ek Killing Field in Cambodia, to take just two examples, are places of horror for most. To their pathological creators, however, they were places of cleansing, places which, they believed, history would look back on with gratitude for the service they performed for humanity (Haffner 2000).

Pathological individuals do not, of course, have a monopoly on violence and greed. Identifying the central perpetrators of mass political violence as being psychologically disordered does not absolve the majority of psychologically normal human beings from participation in acts of evil. It is estimated that up to half a million people took part in the killings of the Nazi Holocaust (Goldhagen 1996). Up to 150,000 Hutus are thought to have taken part in the Rwandan genocide (Waller 2002). These numbers are simply too large for all of the perpetrators to have been people with personality disorders. To state that psychologically normal people can and do commit evil is to state the obvious. To reach this point, however, there is often a central and catalytic role on the part of a disordered leader. We should not underestimate the influence of people with the above-mentioned disorders in engendering tyranny and mass murder.

Democracy as Defense

The recognition of the presence of a psychologically dangerous minority within every society on earth demands that we view democracy in a radically different light (Hughes 2018). From this psychological perspective, the primary purpose of democracy is to safeguard society against the devastation that people with dangerous disorders cause when they come to power. The institutions of democracy are pillars in a system of defenses that act to prevent pathological groups from seizing control of society.

The established story of democracy is a familiar one. After its brief flowering in Ancient Greece, democracy almost vanished for more than two thousand years, during which time monarchs, emperors, and sultans ruled the world. While there were exceptions to this general rule, most notably in the medieval city-states of northern Italy, in general, despotism was the global norm. It was only after its forceful reappearance in the American Revolution and the French Revolution that democracy began its dramatic ascent. During the course of the nineteenth and twentieth centuries, democratic governments grew from a minority to becoming, on paper at least, the predominant form of government. Today, despite the current democratic recession, over half of the countries in the world are fully or partially democratic.

A psychological perspective allows for a retelling of this familiar story. In this retelling, our modern system of liberal representative democracy was constructed piece by piece by those who went before us, often in the aftermath of war and genocide, to protect against the destructiveness of a dangerous minority. While the scientific evidence for the existence and prevalence of dangerous disorders was not available to the ancient Athenians, the Founding Fathers, or the signatories to the Universal Declaration of Human Rights, the destructive consequences of this minority were painfully evident to them all. Without describing what they were doing in the language of psychology, the architects of liberal democracy were nevertheless constructing a defensive system to protect against psychologically disordered leaders and their followers.

Through conflict after conflict, the democrats of previous generations created the following seven pillars that make up our modern system of liberal representative democracy. The rule of law, which applies equally to all regardless of wealth or power. Electoral democracy, which provides the opportunity to keep dangerously disordered individuals out of power and to remove them from power once their destructive nature has become apparent. The separation of church and state, which prevents governments from promoting a single religion and denies zealots the opportunity to use religion as a pretext for discrimination and persecution. Social democracy, which aims to limit social inequality and avoid the type of social breakdown that can propel tyrants to power. Legal protection for human rights, which aims to safeguard every citizen from arbitrary abuse of power by national governments and prevent discrimination and persecution of minorities by the majority. Pooled sovereignty, in which former enemies pool aspects of their sovereignty in an explicit attempt to secure lasting peace. And cultures of tolerance, which enable all sections of society the freedom to develop their abilities and contribute fully to society, while denying pathological elites scapegoats for their campaigns of oppression.

Acting together, this system of defenses serves to limit the power of people with dangerous disorders and allows the majority to live free of oppression, state violence, and exploitation. As political scientist Ronald Inglehart (2018) explains, democratic institutions do not guarantee that the people will elect wise and benevolent rulers, but they do provide a regular and nonviolent way to replace unwise and malevolent ones. And the institutions of democracy place stringent limits on the actions of malevolent leaders during the time that they are in power.

Strengthening Democracy

A democratic society demands that its members limit the pursuit of their self-interest to the extent that the rights of their fellow citizens require it. It requires that citizens treat each other with the respect due them as autonomous individuals with the right to pursue their lives as they see fit. It also requires a commitment to the common good. In return for complying with these demands, democracy produces the public goods that people have struggled for centuries to achieve, namely peace, justice, freedom, equality, and community. For people with dangerous disorders, however, these are demands that they are psychologically incapable of complying with. When the opportunity presents itself, people with these disorders will attempt to remove the constraints of liberal democracy to create the conditions in which their narcissistic needs and paranoid fantasies can become manifest without limit.

Unfortunately, the conditions that empower people with these disorders are endemic today. In the United States and Europe, major political and economic institutions have for decades fostered a culture of selfish individualism and greed, fueling levels of inequality not seen in generations. The 2008 financial crash undermined public faith in democracy by transferring the consequences of the crash onto ordinary citizens while allowing the leaders of financial institutions to walk away. The profound changes being wrought by technology and globalization are further increasing insecurity and undermining the sense of identity for many. These conditions have created a perfect storm that is providing fertile ground for leaders adept at harnessing anger and anxiety to attract public support.

To defend against the rise of dangerous leaders and the further erosion of democracy requires that we reassert the norms and values of democracy, reduce inequalities, ameliorate the insecurities that are fracturing societies, and choose leaders who can heal the divisions within and between countries. The alarming alternative is the continuing decline of democracy, the further spread of authoritarian regimes, and the potential return of an era of devastating wars and unspeakable horrors. There are already too many monuments to the victims of pathological leaders. Given the scale of suffering they cause, and the existential challenges we face, strengthening democracy to reduce this dangerous minority's malignant influence has become the overriding moral imperative of our time.

Cloud of Confusion

History and society have been profoundly shaped by a minority of people with dangerous disorders. This minority's unquenchable drive for power means that they regularly succeed in attaining leadership positions in politics, often with disastrous results.

So why is this vital link between politics and psychological pathology not recognized more clearly?

There are three major reasons for this. The first reason is a general lack of public understanding of what dangerous disorders are. This general lack of understanding has two consequences. First, many people object to discussing the mental health of political leaders out of fear of insulting the leaders or stigmatizing those with mental illness. This is a valid concern. The response, however, is that more education is needed. Mental illnesses are extremely varied, like physical illnesses, and one variety should not define the rest. There are illnesses that impact primarily the person suffering from the condition, such as depression, schizophrenia, and eating disorders, for example. If such persons commit violence, it is far more likely that they will do it against themselves and pose less threat to others than the average person. Then there are outwardly dangerous disorders that visit negative consequences upon society. Individuals with these disorders have a higher propensity for outward violence and aggression, and it is important to distinguish them because their pathological greed and paranoia can undermine the social fabric of families, communities, and entire societies.

A second consequence of the general lack of public understanding is that many people equate dangerous disorders with movie depictions of characters such as Norman Bates in *Psycho*, and Hannibal Lecter in *The Silence of the Lambs*. This means that most people expect psychopaths to be mass murderers who are visibly dangerous, and believe too that people with dangerous disorders are rare. Both views are wrong. Most people with dangerous personalities are not murderers. They generally appear ordinary, if "difficult," "aggressive," "boastful," or "selfish," and we are likely to cross paths with them every day.

A second objection to discussing the mental health of political leaders stems from an understandable concern about the possible misuse of mental categorization. This too is, of course, a valid fear, since examples of abuse of psychiatric classification are rife in history. The systematic political abuse of psychiatry in the Soviet Union, where approximately one-third of the political prisoners were locked up in psychiatric hospitals, is just one of a large number of examples in which psychiatry has been used as a means to stifle political opponents (Van Voren 2010). One need only recall too the classification of homosexuality as a mental illness and the incarceration and forced electroshock treatment of thousands of gay men to be reminded of the dangers.

A third, unsettling, reason that pathological leaders regularly go unrecognized, and that a rational discussion of a leader's possible mental pathology is often impossible, is that they often appeal to us, particularly in times of social and political unrest. Freed from anxiety, self-doubt, and guilt, they strike many of us as having qualities we ourselves would like to possess. They "say what they think," they "get things done," they doggedly pursue their agenda and "don't care what others think." The potent attraction that pathological individuals hold for many of us means that, tragically, not only do we fail to see and name these most dangerous of human psychopathologies, but we tend to reward those affected by them with the power and adulation they crave. And once they are in power, many of us continue to support them with a fervor that makes discussion of their possible mental pathology a deeply divisive undertaking.

It Is Time to Have a Civilizing Conversation About Politics and Mental Health

It is crucial that democratic societies begin to have a civilizing conversation about politics and mental health. Such a conversation is urgently needed in order to dispel the cloud of confusion that surrounds dangerous disorders and to remove the mask of sanity that enables dangerous leaders to rise to power.

Unfortunately, the very specialists who are in the best position to educate the public on this vital issue have been largely silent. The professional code of ethics that governs the conduct of psychiatrists and mental health professionals states that it is unethical for a psychiatrist to offer a professional opinion concerning a public figure unless he/she has conducted an examination of that public figure and has been authorized to do so. This so-called Goldwater rule is hindering mental health experts from participating fully in the public discussion needed to strengthen democracy against the dangers that it currently faces.

Mental health knowledge is central to this debate. First, mental health professionals can help clear the cloud of confusion that currently smothers rational debate by clarifying in the public mind the nature, prevalence, and potential dangers of certain disorders. They can contribute to the discussion of how leaders with dangerous disorders come to power, and how the psychology of the majority of people can contribute to this process.

Second, mental health professionals can increase public understanding, without necessarily diagnosing individual leaders, by pointing out that certain disturbing behaviors make sense when looked at in terms of these disorders. Let us take an example. Trump's alarming behavior at the NATO Summit, at the United Nations, and with allies in the European Union clearly show his aversion to alliances, which he invariably views as "ripping off" the United States. One way of understanding this behavior is in the context of paranoia. People who are paranoid are psychologically incapable of conceiving of alliances and cooperative partnerships. The only relationships they can conceive of are ones in which the other partner is likely to betray them. They strongly believe, therefore, that such alliances are threatening and must be avoided. Trump's behavior is what mental health professionals would expect from someone with such a disposition.

Third, the framework of dangerous disorders has predictive value. Mental health professionals know that the mind-set of people with personality defects does not suddenly change. There was much discussion during and after Trump's election that he might pivot, that his most divisive pronouncements about immigration, international alliances, and race, for example, were simply campaign rhetoric, and that he would change tack on assuming office. A broader public understanding, based on the nature of mental defects, would create a greater collective realism about what to expect when such personalities get into power.

Fourth, mental health professionals have specialist knowledge of how dangerous these disorders can be. The barbarity and the depth of inhumanity that have resulted time and again when individuals with these disorders have gained power are clear from the historical record. Systematic mass murder, the killing of infants and children, the sexual plunder of women and girls by combatants, medical experimentation on civilians, forced starvation of populations, mass enslavement and forced labor, prohibition on love between parents and children, and much, much more. The terrifying wastelands that psychologically disordered leaders produce when their pathology becomes manifest in the world are incomprehensible and thus unimaginable to most people. Part of the role that mental health professionals can play in the civilizing conversation we need to have is to make the incomprehensible comprehensible so that we can confront it, based on their specialist knowledge of what people with dangerous disorders can be capable of.

In the end, the aim of having a civilizing conversation on politics and mental health is to strengthen democracy and to preserve and protect our humanity. The story of human development and the nature of the human being that psychology reveals is a story that is normative at its core. The story it tells is that, if human development goes well, we grow up to be adults capable of love, empathy, and altruism. When human development goes well, we gain meaning primarily from relationships with others. The story psychology tells is that dangerous disorders and the behaviors of violence, paranoia, and excessive selfishness that characterize them are failures of development.

The consequences of allowing dangerous personalities to normalize their pathology is to have the rest of us believing in a false sense of human nature—that violence, paranoia, and excessive selfishness are reflections of our true nature; that cooperation, empathy, trust, and respect for others are for "losers." The longer dangerous leaders remain in power, the more normalized such malignant forms of psychological pathology become in society.

A host of obstacles lie in the way of having a civilizing discussion on the mental health of political leaders. But such a discussion, although difficult, is urgently needed. Mental health professionals and their professional organizations cannot remain aloof from this conversation. They must engage with their duty to educate, their duty to engage with other disciplines to understand better the role of dangerous individuals in our current malaise, and their duty to elucidate the vital role of ethical leadership in the preservation of social stability. At this critically important moment, the profession must do so to fulfill its mission to apply psychological knowledge to help benefit society and improve people's lives. To withhold this critical knowledge is itself deeply unethical.

Ian Hughes, Ph.D., is a scientist and author. He has a doctorate in experimental atomic physics from Queen's University in Belfast and a Postgraduate Diploma in Psychoanalytic Psychotherapy from the Irish Institute for Psychoanalytic Psychotherapy, which has informed his work. He is a Senior Research Fellow at the Environmental Research Institute, University College Cork, Ireland, and a policy adviser on science, technology, and innovation policy. His book Disordered Minds *explores how a small proportion of people with dangerous personality disorders are responsible for most of the violence and greed that scar our world.*

References

Goldhagen, Daniel Jonah. 1996. *Hitler's Willing Executioners: Ordinary Germans and the Holocaust*. New York: Alfred A. Knopf, p. 166.

Grant, Bridget F., Deborah S. Hasin, and Frederick S. Stinson. 2006. "Prevalence, Correlates, and Disability of Personality Disorders in the United States: Results from the National Epidemiologic Survey on Alcohol and Related Conditions." *Year Book of Psychiatry & Applied Mental Health* (January): 133–134.

Haffner, Sebastian. 2000. *The Meaning of Hitler*. London: Phoenix Books.

Hughes, Ian. 2018. *Disordered Minds: How Dangerous Personalities Are Destroying Democracy*. London: Zero Books.

Inglehart, Ronald. 2018. "The Age of Insecurity: Can Democracy Save Itself?" *Foreign Affairs*, May/June, Vol. 97, Number 3. https://www.foreignaffairs.com/articles/2018-04-16/age-insecurity.

Kiehl, Kent A., and Joshua W. Buckholtz. 2010. "Inside the Mind of a Psychopath." *Scientific American Mind* (September/October): 28.

Lobaczewski, Andrew M. 2009. *Political Ponerology: A Science on the Nature of Evil Adjusted for Political Purposes.* Otto, NC: Red Pill Press.

McMurran, Mary, and Richard Howard (eds.). 2009. *Personality, Personality Disorder and Violence.* Hoboken, NJ: Wiley-Blackwell, p. 90.

Padilla, Art, Robert Hogan, and Robert B. Kaiser. 2007. "The Toxic Triangle: Destructive Leaders, Susceptible Followers and Conducive Followers." *Leadership Quarterly* 18: 176–94.

Van Voren, R. 2010. "Political Abuse of Psychiatry—An Historical Overview." *Schizophrenia Bulletin* 36 (1): 33–35.

Waller, James. 2002. *Becoming Evil: How Ordinary People Commit Genocide and Mass Killing.* London and New York: Oxford University Press, p. 14.

CONGRESS SHOULD ESTABLISH AN ALTERNATIVE BODY TO ASSESS THE PRESIDENT

NORMAN EISEN, ESQ., AND RICHARD PAINTER, ESQ.

In 1987, President Ronald Reagan attended a meeting with investigators who were probing his involvement in the Iran-Contra scandal. Senior administration officials were under investigation for facilitating illegal arms sales to Iran and using some of the proceeds to fund an armed rebel group—the Contras—in Nicaragua. During the meeting Senator John Tower explained to President Reagan that a member of his Cabinet had recently testified that "the President was clearly unaware of the Israeli arms shipment to Iran." At that moment, President Reagan rose, whispered to an aide, and walked to the Resolute desk to remove a piece of paper. To the surprise of everyone, the president began reading aloud a note that was clearly intended just for him—"If the question comes up at the Tower board meeting, you might want to say you were surprised." The room fell silent. Senator Tower's jaw went slack. The blood drained from the faces of the other commission members.

In the wake of this incident, the president's new Chief of Staff Howard Baker reportedly considered invoking the never-before-used Section 4 of the Twenty-Fifth Amendment to relieve the president of his office. Ratified in 1967, the Twenty-Fifth Amendment established clear rules for succession and continuity in the event of permanent or temporary vacancies of the presidency and the vice presidency. Section 4 of the amendment authorizes the temporary removal of the president from office for up to twenty-one days if the "Vice President and a majority of either the principal heads of the executive departments or of such other body as Congress may by law provide" a written declaration to the president *pro tempore* of the Senate (the longest serving member of the majority party) and the Speaker of the House that the president is "unable to discharge the powers and duties of his office." While Baker could have gone to Vice President George H. W. Bush and the heads of the executive departments, at the time there was not (and there still is not) a congressionally created body to serve as an alternative to the Cabinet.

Renewed interest in the Twenty-Fifth Amendment, the Constitutional tool to ensure an orderly transfer of power when the president is disabled, makes this as good a time as any to consider what kind of body Congress might create—not least because members of Congress have for the first time introduced legislation with competing visions of what it should look like. Our discussion begins by laying out the rationale for creating an alternative to the Cabinet, summarizes existing proposals, and then turns to the key design questions in creating such a body.

Why Bother Creating an Alternative?

The best reason for establishing an alternative body is that there is evidence suggesting that the Twenty-Fifth Amendment has not been employed when it should have been. President Reagan's mental decline in the late 1980s and President Nixon's period of alcoholism and depression during his final months in the White House were both moments that might have justified invocation of Section 4, especially since there was evidence that neither was in a state to understand his own impairment. Had the Twenty-Fifth Amendment been adopted earlier, it might have been invoked after President Woodrow Wilson suffered a massive stroke (and accompanying mental impairment) in October of 1919.

The crafters of the Twenty-Fifth Amendment foresaw this possibility that the proximity (and accompanying loyalty) of the Cabinet to the president might prove an obstacle to invocation of the amendment and so gave Congress authority to establish an alternative. During his colloquy with Chairman Emanuel Celler following his statement in support of the amendment, Senator Birch Bayh noted that Section 4 provided for the "unforeseen contingency that the Cabinet may not prove to be the best body to determine presidential inability in conjunction with the Vice President" by allowing Congress to create another body to participate in the decision.

The risks associated with establishing such a body are small. Any invocation of Section 4—whether by the Cabinet or by a congressionally established body—requires the assent of the vice president. That is an enormous check against misuse of the process because the vice president is almost certain to be a close political ally of the president. Section 4 also limits potential abuse of Section 4 by permitting the president to challenge a declaration that he is unable to discharge the powers and duties of his office and resume the office. The president's challenge can be overcome, but only with the approval of two-thirds majorities in both the House and the Senate.

Existing Proposals

Although Congress has never established such a body, two proposals have recently been introduced: Rep. Jamie Raskin's Oversight Commission on Presidential Capacity Act and Rep. Earl Blumenauer's Strengthening and Clarifying the 25th Amendment Act of 2017.

The Oversight Commission on Presidential Capacity Act

Representative Raskin's bill would establish an eleven-member bipartisan commission composed of at least eight physicians and at least two former high-ranking executive branch officials. The eleven members would be appointed within thirty days of a presidential election and could serve until their replacement is appointed. Responsibility for appointing eight physicians to the commission would be distributed among congressional leadership: the Speaker of the House, the House minority leader, the Senate majority leader, and the Senate minority leader each would appoint two such members. Two additional members, who would be required to have served as president, vice president, secretary of state, attorney general, secretary of the treasury, secretary of defense, or surgeon general, would be appointed jointly by each party's congressional leadership: one by the two Republican leaders and one by the two Democratic leaders. The final member of the commission—who would be required to be either a physician or a former high-ranking executive branch official—would be appointed by simple majority vote of the other members and would serve as chair.

This commission would not initiate an investigation of the president's fitness for office of its own accord without the prior consent of Congress. Within seventy-two hours of the passage of a resolution by both houses of Congress directing it to do so, however, the commission would be charged with carrying out a medical examination of the president to determine if he or she is mentally or physically unable to discharge the powers and duties of the office. Within seventy-two hours after completing the examination the commission is required to report its findings and conclusions to the Speaker of the House of Representatives and the president *pro tempore* of the Senate. Although the president would be permitted to refuse an examination, such refusal would be "considered by the Commission in reaching a conclusion in the report."

The Strengthening and Clarifying the 25th Amendment Act of 2017

Representative Blumenauer's bill adopts a different tack. It would establish a body consisting of each living former president and each living former vice president, except for any such officials who were impeached by the House and convicted in the Senate or who are currently serving as president and vice president. The bill does not lay out the parameters for an examination of the president or standards for determining a president's inability; rather, the body's sole function would be to provide a written declaration of the president's inability—a decision presumably based in judgment and experience rather than medical evaluation.

Key Considerations
What Body?

The two proposals thus far differ most widely in the manner that they select members to the Twenty-Fifth Amendment body. Representative Raskin proposes a body with eleven members, most of whom would be selected by the leadership of a lame-duck Congress in the immediate wake of a presidential election, while Representative Blumenauer's body would be populated by all living former presidents and vice presidents who were not impeached. There are of course an infinite number of other choices available—Congress could, for instance, select a congressional committee to serve as the body, allow state medical boards to appoint members to a body, or create a body consisting of the individuals serving as surgeons general of the United States Army, Navy, and Air Force.

Congress could also combine aspects of both bills by adopting the easily defined body set forth in the Blumenauer bill while instructing that body, consisting solely of past presidents and vice presidents, to appoint a commission of experts similar to that set forth in the Raskin bill. The bill could then instruct the body of former officials implementing the Twenty-Fifth Amendment that it should give substantial deference in its decisions to the commission of experts it had appointed to discharge that task.

What size body is appropriate for the task of determining the ability of a president to perform the duties of the office? A body composed of too many members might be too unwieldy to act in a moment of genuine need; a body composed of too few might act with undue haste. The drafters of the Twenty-Fifth Amendment saw fit to entrust the same responsibility to the "principal officers of the executive departments"—a body that at the time of ratification was eleven individuals and has since expanded to fifteen. Representative Raskin's proposal comes in at a similar number—eleven. Representative Blumenauer's body would fluctuate according to the number of living presidents and vice presidents (though the body would be automatically "terminated" if at any time it had fewer than two members). If it were in existence now, it would include ten members; however, it would have included only two in 1973 (former vice presidents Spiro Agnew and Hubert Humphrey Jr.). Giving three individuals (a body with as few as two members plus the sitting vice president) the power to declare the president unfit for office on a temporary basis seems rash.

How Will Members Be Selected?

Should members be appointed to the body or simply gain membership automatically on the basis of some other quality? An appointments scheme creates a set of administrative hurdles to the formation of a body that can perform Twenty-Fifth Amendment responsibilities. For example, Representative Raskin's bill requires the participation and cooperation of four congressional leaders as well as the cooperation of the members they select to, in turn, select a chair. By contrast, Representative Blumenauer's bill ensures that a body exists without any further action by one or more third parties.

At the same time, automatic appointment allows no discretion to be employed in the appointment. Representative Raskin's body is designed to ensure nearly equal bipartisan representation because no matter which party controls the House and Senate, each party through its leadership would appoint five members, and the eleventh member (the chair) would be selected by the two parties' ten appointees. By contrast, the composition of Representative Blumenauer's body would depend on how many previous elections were won by a particular party and how many of those representatives were still alive. This imbalance could easily be addressed by modifying the bill to require an equal number of members from each political party, with more recent presidents and vice presidents being appointed to the body before those who are less recent.

What Qualifications Will Be Required of Members?

Eligibility for service in the body is another key design choice. Senator Birch Bayh, the chief architect of the Twenty-Fifth Amendment, in defending the Cabinet model for Section 4, noted that "no mechanical or procedural solution will provide a complete answer if one assumes hypothetical cases in which most of the parties are rogues and in which no popular sense of constitutional propriety exists." He's right, of course. The Twenty-Fifth Amendment could always be grounds for the "usurpation" of the presidency, regardless of who composes the fact-finding body that is in charge of determining the president unable. This potential must be mitigated. In Bayh's case it meant trusting that the Cabinet officials would be "reasonable men" guided by their "sense of 'constitutional morality.'" In their two bills, Representatives Raskin and Blumenauer place that trust in other combinations of officials who might have fewer incentives to protect a mentally or physically unable president or to remove one without a sound basis.

Both Representative Raskin's and Representative Blumenauer's proposals allow previous high-ranking executive branch officials to serve, presumably because their experience as or close to the president makes them well-suited to judge whether another individual can serve constitutionally required functions. That said, one concern with this choice—particularly as executed in Representative Blumenauer's bill—is that the body created will be composed of members who may themselves have trouble fulfilling their duties. Although presidents and vice presidents assume office at a variety of ages, one universal truth is that they are all older when they leave office than when they assume it.

Representative Raskin's bill also incorporates a different form of expertise: by requiring that at least eight of the eleven members be licensed physicians, his proposal places even greater primacy on medical expertise than on high-level executive branch experience. In so doing, Representative Raskin appears to envision his body operating only in cases of medical inability—perhaps because the principal officers of the executive Cabinet may be better placed to make a determination that rests on nonmedical considerations.

What Procedures Should the Body Follow?

There are two key procedural questions: First, can the body act on its own initiative or must it wait for a congressional directive before proceeding? Second, what procedures must the body employ in reaching a determination about the president's fitness?

Representative Raskin's proposal is the more procedurally burdensome on both counts. Raskin's proposal would not have the body entertain the question of a president's fitness until the passage of a congressional resolution seeking an evaluation. The requirement that Congress act first is a significant procedural hurdle in its own right, even though Raskin's proposal incorporates modified fast-track congressional procedures that would likely ensure speedy consideration and a vote on the resolution in both the House and the Senate. Representative Raskin's proposal also requires that the body conduct an examination of the president within seventy-two hours of the passage of such a resolution and then submit a written determination to Congress within seventy-two hours of conducting its examination.

Representative Blumenauer's proposal by contrast neither requires congressional action nor lays out procedural requirements for the body to fulfil before submitting a determination to Congress. Those features would put his body on equal footing to the body of "principal officers of the executive departments," which also does not need external permission to act or to conduct an examination of the president before transmitting its decision. The danger with this proposal is that a body heavily laden with former presidents and vice presidents of one political party could use its power under the Twenty-

Fifth Amendment to interfere with official duties of, and to embarrass, a president of a different political party. Imagine, for example a string of three different Republican presidencies (as we had in the 1920s) followed by a popular but controversial Democrat (as we had with President Roosevelt in the 1930s). It is particularly important that a body be impartial if it is empowered to even temporarily remove the president without first being invited to consider that option by Congress.

What Standards Should Govern the Body's Analysis of a President's Fitness?

There have been, generally, two sides to the debate about the extent of the definition of presidential inability. On one side were senators like John Eaton and scholars like Theodore Dwight (both cited by the framers of the Twenty-Fifth Amendment), who argued that the succession clause covered "no disability of which the president could be aware," and that only an insane president could be considered disabled, for "as long as the president possesses reason [. . .] he is not disabled in the constitutional sense." On the other side were senators like Elbridge Lapham and representatives like George M. Robeson, who argued that a president was unable whenever "the public interest suffers because the president is unable to exercise his powers."

These debates carried over into the framing of the Twenty-Fifth Amendment. At a 1965 hearing, Senator Bayh introduced the "conclusions reached by the Committee on Economic Development" into the record. That report stated "[t]he word 'inability' should continue to be understood to include every situation where the president, for whatever reason, is unable to exercise the powers and duties of his office." Senator Bayh also noted that Section 4 was designed specifically to "provide for the contingency that the nature of the president's disability precludes him from declaring his own inability." The text of the ratified amendment did not settle this debate, for it did not delineate the circumstances in which a declaration of presidential inability is appropriate.

Perhaps unsurprisingly, then, Representative Raskin's and Representative Blumenauer's proposals establish different standards for inability. Representative Raskin's body's determination must be based on a medical finding "that the President is temporarily or permanently impaired by physical illness or disability, mental illness, mental deficiency, or alcohol or drug use to the extent that the person lacks sufficient understanding or capacity to execute the powers and duties of the office of the President." Representative Blumenauer's proposal by contrast adds no elaboration of the Twenty-Fifth Amendment standard—inability to discharge the powers and duties of the office. (Note that neither proposal impacts the circumstances in which the Cabinet might issue a declaration of inability.)

Representative Raskin's proposal to ground the concept of presidential inability in medical terms—whether the president "lacks sufficient understanding or capacity to execute the powers and duties of the office of President"—provides for a narrower but perhaps more objective set of circumstances in which a declaration might issue. The determination is made by the physicians on the commission as to whether the president meets this standard from their medical perspective. This text appears to require that the commission be confident that the president both can understand the complexities inherent to the office, *and* has the mental capacity to make and communicate decisions based on a large volume of complex, interwoven evidence. Representative Raskin's introduction of a medical standard has the benefit of objectivity, which, at least in theory, could insulate a determination of inability from accusations of misuse or even partisanship.

In contrast to Representative Raskin's medical definition of "unable," Representative Blumenauer's bill emphasizes the unique challenges and responsibilities of the presidency and eschews medical procedure to determine presidential inability. The definition of "unable" in Representative Blumenauer's bill, then, is closer to one of "threat to the public interest"—a standard that is, perhaps, supported by the legislative history of the amendment, but that is also inherently subjective. Instead of specifying a standard for presidential inability, Representative Blumenauer leaves such considerations to the body of former executives that his bill would establish. This choice allows Blumenauer's body to make a determination of inability in a wider set of circumstances—not just those that are amenable to medical diagnosis; however, it also leaves any determination more exposed to accusations of misuse and illegitimacy. There is a case to be made for leaving open the question of what forms of disability can justify invocation of Section 4 and leaving it to a body of individuals who understand the quantity and type of mental and physical burdens of the presidency.

Conclusion

Congress's failure to establish an alternative body to assess the president's ability to discharge the powers and duties of his or her office leaves the country without one of the emergency options envisioned by the crafters of the Twenty-Fifth Amendment. The bodies envisioned by Representatives Raskin and Blumenauer reflect very different visions, but both merit consideration because either could be relied on to conduct a fair and independent assessment of a president. Raskin's body would rely on medical professionals and standards, while Blumenauer would place faith in the judgment of previous occupants of the highest offices in our land. In an age where bipartisan consensus and objective standards are hard to establish, Congress would be wise to consider these proactive proposals. Preparing for a worst-case scenario is much easier than trying to react to one.

Ambassador (ret.) Norman Eisen, Esq., is a senior fellow in Governance Studies at Brookings, a CNN political commentator, and the chair and cofounder of the government watchdog group Citizens for Responsibility and Ethics in Washington (CREW). Eisen served from 2009 to 2011 in the White House as President Obama's "Ethics Czar" and was the U.S. Ambas-

sador to the Czech Republic from 2011 to 2014. He is the author of the The Last Palace *(2018), an account of the struggle between democracy and illiberalism over the past century. His writing has also appeared in the* New York Times, *the* Washington Post, USA Today, *and many other publications. He received his J.D. from Harvard Law School and his B.A. from Brown University.*

Richard W. Painter, Esq., is Professor of Corporate Law at the University of Minnesota Law School. Painter served from 2005 to 2007 as associate counsel to the president and ethics counsel to President George W. Bush and is a founding board member of Take Back Our Republic, a campaign finance reform organization. His books include Getting the Government America Deserves: How Ethics Reform Can Make a Difference *(2009) and* Taxation Only with Representation: The Conservative Conscience and Campaign Finance Reform *(2016). His writing has also appeared in the* New York Times, *the* Washington Post, *and the* Los Angeles Times, *in addition to scholarly publications. He received his B.A.,* summa cum laude, *from Harvard University and his J.D. from Yale University.*

Acknowledgments

The authors gratefully acknowledge the invaluable assistance of Conor Shaw and Gabe Lezra of Citizens for Responsibility and Ethics in Washington (CREW) and Andrew Kenealy of Brookings.

References

Abshire, David. 2005. *Saving the Reagan Presidency: Trust Is the Coin of the Realm.* College Station: Texas A&M University Press.

Cannon, Lou. 2001. *President Reagan: The Role of a Lifetime.* New York: PublicAffairs.

Committee on the Judiciary, U.S. House of Representatives. 1956. *Presidential Inability.* Washington, DC: U.S. Government Printing Office.

Committee on the Judiciary, U.S. House of Representatives. 1965. *Hearings on Miscellaneous Proposals Relating to Presidential Inability*. Washington, DC: U.S. Government Printing Office.

Link, Arthur S. 1995. "Woodrow Wilson: A Cautionary Tale." *Wake Forest Law Review* 30: 585–92.

Senate Committee on the Judiciary. 1965. *Report Together with Individual Views*. U.S. Senate. February 10.

Subcommittee on Constitutional Amendments, Committee on the Judiciary. 1965. *Hearing Relating to the Problem of Presidential Inability and Filling of Vacancies in the Office of Vice President*. U.S. Senate. Washington, DC: U.S. Government Printing Office.

Tarr, Ralph W. 1985. *Operation of the Twenty-Fifth Amendment Respecting Presidential Succession*. U.S. Department of Justice, Office of Legal Counsel. June 14.

EPILOGUE

Reaching Beyond the Professions

NOAM CHOMSKY, PH.D., AND BANDY X. LEE, M.D., M.DIV.

Expertise can either be shared with the people to affirm their voice and deepen understanding, or it could be used to insulate and exclude. Linguist and philosopher-historian Dr. Noam Chomsky has been exemplary in using expertise to empower others. Even though we do not count him among the thirty-seven mental health experts, he applies his own critical thinking skills to serve suffering humanity, just as would any mental health professional. He edited the quotes below just after Donald Trump's inauguration, but two years later they are more accurate than ever: the Bulletin of the Atomic Scientists *moved the hands of its Doomsday Clock as close to midnight as they had been in 1953; the Anthropocene era is no longer theoretical but has arrived in the form of apocalyptic hurricanes and fires; and the false populism "built on sand" is crumbling as a billionaire cabinet, tax breaks for the wealthy, and trade wars hurt the president's supporters the most. Since the first edition of this book, Dr. Chomsky has moved out to Arizona after sixty-two years at the Massachusetts Institute of Technology, but continues to be a voice of clarity, while*

I write from Alabama, which has taught me that our nation is one people.

Bandy Lee

It is pretty clear what is responsible for the rise of the support for Trump, and there is general agreement about it. If you take a simple look at economic statistics, much of the support for Trump is coming from mostly white, working-class people who have been cast by the wayside during the neoliberal period. They have lived through a generation of stagnation or decline—real male wages are about where they were in the 1960s. There has also been a decline in a functioning democracy, overwhelming evidence that their own elected officials barely reflect their interests and concerns. Contempt for institutions, especially Congress, has just skyrocketed. Meanwhile, there has of course been wealth created. It has gone into very few hands: mostly into a fraction of the top 1 percent, so there is enormous opulence.

There are two huge dangers that the human species face. We are in a situation where we need to decide whether the species survives in any decent form. One is the rising danger of nuclear war, which is quite serious, and the other is environmental catastrophe. Trump wants to virtually eliminate the Environmental Protection Agency, Richard Nixon's legacy, to cut back regulations, and race toward the precipice as quickly as possible. On militarism, he wants to raise the military budget, already over half of discretionary spending, leading right now to confrontations which could be extremely hazardous (Newman 2016).

The Bulletin of Atomic Scientists regularly brings together a group of scientists, political analysts, other serious people, to try to give some kind of estimate of what the situation of the world is. The question is: How close are we to termination of the species? And they have a clock, the Doomsday Clock. When it hits midnight, we are finished. End of the human species and much else. And the question every year is: How far is the minute hand from midnight?

At the beginning, in 1947, the beginning of the nuclear age, it was placed at seven minutes to midnight. It has been moving up and back ever since. The closest it has come to midnight was 1953. In 1953, the United States and Russia both exploded hydrogen bombs, which are an extremely serious threat to survival. Intercontinental ballistic missiles were all being developed. This, in fact, was the first serious threat to the security of the United States. Then, it came to two minutes to midnight. And it has been moving up and back since.

In 2014, the analysts took into account for the first time something that had been ignored: the fact that the nuclear age—the beginning of the nuclear age—coincided with the beginning of a new geological epoch, the so-called Anthropocene. There has been some debate about the epoch in which human activity is drastically affecting the general environment; there has been debate about its inception. But the World Geological Organization is settling on the conclusion that it is about the same time as the beginning of the nuclear age. So, we are in these two eras in which the possibility of human survival is very much at stake, and, with us, everything else, too, of course, all living—most living things, which are already under very severe threat. Well, a couple of years ago, the *Bulletin* began to take that into account and moved the minute hand up to three minutes to midnight, where it remained last year.

About a week into Trump's term, the clock was moved again, to two-and-a-half minutes to midnight. That is the closest it has been since 1953. And that means extermination of the species is very much an open question. I do not want to say it is solely the impact of the Republican Party—obviously, that is false—but they certainly are in the lead in openly advocating and working for the destruction of the human species. I agree that is a very outrageous statement (Goodman and González 2017), but extreme dynamics are behind it, and we are all responsible.

Sooner or later the white working-class constituency will recognize, and in fact, much of the rural population will come to recognize, that the promises are built on sand. There is nothing there.

And then what happens becomes significant. In order to maintain his popularity, the Trump administration will have to try to find some means of rallying the support and changing the discourse from the policies that they are carrying out, which are basically a wrecking ball, to something else. Maybe scapegoating, saying, "Well, I'm sorry, I can't bring your jobs back because these bad people are preventing it." And the typical scapegoating goes to vulnerable people: immigrants, "terrorists," Muslims, and elitists, whoever it may be. And that can turn out to be very ugly.

I think that we should not put aside the possibility that there would be some kind of staged or alleged terrorist act, which can change the country instantly (Frel 2017).

In the United States, power is overwhelmingly and increasingly in the hands of a very narrow sector of corporate wealth, private wealth, and power—and they have counterparts elsewhere, who agree with them and interact with them partly. There is another dimension of "who rules the world." The public can have, sometimes does have, enormous power. We can go back to David Hume's first major modern work on political philosophy: *On the First Principles of Government*. He pointed out that force is on the side of the governed. Those who are governed have the force if they are willing to and eager to recognize the possibility to exercise it. Sometimes they do (Newman 2016).

Noam Chomsky

The people's movements have been numerous, perhaps representing the force within humankind that resists annihilation and gropes toward health and survival. Like Dr. Chomsky, who has worked tirelessly to inform and engage the public, we as mental health professionals and healers should welcome and assist any action in this direction. The National Coalition of Concerned Mental Health Experts, stepping in where we believe the APA failed, has grown into an international organization, soon to rename itself the World Mental Health Coalition. There will be a lot to do after Mr. Trump, when we must actively work together to foster a safer, saner world.

Bandy Lee

Noam Chomsky, Ph.D., is Laureate Professor at University of Arizona since 2017 and Institute Professor Emeritus at the Massachusetts Institute of Technology, which he joined in 1955. Dr. Chomsky has written and lectured widely on linguistics, philosophy, intellectual history, contemporary issues, international affairs, and U.S. foreign policy, and is the recipient of numerous honorary degrees and awards and is one of the most cited scholars in modern history. Among his more recent books are The Essential Chomsky; On Language; Fateful Triangle; Hegemony or Survival; World Orders Old and New; Hopes and Prospects; What Kind of Creatures Are We?; Why Only Us: Language and Evolution *(with Robert C. Berwick);* Who Rules the World?; *and* Requiem for the American Dream.

References

Frel, Jan. 2017. "Noam Chomsky: If Trump Falters with Supporters, Don't Put 'Aside the Possibility' of a 'Staged or Alleged Terrorist Attack.'" *Alternet*, March 27. www.alternet.org/right-wing/noam-chomsky-it -fair-worry-about-trump-staging-false-flag-terrorist-attack.

Goodman, Amy, and Juan González. 2017. "Full Interview: Noam Chomsky on Trump's First 75 Days & Much More." *Democracy Now*, April 4. www.democracynow.org/2017/4/4/full_interview_noam_chomsky_on _democracy.

Newman, Cathy. 2016. "Noam Chomsky Full Length Interview: Who Rules the World Now?" *Channel 4 News*, May 14. www.youtube.com/watch ?v=P2lsEVlqts0&list=PLuXactkt8wQg9av3Wtu_xhZaAcTi4lF1M.

ABOUT THE AUTHOR

Bandy X. Lee, M.D., M.Div., is a forensic psychiatrist at Yale School of Medicine and a project group leader for the World Health Organization Violence Prevention Alliance. She earned her degrees at Yale, interned at Bellevue, was chief resident at Mass. General, and was a research fellow at Harvard Medical School. She was also a fellow of the National Institute of Mental Health. She has taught at Yale Law School for over fifteen years, as well as at Yale College and Yale Schools of Medicine and Public Health. She has spearheaded several prison reform projects around the country, including of New York City's Rikers Island jail complex, and consults globally with governments on violence prevention. She has written more than one hundred peer-reviewed articles and chapters, edited thirteen academic books, and authored the textbook *Violence*.

APPENDIX:

TRANSCRIPT OF THE YALE CONFERENCE

https://us.macmillan.com/static/duty-to-warn-
conference-transcript.pdf